MIDI

POWER!

Second Edition

Robert Guérin

THOMSON

™

COURSE TECHNOLOGY

Professional ■ Technical ■ Reference

Educational facilities, companies, and organizations interested in multiple copies or licensing of this book should contact the publisher for quantity discount information. Training manuals, CD-ROMs, and portions of this book are also available individually or can be tailored for specific needs.

ISBN: 1-59863-084-9

Library of Congress Catalog Card Number: 2005929811

Printed in the United States of America

06 07 08 09 10 PH 10 9 8 7 6 5 4 3 2

THOMSON

COURSE TECHNOLOGY

Professional ■ Technical ■ Reference

Thomson Course Technology PTR, a division of Thomson Course Technology
25 Thomson Place
Boston, MA 02210
http://www.courseptr.com

Publisher and General Manager, Thomson Course Technology PTR:
Stacy L. Hiquet

Associate Director of Marketing:
Sarah O'Donnell

Manager of Editorial Services:
Heather Talbot

Marketing Manager:
Cathleen Snyder

Senior Acquisitions Editor:
Todd Jensen

Marketing Coordinator:
Jordan Casey

Project Editor:
Brian Proffitt

Technical Reviewer:
Len Sasso

Thomson Course Technology PTR Editorial Services Coordinator:
Elizabeth Furbish

Copyeditor:
Brian Proffitt

Interior Layout Tech:
Digital Publishing Solutions

Cover Designers:
Mike Tanamachi and Nancy Goulet

Indexer:
Sharon Hilgenberg

Proofreader:
Gene Redding

Acknowledgments

Thank you Sang Hee, for all your support, wonderful meals, and back rubs when they were needed the most.

I would like to give thanks to the following people for their help and support throughout the writing process, and for putting up with my caffeine-induced personality at times: Colin MacQueen and Christopher Hawkins, Andy Shafran for taking a chance, Stacy Hiquet for keeping things running smoothly, Todd Jensen and Brian Proffitt during the editing process.

Merci à tous!

About the Author

A composer since 1990 and a music enthusiast since 1976, **Robert Guérin** has worked on different personal and commercial projects such as feature & short films, television themes, educational and corporate videos, interactive titles and Web sites. Composing, arranging, playing, recording, and mixing most of his material, he has developed working habits that allow him to be creative without losing the sense of efficiency.

As a professor, Robert has put together several courses covering a wide range of topics, such as computer software for musicians, digital audio technologies, sound on the web, sound in multimedia productions, hard disk recording, and many more topics. He has been program coordinator at Trebas Institute in Montreal and a part-time professor at Vanier College, also in Montreal. He has developed online courses on sound integration in Web pages and has written articles for audio- and music-related online magazines.

Robert is also the author of five books on Cubase, and he developed the content for four other interactive titles: *Sound Forge 7 CSi Starter*, *ACID 5 CSi Starter*, and *ACID 5 CSi Master*. He is the co-author of *Nuendo Power!* and *Cubase 3 CSi Starter*.

You can contact the author by visiting his personal website at www.robertguerin.com, or through this book's support site at www.wavedesigners.com.

TABLE OF ᒐ Contents

Introduction

Since its release on the market in the early 1980s, MIDI has played a significant role in the music industry. But more importantly, it has given musicians and enthusiasts alike a tool that enables them to bridge the gap that existed before. MIDI provided, for the first time, a means of communicating musical information from one device to another in a way that was accepted and adopted by an entire industry. This is, in itself, a big deal.

Since its inception, MIDI has taken an important place in professional and project studios. It has also played an important role in live performance and has influenced the types of music composers create. With the rise of music-based computer applications, it then provided an even more important way for musicians to create music using these highly versatile devices. Over the years, MIDI and digital audio became so intertwined as a way to create music, it became difficult to understand where one left off and the other picked up during the creative process.

In the mid 1990s, some believed that MIDI had no future. Digital audio workstations were becoming so affordable and computers were offering so much processing power, that using MIDI was almost considered to be a thing of the past and too slow to bother keeping. But as it turns out, things evolve in cycles.

Now, with software synthesizers, samplers, and drum machines, MIDI and audio multi-track applications and hundreds of MIDI applications making their way into the market, MIDI has reclaimed its place in our creative process once again. As you probably know, there are a good number of books that discuss MIDI. However, while all these books offer information on the subject, I found that very few of them deal strictly with an in-depth look at MIDI itself. Many of these books discuss digital audio applications, or hardware devices such as mixers, monitors, or microphones. This book, on the other hand, is meant as a reference guide to MIDI and MIDI alone. From how it works to how you can connect devices together using MIDI, to how it integrates into a computer environment and how it has evolved since it was created.

This book will discuss different types of MIDI software, but not how to use the software in step-by- step instructions. It will also discuss how to set up your MIDI studio, but it will not tell you which buttons to press on your synthesizer. It will, however, point you in the right direction and give you the necessary information to deal with issues that might arise as you are working with MIDI. *MIDI Power!* also provides an in-depth look at MIDI and its messages and protocols. You'll learn to make sense of the MIDI language and appreciate its potential.

 **Is This Book for You?**

This book is for you if you want to learn about MIDI—how to use it, how to make it work, how to edit it, why you should use it, when you should use it, and how to take advantage of it with your computer.

This book is not for you if you are looking for a book on how to use a specific device, such as a synthesizer, sampler, hardware sequencer, or patch bay—or how to use a specific software application, such as a sequencer, software instrument, or patch editor.

If you are new to MIDI and would like to learn what all the fuss is about, or if you're an old-school MIDI user looking to find out where MIDI is going or how it integrates in today's computer world, you will definitely find answers in these pages. This book is meant as a reference book: something to come back to when you need it.

How This Book Is Organized

Let's take a look at what you will find in the pages that follow. At the end of this book, you will also find six appendices that will come in handy once you have a firm understanding of what MIDI is all about.

* Chapter 1, "The Basics" covers the history of MIDI as well as a definition of MIDI itself, offering you the foundation needed to understand the different components involved in MIDI, its vocabulary, and hierarchical organization.

* Chapter 2, "Basic MIDI Messages" looks at the information contained in a MIDI communication. As in any language, understanding how sentences are created allows you to better control your communication. For example, in a sentence, you could have a

subject, verb, and a noun, "John eats chocolate." In a MIDI message you have the same kind of structure "Play note on channel 1, C3 softly." This chapter looks at the different types of messages and how, when, and why they are used.

✳ Chapter 3, "Control Change Messages" is an extension of what was covered in the previous chapter. It looks at a specific type of MIDI message called control changes, learning how to use those messages to control certain aspects of a musical performance.

✳ Chapter 4, "General MIDI and Standard MIDI Files" are two major additions made to the MIDI specification since it was introduced. These additions address compatibility issues when sharing MIDI files with others. This chapter discusses what General MIDI is and how to use it. It will also address the standard MIDI file format as well as extensions made to the General MIDI specification through the GS and XG standards.

✳ Chapter 5, "MIDI Hardware Devices" takes a look at MIDI-enabled devices from sound modules to MIDI patch bays, passing through a wide range of audio devices that support MIDI. It will also look at some basic and more complex MIDI setups, without the use of a computer.

✳ Chapter 6, "MIDI and the Computer" looks at what you need to start using your computer with your external MIDI devices. For example, we'll discuss MIDI interfaces, MIDI remote control surfaces and audio hardware with MIDI integration. We'll also look at some basic and more complex MIDI setups, this time integrating the computer into the setups.

✳ Chapter 7, "MIDI Inside Your Computer" discusses how to get a computer working properly with MIDI and audio applications as well as MIDI/audio related peripherals.

✳ Chapter 8, "Sequencing with MIDI" takes a look at the most popular type of MIDI application inside your computer—covering its configuration, the recording process, and editing environments. You will also find information about converting MIDI to music notation through specialized software as well as integrated features in sequencers.

❋ Chapter 9, "MIDI Software: A Sound Creation Environment" brings you into the world of software instruments, which are taking MIDI to a new level by giving a new meaning to the term Virtual Studio. Patch editors and librarians are also covered in this chapter. Keeping track of your synthesizer patch settings, editing your synthesizer's sounds through your computer, and saving them for later use has never been easier than it is now, thanks to these applications.

❋ Chapter 10, "MIDI Software Applications" is an extension of the two previous chapters, offering an overview of the different ways programmers have used their skills to make MIDI more versatile than ever. This chapter will also look at MIDI and the web, offering solutions for a variety of needs and giving tips on how to create MIDI-enabled web pages.

❋ Chapter 11, "Deeper Into MIDI: System Exclusive and Synchronization" is for those of you who always wondered about these two advanced MIDI features—you'll be surprised at how easy and useful they can be. Learn how SysEx (System Exclusive) works, when you can use it creatively, and why you would want to bother with it in the first place. Along with SysEx, we will look at how you can synchronize different devices, software, and video using MIDI's own synchronization options.

❋ Chapter 12, "The Standard MIDI File Format" completes Chapter 4's introduction to SMF by looking at the construction of a MIDI file, its parameters, and the values within those parameters. This is where you find out how to repair a corrupted MIDI file!

❋ Appendix A, "Understanding Binary, Decimal, and Hexadecimal" will help you understand these three common numbering systems that are part of MIDI. MIDI is transmitted using binary codes, which are usually represented in hexadecimals in technical documents, which, in turn, are displayed as decimal values inside your MIDI applications. To get the whole picture, you will need to understand how to convert from one to another easily.

❋ Appendix B, "MIDI 1.0 Specification" is a reference guide to the MIDI specification, giving you a table view of MIDI and how it works, as defined by the organization that oversees the dissemination of this standard.

* Appendix C, "Understanding Timing Concepts" sheds light on the different ways MIDI deals with time as defined by musicians and also as defined by the applications that use it, such as sequencers.

* Appendix D, "The MIDI Troubleshooting Checklist" offers a series of questions you should ask yourself when you are confronted with MIDI problems, with or without a computer involved.

* Appendix E, "MIDI Arrangements: Tips and Tricks" offers you ideas for making MIDI files using a basic General MIDI sound module.

* Appendix F, "Review Questions: Answers" gives the answers to the review questions found at the end of each chapter in this book. Use these questions to test your comprehension of the topics covered in each chapter.

1 } The Basics

MIDI, pronounced "MID-ee," is an acronym for Musical Instrument Digital Interface. It is a communication standard that allows musical instruments and computers to talk to each other using a common language. At this point, you might be thinking, "Well, I knew that." If so, great; if not, you have just taken your first step toward understanding what MIDI is all about. Let us now look at how it all started and what the basic principles are behind MIDI.

Here's a summary of what you will learn in this chapter:

* ❋ Why MIDI was introduced and how it all started.
* ❋ The different components that make up the MIDI communication protocol.
* ❋ How MIDI is transmitted.
* ❋ What type of connectors, cables, and jacks are used to transport the MIDI data.
* ❋ What the differences are between MIDI In, Out, and Thru (same as Through).
* ❋ How you can hook devices together using MIDI.
* ❋ How MIDI can be saved in a standard file format.
* ❋ What a multi-timbral instrument is.
* ❋ What MIDI channels are and how they work.
* ❋ What MIDI busses, MIDI ports, and MIDI patch bays are.

MIDI is a standard, a protocol, a language, and a list of specifications. It identifies not only how information is transmitted but also what transmits this information. Just like AC/DC current identifies the type of electrical current, it also defines how the cables are connected and what type of cables should be used to transmit this current. Another example of this could be a USB connection. It is both a protocol that defines how devices communicate and the type of connectors linking these devices. MIDI has as many software implementations as it has hardware ones.

A Bit of History

Where to begin? I could start at the very beginning of music, when humans used sticks to create rhythms, and work my way up from there. But, I guess knowing how we got to where we are musically is not the main reason you bought this book. You want to become the MIDI expert, or at least be able to get things working in your musical setup. So with this in mind, we'll start by looking at MIDI from its beginning and find out why and how it evolved from there. Does that seem like a long trip? Well, indulge me a little here, and you might be able to impress your friends with the knowledge you get from these few history pages the next time you're at a party with other musician friends.

Let's skip ahead to the time when synthesizers were introduced—those big monophonic machines that used wires to connect different modules together in order to produce sounds. Eventually, they became polyphonic instruments and later evolved into programmable synthesizers. But yes, there was a time when synthesizers could only play one sound at a time. Where are we? Well, somewhere in the late 1970s. At that time, the main synthesizer manufacturers were ARP, Fairlight, Moog, Oberheim, Roland, Sequential Circuits, Synclavier, and Yamaha. In 1979, the Prophet 5 (see Figure 1.1), built by Sequential Circuits and offering polyphony and programmability, was one of the hottest items you could buy if you had $5,000 to spare.

Figure 1.1   The Prophet 5 synthesizer from Sequential Circuits.

At this point in time, just before the Prophet arrived, if you wanted to play a melodic line with the sound coming from two synthesizers made by different manufacturers, you'd have to play them simultaneously with your two hands. This was a nice way to get a rich synth texture, but not very player friendly, since typically both hands would be occupied with a single musical element.

One solution was to buy only synthesizers from a single company and lock them together using a sequencing machine developed by that same company. Since many companies developed their own hardware analog sequencers, they were all proprietary. These sequencers were nice in the sense that you could record a series of events to create a musical or melodic line and later trigger the sequence using a keypad or pedal. While this was pretty handy at the time, it still fell short of what musicians wanted. These sequencers recorded events

❖ ❖ ❖

one step at a time in a way some pattern-based drum machines still use today. Each step corresponded to a bar subdivision, such as 16th notes. So, for example, if the sequencer offered 64 steps, you could program the sequencer to play up to four complete bars with a 16th-note resolution or set each step to play at half the speed and have eight bars of eighth-note events. Using steps implied that you had to choose a duration value for a note, play a note to record it, then select either a silence or another note to advance, then add another note, and so on. Today, software drum machine sequencers use a similar method of sequencing to produce drum patterns that are stored and recalled at will, a feature that didn't exist yet when sequencers started to make their way into the musician's toolbox.

In 1982, during a trade show called NAMM (National Association of Music Merchants), two guys met—Dave Smith, founder of Sequential in the USA, and Ikutaro Kakehahshi, founder of Roland Corp. in Japan. They started looking at a way to make a communication system that would allow synthesizers to talk to one another. Obviously, these were big companies, and each had its own agenda. One wanted a higher end system; the other was thinking low-cost, mass-market production. But one fact remained: they both agreed to work on this protocol, which at that time was tentatively called UMI: Universal Musical Instrument.

Other companies, such as Oberheim and Yamaha, got involved, and after many revisions, in 1983 the MIDI standard was adopted. Not long after that, Sequential Circuits and Roland came out with their first MIDI-compatible instrument. Simultaneously, the personal computer (PC) was emerging as a potential tool for musicians because of its programmability. Roland seized that opportunity and began work on a musical interface device for the IBM PC. Roland saw the PC as being a digital alternative to its analog sequencers, and since this hardware device would allow musical instruments to communicate with IBM PC computers, it was the perfect interface tool to penetrate new markets, since other companies could develop tools that could be used with the interface. Roland figured that it made good business sense to take advantage of the fact the PC had no built-in sound chip, and Roland could develop an interface for the PC that would be compatible with the company's entire line of new keyboards. It would then have the upper hand, and musicians would buy their keyboards in droves. Roland then decided to build an ISA hardware card that plugged into one of the slots of an AT-style IBM PC, to which you could attach a box containing additional circuitry that would serve as the "musical interface" (see Figure 1.2) for the PC. Thus was born the MPU-401 (Musical Processing Unit–Model 401) card that would allow computer users to interface with other MIDI-enabled devices. To this day, the MIDI interfaces built into some computer audio hardware still offer hardware compatibility to the original MPU-401, since it became such a widely used MIDI interface for IBM PC-compatible computers.

Also in 1983, Yamaha released its DX7 synthesizer (see Figure 1.3), which was MIDI compatible. The DX7 was a milestone in synthesizer design because it was the first synth with completely digital sound generation. It was extremely successful and became very popular. The fact that MIDI was integrated into the DX7 probably helped the new protocol establish itself as a professional standard.

Figure 1.2   The MPU-401 musical interface box from Roland.

Figure 1.3   The DX7 digital synthesizer from Yamaha.

Roland made the specifications for the MPU-401 card available to other parties, and soon other computer software was being written that supported this standard. By 1985, the Commodore 64, Apple II, and IBM PC could all be adapted for MIDI. One computer, the Atari 512, even had a MIDI interface built in. In 1986, Apple came out with the very popular Macintosh Plus, which quickly became a favorite with musicians because of its Graphical User Interface (GUI). As these computers were now equipped with MIDI capability, many software companies such as Steinberg Research GmbH (now known as Steinberg Media Technologies GmbH), Twelve Tone Systems (now known as Cakewalk), C-Lab (which became Emagic, then part of Apple), Hybrid Arts, and others were already producing software sequencers. This was a good thing for musicians and went way beyond Roland's expectation. In fact, software sequencers were much more popular than Roland's hardware sequencers due to their flexibility and wide screen interface.

At this point in time, no one had thought of a way to save MIDI data to a file for later use or outside of the real-time performance applications, other than proprietary solutions provided by individual software makers. Up until then, each sequencer used a proprietary file format that made it impossible to read or write each other's files. It was a company called Opcode, which later provided a software application called OMS (Open Music System) for Macintosh users that offered the MIDI File format specifications to the MMA, opening the road to a common MIDI file format that could be used between software sequencers.

Then, Digidesign came up with the MIDI Time Code (MTC) protocol, which standardized MIDI synchronization between MIDI devices such as hardware and software sequencers, other time-code devices using SMPTE (Society of Motion Picture and Television Engineers) through a SMPTE/MIDI converter, and so on. Before this, the only way to synchronize such devices was an often-perilous method involving FSK (Frequency Shift Key) synchronization, which would not necessarily be the same for every device or software. FSK was also strictly a synchronization to TAPE protocol (audio based). It was not meant for machine-machine sync.

Since then, the MMA, in conjunction with the AMEI (Association of Music Electronics Industries, created in 1996 for Japan's manufacturers), has created new standards and recommended practices for the use of MIDI. The MMA performs this through the work of a Technical Standards Board, which supervises working groups dedicated to a wide range of subjects. Some other advances in MIDI protocol pertain to tape machine control through MIDI via a MIDI Machine Control (MMC) protocol, theatrical staging and presentation controls with the MIDI Show Control (MSC) used by lighting engineers, and music delivery with the implementation of General MIDI, Standard MIDI Files (SMF), Downloadable Sounds (DLS), and Extensible Music Format (XMF), all of which will be described in greater detail in this book.

What Is MIDI?

The Musical Instrument Digital Interface (MIDI) allows musicians, sound and lighting engineers, computer enthusiasts, or anybody else for that matter to use computers and electronic musical instruments to create, listen to, and learn about music by offering a common language that is shared between compatible devices and software. MIDI can be divided into three separate entities: the language it uses, also known as its protocol; the hardware interface it uses to transmit and receive its information (such as connectors and wires); and its distribution formats, such as Standard MIDI Files (SMF). Let's take a closer look at these three aspects of MIDI to better understand how they work together and why MIDI works the way it does, offering you interconnectivity, flexibility, and (in terms of file size) portability.

Fundamentally, MIDI is a music description language in binary form, in which each binary word describes an event of a musical performance. As you saw earlier in this chapter, in the beginning, MIDI was intended for keyboard instruments, so many of its events are keyboard oriented, where the action of pressing a note is like activating an On switch, and the release of that note is like turning a switch Off.

Each musical instrument makes a sound, which is under the control of a musician. The musician controls when the instrument will start to make sounds—a cellist will pull a bow, a bassist will pluck a string, a trumpeter will blow air, and a keyboardist will press a key. Consider this action as the Note On event. The MIDI message itself does not contain the actual sound the instrument makes, but rather the action of playing the note, which note was played, how fast or slow it was played, which program number can be used to play this note back, and as you will discover later, a moment when a note is played.

When a musician stops pulling on the bow, plucking the string, blowing in the trumpet or lifts the finger from the key, the sound stops. With MIDI, when such an action is produced, a Note Off message is sent for that note, and the sound stops as well. Figure 1.4 displays the Note On and Note Off actions and their musical equivalents along the bars and beats time line.

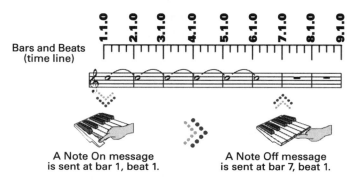

Figure 1.4 MIDI Note On and Note Off messages.

In order to identify which note is flicked on or off on the keyboard (or any other device, for that matter), a number is assigned to each note. MIDI also handles interpretive values, like how fast you strike that note and how hard you press on that note once it's down. MIDI sends all this information as binary encoded messages, along with mixing and panning of sounds, controlling parameters that tell various electronic musical instruments which sound to play and even when to make changes in the instrument's setup.

This is the starting point; we will look at how all this information is encoded and what you can find in an actual MIDI message a little bit later.

How MIDI Is Transmitted

MIDI uses a serial transmission protocol rather than a parallel protocol. A parallel transmission, as the name would imply, sends every piece of information in simultaneously. The amount of data it can send simultaneously depends on the physical capability of the wire and on the speed at which the devices can send their information. In Figure 1.5, the parallel transmission shows that four pieces of information can travel simultaneously. A serial transmission, on the other hand, sends pieces of information one after the other over its wire. As with the parallel transmission protocol, the amount of information serial transmissions can handle depends on the wire and on the speed at which the devices can send information. But since there is only one stream of data in a serial transmission, it can only be as fast as that single stream, whereas a parallel transmission can be as fast as the total number of streams it can send.

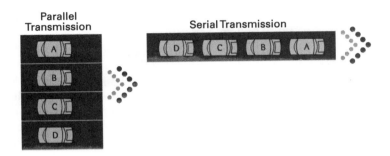

Figure 1.5 Parallel versus serial transmissions.

You might ask why MIDI uses serial transmission rather than parallel transmission. To answer that question, we have to look back at the time when the protocol was developed. Parallel transmission had some disadvantages that outweighed its advantages and was much more expensive to mass market, since the wires, connectors, and jacks were more intricate. Serial transmission, on the other hand, was easy to mass produce, so it was more affordable for the consumer market. It was also fast enough for what manufacturers and potential users had in mind at that point, not to mention more reliable. Things have changed since then and, in terms of technology, this means faster and better. However, to keep MIDI compatible with all previous devices, the way it is transmitted has not changed since it was introduced.

MIDI sends information at a rate of 31,250 bps (or bits per second). This speed is called baud rate. Since MIDI is transferred using a serial transmission protocol, it sends the information one bit at a time. Every byte in a MIDI message uses 10 bits of data (8 bits for the information and 2 bits for error correction). This means that MIDI sends about 3,125 bytes of data every second (31,250 bps divided by 8 bits to convert into bytes). If you compare that with the 176,400-bytes (or 172.3-kilobytes) transfer rate required for digital audio transmission (playback and recording) in CD audio format, MIDI might seem a bit slow. But since MIDI does not need to transfer as much information as digital audio, it worked well under most circumstances in the early days of MIDI, but not so well in today's musical environment. In fact, at that speed, you could play, in theory, up to 500 MIDI notes per second. In reality, it takes about one millisecond to transmit a single note. The threshold for distinguishing individual sound events is roughly 10 milliseconds, so you'll start to perceive flaming with 10 or more simultaneous events.

The Hardware and Connectors

MIDI information flows through cables, the connectors at each end of the cable, and the jacks into which the connectors go. Physical cables between devices can be as long as 15 meters (50 feet). Remember, this is a serial cable; everything is transmitted over one main wire, so the longer the cable is, the more signal degradation occurs, which increases the risk of losing information or making some MIDI messages unreadable as the events go from point A to point B. This is why cable companies have to put signal amplifiers along the way between the cable company distribution point and your house.

MIDI Connector

The MIDI connector itself is a 5-pin DIN jack (see Figure 1.6). You can find the same type of male connector at both ends of a wire, unless you want to extend an existing cable with a special female/male MIDI cable. This type of design allows peer-to-peer connections, unlike USB connectors for example, which allow only host-centric connections. In other words, with MIDI connectors, you can connect a computer to a keyboard to a sound module and so on. With a USB connector, you can connect a computer to a keyboard, but you will need to connect the sound module to the computer as well, either directly through a USB port or through a USB hub. We will discuss MIDI-USB support in greater detail in Chapter 7.

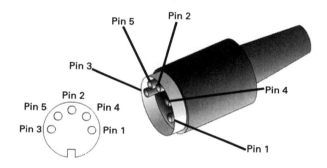

Figure 1.6   The MIDI 5-pin DIN jack.

The five pins in the MIDI connector are not all active. As mentioned earlier, MIDI sends information using a serial transmission protocol, so in reality, only one of the five pins is sending the actual MIDI information. Table 1.1 describes each pin in the MIDI connector and its purpose.

Table. 1.1   MIDI Pin Description

Pin No.	Description (see Figure 1.6)
1	Not used; in most MIDI cables, this pin is not even connected to a wire.
2	This is used as electrical shielding (ground). This shielding protects the MIDI cable from transmitting undesirable electrical or radio interference.
3	Like Pin 1, Pin 3 is not used, and in most MIDI cables it is not connected to a wire.
4	This is the actual MIDI data receiver. Information on this cable flows in one direction only.
5	This is the actual MIDI data transmitter. As with Pin 4, the information on this cable flows in one direction.

MIDI Jacks

The jacks on MIDI-compatible instruments, patch bays, or interfaces are the female version of these connectors. Keyboards usually have two or three jacks: one labeled In, another labeled Out. The third optional jack is labeled "Thru" (see Figure 1.7), which in the MIDI world means "Through." Note that the MIDI Thru connector is usually not found on computer interfaces or MIDI patch bays. The reason for this is explained below.

Figure 1.7 A 3-connector MIDI configuration.

MIDI information flows in one direction, like an audio cable; it doesn't really matter which side of the wire you plug into your guitar and which side you plug into your amplifier, as the flow of electricity will go from your guitar to the amplifier. MIDI cables are the same. This is because the audio jack on your guitar is an output, and the audio jack on your amplifier is an input. Plug your guitar into the headphone output of your amplifier, and all of a sudden, nothing happens. MIDI works the same way.

MIDI Out

The MIDI Out serves as a MIDI output. What comes out of this connector is the MIDI messages that the device or software generates. We'll get into what these messages are further in this chapter. What comes out here originates from the sending or master device, which could be a keyboard, sound module, sequencer, or any other software or hardware transmitting MIDI. Therefore, if you have more than one device in your setup and want to chain them together (peer-to-peer), you need to use the MIDI Thru to echo the information that comes from the MIDI In. The MIDI Thru can be either the physical Thru on your device or a Thru setting inside your software. The MIDI Out does not send audio information, simply MIDI messages that are interpreted by the receiving MIDI In of another MIDI device. These MIDI messages are digital codes that represent what and how music or events are being played on the master instrument. For example, MIDI events can include foot pedals being pressed, faders being moved, or program numbers being changed. MIDI Outs should always be hooked up to MIDI Ins, no matter what type of setup you have.

MIDI In

The MIDI In serves as a MIDI input. That's where MIDI data comes in and is sent to the hardware or software's processor. Whatever comes in here is processed and can be sent back through the MIDI Thru if you want to use the MIDI data in another device. For example, the MIDI data tells a sound module to play a certain note at a certain velocity, on a certain MIDI channel, using a certain sound in its memory, thus triggering the synthesizer to produce a sound through its audio outputs. The audio output can then be monitored or recorded. But make no mistake: What you are recording or monitoring is the audio outputs, not the MIDI outputs.

MIDI Ins can receive their information from MIDI Outs if the previous module in the chain is the master, or MIDI Thru if the previous module in the chain is echoing the information sent by another master module in a chain.

MIDI Thru

The MIDI Thru serves as an echo of the MIDI In connector port, which means that whatever comes in the MIDI In goes out to the MIDI Thru, not the MIDI Out. In other words, it repeats the information coming from the MIDI In of this same device. MIDI Thru will not, however, echo information played from its module. For example, in Figure 1.8, anything you play on synthesizer A will be sent out to synthesizer B through its Out jack, not its Thru jack. Synthesizer B will need to use the MIDI Thru to send the information from synthesizer A to synthesizer C, but if you want to send information to synthesizer C that is triggered on synthesizer B, you will need to use the MIDI Out of this synthesizer.

Still in Figure 1.8, the note played on keyboard A is sent to keyboard B using the MIDI Out to MIDI In connection, whereas keyboard B in the upper part of the figure will not send the information from keyboard A to keyboard C if it uses the MIDI Out on keyboard B. The proper connection is shown in the lower portion of this figure. By making your MIDI connections this way, whatever you play on A will be transmitted to both B and C keyboards, using the Thru as a bridge between them.

Daisy-Chaining Devices

The method just described, chaining different MIDI devices together, is referred to as "daisy chaining." This will allow you to echo MIDI information from one controller (master) to multiple (slave) devices such as sound modules, for example. You can also use a daisy chain with your computer configuration to send the computer's MIDI output to multiple receiving devices in the absence of a multi-port MIDI interface or a MIDI patch bay connected to your computer. A multi-port MIDI interface simply offers more than one MIDI output on it, while a MIDI patch bay is a MIDI device that works as a MIDI matrix, usually with multiple inputs and outputs.

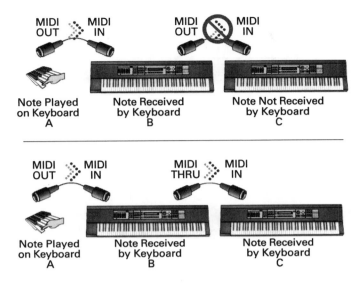

Figure 1.8 MIDI In, Out, and Thru connectivity.

Although this is an effective way of using more than one MIDI sound module in a simple setup, it has some drawbacks. In theory, you can daisy chain as many devices together as you wish, but in reality, things are quite different.

Remember that MIDI information travels in series, so the longer it has to travel along different cables and devices, the more potential for data loss. Although the Thru connector does not, in theory, add to the processing time, in practice, messages always go through interface chips that have some minor processing delays. The cumulative effect of daisy chaining does result in measurable and, as the chain is increased, audible delays. A good rule of thumb to observe is to keep your chain as short as possible, not exceeding a three-device chain. If you have many devices to control, a good way to hook them up is by using either a multi-port MIDI interface or a MIDI patch bay, both of which will be discussed later in this chapter.

In a daisy chain, each device responds to its own MIDI channel, so you can use this setup to trigger multiple sounds from different sound modules in a live performance setup. As long as you limit your chain to three devices, you ensure the events from the master device are received on time by the rest of the devices in that chain. It doesn't really matter if an instrument is active or not in the chain, as its mere presence may introduce loss.

Figure 1.9 displays an example of how MIDI cables are connected between devices in a chain. Only the first keyboard (controller or master) uses the MIDI Out to send whatever the musician plays to other devices in this chain. This type of setup makes it possible to trigger sounds from other devices in the chain, provided that you set all the devices properly in this chain. If you're wondering what needs to be set up, don't worry, we will get into that later.

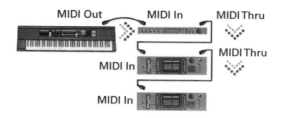

Figure 1.9 MIDI daisy-chain setup for live performances.

This said, in many project studios today more and more musicians rely on software instruments that are controlled by a single MIDI keyboard, which reduces the need for daisy-chained MIDI devices, multi-port MIDI interfaces, and MIDI patch bays altogether.

In Figure 1.10, you can see another example of a daisy chain, but this time with a computer at the top of the chain (master). Here the keyboard uses the MIDI Thru to echo the information coming from the computer to other devices in the chain. As mentioned above, computer MIDI interfaces don't normally have MIDI Thrus because they can be programmed within the MIDI application itself to turn the MIDI Out into a MIDI Thru. Using the MIDI Out of the computer will send any MIDI information out to the device that's hooked up to it, just as Figure 1.9 demonstrated. If you look at the keyboard, however, all three MIDI jacks are used. The MIDI In receives the information coming from the computer, the MIDI Thru echoes it out to the rest of the chain, and the MIDI Out sends information that you would play (like an additional musical line) into the computer, allowing you to record it in a sequencer, for example. If you were to use the MIDI Out of the keyboard to feed the rest of the chain, the only thing the other sound modules would receive is the MIDI data coming from this keyboard, not what is coming out of the computer.

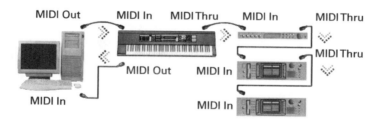

Figure 1.10 MIDI daisy-chain setup with computer.

One disadvantage of using daisy chains, besides the practical limit on the number of devices you can hook up to the chain, is that the devices that are past the keyboard in the chain cannot send MIDI data back to the computer to be recorded, such as instrument parameter settings. If the computer has only one MIDI In, it is logical that you use it to receive MIDI notes from the keyboard; therefore, if you wanted to transmit information from other devices, you would need to make manual changes to your wires in order to send pertinent information back to the computer. Using a MIDI patch bay, multi-port MIDI device on your computer, or external MIDI devices with USB compatibility would solve this problem quite nicely. But for now, understand that chaining devices together will allow you to control several instruments from one master source, as shown in Figure 1.10. Lastly, any MIDI data sent out by the keyboard above can be echoed through the MIDI Out of the computer back into the keyboard and the other devices in the chain. So in reality, the only true MIDI Out here is the one coming from the keyboard. When a keyboard also doubles as a sound module, playing, as is the case in this example, notes played on the keyboard triggers the integrated sound module while it sends the same events to the computer. If the computer sends these events back to the keyboard, the same events will play again, duplicating the note events, which sometimes causes problems with the MIDI data flow. We will see later how to prevent this from happening. This is not a problem when using keyboard controllers that don't offer onboard sounds.

The File Formats

MIDI is also about saving musical performances for later use. Once you've had time to sleep, you want to be able to listen to your MIDI performance and tweak it a little or add layers to it. That's where MIDI files come in handy. There are many different types of files that contain MIDI data. For example, files saved in a sequencer such as Cubase use proprietary formats with its own file extension. The same applies to any other software. This is because each software application saves everything it needs, and this might include non-MIDI information. But somewhere in that file, MIDI data does find its place.

MIDI provides a standard format to save MIDI performances to a file called Standard MIDI File format, or SMF for short. An SMF holds all the information needed to reproduce all the performance parameters supported by MIDI. Furthermore, it adds a time stamp on each event so that MIDI sequencers know when to play these events. The sequencer makes sure each event is played at the correct time. Along with live MIDI keyboard setups, recording MIDI into a sequencer is probably one of the most popular uses of MIDI today.

MIDI has the advantage of being compact, since you don't record the actual sound when you record MIDI. You record events, just as a database collects information. A database can have links to large content files such as video, audio, or image files, but the actual size of the links, or pointers from within the database, is much smaller than the content they represent. In the same way, MIDI files, though small themselves, can be used to trigger sounds in, for example, a sampler keyboard that might require a lot of space in your sampler's memory. Again, the MIDI files don't contain the actual sample; they act in the same way as the link does in the database. As an example, if you were to record a single four-note chord played over one minute in digital audio using a CD audio format, the end result would be a file using about 10 megabytes, whereas recording the same chord and holding it for a minute in MIDI format would generate an SMF document with less than 10 kilobytes.

The fact that MIDI does not record audio is perhaps its one disadvantage. When you record the actual audio, you are in full control of the final audio output, whereas with MIDI, the audio output depends on the device or software that is used to reproduce the audio. In the mid-1990s MIDI was the most popular way of using music in games and applications because it required only a basic audio hardware device, files required very little space, and it was CPU friendly since it didn't require much processing power. Today, things have changed in this respect since CD-ROMs and DVDs, combined with increased CPU power and more demanding customers, have made MIDI in games a thing of the past. But the fact remains that MIDI is still a great tool for creating and editing music in both live and studio environments.

MIDI is a binary communication system that is used to transmit music-related information. A MIDI file is a way to save this content to a file on disk for later use. If you were to load a MIDI file into a text editor, you'd find a bunch of nondescript binary codes. You can, however, use a MIDI file disassembler/assembler utility to convert MIDI data into something you could edit. For this, though, you need to understand how everything is encoded. By the end of this book you'll be able to do so, but for now remember that MIDI files are usually easier to edit in a sequencer than in disassembler or MIDI converter software.

The Standard MIDI File comes in three formats, which are described in the following table.

Table. 1.2   Standard MIDI File Format Types Explained

MIDI Type	Number of Tracks	Contains All MIDI Messages	Number of Songs, Patterns, or Musical Performance Saved in the File
0	1	yes	1
1	1 per channel	yes	1
2	1 per channel	yes	unlimited

Type 0 contains only one song with all the MIDI channels merged into one MIDI track. Type 1 contains only one song as well, but each MIDI channel can be saved on its own track in this song. Finally, Type 2 may contain different songs or patterns, each one with its own tempo settings, and each pattern or song can save MIDI channels on its own tracks.

When you record MIDI sequences in a software sequencer, the MIDI files will not be saved in one of those three formats unless you tell the software to do so. Your MIDI sequencer application saves more than MIDI information when it saves to file. Saving as an SMF is a good way to make a file cross-platform and cross software compatible, since SMF format is a standard endorsed by most software developers. SMF can also allow you to save track names (in Type 1 and Type 2 format) to identify the content of each track in your MIDI sequence. Note however that much sequencer-specific information will be lost by saving in Standard MIDI Format, such as score formatting and other non-MIDI related information. We'll discuss more on this in Chapter 8.

The MIDI Hierarchy

We've seen that MIDI is a series of binary messages sent to capture and later be translated back into musical performances. Chances are you will want to have more than one musical performance playing at a time. That's where MIDI channels and MIDI ports or busses come into play.

MIDI Channels

A MIDI channel is like a television or radio channel. It is a way for MIDI to isolate information so that a receiving instrument set to a certain channel will filter out all the other information in the transmission and reproduce or process only the information to which it is tuned. When you are watching channel 3 on your television set, your television set is processing only what is meant for channel 3. This doesn't mean that the rest of the channels aren't there or that the information doesn't enter your television. MIDI channels work the same way. When an instrument receives MIDI from its MIDI In (see Figure 1.11), it matches the MIDI data with the appropriate MIDI channel settings in the instrument, playing or reproducing what is set in this instrument as active and ignoring what is set as inactive.

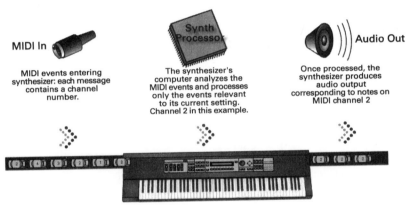

MIDI In

MIDI events entering synthesizer: each message contains a channel number.

The synthesizer's computer analyzes the MIDI events and processes only the events relevant to its current setting. Channel 2 in this example.

Audio Out

Once processed, the synthesizer produces audio output corresponding to notes on MIDI channel 2

Figure 1.11 How musical instruments handle MIDI channels.

MIDI Ports and MIDI Busses

Until now, we have referred to a MIDI connection as a series of cables being hooked up to a physical device's MIDI jacks: MIDI In, Out, and Thru. This set of three jacks can be called a MIDI port or MIDI bus. Most keyboards and sound modules have one MIDI port, while others might have more. Each port usually offers a set of MIDI In, Out, and sometimes Thru connections, either physical or virtual in some software applications such as software synthesizers, for example.

Each MIDI port can handle up to 16 simultaneous MIDI channels, from channel 1 through channel 16. In other words, you can choose one of 16 different channels to transmit MIDI events or have up to 16 different instruments playing different MIDI events at the same time if the receiving MIDI instrument supports more than one channel at a time.

Some MIDI devices will offer more than one set of MIDI outputs, inputs, and thrus. In most recent devices, this probably means that you will have one MIDI port per MIDI set of connectors (In, Out, and Thru). For example, you might have two MIDI inputs and two MIDI outputs, which would give you two MIDI ports for a total of 32 MIDI channels (16 per port). On some older devices, this can also mean that it can send the same MIDI information over multiple MIDI Outs. To find out if this is the case, review the device's documentation and find out if it is a multi-port (or multi-bus) device or simply a multi-output device, which transmits the same 16 channels over all its outputs. The difference is quite important.

On one hand, you have a multi-port device that can transmit on up to 16 MIDI channels simultaneously on each MIDI port it offers. For example, a four-MIDI port device offers four times 16 channels, or 64 simultaneous MIDI channels. On the other hand, you have a single port device with multiple MIDI outputs, all sending the same 16 channels. Same amount of MIDI outputs, but in the latter case, 48 fewer MIDI channels! Because each channel can be a different musical instrument, more ports, especially hardware ones, often translate into more creative flexibility. As you will discover shortly, however, software instruments provide their own virtual MIDI ports, thus reducing the need to have multiple physical MIDI ports connecting a keyboard controller to its sound sources.

In Figure 1.12, on the left you can see a device with one MIDI Out, offering 16 MIDI channels through its connection. The second column to the left is a single MIDI port, but one that offers more than one MIDI Out jack. This is useful if you want to send the same information to different instruments but don't want the MIDI chain to be too long. However, it still offers only 16 MIDI channels. This is the case with some older MIDI patch bays (a matrix offering multiple MIDI inputs and outputs). Finally, the two columns on the right show a device that offers two separate ports, one labeled A and another labeled B, each of which offers 16 MIDI channels. In this setup, two different instruments can receive different MIDI information on channel 1, provided that you tell the sending (or master) device where the desired information should go and set up your MIDI connections properly. The numbers in parentheses correspond to the total number of MIDI channels available. Even if you have more than 16 MIDI channels in your MIDI studio setup, they will always be numbered from 1 to 16. The device sending the MIDI through different ports will identify each set of 16 channels by giving each port its own name. This name is usually defined by the multi-port MIDI interface itself, which is how a sequencer software can send recorded MIDI events to a device connected to one port rather than another. Imagine that you connect a multi-timbral synthesizer to port A in Figure 1.12 and a sampler to port B in the same figure. You will need to tell your sequencer that the information contained on one track goes to port A, channel 1 and the information contained on another track goes to port B, channel 1. Both devices will receive separate MIDI information, even though they both use the same MIDI channel number.

As you just saw, using a single MIDI port, you can control up to 16 simultaneous instruments, either through 16 separate devices or through one multi-timbral device. But what if you have two or three multi-timbral devices? Then what? If one sound module uses all 16 channels, you are left with no other MIDI channels for these additional sound modules. That's when multiple MIDI ports come in handy, since each port offers 16 channels. Simply multiply

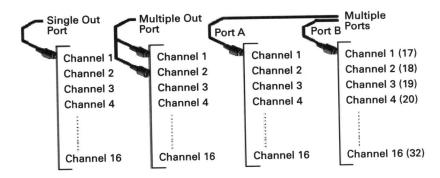

Figure 1.12 Different types of MIDI ports (busses).

the number of available ports by 16 to get the total number of MIDI channels available in your system.

Using a multiple port or multi-port MIDI device offers another advantage: Since all MIDI data is streamed through a serial transmission protocol, it implies that everything is sent in a line, one bit of information after another. The longer this line of data is, the slower the information moves from point A to point B. Take the beginning chord of a symphony, for example, where you might have 16 instruments playing three notes each. It takes a total of 960 microseconds for MIDI to transmit the note from a struck key to the sound module connected to it. This is so fast that your ear won't hear the delay. Now multiply that short delay by 16 instruments, then by three notes each (960×16×3) and you now have 46,080 microseconds between the time the notes are played and the last note is transmitted to the sound module. That's 46 milliseconds... a very audible delay indeed. Some might argue that if all these instruments play together, you won't feel that delay, which is accurate. But nonetheless, if you are going to send a large amount of MIDI data over one single MIDI port, you may end up with what is affectionately called a "MIDI data clog" or "MIDI choking." This is when the data flow breaks down and loss occurs during playback, effectively stopping some instruments from receiving MIDI as they should.

Dividing the MIDI flow over two or more MIDI ports, making sure each receiving MIDI device is hooked up to its proper MIDI port, can reduce the possibility of "choking" the MIDI (see Figure 1.13). The information will reach your device quicker, and the device will respond to it in a more natural way since it doesn't have to wait for the information to come in.

One Channel, One Sound

No matter how many different sounds you might have in your synthesizer, sampler, or sound module, you can access only one sound at a time per MIDI channel. Now, some synthesizers use names like combis, combos, performances, programs, patches, presets, voices, and what not. When you assign a sound, no matter what the module's manufacturer calls it, and press a key on your controller keyboard, a sound is generated. If you decide that this sound will

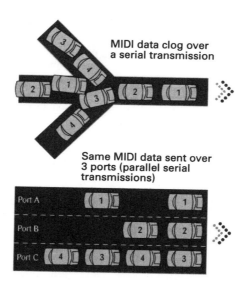

MIDI data clog over
a serial transmission

Same MIDI data sent over
3 ports (parallel serial
transmissions)

Port A

Port B

Port C

Figure 1.13 Data over a single port (top) and data splitting it over multiple ports (bottom).

play on channel 1, then you can hear that sound only on channel 1 until you decide to hear another sound on channel 1. In other words, think of your 16 channels as a 16-member band, where each channel is the equivalent of a musical part. Let's take the example of a big band. Some musicians in this formation often switch instruments, going from a saxophone to a flute during a performance. The number of musicians in the band doesn't change, but the instruments being played do. MIDI works the same way. Sounds or instruments playing on a particular channel can be changed during the course of a song.

Changing a sound while you're playing is just like changing notes. It's as simple as selecting another patch, preset, or program number on your keyboard's control panel. Just as with playing notes, when changing a sound manually on one machine, every machine (device or software) down the chain will respond to this information if they are receiving MIDI from the "master" device. In other words, any change made in the sound patch number is sent out through MIDI just like any other information. So any slave device that is set to receive MIDI information from this port's specific channel number will respond by changing as well. Just as you can record MIDI events such as Note On and Note Off, you can also record changes like Patch Changes.

With most rules, there are exceptions: Some MIDI devices offer key or zone splits. When a MIDI device supports such a feature, you can assign one sound over a note range and another sound over another range. For example, assigning a bass sound to the lower part of a keyboard while the higher portion plays an electronic piano makes it possible to play a two-part rhythm section with a single keyboard and player. While this can be very convenient in live performances, it is usually a feature offered by the hardware/software instrument and not a function specific to MIDI. As a result, such key/zone splits, unless otherwise mentioned in the device's documentation, are not supported by a specific MIDI message.

Multi-Timbral Instruments

When a sound module can listen to and play back sounds on more than one MIDI channel at a time, it is referred to as multi-timbral. Multi-timbral devices (hardware and software) have the ability to reproduce more than one sound over more than one MIDI channel at a time. By enabling instruments, selecting different sounds for each instrument, and associating a MIDI channel for enabled instruments, multi-timbral sound modules are like having several musicians playing different instruments. Multi-timbral instruments can isolate MIDI data coming in on any MIDI channel and route this data to the proper sound patch. Most multi-timbral sound modules can also turn on or turn off a MIDI channel to better control which channel it will process and which ones it will ignore. When a MIDI channel is selected, any MIDI message coming in on that channel will play back the sound (patch, preset, or settings) you assign to this channel.

For example, to record or play back a keyboard, bass, and drums trio, assign and enable channels to each of these instruments on the multi-timbral device and set the appropriate patch to the corresponding MIDI channel, and the multi-timbral instrument will play all three instruments simultaneously (see Figure 1.14).

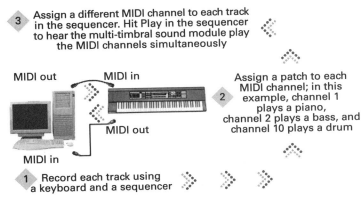

Figure 1.14 Using multi-timbral instruments to play back more than one MIDI channel at a time.

In Figure 1.14, the controller keyboard is hooked up to the computer's MIDI interface and sequencer application. Because some multi-timbral devices have built-in sequencers, a computer hook-up is not a required at that point as the built-in sequencer replaces the software application in this example.

Each instrument or sound playing in a multi-timbral sound module is often referred to as a "part." In our example, the sound module would play three parts: piano, bass, and drums. A part will respond to all the MIDI messages it receives, including volume, pan, and program settings, for example.

Where each part ends up in terms of audio output depends on the individual sound module's physical audio output settings or its internal software settings in the case of a software multi-timbral instrument. This setting is independent from MIDI, since it refers to how you assign the MIDI channel's audio output on your sound module. In terms of MIDI, there is a good chance that all channels will come from the sound module's MIDI In and will be echoed through its MIDI Thru. This said, the internal audio routing parameter of a MIDI-compatible device can be modified and stored along with a sequence through System Exclusive (SysEx) messages, the discussed in Chapter 11.

About MIDI Patch Bays

MIDI patch bays are similar to MIDI ports in that they effectively connect multiple MIDI devices together to a common port. Many MIDI patch bays also offer multiple MIDI ports. However, a MIDI patch bay might only represent one MIDI port in your MIDI studio setup. For example, if you connect all your MIDI devices to a patch bay, there will still only be 16 MIDI channels available, even though there is more than one set of MIDI Ins and Outs. This is not the case with MIDI ports. By definition, a MIDI port is any device that can handle 16 MIDI channels. If you can hook up your MIDI patch bay to your computer using a PCI host card or a USB or FireWire connection, your computer may allow you to address each MIDI set of inputs and outputs as an individual MIDI port. At this point, your MIDI patch bay becomes a multi-port MIDI patch bay.

In Figure 1.15, the back of the patch bay displays eight inputs and outputs. There is usually no MIDI Thru on patch bays because they are part hardware, part software. You can plug in up to eight devices—in this example, hooking up the MIDI Out of your devices to the MIDI In of the patch bay and vice versa. Once your connections are made, you can configure the path as you wish, using the front panel controls of the patch bay or even a software interface in some cases.

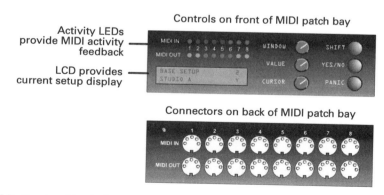

Figure 1.15   Front and back of a typical single-port MIDI patch bay (with eight Ins and eight Outs).

❋ **Connecting a MIDI Patch Bay to Your Computer**

Figure 1.15 does not show any connectors that would allow you to connect your computer to the patch bay other than by using MIDI connectors. However, many patch bays today use either parallel or USB connectors to make the connection with a computer. With such connections, the MIDI patch bay may appear as a multi-port MIDI patch bay with one port for each pair of MIDI In/Out. We'll get to that a little bit later.

The patch bay acts as a MIDI matrix, sending what comes from MIDI In 1 to MIDI Out 4, 5, and 6, for example. On the top part of Figure 1.16, you can see how a signal is taken from MIDI In 3 and sent out only to MIDI Out 2. MIDI In 3 comes from the MIDI Out of that device, and MIDI Out 2 is hooked up to the MIDI In of that device. In the lower part of this same figure, the MIDI signal coming from MIDI In 4 is distributed to two devices through MIDI Out 3 and 5. In both examples, the left-hand side displays a matrix point of view, and the right-hand side displays how the actual MIDI data flows from the patch bay's MIDI In to MIDI Out. This type of operation in a MIDI patch bay is called *MIDI routing*. MIDI routing is probably one of the most difficult aspects for beginners to grasp and even for some intermediate users, since making sure your MIDI data flows properly between devices without creating MIDI loops or connections that go nowhere may require some trial and error. But once you understand the principle of MIDI data flow, you will also reduce your troubleshooting time considerably. Until now, the different MIDI setups that were illustrated were quite simple. As we progress, this MIDI routing will get a bit more interesting, especially when a combination of hardware and software settings is involved.

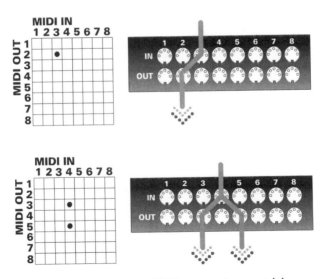

Figure 1.16 Directing a MIDI stream using a patch bay.

These simple examples show you how 16 channels of MIDI data can be routed from point A to point B; however, we are still talking about 16 MIDI channels. If a MIDI patch bay is connected to your computer through a parallel port, serial port, USB, or any type of connection other than a simple MIDI cable, it might support multiple ports as well. For example, the MOTU (Mark Of The Unicorn) MIDI Time Piece AV offers, among other things, 128 MIDI channels distributed over eight separate MIDI ports (8 ports ×16 channels = 128 MIDI channels).

MIDI patch bays are not only used to route devices; some of them allow you to convert SMPTE time code into MIDI Time Code (this will be discussed later in Chapter 11), save different settings such as MIDI routing configurations, and filter certain types of MIDI messages.

Review Questions

1. At the 1982 National Association of Music Merchandisers (NAMM) convention, what were the names of the two companies that met to look at ways to make a communication system possible between synthesizers from different manufacturers?

   a) Yamaha and Roland

   b) General MIDI and General Tao

   c) Roland and Sequential Circuits

   d) Oberheim and Hybrid Arts

2. What does the acronym MIDI stand for?

   a) Many Instruments Dialog Interface

   b) Musical Instrument Digital Interface

   c) MIDdle Instrument

   d) Master Interface Direct Input

3. What was the first MIDI-compatible synthesizer developed by Yamaha in 1983?

   a) The Commodore 64

   b) The Prophet 5

   c) The MPU-401

   d) The DX-7

4. The basis for MIDI is:

   a) A music description language in binary form, where each binary word describes an action of a musical performance.

   b) An electronic impulse in analog form, where impulses record audio wave lengths.

   c) A set of rules that determines how musical notation appear in a staff, which can be used to record and play back audio events.

   d) All of the above.

5. A single MIDI port can support up to how many simultaneous channels?

   a) 1
   b) 16
   c) 64
   d) 128

6. Which Standard MIDI File format supports one track per channel?

   a) Type 0
   b) Type 1
   c) Type 2
   d) Type 1 and 2

7. In a 3-device MIDI daisy chain, which MIDI connection should the second device use to echo the MIDI events from the first device to the third?

   a) MIDI In
   b) MIDI Out
   c) MIDI Thru
   d) Any of the above

8. Which pin(s) of the 5-pin DIN connector does MIDI travel on?

   a) Pins 4 and 5
   b) Pins 1 and 3
   c) Only Pin 2
   d) Only Pin 4

9. MIDI uses what type of transmission protocol?

   a) IP transmission
   b) Serial transmission
   c) Parallel transmission
   d) Longitudinal transmission

10. True or False: The MIDI Manufacturer's Association is the body that recommends practices and uses for MIDI through the work of a technical standards board.

2 } Basic MIDI Messages

Before you could learn how to ride a bike, you had to learn how to walk. You started with one step at a time. You had to learn how to control your balance to stand still long enough, and when you felt confident that you could put one foot forward without falling, you did it. This chapter will give you the necessary confidence to take your first step into MIDI messages—your first steps into a world that will help you advance in your creations later. When you understand MIDI messages—when you know why MIDI works, what it can do, and how it does it—you get a glimpse of the possibilities that lie ahead. Here's a summary of what you will learn in this chapter:

* The structure of a MIDI message.
* The difference between types of MIDI messages.
* What these messages contain and what their values represent.
* Which messages control how your MIDI devices react to MIDI messages.
* How MIDI messages transmit information about a performance, store it, and then reproduce it in time.
* What kind of MIDI messages will allow your device to send and receive information about its parameters.
* How MIDI assigns note names and note numbers to note pitches.

MIDI messages are the building blocks of every performance recorded through MIDI. The content of a message is fairly simple. All MIDI messages contain a component called a *Status byte*. The Status byte is accompanied by a value that is defined by one or more *Data bytes*. In other words, a MIDI message can be as short as one Status byte and can have as many Data bytes as needed for the values it is transmitting. In most cases, however, MIDI messages will have one or two values—Data bytes—attached. The only exception to this rule, as discussed in this chapter, is System Exclusive messages.

Status and Data Messages

As seen in the previous chapter, MIDI uses an 8-bit word (1 byte) to transmit its information across a serial transmission. A bit is a switch; it can be on or off, a 1 or a 0. It takes eight switches (bits) to form one byte. For example, your computer needs eight bits to represent the letter "A" in ASCII (American Standard Code for Information Interchange) text. In other words, you read "A," but your computer reads "0100 0001" and understands that if this is supposed to represent a text character, it should display the capital letter "A." An 8-bit word (a word in this case represents the total number of bits needed to represent a character) implies that each message can hold a value from 0 to 255, for a total of 256 different combinations (2 to the power of 8, or 2^8). These messages are divided into two categories: *Status* and *Data* (see Figure 2.1). In Chapter 1, you learned about MIDI channels and Note On/Off messages. Both pieces of information are part of the Status byte.

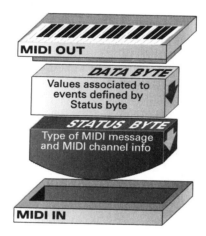

Figure 2.1 Status and Data bytes.

The Status byte portion of the MIDI message serves to identify the kind of information being sent. It tells the receiving device which MIDI channel the event belongs to and what the event is. An event can be a "Note On," for example, or a pitch wheel bend, a patch change, or an Aftertouch Control, which occurs when you bear down on a note after it has been pressed initially.

The Data byte portion of the MIDI message tells the receiving device what values are associated with the event found in the Status byte portion of the message. For example, if you strike a middle C with medium force, the Status byte would send a "Note On" event, and the Data byte would pass the corresponding note value number of 60 for a C5 and a velocity level of about 64, with the velocity being the speed at which you hit a key.

The Status byte uses numbers ranging from 128 to 255 (1000 0000 to 1111 1111 in binary numbers), and the Data byte uses numbers ranging from 0 to 127 (0000 0000 to 0111 1111 in binary numbers). In the binary representation of these numbers, the Status byte's first digit on the left (also known as the *most significant value* and also known as Most Significant Bit or MSB) is a 1, and in the Data byte, this value is 0. In other words, any receiving MIDI device will immediately interpret a message as a Status byte or a Data byte, depending on whether the byte begins with a 1 or a 0.

❋ **About MSB and LSB**

It is important to grasp the concept of Most Significant Bit (MSB) and Least Significant Bit (LSB). In any numbering system, the value found on the left always represents a greater number of variables than the values found to its right. For example, in the number 56, 5 represents a multiple of 10, or 5 times 10, and 6 adds only 6 values to this number, changing its value by 6. So 56 is (5×10)+6. If you change the 6 to 7, you only add one to the value of 56, whereas if you add one to the 5, you add 10 to the value of 56. Imagine now if you go to a store and the salesperson charges you $56 instead of $57. You'd be happy about it, but you'd be even happier if he charged you $47 instead of $57!

In a binary system, when the first bit on the left changes, the change is also more important than when the first bit to the right changes. Therefore, the first bit or byte (when there is more than one byte) to the left is called the Most Significant Bit (or Most Significant Byte when a binary word has more than one byte). The bits (or bytes) to the right are called Least Significant Bits (or Least Significant Bytes when a binary word has more than one byte).

MIDI uses 8-bit words to transmit its information (two extra bits that are never displayed as part of the MIDI message but are used for error correction). As stated previously eight bits can communicate up to 256 different values (2 to the power of 8 = 2×2×2×2×2×2×2×2 = 256), or 0 to 255. Since MIDI separates its messages into Status and Data byte messages, it uses the eighth bit (the highest value or Most Significant Bit) to be the toggle bit, telling the receiving device that what follows in the word (the remaining seven bits of information) is status or data information. Thus, when a binary word starts with 1, it is interpreted as the Status byte portion of the message, and when it starts with a 0, it is interpreted as a Data byte portion of the same message. This use of the eighth bit then limits the range of possible values within MIDI to a 7-bit word, or 128 different values, ranging from 0 to 127. This is why you will notice that values in MIDI, such as MIDI note numbers, for example, are often numbered from 0 to 127.

Here's an example of how this works. Let's say the MIDI device receives the three following values: 200, 127, and 120. It will know that 200 is a Status byte because it is between 128 and 255 and that 127 and 120 are the two accompanying Data bytes to this Status byte because they are between 0 and 127.

Here's another example where the MIDI device receives the following three values: 190, 245, and 98. It will interpret the first number (190) as a Status byte, and since the second one is also between 128 and 255, it too will be considered a Status byte. However, the last value (98) will be interpreted as the Data byte for the number 245's Status byte.

MIDI messages are often represented in one of three formats: decimal values, such as 127; binary values, such as 01111111; and hexadecimal, such as 7F. To better understand how to convert binary numbers into decimal or hexadecimal numbers, please refer to Appendix A.

An entire MIDI message can contain up to three bytes of information, depending on the MIDI function. In Figure 2.2, you can see a binary message with three bytes of information. The first byte begins with a 1. This tells the receiving MIDI device that it is a Status message and that the device should expect to receive Data messages subsequently. Note that both the second and third bytes start with 0. Every time a byte starts with a 1, it is considered the locomotive (Status) pulling its cars (Data). The next three bits identify the MIDI function. For a complete list of these functions, refer to Appendix B, in the section called "Expanded Status Bytes List." The remaining four bits in the first byte serve to identify the MIDI channel. Because 4 bits define up to 16 values, you will understand that each value corresponds to a MIDI channel and is displayed in Table 2.1 below.

In this example, the MIDI function is called Polyphonic Aftertouch (described later in this chapter). This function is applied to a pressed key, which is identified in the second byte. The amount or level of this function for this specific note number is then determined by the third byte. In this example, the Polyphonic Aftertouch was played at a level of 95.

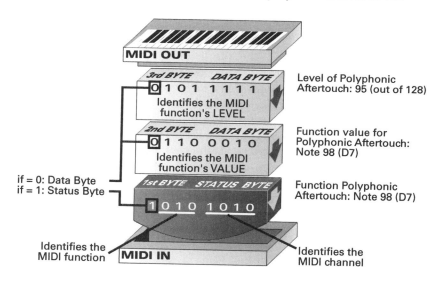

Figure 2.2 Components of a sample MIDI message.

Table 2.1   How MIDI Channels Are Represented in the Last Four Bits of the Status Byte

Bits	MIDI Channel	Bits	MIDI Channel	Bits	MIDI Channel	Bits	MIDI Channel
0000	1	0100	5	1000	9	1100	13
0001	2	0101	6	1001	10	1101	14
0010	3	0110	7	1010	11	1110	15
0011	4	0111	8	1011	12	1111	16

A musical instrument can receive events on all the MIDI channels simultaneously but can make only one channel active at a time, unless this instrument is multi-timbral. As mentioned previously, a TV set receives all the channels through its antenna/cable but can tune into only one channel at a time. Determining which channel the message belongs to is an important part of the Status byte of a MIDI message because it determines whether or not the message belongs to the channel the receiving device is set at so that the information is processed or filtered accordingly.

If your instrument is multi-timbral, it will retain only the MIDI messages that apply to its active channels. For example, an instrument set to play channels 1 through 5 will ignore all messages not containing the appropriate bits in the Status byte. In other words, it will ignore all messages where the Status byte indicates the events are set to channels 6 through 16.

Most aspects of your musical performance can be represented in a MIDI message. The following sections will identify these aspects and explain how they work and what values are attached to them. To better understand these aspects of MIDI messages, they have been divided into five categories:

- ❄ **Channel Voice** messages are the basic MIDI events representing a musical performance. The most common channel voice messages are Note On and Note Off.
- ❄ **Channel Mode** messages tell devices to send or receive information in a certain way, which is defined by the mode being sent. An example of this would be to turn all sounds off or all notes off.
- ❄ **System Common** messages are, as the name would suggest, common to all instruments, devices, or software in your MIDI setup. Sequencers use system common messages for MIDI time references (through MIDI Time Code), song position, song selection, and tuning.
- ❄ **System Real Time** messages are synchronization commands used by MIDI to control sequences, such as Start and Stop commands imbedded as a MIDI command, along with the MIDI Timing Clock.
- ❄ **System Exclusive** messages are used to send or receive instrument settings such as patch or performance memories. You can also use System Exclusive (SysEx) messages to transfer sample waveforms via MIDI along with other non-music related functions or use

SysEx messages to record parameter automations on software synthesizers using a remote MIDI controller.

You will find a complete list of these messages and their settings in Appendix B.

Channel Voice Messages

Channel voice messages are the backbone of MIDI because they represent the bulk of what MIDI transmits during a live performance. The following section describes these messages so that you can understand what is transmitted through MIDI and where to look when editing a MIDI sequence of events recorded in a sequencer. You will find a general discussion on sequencers in Chapter 8.

Note On

Every time you press on a note, a *Note On* message is sent. This Note On message contains two pieces of information: the note number corresponding to the key pressed and the velocity at which this note was pressed. This information is passed as values between 0 and 127. Note numbers are discussed later in this chapter. As for velocity, higher values represent notes played faster and subsequently usually feel as if they are struck with more force. This value represents the dynamic value of the note, which is usually musically represented by names such as pianissimo, piano, mezzo piano, mezzo forte, forte, and fortissimo.

A velocity of 0 means that the note wasn't struck, so velocity levels are between 1 and 127 rather than 0 and 127. Zero velocity represents a Note Off message, which is described in the next section. How fast you have to press a note to get the appropriate dynamic depends on the actual sound itself and the mechanics of your instrument. Table 2.2 gives you an idea of the musical equivalent for a range of velocity values when using a standard linear velocity sensitive instrument. Some instruments actually provide different velocity curves to help musicians with different playing styles. With a standard linear velocity response, the loudness or intensity of the instrument increases at the same rate as the value of the velocity. This loudness or intensity does not affect the actual volume or level setting for this MIDI instrument, but rather how the note will be played back, depending on how it was hit.

Table 2.2 Velocity Range Explained Through Corresponding Musical Intensity Indications

Musical Value	Musical Notation	MIDI Velocity Range
Extremely soft	ppp	1 to 15
Pianissimo (very soft)	pp	16 to 31
Piano (soft)	p	32 to 47
Mezzo piano (softly or moderately soft)	mp	48 to 63
Mezzo forte (moderate, not too soft, not too hard)	mf	64 to 79

Musical Value	Musical Notation	MIDI Velocity Range
Forte (loud or hard)	f	80 to 95
Fortissimo (very loud or hard)	ff	96 to 111
Extremely loud or aggressive	fff	112 to 127

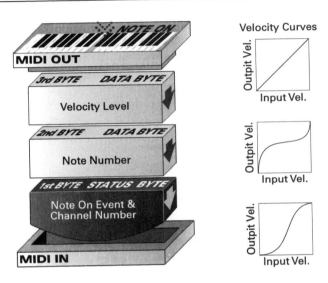

Figure 2.3   Note On message.

Table 2.3   Different Ways to Look at the Same Values Found in Figure 2.3: as Sequencer MIDI Values, Binary Values, and Hexadecimal Values

	Note On & Channel Number	Note Number	Velocity Level
MIDI values	Note On, Ch. 3	60	100
Binary equivalent	1001 0010	0011 1100	0110 0100
Hex equivalent	92	3C	64

In Figure 2.3, you can see an example of the Note On message with the content of its Status and Data bytes in MIDI, binary, and hex equivalents.

Most new keyboards or controllers support velocity levels, but if you have an older model, it might transmit only one velocity level, which is usually set at 64. In this case, it wouldn't matter how fast or slow you hit the key, since it would always be sending a velocity level of 64.

How velocity affects the sound is also determined by the device's preset settings. Sometimes, hitting the keys with high velocity (quick or hard) will make the sound brighter; other times, it will be louder or actually trigger a different sample altogether if your sound module is programmed as such. In other words, the velocity always affects how the sound will react, but not necessarily in the same way for each sound. This is different for the volume level, which always makes a sound louder as the MIDI volume level gets higher.

Note Off

This message is sent when you release a note after striking it. Most devices will use a Note On message with a velocity value of 0 to indicate that the note is off. If your keyboard supports Release Velocity sensing, which detects how fast you release the key once it has been hit, then a Note Off message is sent with its corresponding Release Velocity value as shown in Table 2.4. In this case, the Release Velocity value will affect the release envelope of your sound module. This is not implemented on every sound module, so if it is not, the Release Velocity value will act just as a Note On with a velocity at 0 (see Table 2.5), releasing the note and ignoring the speed at which it is released.

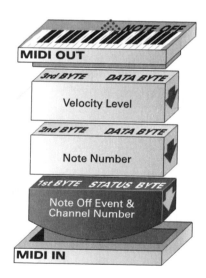

Figure 2.4 Note Off message.

Table 2.4   MIDI, Binary, and Hexadecimal Values Passed when a MIDI Controller Supports Release Velocity Levels

	Note On & Channel Number	Note Number	Velocity Level
MIDI values	Note Off, Ch. 3	60	100
Binary equivalent	1000 0010	0011 1100	0110 0100
Hex equivalent	82	3C	64

Table 2.5   MIDI, Binary, and Hexadecimal Values Passed when a MIDI Controller Does Not Support Release Velocity Levels

	Note On & Channel Number	Note Number	Velocity Level
MIDI values	Note Off, Ch. 3	60	0
Binary equivalent	1000 0010	0011 1100	0000 0000
Hex equivalent	82	3C	00

Figure 2.4 illustrates a complete MIDI message with the MIDI Note Off Status byte and the associated Data bytes, the note number being released and, when supported by the MIDI controller, its release velocity. If your MIDI controller supports the Release Velocity level parameter, this will affect how quickly the note will fade once the key is released. On the other hand, if the sound module receiving this data doesn't support the parameter, it will simply interpret it as normal Note Off data (Note On with velocity set at 0).

❋ **How Sequencers Handle Note Off Messages**

Most popular sequencers offer a list view of MIDI events but in many cases will not display Note Off messages as separate messages to avoid cluttering the list with additional messages. However, they will most likely display a length value for each Note On message, which corresponds to the difference in time between the Note On message timestamp and the Note Off message timestamp. When editing the length of a MIDI Note On event, you essentially modify the position of the Note Off event that will be sent to the receiving MIDI device.

Channel Pressure or Channel Aftertouch

This function comes into action once you've pressed a key and then decide to press harder while you're holding the note down. This will, in most cases, add some kind of vibrato-like modulation to the sound being played, which is similar to a cello player moving his finger on a string while holding it, creating a vibrato on the sustained note. Many MIDI controllers support this type of function; if yours doesn't, no Channel Aftertouch information will be sent.

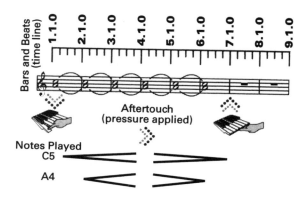

Figure 2.5 Channel pressure applied to a two-note harmony.

The harder you press on a key (after the initial key strike), the higher the aftertouch (or channel pressure) value will be. When playing more than one note, the hardest pressed key will determine the channel pressure value sent over MIDI.

In Figure 2.5, a two-note harmony is played, but one is being pressed harder than the other. The resulting channel pressure will always be the higher value. The following table illustrates the MIDI messages that would be sent.

In Table 2.6, the Status byte for a channel pressure or aftertouch message tells the receiving device the name of the function and the channel for this message. The first Data byte represents the amount or value for this aftertouch. The second Data byte is not used in the channel pressure message. The last column represents the point in time when this event occurs, but it does not represent the actual MIDI message itself, since it is written in bar and beat format. This is just to give you an idea of where to look in the figure.

Table 2.6   The Result of Figure 2.5's Channel Pressure Messages Sent by a Keyboard Supporting This Function

Status Byte	Data Byte 1	Data Byte 2	Bar & Beat
Note On, Ch. 3	C5	100	1.1.0
Note On, Ch. 3	A4	100	1.1.0
Channel Aftertouch, Ch. 3	64	none	2.1.0
Channel Aftertouch, Ch. 3	127	none	3.3.0
Channel Aftertouch, Ch. 3	64	none	4.3.0
Channel Aftertouch, Ch. 3	0	none	6.1.0
Note On, Ch. 3	C5	0 (Note Off)	7.1.0
Note On, Ch. 3	A4	0 (Note Off)	7.1.0

Polyphonic Key Pressure or Polyphonic Aftertouch

This function is like Channel Aftertouch but determines the amount of pressure you exercise on a series of keys once they are pressed. The word *polyphonic* means that each note, or key, can have its own pressure value. Unlike the Channel Aftertouch or channel key pressure, each note can have its own pressure level value. For example, play a three-note C major chord and then apply pressure (press harder) on the keys; a series of MIDI messages will be sent out to account for this variation in key pressure, which is also called *aftertouch*.

Note that not all keyboard controllers or MIDI input devices support Polyphonic Aftertouch. If your device does not support this parameter, it will not send Polyphonic Key Pressure messages as you press harder on the keys.

The following table displays a list of MIDI messages that would be sent as a result of the actions illustrated in Figure 2.5. The Status byte describes the actual function, in this case, Note On events and polyphonic aftertouch (or polyphonic key pressure) and its channel number. The first Data byte is used to identify the note number (in this table, the note name is displayed to better relate with the corresponding figure). The second Data byte represents the amount of Polyphonic Aftertouch for that specific note.

Table 2.7   The Result of Figure 2.5's Polyphonic Key Pressure Messages Sent by a Keyboard Supporting This Function

Status Byte	Data Byte 1	Data Byte 2	Bar & Beat
Note On, Ch. 3	C5	100	1.1.0
Note On, Ch. 3	A4	100	1.1.0
Polyphonic Key Pressure, Ch. 3	C5	32	2.1.0
Polyphonic Key Pressure, Ch. 3	A4	64	2.1.0
Polyphonic Key Pressure, Ch. 3	C5	78	3.3.0
Polyphonic Key Pressure, Ch. 3	A4	127	3.3.0
Polyphonic Key Pressure, Ch. 3	C5	32	4.3.0
Polyphonic Key Pressure, Ch. 3	A4	64	4.3.0
Polyphonic Key Pressure, Ch. 3	C5	0	6.1.0
Polyphonic Key Pressure, Ch. 3	A4	0	6.1.0
Note On, Ch. 3	C5	0 (Note Off)	7.1.0
Note On, Ch. 3	A4	0 (Note Off)	7.1.0

If you compare Tables 2.6 and 2.7, you can see the difference between Channel Aftertouch and Polyphonic Key Aftertouch. One offers one level of aftertouch, which it applies to all notes played simultaneously, and the other offers a more precise aftertouch control, assigning each note its own value.

> ❄ **The Cost of Polyphonic Key Pressure**
>
> Polyphonic Aftertouch messages use a greater number of bytes than Channel Aftertouch messages. As a result, they use a greater portion of the MIDI bandwidth. Furthermore, to support Polyphonic Key Pressure, a MIDI controller such as a keyboard will require additional pressure sensors on each key. These sensors result in higher manufacturing costs and usually translate into more expensive keyboards. Manufacturers will often omit these sensors to keep the price of a controller keyboard affordable. While Polyphonic Key Pressure allows for greater expressivity in a performance when using sustained pads, it is not essential with shorter, more percussive sounds. If you are looking for a MIDI controller to emulate the behavior of a piano keyboard, keep this fact in mind, since it could save you a few dollars.

Program Change

Most sound modules and keyboards today have memories in which presets are stored as programs or spaces where you can store your own programs. You can later recall these sounds by selecting the appropriate program number. Some manufacturers might called them presets; others call them programs, instruments, patches, or whatever. When a specific number can access a sound, you can change that sound using a *Program Change* message. If you have a MIDI device that doesn't contain sounds, like a MIDI-enabled reverb, for example, you can access preset or program numbers stored in the device's memory just as you would with a sound module.

You can access up to 128 sounds using the Program Change function. When sending a Program Change message, the MIDI device associated with that specific MIDI channel will respond by changing the sound or program for this channel. In other words, if you have a multi-timbral device and wish to change the program for the part playing on channel 5, sending a Program Change for this channel will affect only this part and not the others.

Program Change messages contain only one byte of data following the Status byte. This Data byte holds the program number, and the Status byte tells the device that this is a Program Change for a specific MIDI channel, as displayed in Figure 2.6.

Program Changes are different from sound banks: Program numbers identify a specific sound, while sound banks identify a specific set of sounds. To select a specific set of sounds, such as a sound bank, you would use a *Sound Bank Control Change*, described later in this chapter.

On sound modules it became useful to define an ordered and standard set of programs in order to make the playback of MIDI songs more compatible from machine to machine. This would, for example, set a Program Change 01, which plays a piano on your sound module, and then have the same Program Change set a similar piano sound on another sound module rather than a completely different type of sound. This standard set of numbered and named sounds is called General MIDI. We will talk more on this in Chapter 4.

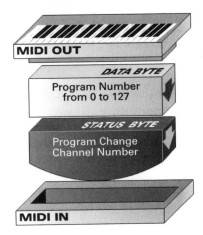

Figure 2.6   Program Change MIDI message.

❋ **MIDI Channel Numbering Convention**

MIDI uses values 0 to 15 in order to pass MIDI channel information. However, MIDI channels are always displayed as channels 1 to 16 to musicians.

Many MIDI devices display their program numbers starting from 1, even if a program number of 0 in a Program Change message selects the first program in the device. However, this approach was never standardized, and some devices use different methods to select a program. For example, some devices require the user to specify a bank of programs and then select one within the bank. Older sound modules might have two LEDs, each one having digits allowing numbers from 0 to 9, for example. In this case, to get to program 55, you would need to set your first bank to 5 and then select program 5. This is different than the Sound Bank Control Change presented above and described later in this chapter. Here, since it is actually an interface issue, which does not allow for more than nine digits per LED, you would still use a Program Change message to access your specific program number.

Table 2.8 Examples of Program Number Correspondence

MIDI Program Numbers	Device Using 3 LEDs with Numbers 0 to 9	Device Using Two LEDs with Numbers from 0 to 8	Device Using a Digital Display Starting at Program 1
0	000	00	1
1	001	01	2
…	…	…	…

MIDI Program Numbers	Device Using 3 LEDs with Numbers 0 to 9	Device Using Two LEDs with Numbers from 0 to 8	Device Using a Digital Display Starting at Program 1
8	008	08	9
9	009	10	10
10	010	11	11
...	...	...	...
17	017	18	18
18	018	20	19
Etc.	Etc.	Etc.	Etc.

Pitch Bend Change

Pitch bending can make keyboards more expressive, somewhat like a wind instrument, as when a saxophone player uses inflections in the attack of a sound to accentuate certain melodic lines by bending into a note. Most keyboards today have some kind of pitch bend controller. Some use a wheel, others a joystick. The goal is to be able to slide from one note to another smoothly by bending its pitch up or down. Because the human ear is very sensitive to pitch changes, the pitch bend message contains two Data bytes to determine the bend value. In fact, the pitch bend has a resolution of 16,384 steps, which is usually split in two: 8,192 steps above and the same number of steps below the original pitch, or a range from minus 8,192 to plus 8,191, with 0 being the original pitch. How much pitch bending this represents depends on the sound module's program setting. The pitch bend wheel range is programmable, so its Data bytes values do not determine a range, but rather a percentage over the programmed range. The General MIDI specification recommends that a pitch bend should have a range of plus or minus 2 half steps. In reality, you can program your sound to pitch bend over as much as a full octave if your instrument allows.

The pitch wheel range can also be adjusted via an RPN controller message as described below.

As you can see in Figure 2.7, the center pitch is represented by the MIDI values 0 (Data byte 1) and 64 (Data byte 2). One step above this would be MIDI values 1 (for Data byte 1) and 64 (for Data byte 2). One step below the center would be 127 (for Data byte 1) and 63 (for Data byte 2).

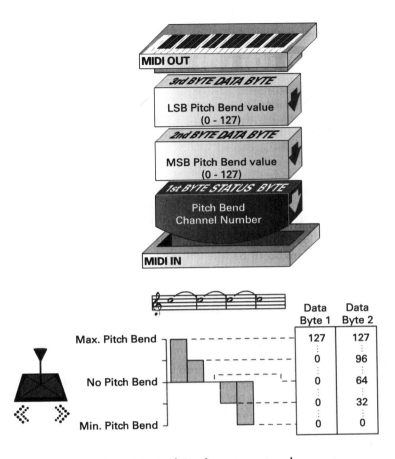

Figure 2.7 Pitch Bend messages at work.

Control Change

Control Changes are a set of a 128 different numbers assigned to different functions. Because there are so many functions to describe, the next chapter is dedicated exclusively to the description of these functions and their corresponding controller numbers. At this point, remember that the first numbers (0 to 119) are reserved for Channel Voice messages and that the Control Change numbers 120 to 127 are reserved for the next category of MIDI messages: *Channel Mode* messages.

Channel Mode Messages

MIDI modes affect how the device will respond to incoming MIDI messages and how it will send outgoing messages. The MIDI Specification allows four modes of operation, using two sets of Channel Mode messages:

❋ **Omni On** mode implies that a device can respond to all or any incoming MIDI channel data, regardless of its channel.

❋ **Omni Off** mode implies that a device can only respond to its base MIDI channel. The base MIDI channel is the default channel on which the MIDI device is set. This channel can be set directly in the device's MIDI preferences. For example, if you set your keyboard to channel 1, it will send and receive information only on this channel in Omni Off mode. Channel 1 in this case will be its base channel. On the other hand, a multitimbral device can send and receive over any MIDI channel. However, in Omni Off mode, the base channel setting will determine which channel will be used to transmit MIDI and which channel it will respond to when receiving MIDI messages. For example, if you set the base channel to 1, any messages the Status byte doesn't identify as being channel 1 would be ignored in this mode.

❋ **Poly** mode implies that a device is capable of polyphony and will enable polyphonic playing on any MIDI channel. You have polyphony when you can play more than one note simultaneously (chords) on a given MIDI channel. The number of simultaneous polyphonic voices you can have depends on the device itself, since this is not a MIDI specification but rather a limitation of the device's design.

❋ **Mono** mode implies that a device will not play more than one note at a time on any given channel. Multi-timbral instruments may play two or more notes on two or more separate channels, just not on the same channel.

 About the Base Channel

A receiving device will respond to Channel Mode messages only if they are on the same MIDI channel as its base channel. A device always has a base channel for the purpose of these Channel Mode messages, even when you are in Omni mode.

These modes can be combined in four ways, which are often referred to as Mode 1, Mode 2, Mode 3, and Mode 4:

❋ **Mode 1: Omni On/Poly**—In this mode, a device plays MIDI data coming from any MIDI channel and will redirect these channels to the instrument's base channel. It will also play polyphony normally. Voice messages are received from all voice channels and assigned to voices polyphonically. All voices are transmitted on the base channel. This is rarely used because in this mode the receiving device doesn't care which channel the data is from and will play back everything. However, if you are playing in a live show and want to layer different instrument sounds coming from different sources, it is a good setting. Otherwise, stay away from this mode.

❋ **Mode 2: Omni On/Mono**—This mode is similar to Mode 1, since the receiving device does not discriminate any MIDI channel information. In Mode 2, it will play only one note at a time. Voice messages are received from all voice channels and control only one voice, monophonically. This mode is the rarest one of all since its purpose is quite limited, being that you can't isolate MIDI channels, and you can play only one note at a time.

❋ **Mode 3: Omni Off/Poly**—From the least used (Mode 2) to the most used, this is as common as common gets in today's MIDI world. In this mode, a single channel device (as opposed to a multi-timbral one) will respond to only the MIDI messages set to that device's channel and will ignore all other MIDI messages. In a multi-timbral instrument, the device will respond to all the active channels as separate devices. For example, you could have a sequencer send up to 16 channels of MIDI data to a 16-instrument multi-timbral device, all playing their respective parts. Since it is in Poly mode, each part will play its dedicated polyphony.

❋ **Mode 4: Omni Off/Mono**—In this case, each active MIDI channel on a receiving device will play only monophonic lines. The base channel determines which will be the active channel on a single timbre instrument, whereas a multi-timbral instrument will treat each MIDI channel as it is internally set up for. In other words, if you have made a MIDI channel active on your device, it will accept and play the MIDI information in monophony. This is not a common mode; however, it can be effective if used with a guitar controller where each string is assigned a MIDI channel and each MIDI channel plays one note at a time.

The Channel Mode messages are nested in the last eight values of the Control Change set (Control Change numbers 120 to 127). So their Status byte is identical to a channel voice message containing a Control Change function. This subset of control changes is called Channel mode because it tells the device how to handle data sent or received. It has control over monophonic and polyphonic operations as well as how it handles MIDI channels when receiving a stream of MIDI with multiple channels embedded.

MIDI modes and Local Control messages are described in the following sections. You will find a further discussion on the other Channel Mode messages in Chapter 3. These messages are All Sound Off, Reset All Controllers, and All Notes Off, which serve to reset parameters to default values (controller 121) or stop Note On messages (controllers 120 and 123).

About Local Control

MIDI keyboards often come with a sound module programmed with sounds. On the other hand, rack-mounted sound modules don't have any keyboard controllers. In fact, you can find many models of synthesizers that offer both keyboard and rack-mounted versions of the same model. Keyboards are really two devices in one: a controller device and a sound module device, as shown on the left side of Figure 2.8.

The *Local Control* message disconnects the controller part from the sound module part of a keyboard. This message is sent by the Control Change number 122 (see Chapter 3 for a full description of this controller). When the Local Control is Off, the MIDI is sent out but the sound module does not produce the sounds triggered by the keyboard portion. When the Local Control is On, the MIDI device produces sounds at the same time as it sends MIDI information to its MIDI output. Regardless of the Local Control's state, the sound generators or circuitry will receive the MIDI information coming from the MIDI input.

> ❅ **Local Control Support**
>
> Some synthesizers, especially older ones, may not support Local Control switching. When this is the case, you will need to disable MIDI echoing from the sequencer application. This option will most likely be found in the sequencer's MIDI preference settings. By default, most sequencers will echo MIDI events coming in record-enabled MIDI tracks. Turning off this option will essentially have the same effect as turning off the Local Control setting on your synth.

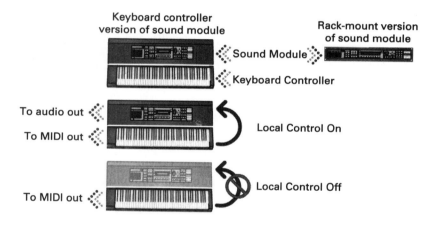

Figure 2.8   Local control.

System Common Messages

System Common messages are intended for all channels in a system and enhance the functions of other MIDI commands. They are not related to any specific channel. In most cases, System Common messages relate to synchronization features and are used with sequencers since they relate to time positioning, song selection, and tuning features on your MIDI device. Here's a look at these messages.

MIDI Time Code (MTC) Quarter Frame

MIDI Time Code (MTC) will be the subject of a longer discussion in Chapter 11, but suffice to say at this point that the MTC message allows sequencers to lock up to video devices containing SMPTE (Society of Motion Picture and Television Engineers) Time Code. SMPTE is the standard protocol for video synchronization, and it works by giving each frame in a film strip a specific address. This address looks like a time stamp with hours, minutes, seconds, and frames (sometimes even sub-frames). It looks something like this: 00:00:00:00, where the first two digits to the left represent hours, then the minutes, and so on, just as if you were reading the time of day. In this time display, each second can be divided into individual frames.

MTC is basically a MIDI version of this protocol. To use MTC, you will need to have a device that converts the SMPTE into its MTC equivalent and finally, sends the MTC data along a MIDI cable, just like any other MIDI message. Once your sequencer receives this MTC, it can lock to it and play in sync with the video, allowing you to score music, for example, to a video.

The System Common message sends Quarter Frame messages, which tells the sequencer the time stamp address in hours, minutes, seconds, and frames and which type of time code is being used (if it's PAL, NTSC, drop-frame, non-drop, and so on. This will be explained further in Chapter 11).

Note that MTC is an alternative to another type of synchronization method called MIDI Timing Clock, also referred to as Timing Clock to avoid acronym confusion. Timing Clock is not as precise as MTC, since it does not support any shuttle functions. For example, you can't fast forward and rewind a video while having a MIDI sequence follow the video as you fast forward.

MTC is meant for video synchronization and refers to a fixed time or absolute reference. Timing Clock is a relative reference: It is relative to the tempo of a sequence, since it subdivides each beat into 24 ticks (ticks are sub-divisions of beats), no matter the tempo of the sequence.

The MTC message contains only one Data byte that holds the type of time code and the value for the time address, as shown in Figure 2.9. This message is called Quarter Frame because each message contains a quarter of the information: In the first MIDI message, it gives the hour value, the second represents the minutes, the third represents the seconds, and the fourth gives the frame number. In other words, it takes four MIDI messages (each one containing a Status byte and a Data byte) to represent a full SMPTE time.

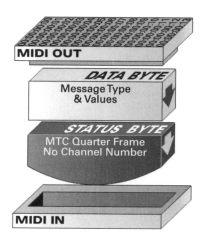

Figure 2.9   Content of a MIDI Time Code Quarter Frame message.

Song Position Pointer (SPP)

The *Song Position Pointer* message tells receiving MIDI devices the position of a song in a sequence. When a sequencer is set to transmit SPP messages through its MIDI output ports, a Start command is sent out when playback is initiated. Every clock-driven instrument then starts playing from the beginning of this sequence to its end unless the playback is stopped and a Stop command is received. It then holds its position until you send a Continue command. What the SPP message does is simple: It gives an address to each 16th note step in a song, starting with beat 0 at the beginning. SPP messages don't actually tell the sequence to start or stop, but rather tell the devices where to start again once stopped. This 16th note step is set every six MIDI Timing Clocks from the start of the sequence. Since there are 24 ticks per beat and the SPP identifies every sixth one, you have an even four SPP addresses per beat, or one SPP address per 16th note (24 ticks/6 ticks = 4 times per beat or quarter note = 1 16th note).

To accommodate long songs, two Data bytes are used to identify each 16th note step. This gives you a total of 14 bits of data to identify each 16th note step, or a total of 16,384 16th notes. That's 1,024 bars of 4/4 time signature (four beats of quarter notes per bar). This information is divided in two Data bytes, called Most Significant Byte (MSB) and Least Significant Byte (LSB), as shown in Figure 2.10. As the name suggests, when a value changes in the MSB portion of the message, the increments are greater than in the LSB, even though they all represent 16th note steps. Look at the MSB as the integer values and the LSB as the decimal values. You can have as many numbers to the left of a decimal point as you can have to the right, but the ones on the left will always represent greater values than the ones on the right. This principle will be further developed in Chapter 3.

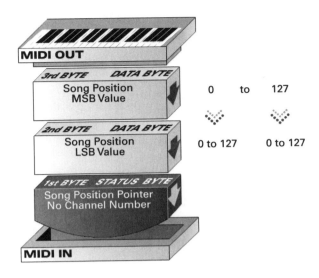

Figure 2.10 Song Position Pointer message.

Let's look at this through an example: To send a sequencer to the second beat of bar 33 in a song with a 4/4 time signature, the SPP would point to the 517th 16th note step in the sequence ((32 bars×4 beats×4 16th notes) + (1 beats×4 16th notes)) = 516, which is the last 16th note of the first beat of the thirty-second bar. The next 16th note step would be number 517, and this is our target. This would be represented by the LSB's sixth value (5) and the MSB's fifth value (4) ((5×1) + (4×128) = 517).

While these calculations seem tedious, they are all done without your knowledge, and don't worry, you won't have to do the math every time you want to start a sequence. Once the Song Position Pointer (SPP) message has identified the song's position, the other slaved devices will know where to start once they receive the appropriate command. A device is slaved when a master device sending synchronization information, such as a Song Position Pointer message, controls its transport functions, such as play and stop.

Song Select

A *Song Select* message tells receiving devices that support this message to load a specific song number into a sequencer's song memory. Imagine, for example, that you have a sequencer in your keyboard, and this keyboard is hooked up to a drum machine that holds drum sequences for songs. When practicing a set at home, you can assign the same numbers (or song order) to both sequenced devices. When it's time to perform live, simply send a Song Select message through MIDI, and the keyboard and drum machine will load the appropriate song in the set. The Song Select message can store up to 128 songs in a set and sends only one Data byte representing the song number.

Most devices display song numbers starting at number 1 instead of 0. Some devices might even use different labeling systems for song: for example, Bank A, Number 1 song. However, a Song Select message with song number 0 should always select the first song, just as the first program number on your sound module will always be Program Number 0 in a Program Change message.

Once the Song Select message is received, it will cue the song at the beginning of the sequence unless a subsequent Song Position Pointer message is sent to this device, telling it to start somewhere else. Songs always default to Song Position 0.

> ❄ **Synchronizing More Than One Sequencer Using MIDI Clock**
>
> For both devices to play properly once their Song Select has been cued, they should be synchronized using a common MIDI Clock. Otherwise, the sequences might start together, but they would quickly drift apart, especially if the tempo setting is different. MIDI Clock is described in Chapter 11.

Tune Request

This message is mostly used for sound modules that have analog circuitry. Once the device receives this message, it usually initiates a self-tuning operation, which calibrates its oscillators (the actual sound-making portion of the synthesizer) to match up. Older analog synthesizers were known to go out of tune as they warmed up, so during a performance they sometimes would have to be retuned in order to stay in tune with the other instruments, just as you retune a guitar or a bass. The Tune Request message doesn't contain any Data bytes, and its default value is 0. This message is useless on digital synthesizers.

End Of Exclusive Message

This message marks the end of a System Exclusive message. It's like the caboose at the end of a train. System Exclusive messages are discussed in the coming paragraphs. However, the end of a System Exclusive (SysEx) message is always identified using this System Common message. End Of Exclusive messages don't have any Data bytes, and their value defaults to 0.

System Real Time Messages

System Real Time messages control, in real time, all devices in your system, and are channel independent. These messages are used for synchronizing clock-based devices such as sequencers and drum machines, using single Status byte messages. If a System Real Time message is not implemented, as in a sound module that doesn't have a built-in sequencer, for example, it is simply ignored.

System Real Time messages can be sent at any point in time at regular intervals, even in between bytes of other messages, to maintain timing precision. Once the System Real Time passes, the remaining bytes from other messages resume their previous status without any hiccups. In comparison to this, System Common messages such as MIDI Time Code (MTC) are time based, rather than clock based. The time is absolute, and the clock is relative to the speed of the sequence. Both types of messages serve a similar synchronization purpose; however, Real Time messages are music oriented and will serve their purpose when trying to lock two sequences together rather than a sequence and a video, for example. If you take a stick and a rubber band of the same length and draw equally spaced markings on both, you will have lines that will match up. Imagine the stick is a System Common message and the rubber band is a Real Time message. Now, stretch the rubber band; notice that the markings on the rubber band no longer match up with the markings on the stick. Notice also that the spaces separating the marks are still of equal distance in relation to each other. There lies the difference between these two types of synchronizing messages: One is relative to the tempo of a sequence, the other is absolute and will not vary with the tempo of the sequence.

There are six defined System Real Time messages.

Timing Clock

This message is used to synchronize timing across sequencers in a MIDI system. It is sent 24 times per beat (or quarter note), no matter what the tempo of a song (as displayed in Figure 2.11). Look at this as being a ruler with major markings, like inches or centimeters, and minor subdivisions, like fractions of an inch or millimeters. It is simply a way to divide time in an equally spaced format.

When a sequencer is recording MIDI, it starts counting ticks at the beginning of a song and then looks for incoming MIDI events. When other MIDI messages are sent, they are recorded and assigned a tick count so that when they are played back, they will play at the exact same time as recorded or later quantized to. This clock can be sent to other devices, and once these devices are set to follow an incoming Timing Clock, they can play back MIDI events in perfect synchronization. Some might debate the accuracy of MIDI timing when compared to digital audio timing, but we'll get back to this later when we will discuss software sequencers that handle both MIDI and audio.

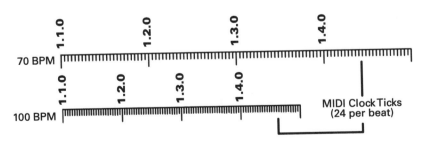

Figure 2.11 MIDI Clock ticks.

How fast is this Timing Clock? Well, there are 1,000,000 microseconds in a second. At a speed of 100 BPM (beat per minute), or 100 quarter notes per minute, the sequencer sends

24 ticks per beat for a total of 2,400 ticks in a minute. If there are 1,000,000 microseconds in a second, it means there are 60,000,000 of those in a minute. So 60,000,000/2,400 ticks = 1 tick every 25,000 microseconds, or 1 tick every 25 milliseconds. Now change the tempo to 120 BPM, and you have one tick every 20,833 microseconds. So how fast the Timing Clock is depends on the speed (tempo) of the sequence. The only consistency in the Timing Clock is that it subdivides each beat by 24. Compared to most sequencing software, which often runs at resolutions of 384 to 960 ticks per beat, MIDI Clock is considered to be a very coarse timing tool. Looking at the example in Figure 2.12, a master device can send a Song Select message to cue a specific song to play in the slave device, a series of Note On messages when you play a chord, a Foot Controller message when you want to sustain these Note On messages, periodic MIDI Clocks in order to keep the playback in sync with the master, a MIDI Program Change, and, eventually, a MIDI Stop to halt playback.

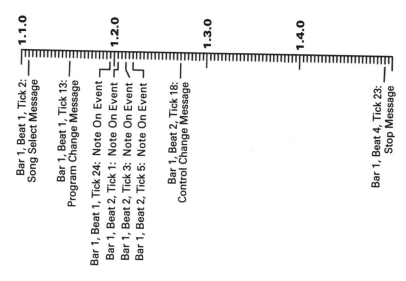

Figure 2.12   MIDI events as they occur along the MIDI Clock tick time line—each beat is divided into 24 equally spaced ticks, and the time between each tick is determined by the sequencer's tempo (BPM) value.

Timing Clock messages do not contain any Data bytes and act like pulses, or square waves. Imagine this as being a very fast pulsating metronome, which the sequencer uses to keep track of timing.

Start, Stop, and Continue

These three System Real Time messages control a slaved sequencer or drum machine from a master sequencer or drum machine. The *Start* message sends the sequence to Song Position 0 at the beginning of the sequence and begins playback. The *Stop* message interrupts the playback of the sequencer, and the *Continue* message tells the sequencer to pursue playback from the point it was last stopped until you send a Stop command again or reach the end of the sequence. When a slave sequencer or drum machine receives these messages, it immediately positions its sequencer at the appropriate location in the time line. If a Song Position Pointer message precedes the Continue command, the sequencer will then locate the position found in the SPP message and will continue from there. In other words, to start a sequence from anywhere else but the Song Position 0, you would use the Continue command rather than the Start command, which always starts at the beginning. The Stop command always acts as a pause, leaving the sequence at the position where it receives the Stop command.

Sending a Start command to a slaved sequencer sends it to Song Position 0 where it waits for an incoming Timing Clock from an external MIDI Clock. To stop a sequence and start it again from Song Position 0, you will need to send a Stop message before sending another Start message or the device will ignore this second Start message.

These three messages do not contain any Data bytes. All the MIDI sequencer needs is the Status byte telling it what to do: Start, Stop, or Continue.

Active Sensing

Sometimes MIDI connections are done virtually inside a computer's software, while other times, MIDI devices are often connected together through USB connections. Traditionally, all MIDI devices were connected using MIDI cables and connectors. Now, what would happen if one of your cables got disconnected while you were playing, or in MIDI language, just after you sent a bunch of Note On messages? Well, these *note on* messages would get stuck, since the cable carrying the Note Off message isn't connected to the device anymore. Remember, MIDI goes in one direction only, so a sending device such as a sequencer would not know if the receiving end has received events or not. The receiving device, on the other hand, has no way of knowing if more MIDI data should be coming its way either. So it just holds the notes until it receives a Note Off event message.

That's where *Active Sensing* messages come in handy. What this message does is simple, yet very clever. It sends a message to a receiving device. Once this receiving device gets an Active Sensing command, it will expect at least one MIDI event every 300 ms on the MIDI port through which it received this message. If there is no MIDI activity over this MIDI port for 270 ms, then when Active Sensing is enabled, the sending device will know to send another Active Sensing message to reassure the receiving device that everything is all right and that the connection is not dead. If the receiving device, which is expecting a MIDI event at least once every 300 ms, doesn't receive anything, it then considers this port connection to be dead and sends an All Note Off command to its sound module, effectively killing any stuck notes. It acts in many ways like a carrier signal for a modem; it indicates that the line is still operational.

This is an optional feature that some devices implement. Many devices don't ever initiate this minimal security feature. To verify if your device supports this feature, you will need to consult your device's MIDI implementation chart or look at your MIDI interface to see if there's a constant flashing LED, which would indicate it is receiving active sensing messages.

System Reset

When you turn on a MIDI device, it usually sets itself up using default device parameters. These parameters sometimes vary from one device to the next. Obviously, these parameters can be changed using MIDI messages, as you have seen up until now and will continue to discover as you read the rest of the book. The System Reset sends a Status byte ordering the receiving devices to reset their parameters to a nominal state, or as they were when you powered up your device. Because the System Reset message is part of the System Real Time messages, it doesn't matter which MIDI channel the receiving device is set to. It is more likely that a sequencer will send a System Reset message than a synthesizer. That's why System Resets are not found under the next category of messages (System Exclusive). It should be noted that a sending device should not use this message automatically, but it should rather be sent when a musician specifically wants to tell a device to do so. Otherwise, this could lead to a situation where two devices endlessly reset each other. A System Reset message can be useful to bring all the parameters of a MIDI device to their default values. For example, if you've been working on a project and have been tweaking certain parameters on your device to see how these parameters affect the sound, using the System Reset message serves as a one-touch button that brings everything back to the way it was before you started.

Like other System Real Time messages, the System Reset message only contains a Status byte.

System Exclusive Messages

Until now, we have discussed messages common to all devices, keyboard, sound modules, and sequencers. No matter which manufacturer built the device, they all share a common language through these commands. As the word "Exclusive" might suggest, these messages are different from all others. In fact, System Exclusive, or SysEx for short, is used to send some data that is specific to a particular MIDI device. For example, a SysEx message can be used to set the feedback level for an operator in an FM synthesis device, a dump of its patch memory, sequencer data, or even waveform data. If you consider the last example, it would be useless to send this type of information to a non-waveform based synthesizer. However, most devices will support Pitch Bend, Foot Pedal, Modulation Wheel, and Program Change functions; therefore, they are part of the MIDI standard. In other words, whenever functions are manufacturer dependent, they become part of the SysEx family. That's why this is called System Exclusive: It sends specific information to a specific device, "excluding" the other devices from the conversation.

Every SysEx message starts and ends the same way. However, almost every MIDI device defines the format of its own set of SysEx messages, and a device will understand the values these messages contain if it is being addressed by name. At the beginning of the SysEx message, there is a manufacturer identification message (Manufacturer ID number) telling a receiving device, "Hey, I'm talking to you," and a SysEx message ends when it receives an End SysEx Real Time message (or if it receives any other non-system real time message). In between these two Status bytes (see Figure 2.13), any number of 7-bit Data bytes may be sent (remember that the first bit is always used to identify the Status byte). Once the device understands for whom the incoming SysEx is intended, it either ignores it or processes it, depending on the Manufacturer's ID number.

SysEx messages can be used in different ways. Here are a few examples:

❋ When saving a song in a sequencer, you can include a series of SysEx messages at the beginning of the sequence that will configure the custom patches you have created for this song. If you change your programs for another song, every time you load this one, your custom settings will be sent back to your specific device, as you saved them in the sequence.

❋ You may also want to send all the parameter settings of a MIDI device into patch editing software (editor/librarian) in order to use your computer's graphical interface to make changes to these parameters, rather than your device's front LCD panel. Once you've edited your parameters and saved them in a file on your computer, you can use a SysEx transfer to send the modified information back to your MIDI device.

❋ You can use SysEx to transmit the patterns from a drum machine to another drum machine, or better yet, to your computer.

❋ Remote MIDI control surface devices use SysEx messages to communicate with digital audio workstations (DAWs). This communication makes it possible to associate any physical control on the external device to a virtual control inside the DAW application, for example, associating a volume slider control to a volume channel fader inside a DAW mixer.

Hardware manufacturers can apply for a System Exclusive Manufacturer ID number. It is the MMA's (MIDI Manufacturer's Association) responsibility to assign Manufacturer's ID numbers that are adopted as a standard. You will find a complete list of Manufacturer ID numbers in Appendix B of this book.

The manufacturer of a product determines the purpose of the remaining Data bytes, no matter how many there may be. Usually, what follows the Manufacturer ID number is the Model Number ID as defined by that specific manufacturer. This way, you may have a Korg Triton and a Korg M1 in your MIDI setup, and they will both respond to the same Manufacturer ID, but since the model is different, the Triton will know if the rest of the bytes are for it, or for the M1. After this Model ID number, you might find information that will tell the device what the rest of the SysEx message is supposed to do, how many more Data bytes the device should expect, and so on. Some manufacturers even have a checksum byte, which is used to check the integrity of the message's transmission.

Imagine you're on a tour that brings you by plane into the middle of the Amazon forest. As you get off the plane, your tour guide counts everybody and lets you go off in the wilderness, telling you to be back in an hour. After the hour passes, the tour guide counts the passengers again to make sure everybody made it back. Your tour guide checks to make sure that everyone who came off the plane is back on it; otherwise, the plane won't leave. A checksum byte does a similar process, counting the sum of bytes that pass by and comparing it with a checksum value. If both values match, it accepts the transfer as successful; otherwise, it tells you the transfer failed and waits for further instructions.

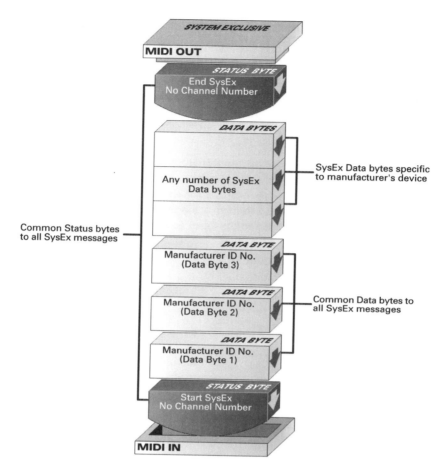

Figure 2.13 The construction of a System Exclusive (SysEx) message.

As mentioned above, if for some reason a device should receive a MIDI message other than a SysEx Data byte, a System Real Time message, or an End Of SysEx message, it would consider the transfer as being aborted, since such a scenario would indicate an abnormal MIDI condition.

Note Names and Numbers

As a musician, you know that notes are given names. These names might vary, depending on the language you speak. For example, in English, notes in a scale are named with letters from A to G, with the most common scale being C (C, D, E, F, G, A, B). Germans have a similar naming system; however, B is replaced with the letter H. In French, this same scale is represented with the following names: C = Do, D = Re, E = Mi, and so on. Between these notes, you have accidental notes, which are half-tones between some notes, so you will have C sharp (C#), D sharp (D#), and so on when going upward, and B flat (Bb), A flat (Ab), and so on when going downward. On a piano—and since MIDI was developed with the keyboard in mind, many of its references can be made to this instrument—the center of a keyboard is often referred to as middle C. Since most pianos have the same number of keys (88 keys), it's not difficult to find this center C.

Since MIDI is a digital language, numbers have replaced key names. As you might recall, out of the eight available bits in a message, one is used to indicate whether the byte is a Status message or a Data message. Therefore, with the remaining 7 bits, MIDI can give up to 128 different note values, which it distributes over the whole range of notes.

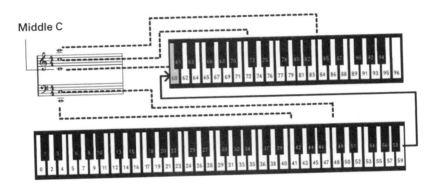

Figure 2.14 MIDI key numbers over a keyboard range.

Figure 2.14 illustrates how these numbers are distributed over a 96-key keyboard, which is already 12 keys more than any controller keyboard you will find on the market. However, MIDI can expand this range up to 127 (0 to 127 represents 128 values). The middle C in MIDI is always key number 60. So when you play the middle C on your keyboard, the MIDI value sent out is 60.

Because as humans, and as musicians, we are more familiar with note names, references made to MIDI numbers are very rare in both software and hardware interfaces. This is why the note names remain the best way to identify notes. To know which C is being played over a keyboard range, a number is assigned to it so that we know if it's high or low on the keyboard. Now, logic would have it that the lowest C (MIDI value 0 in Figure 2.14) would be considered the C0 octave, then the C above that the C1 octave to differentiate the first octave from the second. The following C would be C2, and so on. Middle C in this case would be C5. But in reality, there are discrepancies on how this is interpreted, depending on the software or hardware you are using. The discrepancy lies in the octave number. Roland documentation always refers to middle C as C4, while Yamaha refers to the same note as C3. The MIDI protocol assigns the MIDI note number 60 to middle C, no matter whether it is named

C3, C4, or C5. In fact, if you were to play a C major chord on your keyboard, starting on the middle C and doubling the C one octave higher, you would be sending the following numeric values through MIDI: 60, 64, 67, and 72 as MIDI note number values. However, unlike pianos, the actual pitch (if any) associated with MIDI note numbers depends on the receiving device because some keyboards have transposition parameters built in.

As you saw earlier and will see later, these are not the only values you are sending through MIDI. However, note numbers along with Note On or Note Off values are the basic stepping stones of MIDI, and it should be clear to you by now why this is done.

Review Questions

1. How does MIDI see the difference between a Status byte and a Data byte?
   a) A Status byte has 8-bits and a Data byte has 7.
   b) A Status byte always begins with a 1, while a Data byte always begins with a 0.
   c) A MIDI message always begins with a Status byte, followed by a Data byte, so even bytes are always Data bytes and uneven bytes are always Status bytes.
   d) Status bytes always begin with a Note On message, and Data bytes always begin with a Note Off message.

2. MIDI Note On and Note Off events are part of which category of messages?
   a) System Real Time messages
   b) System Common messages
   c) Channel Mode messages
   d) Channel Voice messages

3. What is the most commonly used MIDI mode in today's MIDI world?
   a) Mode 1, Omni On/Poly
   b) Mode 2, Omni On/Mono
   c) Mode 3, Omni Off/Poly
   d) Mode 4, Omni Off/Mono

4. Which of the following System Common messages would be completely useless with digital samplers or synthesizers but very useful with older MIDI-compatible analog synthesizers?
   a) End Of Exclusive message
   b) Tune Request
   c) Song Select
   d) Song Position Pointer

5. In a MIDI signal containing a MIDI Timing Clock, how many ticks per beat are there?

   a) 24 ticks
   b) 29.97 ticks
   c) 128 ticks
   d) 44,100 ticks

6. Which of the following statements does not describe a standard use for System Exclusive messages?

   a) Store an external device's parameter settings used in a song by including them in your MIDI song file.
   b) Edit some parameters and save the changes as a patch inside an editor/librarian application, or transfer them back to the MIDI device once they have been edited.
   c) Use MIDI to transmit drum patterns from one drum machine to the next.
   d) Save the music played during a performance.

7. MIDI note numbers support how many different notes (pitches)?

   a) 12
   b) 60
   c) 88
   d) 128

8. Which of the following messages is not a System Real Time message?

   a) Control Change
   b) Timing Clock
   c) Active Sensing
   d) System Reset

9. In a Channel Aftertouch (channel pressure) message, what information is transmitted in the second Data byte?

   a) A key pressure value
   b) The note number
   c) The bar and beat location in the sequence
   d) None of the above

10. True or False: A Note On message with a velocity of 0 has the same effect in MIDI as a Note Off message.

3 } Control Change Messages

Until now, we have discussed only one type of MIDI controller: the keys, those little black and white rectangles laid out in a row. That's one type of controlling device MIDI offers you. A keyboard is probably the best known but not the only type of MIDI controller. You can also find on most keyboards devices such as pitch bend wheels, modulation wheels, sustain foot switches, volume foot switches, and joysticks (acting as modulation and pitch bend controllers). Some devices also have breath controllers that control the sound of a device using your breath. All of these devices have one thing in common: They are meant to give you physical control over the parameters of a sound module or software application in a live or mixing performance. Like a keyboard, other control devices generate MIDI messages that can be recorded and played back to reproduce the original performance as precisely as possible.

Here's a summary of what you will learn in this chapter:

* What Control Change messages are and how they work.
* The functions and values associated with each Control Change message and how they affect a performance.
* The difference between a low-resolution and high-resolution Control Change message.
* Which Control Change messages are meant as switches.
* How Channel Mode messages work.

What Are Control Change Messages?

As you saw in Chapter 2, playing a note on a MIDI keyboard sends a Note On message. In this message, two types of information are transmitted: the actual event—in this case, the Note On, and the number value of the actual note you played. This information is divided into the Status byte that identifies the message as being a Note On event and the Data bytes representing the note number value for this event and its velocity. A Control Change is similar to this as it also uses a Status byte to identify the event and one or two Data bytes representing the values for this event. For example, when moving the pitch bend wheel, a MIDI message identifies the event as a pitch bend on a specific channel and tells the receiving device the position of this pitch bend. The MIDI message, in other words, always identifies what event or action is being performed along with its associated values.

Considered as part of the Channel Voice messages family, Control Change messages are a set of 128 such events or actions that are transmitted through MIDI. Each event is identified by its own number, just like note numbers.

For example, when you move the modulation wheel (mod wheel) on your synthesizer or depressing a foot pedal during a performance, a string of MIDI information—called a Control Change message—is sent out to indicate the precise position of that mod wheel or foot pedal. Just like Note On/Off messages, Control Change messages can be recorded and, when combined with the recorded Note On/Off MIDI information, constitute the complete performance information of a given piece as captured by MIDI.

With multi-timbral modules, each part assigned to a different MIDI channel can respond independently to a particular controller number. In other words, controller messages only affect the parts in a multi-timbral/multi-channel module for which they are intended, even if other parts are playing at the same time.

In Table 3.1, the names of control changes implemented in the MIDI specification are listed. There is also a provision in this specification for additional controllers that have not yet been defined. These undefined controllers do not figure in this list, since they have no standard function associated with them at the present time and, when used, are defined by the manufacturer in the device's documentation.

Table 3.1   List of Control Change Names in Alphabetical Order

All Notes off	Modulation wheel
All Sound Off	Non-Registered Parameter Number
Balance	Omni mode off (+ all notes off)
Bank Select	Omni mode on (+ all notes off)
Breath Control	Pan
Channel Volume (formerly Main Volume)	Poly mode on (incl mono=off +all notes off)
Damper Pedal On/Off (Sustain)	Poly mode on/off (+ all notes off)
Data Entry	Portamento Control
Effect Control 1 & 2	Portamento On/Off
Effects 1–5 (Reverb Send and Chorus Send Effect)	Portamento time
Expression Controller	Registered Parameter Number
Foot Controller	Reset All Controllers
General Purpose Controller 1 to 8	Soft pedal On/Off
Hold 2	Sound Controller 1 to 10
Local Control On/Off	Sustenuto On/Off

What each controller does and which number is associated with the controller in the Control Change MIDI message is discussed later in this chapter.

Control Change Message Structure

Control changes follow a similar message structure as other MIDI messages. In Figure 3.1, the Status byte introduces the control change to the receiving MIDI device. The first Data byte that follows corresponds to the actual number associated with the control change being performed, such as a modulation wheel (01 or 33) or foot pedal (04 or 36). The second Data byte represents the value of the actual controller. All Control messages have three bytes of information. You will see later that some Control changes use two sets of Control Change messages to add a level of precision to the position of the controller. However, the principle of identifying each byte remains the same, no matter how many Control Messages are sent.

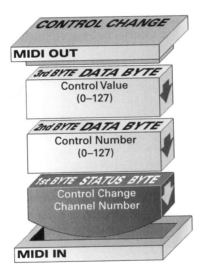

Figure 3.1 The structure of a control change message.

Understanding Controller Numbers

Like other MIDI messages, a Control Change message uses the last seven bits of each byte to identify the position of its controller. These seven bits represent a total of 128 values. Table 3.2 gives a complete list of each available Control Change name and associated number represented by the first Data byte following a Control Change Status byte.

Table 3.2 List of All Control Changes (CC) Numbers and the Functions (MIDI Event) They Represent

CC Number	Function	CC Number	Function
0	Bank Select	69	Hold 2
1	Modulation Wheel	70	Sound Controller 1 (Sound Variation)
2	Breath Control	71	Sound Controller 2 (Timbre)
3	Undefined	72	Sound Controller 3 (Release Time)
4	Foot Controller	73	Sound Controller 4 (Attack Time)
5	Portamento Time	74	Sound Controller 5 (Brightness)
6	Data Entry	75	Sound Controller 6
7	Channel Volume (formerly Main Volume)	76	Sound Controller 7
8	Balance	77	Sound Controller 8
9	Undefined	78	Sound Controller 9
10	Pan	79	Sound Controller 10
11	Expression Controller	80	General Purpose Controller 5
12	Effect Control 1	81	General Purpose Controller 6
13	Effect Control 2	82	General Purpose Controller 7
14 & 15	Undefined	83	General Purpose Controller 8
16-19	General Purpose Controller 1 to 4	84	Portamento Control
20-31	Undefined	85-90	Undefined
32	Bank Select	91	Reverb Send Level
33	Modulation Wheel	92	Effects 2 Depth
34	Breath Control	93	Chorus Send Level
35	Undefined	94	Effects 4 Depth
36	Foot Controller	95	Effects 5 Depth
37	Portamento Time	96	Data Entry +1
38	Data Entry	97	Data Entry -1
39	Channel Volume (formerly Main Volume)	98	Non-Registered Parameter Number LSB
40	Balance	99	Non-Registered Parameter Number MSB
41	Undefined	100	Registered Parameter Number LSB

CC Number	Function	CC Number	Function
42	Pan	101	Registered Parameter Number MSB
43	Expression Controller	102-119	Undefined
44 & 45	Effect Control 1 & 2	120	All Sound Off
46 & 47	Undefined	121	Reset All Controllers
48-51	General Purpose Controller #1 to #4	122	Local Control On/Off
52-63	Undefined	123	All Notes Off
64	Damper Pedal On/Off (Sustain)	124	Omni Mode Off (+ All Notes Off)
65	Portamento On/Off	125	Omni Mode On (+ All Notes Off)
66	Sustenuto On/Off	126	Poly Mode On/Off (+ All Notes Off)
67	Soft pedal On/Off	127	Poly Mode On (Incl Mono=Off +All Notes Off)

To better understand this list, you can divide Control Change messages into three categories:

✳ **Continuous Controllers:** This type of controller sends position information, such as a modulation wheel position or a pan (stereo panorama) position. Moving the modulation wheel to different positions as you record this action is quite common, and continuous controllers can generate a large amount of data to represent these changes as they occur through time. It is therefore named Continuous Controller since it continuously sends MIDI messages to update the receiving MIDI device on the position of its controller, whenever the control is moved.

✳ **Switch Controllers:** As the name implies, this type of controller acts as an on/off switch. Since the value byte (the second Data byte in the Control Change message) is the same as any other byte, your MIDI device will interpret any values from 0 to 63 as being off and values from 64 to 127 as being on. By default, however, a switch controller will send a value of 0 when off and 127 when on. A sustain foot pedal is a good example of the switch controller in action. When you press the pedal, it is on and keeps all previous Note On events sustained until it receives a foot pedal off message. It will then release any sustained notes.

✳ **Channel Mode Message Controllers:** The last set of Control Change functions is not like the other control changes but instead resembles Channel Mode messages, which have been given Control Change numbers between 120 and 127 (see Table 3.2). They are handled and identified as Control Changes even if their content (or function) is similar to Channel Mode messages.

Continuous controller messages can further be divided into two subcategories: low resolution and high resolution. As you might have noticed, two numbers represent some of the controllers. For example, take controller 0 and 32, which are both used to define the bank select.

In order to keep the structure of Control Change messages identical (one Status byte followed by two Data bytes, one to represent the Control Change number and the other to represent its value), some Control Changes use two messages to identify intermediate values. In other words, some controllers might need more than 127 values to represent positions or settings. For example, the modulation wheel has two controllers: numbers 1 and 33. This is to accommo-date future enhancements in MIDI. Controller number 1 is the default controller for a modulation wheel and is supported by all MIDI devices. It sets the modulation applied to a program by sending a value ranging from 0 to 127. This represents a total of 128 different positions. The first controller in this case is considered to be most significant. As for controller number 33, it can also represent values from 0 to 127, or 128 different values. But in this case, it represents a subset of 128 sub-positions found for each position in controller 1. That's why it is called "least significant." Combining the different values of both controllers, you get 128 times 128 different modulation wheel positions. This is why it is called high resolution. It offers a greater number of possible values when both controllers are combined, whereas low-resolution controllers have only one controller number assigned to them and therefore can represent only 128 different values. This said, most MIDI devices today will ignore any values sent by controllers that represent subsets of values, or Least Significant Byte (LSB) information such as the ones found in the Modulation Wheel controller 33.

Figure 3.2 offers a complete look at the control change hierarchy as described above. Some controller numbers are not represented in this hierarchy because the numbers are not defined by the MIDI specification and cannot be categorized in this structure. Perhaps some of them will be implemented in further MIDI revisions. You will, however, find all Control Change

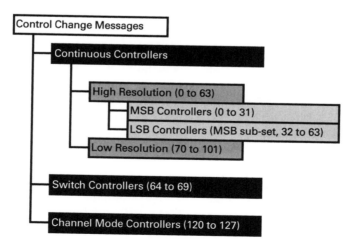

Figure 3.2 The Control Change message hierarchy.

messages listed in Appendix B. Note that even though a controller is not defined by the MIDI implementation, many software synthesizers and MIDI remote control surfaces commonly use all control change addresses, even making use of undefined controllers to add more control power to users. We'll discuss more on associating MIDI control surfaces with virtual controls inside sequencers and software synthesizers in Chapters 6 and 9.

In the sections that follow, you will find a description of each control change and how it controls the sound. Each category and subcategory of Control Change messages is described in its own section. However, remember that all Control Change messages are numbered from 0 to 127 and are addressed by the MIDI specification as a set of 128. Their subdivision into categories and subcategories in this chapter is meant for you to better understand their purpose and their explanation, rather than being an actual part of the MIDI specification.

High-Resolution Continuous Controller Messages

High-resolution and low-resolution continuous controller messages use three bytes: the usual Status byte, which tells the receiving device that this is a Control Change message, a second byte that identifies the actual control change, and a third byte that gives the value for this control change. Where high-resolution control changes differ from their low-resolution counterpart is in their second control number assignment. As discussed earlier, the bank select control change, for example, has two control change numbers referring to this same control change function—numbers 0 and 32. Low-resolution control changes have only one control change number. So, for each high-resolution controller, you have two control change numbers assigned: the first, which represents the most significant values or coarse adjustment, and a second, which represents the least significant values or fine adjustment.

High-resolution controllers can have either 128 values, if the MIDI message refers to one control change, or 16,384 values (128×128), if both control change numbers referring to the same function are being used. In reality, most of the high-resolution controllers are handled as low-resolution controllers since very few MIDI devices will offer support for controller numbers 32 to 63. When they do support these controllers, it is transparent to both the user (you) and the MIDI device receiving the message.

For example, the modulation wheel (controller 1) can have a value of 50 (see Figure 3.3). Then, imagine that a second control change message follows, but now the controller is number 33, which is also a modulation wheel control change message; however, this time, the third byte value represents a fine-tuning of the modulation. So, for every value in controller 1, you have 128 intermediate values.

This is also known as the MSB (Most Significant Byte) and LSB (Least Significant Byte) values, where MSB is the coarse setting and LSB is the fine setting. In our example above, the modulation has a coarse setting of 50; within that coarse setting you can have 128 different values for a total of 16,384 different (7 bits of MSB + 7 bits of LSB = 14 bits = 2 to the power of 14 = 16,384) values for a single control change (see Table 3.3).

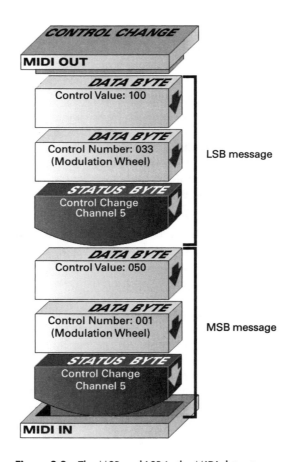

Figure 3.3   The MSB and LSB in the MIDI data stream.

Table 3.3   MSB and LSB Value Combination Table

MSB Values	LSB Values	Possible LSB Values per MSB Value
0	0 to 127	128
1	0 to 127	128
2	0 to 127	128
...	0 to 127	128
127	0 to 127	128
Possible MSB values	128	Possible MSB and LSB combinations (128 × 128) 16,384

Here's how it works:

❋ When the MIDI device sending the MIDI messages (master) doesn't support controllers 32 to 63, the subset controllers representing the fine or LSB values for controllers 0 to 31 will never be used or transmitted. When the same device receives control change messages for these controllers, they will be ignored.

❋ When the MIDI device sending the MIDI messages supports controllers 32 to 63, but the MIDI device receiving the MIDI messages (slave) doesn't, the slave will ignore these messages.

❋ If both master and slave MIDI devices support controllers 32 to 63, the resolution for these controllers is increased. This will enhance each controller by adding 128 fine or LSB values for each one of the 128 coarse or MSB values found in their corresponding control change messages (controllers 0 to 31).

In most cases, the LSB controllers are either not implemented or not used by the devices. The purpose of these higher resolutions is to allow greater precision over changes made by these controllers. However, using LSB controllers will add twice as much additional MIDI information in your MIDI data stream, which can clog at the output, especially if you are hooking up multiple devices in a daisy chain rather than using a multi-port MIDI type of connection. The only control you have over the use of these controllers is by not using them if your MIDI device supports them. To find that out, you will need to consult your MIDI device's documentation to see which control change are implemented. On the other hand, if these controllers are implemented, and you find this improves the control you have over your performance without slowing the MIDI data flow, their use will be transparent to you in most cases.

Bank Select

Controller 0, coarse or MSB

Controller 32, fine or LSB

Some MIDI devices have more than 128 presets (or patches, instruments, programs, etc). MIDI program change messages only support switching between 128 programs. In order to accommodate more than 128 programs, many devices categorize their programs in banks. For example, a device with 512 programs may be divided into four banks of 128 programs (as shown in Figure 3.4). The bank select controller (sometimes called the *bank switch*) switches between groups of programs. How many programs are available in every bank depends on how the MIDI device assigns them; a maximum of 128 programs are available in each bank.

For example, the program number 129 is actually the first program within the second bank (programs and banks always begin with a 0). Programs 1 to 128 are numbered, in a MIDI message, as 0 to 127 of bank 0, and program 129 would be numbered program 0 of bank 1. Sending a bank select controller to switch to the second bank followed with a program change to select the first program in this bank should bring up the appropriate sound into memory. As with program change messages, bank select messages affect only events

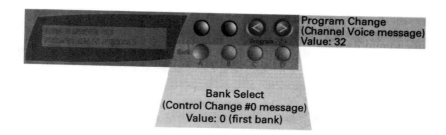

Figure 3.4 Comparing the bank select control change message with the program change channel voice message.

associated to the message's assigned MIDI channel. You can select a bank for a keyboard on channel 5 without affecting any other MIDI devices on other channels.

Controller number 32 is used for fine-tuning, meaning that you could have up to 16,384 banks of 128 sounds.

Modulation Wheel

Controller 1, coarse or MSB

Controller 33, fine or LSB

Sets the modulation wheel (or MOD wheel) to a particular value, which in most cases introduces some sort of vibrato effect. This vibrato effect can be achieved in different ways: through a frequency modulation (changing the pitch with an LFO or Low Frequency Oscillator), for example, or by amplitude modulation (changing the loudness), or a filter modulation.

Controller number 33 adds fine-tuning, or micro amounts of MOD wheel, giving an added resolution to this controller. However, some devices will not support this controller. If that's the case, the messages are simply ignored.

Breath Control

Controller 2, coarse or MSB and controller 34, fine or LSB.

Values for both controllers range from 0 to 127.

This may be used to control a parameter like Aftertouch, since breath control is a wind player's version of how to vary pressure, so it can be assigned to whatever the musician sets this controller to affect.

As with other controllers supporting MSB and LSB, controller 34 adds more definition to the breath control values. If the device does not support the controller, it will simply ignore its information.

Foot Controller

Controller 4, coarse or MSB

Controller 36, fine or LSB

This may be used to control a parameter like Aftertouch as well or whatever the musician sets this controller to affect. This foot pedal is a continuous controller, like a potentiometer or a fader, such as a swell pedal found on B3 organs, where the more you press on the pedal, the louder the sound gets (as suggested in Figure 3.5).

These values are from 0 to 127. However, in a foot switch, values from 0 to 63 are interpreted as being equal to 0 (or as being Off), and values from 64 to 127 are interpreted as being equal to 127 (or as being On). Although in both cases you may have a foot pedal transmitting values from 0 to 127, in the case of a foot controller, all values are interpreted as individual values. In a foot switch, though, only two value ranges (0 to 63 and 64 to 127) determine the value for this controller, as suggested in Figure 3.5.

Figure 3.5   Foot controller (control change 4 and 36) sends a series of values, whereas some other types of foot-like controllers act as On/Off switches (such as controller 64, hold pedal).

As with other controllers supporting MSB and LSB, controller 36 adds more definition to the foot controller values. If the device does not support the controller, it will simply ignore its information.

Portamento Time

Controller 5, coarse or MSB

Controller 37, fine or LSB

Portamento is the time it takes for the pitch of one note to slide to a second note's pitch rather than playing this second note's pitch immediately. This controller determines the rate (in time) at which portamento slides the pitch between two notes.

Controller 37, when supported, adds intermediate values to that rate, making it more precise. If the device does not support the controller, it will simply ignore its information.

Data Entry
Controller 6, coarse or MSB

Controller 38, fine or LSB

Data Entry is the value of some Registered Parameter Number (RPN) or Non-Registered Parameter Number (NRPN). Which parameter is affected depends upon a preceding RPN or NRPN message (which itself identifies the parameter's number). RPN and NRPN are parameters that can be controlled by MIDI but are specific to a MIDI device or not controlled by any other control change messages. For example, the master coarse tuning request message on a multi-timbral MIDI device is an RPN parameter. Sending a control change value using the data entry controller would be interpreted by the RPN controller as a coarse tuning value.

On some devices, this slider may not be used in conjunction with RPN or NRPN messages. Instead, the musician can set the slider to control a single parameter directly, often a parameter such as what aftertouch can control.

Controller 38, when supported, adds intermediate values. If the device does not support the controller, it will simply ignore its information.

Channel Volume
(Formerly known as Main Volume) Controller 7, coarse or MSB

Controller 39, fine or LSB

Channel Volume affects the device's channel or main level but not its master volume if the device is multi-timbral. If this is the case, each part has its own volume (this controller), and the master volume of the instrument or device would be found in a SysEx Master Volume message, take its volume from one of the parts, or be controlled by a general purpose slider controller. The expression controller can also affect the volume level of a channel.

Controller 39 is rarely supported in sound modules, but when supported, it adds intermediate values to the channel volume. If the device does not support the controller, it will simply ignore its information.

Balance
Controller 8, coarse or MSB

Controller 40, fine or LSB

If the device has stereo audio outputs, this controller will have an effect on the stereo balance for the corresponding MIDI channel. If it is a multi-timbral device, then each part usually has its own balance.

Typically, balance is used on a channel that has stereo sounds when you wish to adjust the volume of the stereo elements without changing their pan positions, whereas pan is more appropriate for a channel that is strictly a "mono instrument."

Controller 40 is rarely supported in sound modules, but when supported, it adds intermediate values to the balance. If the device does not support the controller, it will simply ignore its information.

A value of 0 emphasizes the left side in a stereo balance, 64 will center the stereo balance, and 127 would emphasize the right side of a stereo balance.

Pan

Controller 10, coarse or MSB

Controller 42, fine or LSB

This determines where, within the stereo field of a stereo audio output device, the sound will be placed. Typically, pan is used on a channel that has mono sounds, but it also affects stereo panning just as well (see the "Balance" section above).

As Figure 3.6 would suggest, when you change the balance of a stereo sound, the weight of the stereo field shifts toward the audio output channel corresponding to the MIDI value. In this case, the value 32 tilts the stereo balance toward the left. In comparison, the pan positions a sound (usually mono) at the same position. If the sound is stereo, the left channel will be slightly louder than the right channel in this example. A value of 0 pans the sound hard left in a stereo field, 64 will center the sound, and 127 will pan hard right in a stereo field.

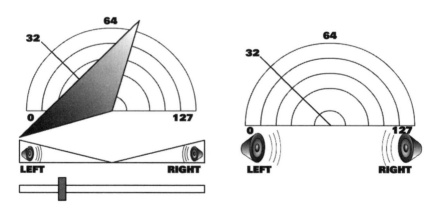

Figure 3.6 Comparing the balance control change to the pan control change.

Controller 42 is rarely supported in sound modules, but when supported, it adds intermediate values to the pan. If the device does not support the controller, it will simply ignore its information.

Expression Controller

Controller 11, coarse or MSB

Controller 43, fine or LSB

The expression controller acts as a percentage of the volume controller. It commonly controls either the sub-volume level or other parameters. For example, commercial sample libraries, such as Garritan's Vienna Symphonic Library, use this controller, among other things, to switch between different samples. Although rarely used since devices don't usually have any knobs, sliders, or buttons assigned to this controller, it can come in handy in certain occasions. This controller divides the current volume into 16,384 steps, acting as an LSB for the volume control, thus adding more "expressive" control over the volume level. While the volume controller already has two controllers taking care of the volume level of a channel, the LSB controller for the volume controller is rarely implemented in MIDI devices. The expression controller, on the other hand, is implemented in most of them. For example, you can set several instrument levels using the volume controller, then without changing these relative volume values, change the expression controller as a way to create crescendos or decrescendos while keeping these relative volume levels the same. Here's a practical example of how this controller can be applied:

Let's say you are mixing a piano, bass, and drum sound and determine that the piano's volume controller should be set at 70, the bass 90, and the drums at 100. You have three options to increase the volume for these three instruments while keeping their relative balance between them: You can either calculate manually the value for each instrument by adding a percentage and then rounding up to the closest value, add a fixed value to the volume of each instrument, or assign the same value to the expression controller for all three instruments.

In Table 3.4, you can see that by adding a value of 32 (out of 128) to the expression controller, all instruments will increase by 25% (0 is 0%, 64 is 50%, and 127 is 100%), bringing the volume of each instrument up by that ratio, therefore keeping the relative balance. However, if you simply add 25 to all instruments, as shown in the table, the end result would upset the relative balance between instruments, as the last row suggests.

Table 3.4   Practical Comparison Between the Use of Volume Controllers and Expression Controllers to Maintain the Relative Balance Between Different Sounds in a MIDI Mix

	Piano	Bass	Drums
Volume level	70	90	100
Expression level with a value of 32, or an increase of 25%	+ 25%	+ 25%	+ 25%
End result	89	113	125
If you add 25 to all the instruments using the volume level	95	115	125

	Piano	Bass	Drums
Percentage louder compared to the original value when using volume control	+ 35 %	+ 28%	+ 25 %

With a software sequencer offering a mixing interface on which series of MIDI volume controllers can be grouped together, you might not have to use the expression controller at all, since it will be easier to use your software mixing features. Otherwise, using the expression controller as described earlier in the example found in Table 3.4 would be one of the ways you could use the expression controller.

Finally, the expression controller may also be assigned to a foot pedal, just like the foot controller, to control the swelling of the volume by the musician. Since it works on a percentage value of the volume, the expression controller may yield a more subtle effect in volume changes than simply applying volume changes everywhere. The LSB version of this controller (controller number 43) is, however, rarely implemented.

Effect Control 1 and 2

Controllers 12 and 13, coarse or MSB

Controllers 44 and 45, fine or LSB

These controllers can be used to control any parameter relating to an effects device such as the reverb decay time for a built-in reverb found in some sound modules. There are separate controllers for setting the volume levels of reverb, chorus, phase shift, and other effects (see controllers 91 to 95).

General Purpose Controllers 1 to 4

Controllers 16 through 19, coarse or MSB

Controllers 48 through 51, fine or LSB

These controllers can be set by musicians to control pretty much anything. They are the equivalent of having four additional general purpose sliders or faders. The general purpose controllers 48 through 51 (the fine or LSB versions) are rarely implemented in MIDI devices.

Low-Resolution Continuous Controller Messages

These controllers operate exactly the same way as high-resolution controllers, with the exception that they don't come in pairs, allowing an MSB and LSB version of the same controller. For the most part, they are used to control sound parameters like knobs on a sound module. These controllers can be assigned as remote controls for MIDI-compatible devices that aren't next to you during a work session or onstage. The controllers make it possible to use control change messages rather than using the onboard physical knob. Which parameters these controllers modify is device dependent, and you will have to consult your device's documentation to know how to implement them.

Low-resolution controllers may come in handy when you want to automate certain parameters of your MIDI device, since you can create a series of control change messages, record them in a sequencer, and then play them back as automation data to control the timbre, attack, or release time of a MIDI device over time.

Once again, all these controllers have a fixed range of 128 values (0 to 127), where unless specified, 0 represents the lowest value or off setting and 127 represents the maximum value.

Sound Controller 1 (Sound Variation)
Controller 70

Affects the parameters associated with the circuitry that produces the sound, such as the sample rate of a sampler's sound, therefore playing on its pitch.

Sound Controller 2 (Timbre)
Controller 71

As with controller 70, this controller affects sound production parameters. In this case, it adds control to the Voltage Control Filter (VCF) and plays on the envelope's levels. In other words, it controls how the filter shapes the brightness or timbre of the sound over time. Higher values create a more audible effect.

Sound Controller 3 (Release Time)
Controller 72

This controls the Voltage Control Amplifier's (VCA) release time envelope. Lower values will make the envelope's release time fade quicker, and higher values will make the envelope's release time longer.

Sound Controller 4 (Attack Time)
Controller 73

This controls the VCA's attack time envelope. Lower values will make the envelope's attack time quicker, and higher values will make the envelope's attack time longer, fading in more gradually.

Sound Controller 5 (Brightness)
Controller 74

This controls the VCF's cutoff frequency by changing its filter frequency, affecting the overall brightness of the sound.

Sound Controllers 6 to 10 (No Default Parameter)
Controllers 75 through 79

These extra five sound controllers can be used to adjust other parameters associated with the sound producing circuitry of a sound module. They are assignable, so they don't modify anything in particular until you assign them to a parameter.

Portamento Control
Controller 84

This controller sends a MIDI note number to set the starting note of a portamento, which will then be glided in a time set by the portamento time controller to the next Note On message. When a Note On message is received after a portamento control message, the voice's pitch glides from the key number specified in this message to the new Note On's pitch at the rate set by the portamento time (controller number 5), ignoring the current status of portamento on/off (controller 65). This message only affects the next Note On received on the relevant MIDI channel.

If your device is set to play in poly mode (see description in Chapter 2), receiving a portamento control message does not affect the pitch of any currently playing notes, whether in their sustain or release phase. However, when in mono mode, or if the legato footswitch (controller 68) is on, a new overlapping note event results in an immediate pitch jump to the note number specified in the portamento control message and then a glide at the current portamento rate to the note number specified in the new Note On. The values for this controller correspond to note numbers as defined in Appendix B.

Reverb Send Level
Controller 91

When a device offers an integrated audio reverb effect, this controller affects the level of dry audio sent to this reverb effect.

Tremolo Level
Controller 92

This can be used to control the level of a device's tremolo, or vibration.

Chorus Send Level
Controller 93

When a device offers an integrated audio chorus effect, this controller affects the level of dry audio sent to this chorus effect.

Celeste (Detune) Level
Controller 94

This can be used to control the effect level of a device's detune amount, also called Celeste.

Phaser Level
Controller 95

This can be used to control the effect level of a device's phaser amount, which is a form of very slow chorus.

Data Increment Button
Controller 96

This button controller function causes data to increase its current value by one. More often, this controller's value is used to set some RPN and NRPN (see below for more detail on RPN and NRPN controllers). It is the preceding RPN or NRPN message that will determine which parameter this switch will affect. This preceding message usually identifies the parameter number itself. Being a switch, values 0 to 63 represent off, and 64 to 127 represent on, which will make the data increment by one. This is slightly different than the usual switch controller, and that's why it is considered a low-resolution controller rather than a true switch controller.

Data Decrement Button
Controller 97

Acts like controller 96, except that in this case it decreases the data button's value by one rather than increasing it.

Non-Registered Parameter Number (NRPN)
Controller 98, fine or LSB

Controller 99, coarse or MSB

These controllers will determine which parameter the data button increment (controller 96), data button decrement (controller 97), or data entry controllers (numbers 6 and 38) will affect. Since these two controllers (98 and 99) work as a pair, you can have 16,384 different non-registered parameters. It is up to each manufacturer to determine which parameter number affects which actual device parameter.

An example of NRPN in use is the way a MIDI mixer manufacturer might address specific controllers, giving them functions corresponding to onboard knobs, such as a compressor level if this mixer has an automatable compressor.

Since each device can define a particular NRPN controller number to control anything, it's possible that two devices may interpret the same NRPN number in different manners. Therefore, a device should allow a musician to disable receipt of NRPN, in the event that there is a conflict between the NRPN implementations of two daisy-chained devices.

It should be mentioned here that the difference between RPN and NRPN is that the former has been adopted, thus registered and approved by the MMA (MIDI Manufacturer Association) and the JMSC (Japan MIDI Standard Committee), whereas the latter has not. As a result, a manufacturer might implement some uses for NRPN, but these parameters won't necessarily be applied the same way for another manufacturer. You should also know that NRPN controllers and their RPN counterparts (described in the next section) are not controllers you will be using very often, since most manufacturers will use them as a way to send and receive information that in most cases remains transparent to the user.

Registered Parameter Number (RPN)

Controller 100, fine or LSB

Controller 101, coarse or MSB

These controllers work like the ones you just saw (98 and 99), with the exception that they work with RPNs (Registered Parameter Numbers) rather than NRPNs (Non-Registered Parameter Numbers). Here are the registered parameters as defined by the MIDI Specification:

❈ Pitch Bend Range Sensitivity, which sets the number of semi-tones or half steps defined by the MSB of the pitch bend (controller number 6, Data Entry) and the number of cents defined by LSB of the same message (controller number 38, Data Entry).

❈ Master Fine Tuning.

❈ Master Coarse Tuning.

❈ Select Tuning Program.

❈ Select Tuning Bank.

❈ Null Function, used to cancel an RPN or NRPN or to indicate the end of the message.

Switches

Switch type control changes come from controllers that are either on or off. For that purpose, only two values are needed: 0 indicates off and 127 indicates on. However, since 7 bits of data are available, most devices will interpret any value less than or equal to 63 as being off and all values greater than or equal to 64 as being on.

Damper Pedal (Sustain)

Controller 64

This acts the same way as a sustain pedal on a piano, holding the notes as if they remained pressed until the sustain or damper pedal is released. It postpones the Note Off event effect. It will also postpone any All Notes Off controller messages (controller 123). This is different from the foot pedal described earlier (see Figure 3.5) since it is like an on/off switch (see Figure 3.7) rather than a foot version of a fader with values ranging from 0 to 127.

Portamento On/Off

Controller 65

This controls the portamento (pitch sliding between two notes). Usually, this controller works with the portamento time controllers 5 and 37. If the portamento is off, the portamento time controller will not have any effect.

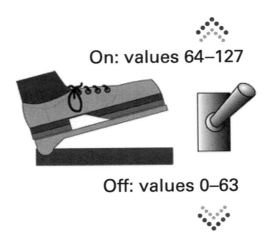

On: values 64–127

Off: values 0–63

Figure 3.7 The damper "switch" pedal.

Sostenuto

Controller 66

This is like the hold pedal controller, except it only sustains notes that are already on when the pedal is pressed, rather than holding all the notes that are played from the moment the pedal is pressed until it is released. When you play new notes after pressing the pedal, they will not be held. In other words, this controller acts as a chord/note holder for the notes that are on when the pedal is pressed.

As Figure 3.8 would suggest, a two-note chord is played. Then, the sostenuto pedal is pressed. From this point on, these two notes will be sustained until the sostenuto pedal is released;

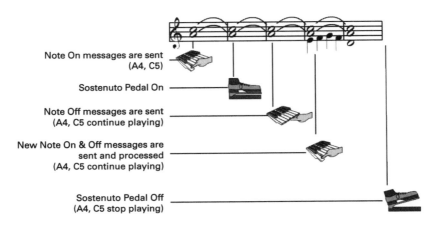

Note On messages are sent
(A4, C5)

Sostenuto Pedal On

Note Off messages are sent
(A4, C5 continue playing)

New Note On & Off messages are
sent and processed
(A4, C5 continue playing)

Sostenuto Pedal Off
(A4, C5 stop playing)

Figure 3.8 Example of a sostenuto message.

however, the other notes that are played will not be sustained because they are pressed after the sostenuto pedal's On action.

Soft Pedal
Controller 67

This pedal softens notes by lowering their volume, acting like the center pedal in a three-pedal piano setup. This controller is not necessarily implemented in all devices, as with many others, so you should read your device's manufacturer documentation to find out if and how it implements this controller.

Legato Footswitch
Controller 68

You can use this to skip the attack portion of the VCA's (Voltage Control Amplifier) envelope, which will give you a legato effect between notes. For example, a violin player can play several notes with the bow going in the same direction, which has the effect of softening the attack. This controller enables the keyboard player to do something similar.

Hold 2
Controller 69

This controller increases the fade out time (release) of notes that have been played. Unlike the hold pedal (controller 64), however, it does not sustain permanently the notes until the musician releases the pedal, even if the notes do take a longer time to release. It acts primarily on the VCA's envelope. The hold 2 controller is an on/off switch.

General Purpose Controllers 5 to 8
Controllers 80 through 83

You can assign these general purpose controllers to any on/off switch you want. They can act as triggers to control a sequencer, for example. Since they are assignable, you will need to associate these controllers with something before you use them.

Channel Mode Messages

Channel mode messages are a subset of control change messages. However, they are not handled as the other control change messages above, since they have a more global affect on a device. And, in most cases, they enable or disable channel-related functions such as MIDI modes, local keyboard control, and the ever-precious Panic functions that send a message to a device to release any Note On messages in case MIDI gets stuck.

All Sound Off
Controller 120

This controller would cause sound generators to immediately cease all sound, muting all sounding notes that were turned on by received Note On messages and that haven't yet been turned off by respective Note Off messages. This message is not supposed to mute any notes that the musician is playing on the local keyboard, so if a device can't distinguish between notes played via its MIDI In and notes played on the local keyboard, it should not implement All Sound Off.

The difference between this message and All Notes Off is that this message immediately mutes all sound on the device regardless of whether the Hold Pedal is on and mutes the sound quickly regardless of any lengthy VCA release times. This controller doesn't use a value range byte but rather sends a default 0 value when this controller is sent in the MIDI message.

Reset All Controllers

Controller 121

Reset All Controllers sets all controllers to their default states. All switches, such as Sostenuto, are turned off, and all continuous controllers, such as Mod Wheel, are set to minimum positions. In other words, the controllers are reset to the most suitable default value. The only value for this is 0, since the value byte isn't used.

Local Keyboard (or Control) On/Off

Controller 122

This controller turns the device's keyboard on or off locally. When a Local Keyboard Off message is sent, the keyboard gets disconnected from the device's internal sound generation circuitry. From this point on, it sends MIDI information but doesn't transmit these events directly to its internal sound generation circuitry (such as a synth module for example). So, when the musician presses keys, the device doesn't trigger any of its internal sounds. This is the best way to eliminate loops in the MIDI messages where the sounds would be generated by the musician as he plays on the keys, where the sound generation circuitry reproduces what comes in from the MIDI input and reproduces the same sounds if the same MIDI data is coming out of the keyboard devices and comes back in to this device. Furthermore, if a device is only going to be played remotely via MIDI, then the keyboard may be turned off in order to allow the device to concentrate more on dealing with MIDI messages rather than scanning the keyboard for depressed notes and varying pressure.

In Figure 3.9, you can see two sample setups that would create such a feedback loop if the Local Keyboard is set to *on*. Let's look at these examples:

1. Play on the keyboard: The notes are sent to the MIDI Out, and the sound circuitry produces the sounds through the keyboard's audio outputs.

2. The receiving sequencer (Setup A in the example) or the sound device (Setup B) processes the MIDI information and sends the MIDI back to its MIDI output.

3. The keyboard receives MIDI information from its MIDI input and plays the sounds through its audio output a second time, since they are already playing the same notes when you pressed the keys, thus creating an undesired note doubling effect that usually sounds like a quick flange.

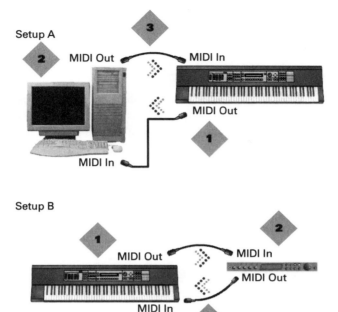

Figure 3.9   Local On/Off message explained in two setup examples.

On the other hand, if the Local Keyboard is set to off, in step 1 of the above example, the keyboard does not produce an audio output, since the MIDI information is sent only to its MIDI output. It will then only process the MIDI information coming from its MIDI input and create the corresponding audio output once.

All Notes Off
Controller 123

Similar to the All Sounds Off (controller 120), this controller turns off all notes that were turned on by received Note On messages that haven't yet been turned off by respective Note Off messages unless these notes are being played on the local keyboard by the musician. If a device can't distinguish between notes played via its MIDI In and notes played on the local keyboard, it should not implement All Notes Off. Furthermore, if a device is in Omni On state, it should ignore this message on any channel. What makes this different than the All Sounds Off controller is that if the device's Hold Pedal controller is on, the notes aren't actually released until the Hold Pedal is turned off. See the All Sound Off controller message for turning off the sound of these notes immediately. The only value for this is 0, since the value byte isn't used.

This is a softer way of releasing all Note On messages, since it will respect the release stage of any notes that are in their Note On phase.

Omni Mode Off
Controller 124

This sends an Omni Off message, which has no value byte (default value is 0) and turns the Omni Mode off. See the discussion in Chapter 2 under "About MIDI Mode." When a device receives an Omni Off message, it automatically turns off all playing notes.

Omni Mode On
Controller 125

This sends an Omni On message, which has no value byte (default value is 0) and turns the Omni Mode on. See the discussion in the Chapter 2 section "About MIDI Mode." When a device receives an Omni On message, it should automatically turn off all playing notes, just as with the Omni Mode Off.

Monophonic Operation
Controller 126

This controller enables the monophonic operation MIDI mode (Mono On), disabling the polyphonic operation MIDI mode as discussed in Chapter 2.

If Omni is off, this value tells how many MIDI channels the device is expected to respond to in Mono mode. In other words, if Omni is off, this value is used to select a limited set of the 16 MIDI channels (i.e., 1 to 16) to respond to. If Omni is on, this value is ignored completely, and the device only plays one note at a time per active channel in a multi-timbral device. The following paragraphs would then be relevant only if the Omni Off mode was active.

When the value is 0, it tells the device it can receive voice messages on any MIDI channels. However, since this is Mono On, only one voice per channel (monophony) can be reproduced.

If the value is between 1 and 16, that tells the device how many channels can be actively receiving voice messages, the number value defining the number of MIDI channels. A value of 3, for example, would restrict the device from receiving data from more than three MIDI channels simultaneously. If it did, they would be ignored.

The base MIDI channel of a device will have an effect on which channel it responds to when in this mode. For example, if your device is set to channel 2 as the base MIDI channel, and the value is set to 3, it will respond to channels 2, 3, and 4 (2 being the base channel and 3–4 completing the set of 3 channels).

Multi-timbral devices operate in a slightly special way. Basically, each part has its own MIDI channel and is usually considered as a separate device, with each part being set to Omni Mode Off and Poly Mode On. Changing the mode to Mono Mode On rather than Poly Mode On would result in a series of monophonic instruments (one for each supported multi-timbral device part).

Polyphonic Operation

Controller 127

This enables polyphonic operations (Poly On), thus disabling monophonic operation (Mono On). You can refer to Chapter 2 in the section "About MIDI Mode" to get more details. The value byte isn't used and defaults to 0. When a device receives a Poly Operation message, it should automatically turn off all playing notes.

Review Questions

1. When combined with the recorded Note On/Off MIDI information, which type of MIDI messages constitute the complete performance information of a given piece as captured by MIDI?

   a) System Real Time messages

   b) Control Change messages

   c) System Common messages

   d) System Exclusive message

2. How many bytes are used to represent Control Change messages?

   a) 1

   b) 2

   c) 3

   d) 4

3. What category of Control Change messages describes controllers that send position information in their values?

   a) Continuous Controllers

   b) Switch Controllers

   c) Channel Mode Message Controllers

   d) None of the above

4. What controller could be used as or compared to a potentiometer or a fader control?

   a) Damper Pedal

   b) Portamento On/Off

   c) Foot Controller

   d) Data Entry

5. Controller 7 is more commonly known to control which MIDI parameter?

    a) The stereo panorama of a MIDI channel

    b) The expression level of a MIDI channel

    c) The balance of a MIDI channel

    d) The volume of a MIDI channel

6. Which of the following controllers doesn't belong in this Registered Parameter Number list?

    a) Select Bank

    b) Master Fine Tuning

    c) Pitch Bend Range Sensitivity

    d) Select Tuning Program

7. The All Sound Off, All Controllers Off, and Local Keyboard On/Off controllers are part of which category of MIDI messages?

    a) Channel Voice messages

    b) Switch Controllers

    c) Continuous Controllers

    d) Channel Mode Controllers

8. Whenever controllers offer a pair of coarse and fine controls, which one is usually considered an MSB controller?

    a) The coarse control

    b) The fine control

    c) The fine and coarse controls

    d) The LSB control

9. What are the controllers responsible for determining which parameter the data increment and decrement buttons or the data entry controllers will affect?

    a) Sound Controllers 1 through 5

    b) General Purpose

    c) Non-Registered Parameter Number

    d) All of the above

10. True or False: On a synthesizer that doubles as a keyboard controller, setting the Local Keyboard to off on this device prevents MIDI note doubling when the synth is connected to a MIDI sequencer.

General MIDI and Standard MIDI Files

Not long after the MIDI 1.0 standard was finalized in the early 1980s, musicians started hooking different manufacturers' devices together using this new standard. They quickly realized that the MIDI 1.0 specification had overlooked an important detail: No provision had been made in this standard for a set of standard patches, nor had they ventured into specifications for multi-timbral instruments, since at this point in time, they did not exist. It took almost a decade for the MMA (MIDI Manufacturers Association) and the JMSC (Japan MIDI Standards Committee) to adopt what is known as the General MIDI System Level 1 specification, or GM for short. When adopted in 1991, this specification was designed to provide a minimum level of performance compatibility among MIDI instruments. It has also helped pave the way for MIDI in the growing consumer and multimedia markets that were emerging at the time.

Here's a summary of what you will learn in this chapter:

* What General MIDI is and why it was developed.
* What a General MIDI sound bank is.
* What other aspects of a device are defined by General MIDI.
* What a Standard MIDI File is and why it was developed.
* What the different types of MIDI files are and how to choose which one to use.
* What makes Standard MIDI Files so different from audio files when it comes to distribution over a network.
* Why other companies expanded on the General MIDI specification by introducing their own standards.
* What the GS standard is.
* What the XG standard is.

To give you an example of how things were before MIDI, consider this: Let's say you had two synthesizers, an EMU Proteus XR sound module and a Yamaha DX-7 keyboard. You hook both of these devices together using a MIDI chain and wish to use the keyboard to send patch change messages to the Proteus sound module. When sending a program change, the DX-7 keyboard sends a program number value, and nothing in that number tells the receiving device what kind of sound it should play. MIDI simply tells the receiving device to change its program number to the same value. If program 32 is a bass sound on the DX-7, entering that number on the DX-7 will also change the Proteus to the same program number as the Proteus, which is probably not a bass sound since it is not a GM module. It is difficult to control or embed program changes in a sequencer, save the sequence, and have the sequence play back on another set of MIDI instruments with the appropriate sounds. Compatibility between different systems was hard to achieve because of this, since no two devices had the same list of sounds or had their sounds in the same order.

To address these concerns, Roland proposed an addendum to the MIDI 1.0 specification. This addendum was called General MIDI (GM). It added some new requirements to the base MIDI 1.0 specification. These additions did not supplant any parts of the 1.0 specification, and the 1.0 specification is still the base level to which all MIDI devices should adhere. GM has now been adopted as part of the MIDI 2.0 specification.

What Is General MIDI?

To be GM compatible, a GM device such as a keyboard, sound module, sound card or audio hardware, software program, or any other product must meet the General MIDI System Level 1 performance requirements described in the following sections. These requirements must be instantaneous upon demand and should not require additional modification, adjustment, or configuration by the user. This way, a specially prepared score transmitted to the module via MIDI, using a sequencer or MIDI file player, will play back with the correct sounds, regardless of the make and model of the sound module. These recorded sequences can then be distributed as Standard MIDI Files on floppy disks or via other mediums such as the Internet.

It is important to know that General MIDI is a recommended practice for manufacturers; they do not legally have to comply with it, but since the market usually dictates what should be done by observing what sells, GM has become widespread across most sound-generator manufacturers. So, if you are a game enthusiast or use MIDI files regularly, GM is a must, and chances are you will probably need a GM-compatible device. However, if you are a serious music composer, you will feel the need for more sounds than GM provides.

Usually, General MIDI devices are meant for musicians who are not into designing their own sounds, but rather need a sound source they can rely on to hear MIDI files or create MIDI files they can distribute. Editing GM sound parameters may be possible, but saving these changes over the original sounds is not. When using GM sound banks, using only the set of 128 programs ensures a song will comply with this standard and play back the same way on any MIDI device equipped with GM sounds. For example, inserting a program change number 0 will always result in hearing a piano sound; program change number 26 will always be a jazz guitar, and so on (see Table 4.2 for complete GM program listing). GM is not meant for musicians who enjoy creating their own sonic textures or personal sound, but rather for musicians who want to distribute or exchange songs in MIDI format. Every GM device should display the logo found in Figure 4.1 somewhere on the device or on the packaging if it is software or computer hardware.

Figure 4.1 The General MIDI logo found on all General MIDI instruments—this usually means that the instrument complies with all GM specifications.

General MIDI Patches

GM's most recognized feature is the defined list of sound presets. However, the GM specification does not specify exactly how a sound should be reproduced. This is still left to the manufacturer's discretion. It is important for a manufacturer to create a sound bank that will provide a good quality sound that adheres to this GM standard. This can result in wide variations in performance and quality from the same song data on different GM sound devices. The creators of this standard felt it was important to allow each manufacturer to have its own ideas when it came to picking the exact timbre for each sound in this sound bank, as long as they provide an acceptable representation of song data written for GM.

You will find in Table 4.1 a list of different instrument families that are identified in the GM specification. In Table 4.2, you will see a list of sounds with their associated program numbers. All GM devices will have these 128 sounds.

Table 4.1   General MIDI Program Numbers Grouped by Instrument Categories

Program #	Instrument Category	Program #	Instrument Category
1–8	Piano	65–72	Reed
9–16	Chromatic Percussion	73–80	Pipe
17–24	Organ	81–88	Synth Lead
25–32	Guitar	89–96	Synth Pad
33–40	Bass	97–104	Synth Effects
41–48	Strings	105–112	Ethnic
49–56	Ensemble	113–120	Percussive
57–64	Brass	121–128	Sound Effects

Table 4.2   General MIDI's 128 Program Names with Their Associated Program Numbers, also Grouped by Instrument Categories

Program #	Instrument	Program #	Instrument
	Pianos		**Guitars**
1	Acoustic Grand Piano	25	Acoustic Guitar (nylon)
2	Bright Acoustic Piano	26	Acoustic Guitar (steel)
3	Electric Grand Piano	27	Electric Guitar (jazz)
4	Honky-Tonk Piano	28	Electric Guitar (clean)
5	Electric Piano 1	29	Electric Guitar (muted)
6	Electric Piano 2	30	Overdriven Guitar
7	Harpsichord	31	Distortion Guitar
8	Clavinet	32	Guitar Harmonics
	Chromatic Percussion		**Basses**
9	Celesta	33	Acoustic Bass
10	Glockenspiel	34	Electric Bass (finger)
11	Music Box	35	Electric Bass (pick)
12	Vibraphone	36	Fretless Bass
13	Marimba	37	Slap Bass 1
14	Xylophone	38	Slap Bass 2
15	Tubular Bells	39	Synth Bass 1
16	Dulcimer	40	Synth Bass 2
	Organs		**Strings**
17	Drawbar Organ	41	Violin
18	Percussive Organ	42	Viola
19	Rock Organ	43	Cello
20	Church Organ	44	Contrabass
21	Reed Organ	45	Tremolo Strings
22	Accordion	46	Pizzicato Strings
23	Harmonica	47	Orchestral Harp
24	Tango Accordion	48	Timpani

Program #	Instrument
	Ensemble
49	String Ensemble 1
50	String Ensemble 2
51	Synth Strings 1
52	Synth Strings 2
53	Choir Aahs
54	Voice Oohs
55	Synth Voice
56	Orchestra Hit
	Brass
57	Trumpet
58	Trombone
59	Tuba
60	Muted Trumpet
61	French Horn
62	Brass Section
63	Synth Brass 1
64	Synth Brass 2
	Reed
65	Soprano Sax
66	Alto Sax
67	Tenor Sax
68	Baritone Sax
69	Oboe
70	English Horn
71	Bassoon
72	Clarinet

Program #	Instrument
	Pipe
73	Piccolo
74	Flute
75	Recorder
76	Pan Flute
77	Blown Bottle
78	Skakuhachi
79	Whistle
80	Ocarina
	Synth Effects
97	FX 1 (rain)
98	FX 2 (soundtrack)
99	FX 3 (crystal)
100	FX 4 (atmosphere)
101	FX 5 (brightness)
102	FX 6 (goblins)
103	FX 7 (echoes)
104	FX 8 (sci-fi)
	Ethnic
105	Sitar
106	Banjo
107	Shamisen
108	Koto
109	Kalimba
110	Bagpipe
111	Fiddle
112	Shanai

Program #	Instrument		Program #	Instrument
	Percussive			Sound Effects
113	Tinkle Bell		121	Guitar Fret Noise
114	Agogo		122	Breath Noise
115	Steel Drums		123	Seashore
116	Woodblock		124	Bird Tweet
117	Taiko Drum		125	Telephone Ring
118	Melodic Tom		126	Helicopter
119	Synth Drum		127	Applause
120	Reverse Cymbal		128	Gunshot

Multi-Timbral Capability

To make sure you can hear all parts in a MIDI sequence properly, GM also provides multi-timbral capability definitions. Any GM device plays and records at least 16 MIDI channels simultaneously, with each channel playing a variable number of polyphonic voices. This might be different from one model to another, but a minimum number of polyphonic voices has been set, which is described in the following paragraphs. Each channel can also be set to play a different instrument or program (sound, patch, or timbre, depending on the sound module's convention).

Since MIDI sequences often use percussions or rhythmic parts, MIDI channel 10 in the GM specification is reserved especially for this. In other words, you can't assign a bass sound to this channel, since it will always be dedicated to the percussion sounds as defined in Table 4.3.

GM Note Numbers

Note numbers were described in Chapter 2. To make sure the pitch of all GM instruments refers to the same pitch values when it comes to note numbers, the GM specification designates that the A-440 pitch is note number 69, making every sound relate to that pitch when a note number is sent through MIDI. In non-GM compatible devices, for example, you might play a melodic part in a high range and would find it was playing an octave higher or lower on other modules due to manufacturers that map middle C on note number 48 or 72, rather than on 60. With GM defining the A-440 (Hz) pitch or the note number 69, middle C will always be note number 60. Obviously, you can change the octave setting for a sound, making it lower or higher. However, the note number in relation to other sounds will be the same, and the default GM sound bank takes that into consideration.

Drum machines were also problematic, since most of the multi-timbral devices came with a built-in set of percussive sounds such as drum kits and percussion. This can be troublesome when recording a percussion part for a song and having it played by another device. Imagine if your bass drum became a tambourine all of a sudden! It could be interesting, but not what you had in mind.

To address this, GM assigns 48 common drum sounds to 48 specific MIDI note numbers, as shown in Table 4.3. Using channel 10 and these instruments, a composer can safely assume that a drum/percussion part will play the right instruments when played on another GM-compatible device. GM drum sounds are not part of the 128 programs defined in the GM sound bank set, but rather an additional set of sounds specific to the number 10 MIDI channel. These sounds are mapped to note numbers on your keyboard in a single special drum map program, which can only be accessed by using MIDI channel 10.

Table 4.3   The GM Drum Map

MIDI Note #	Drum Sound	Note Name	MIDI Note #	Drum Sound	Note Name
35	Acoustic Bass Drum	B0	59	Ride Cymbal 2	B2
36	Bass Drum 1	C1	60	Hi Bongo	C3
37	Side Stick	C#1	61	Low Bongo	C#3
38	Acoustic Snare	D1	62	Mute Hi Conga	D3
39	Hand Clap	D#1	63	Open Hi Conga	D#3
40	Electric Snare	E1	64	Low Conga	E3
41	Low Floor Tom	F1	65	High Timbale	F3
42	Closed Hi-Hat	F#1	66	Low Timbale	F#3
43	High Floor Tom	G1	67	High Agogo	G3
44	Pedal Hi-Hat	G#1	68	Low Agogo	G#3
45	Low Tom	A1	69	Cabasa	A3
46	Open Hi-Hat	A#1	70	Maracas	A#3
47	Low-Mid Tom	B1	71	Short Whistle	B3
48	Hi-Mid Tom	C2	72	Long Whistle	C4
49	Crash Cymbal 1	C#2	73	Short Guiro	C#4
50	High Tom	D2	74	Long Guiro	D4
51	Ride Cymbal 1	D#2	75	Claves	D#4
52	Chinese Cymbal	E2	76	Hi Wood Block	E4
53	Ride Bell	F2	77	Low Wood Block	F4
54	Tambourine	F#2	78	Mute Cuica	F#4
55	Splash Cymbal	G2	79	Open Cuica	G4
56	Cowbell	G#2	80	Mute Triangle	G#4
57	Crash Cymbal 2	A2	81	Open Triangle	A4
58	Vibraslap	A#2			

GM Polyphony

To ensure that all notes recorded are played, the GM standard also provides for a minimum number of polyphonic voice assignments. Therefore, every GM device provides a minimum of 1 voices that can be assigned to any or all MIDI channels simultaneously and eight voices for percussion alone (which are played on channel 10). These 24 voices should also be velocity sensitive.

This is the minimum required by the GM standard. However, many devices such as multi-timbral devices offering GM as a separate bank of sounds may offer more than the required minimum number of voices. This is because GM is, after all, a recommended practice, not a standard dictating the maximum number of polyphonic voices a sound module should offer. For example, the Roland JV-1080 is GM compatible but offers 64-voice polyphony. Restricting your polyphony to 16 voices only provides you with a guideline to follow when writing music that will be distributed using GM devices.

A good example of this would be a MIDI file on a Web page. Since many users don't have fancy synthesizers or audio hardware, chances are they will be using a GM synth built into their audio hardware. Many of them will offer no more than what the GM requires as a minimum.

Other Supported MIDI Messages

Sound banks, note numbers, and channel assignments for percussions and polyphony are not the only parameters defined by General MIDI. As you saw in Chapters 2 and 3, a good portion of what MIDI is lies in its functions. Therefore, GM also provides a set of standard channel messages to ensure that volume changes made in an original song, for example, will be reproduced properly. Here are the MIDI messages to which every GM device should respond:

* **Control Change 1**: Modulation wheel, which is usually hard wired to control LFO amount, or in other words, the amount of vibrato.
* **Control Change 7**: Channel Volume.
* **Control Change 10**: Pan.
* **Control Change 11**: Expression, which can be assigned to anything, including aftertouch.
* **Control Change 64**: Sustain.
* **Control Change 121**: Reset All Controllers (this is actually a Channel Mode message).
* **Control Change 123**: All Notes Off (as with the previous, this is a Channel Mode message as well).
* **Registered Parameter Number 0**: Pitch Wheel Bend Sensitivity.
* **Registered Parameter Number 1**: Fine Tuning.
* **Registered Parameter Number 2**: Coarse Tuning.

Finally, the GM standard has attempted to standardize further by defining a certain number of features. Here's a list of those features:

❋ GM modules respond to velocity; however, what the velocity affects in the sound has not been determined. Typically, this affects the VCA level or volume of each note.

❋ The pitch wheel bend range defaults to plus or minus 2 semitones (or half steps). This way, you can save pitch bends in a GM file without worrying whether the bend will be going one octave up and down.

❋ GM modules respond to channel pressure, which often determines the VCA level or VCO level for vibrato depth. How exactly it responds to the channel pressure is not determined, so you might hear different effects from device to device when using the same sounds in a GM sound bank.

❋ A GM device provides at least a MIDI In, Out, and Thru connector, access to a master volume control, and at least two audio outputs (left and right), with an additional headphone connector.

❋ By default, a GM module powers up with all of its channel volume levels at a default value of 90. Its controllers and effects should be off, and it should be tuned to the A-440 reference.

Standard MIDI Files (SMF)

You've just seen how the MIDI specifications were enhanced to allow for greater control over instruments through the standardization of some basic features. The most prevalent use of GM, however, is through the sequences it plays. Recording a sequence means that you lay down a certain number of tracks on a software- or hardware-based sequencer and play back these tracks. This is fine if you keep your files at home and are the only one listening to them. But what if you wanted to bring them into another studio, using different software and a different set of sound modules? Well, for the different set of sound modules, you've got GM, right? But what about the sequences?

That's what Standard MIDI Files (SMFs) are for. This is a protocol used to transfer MIDI information from one type of device to another. In most cases, this would be from one MIDI sequencer to another. You could even take a Standard MIDI File and open it in notation software to polish your score if your MIDI sequencer doesn't support any notation outputs.

What Is an SMF?

Standard MIDI Files were added to the MIDI specification in 1988 and use a universal language that saves all MIDI notes, velocities, and controller codes as a generic file that may be interpreted by any program that supports this type of file. Most media players (such as Quick-Time, Winamp, Real Player, and Windows Media Player), along with all popular sequencers, support this file type, import it into an existing file, or simply create a file and save it, export it as another type of MIDI file, or save your updated version as a Standard MIDI File.

Most of the time, SMF will use the extension .mid at the end of a document to indicate to the applications installed on your computer that this is a Standard MIDI File.

There are three types of SMF files, which were described in Chapter 1, Table 1.2. *Type 0* combines all tracks or staves into a single track. *Type 1* will save each part (MIDI channel) on a separate track or staff in a score. It will also save the tempo setting and time signature information included in the first track. However, you can save only one song per file with this type. To save patterns, such as drum patterns, the best type of SMF is *Type 2*. A Type 2 MIDI file saves your parts on separate tracks but also saves different tempo and time signature settings for each track in a file or, as you can see in Figure 4.2, one for each section (bar 1, bar 9, and bar 21). While Type 2 is more likely to be used as a way to save a series of drum patterns for a drum machine than it is to save an actual song, Type 1 is the most common MIDI file type.

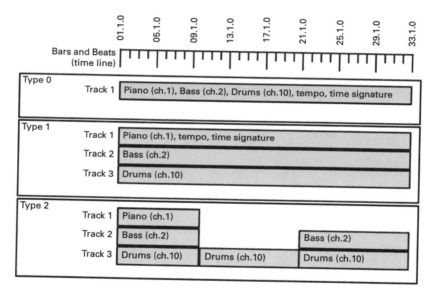

Figure 4.2 Standard MIDI File types.

MIDI files don't hold only events such as channel voice messages, channel mode messages, and system messages. They also hold song tempo and tempo changes, time signatures and signature changes, key signatures, text, lyrics, markers and cue points. Let's not forget time code offsets, which is the time that a song would start at bar 1.1.0 if it were synchronized with a video starting at 09:50:00:00. To start at the first bar of the song, a MIDI file's offset value would need to correspond to this video starting value (09:50:00:00) rather than the default 00:00:00:00 time code. This is called a time code offset, and it is also saved with your MIDI file.

MIDI files were designed to be generic enough for any sequencer or MIDI file player to read or write such files without losing the most important data. They are also flexible enough for sequencers to store their own proprietary information into them as extra data. This extra data is organized in such a way that another application won't mistake it for another type of file but rather will ignore any information it doesn't need and continue loading it into memory.

Think of it this way: You can type a letter in a text editor, such as Notepad, for instance, or you can type a letter in Word or Word Perfect. Both files will contain text; however, the former contains only text, and the latter may also contain formatting, pictures, links, and a page layout. MIDI files are similar to ASCII text files in this sense. All the rest of the formatting, pictures, links, and page layout are things that, in comparison to word processors, sequencers will add to a MIDI file in a form that only the sequencer that saved the information will be able to recognize. Instead of text formatting, sequencers save things like automation of control changes that are not supported in MIDI files or structural information used by the sequencer itself. It does this by inserting a flag byte to indicate certain user settings, like a metronome click, for example. Another application would simply skip this flag byte since it doesn't understand it.

Differences with Audio Files

Why bother with General MIDI if it doesn't allow you to create your own sounds and is limited to 128 sounds from which to choose? As mentioned above, GM is not meant as a creative tool for the working composer/musician but rather as a way to better distribute MIDI content over a wide network while ensuring a certain level of compatibility and quality throughout different MIDI systems. It also provides a common tool that most new electronic musicians can rely on, no matter what GM-compatible device they may own or work with.

GM also opened up markets for the distribution of commercial sequences and karaoke songs. You don't need to know how a sequencer works or how MIDI works to use GM, since it is part of the MIDI specifications of most computers today. So, loading these songs is easily done, and because of its specifications, the creators of these sequences can be sure everybody will hear the content properly. You can also use ready-made sequences to practice songs without having a band in your living room by simply deactivating the MIDI channel in a GM-compliant sequence, thus creating a great educational tool.

With the rise of the Internet's popularity, being able to download music quickly with even the slowest modem has been a major hassle. The GM specification offers a simple, standard way to easily and quickly distribute songs over a network of computers. Let's take a three-minute MIDI file containing J.S. Bach's "Prelude & Fugue No.1." The whole content of the file will take up approximately 30Kb, whereas the same song as a CD-quality audio file would take around 31,007Kb. That's 1,000 times the size of its MIDI equivalent. Even with MP3 compression being very popular, to keep decent quality still requires around 100 times (about 3,000Kb) the size of a MIDI file (*.mid). MIDI stores events that take very little space, as seen in Figure 4.3's top section, whereas digital audio stores data at a rate of 44,100 samples per second, per channel. It does so in order to be able to reproduce an audio waveform as it was recorded (see bottom half of the same figure).

MIDI

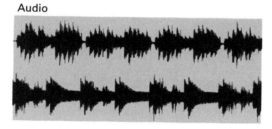

Start-Pos.				Length	Val.1	Val.2	Val.3	Event Type
1.	1.	1.	1	====,==,====	64	127	===	Sustain
1.	1.	1.	1	====,==,====	91	127	===	Effect1Dep
1.	1.	1.	1	====,==,====	64	127	===	Sustain
1.	1.	1.	1	====,==,====	91	127	===	Effect1Dep
1.	1.	1.	1	====,==,====	10	127	===	Pan
1.	1.	1.	32	1. 3.3600	B2	52	0	Note
1.	1.	2.	1	====,==,====	10	95	===	Pan
1.	1.	2.	32	1. 2.3800	D3	48	0	Note
1.	1.	3.	1	====,==,====	10	63	===	Pan
1.	1.	3.	32	0. 0.3800	G3	45	0	Note
1.	1.	4.	1	====,==,====	10	31	===	Pan
1.	1.	4.	32	0. 0.3800	D4	48	0	Note
1.	2.	1.	1	====,==,====	10	0	===	Pan
1.	2.	1.	32	0. 0.3416	F4	52	0	Note
1.	2.	2.	32	0. 0.3800	G3	41	0	Note
1.	2.	2.	33	====,==,====	10	63	===	Pan
1.	2.	3.	32	0. 0.3800	D4	40	0	Note
1.	2.	3.	33	====,==,====	10	31	===	Pan

Audio

Figure 4.3 Comparing MIDI and audio files.

Another difference between MIDI files and audio files is that you can easily change the pitch of a song in a MIDI file if you are using it as a practice tool and wish to adjust the song to your range. With audio, you need specialized software to change the pitch. Furthermore, when changing the pitch of an audio file, the audio quality is also modified. Finally, to change the pitch of a single instrument in a song requires that you have access to all the audio tracks as separate files; otherwise you end up transposing percussive instruments as well.

Another advantage of MIDI over audio is that you can dramatically slow down or speed up the tempo in a MIDI file to fit your needs without affecting the audio quality. With MIDI, working on a solo for a new song your band will be covering is easier because you can slow down the tempo to get all the notes right and then speed it back up when you feel comfortable.

However, if you are trying to get a special sound with creative effects or sound design, MIDI files, especially those using GM sound banks, are probably not what you are looking for. Another drawback of MIDI files with GM devices is that you can't really predict how well the sound module will reproduce your music on someone else's computer, despite recent advances in sound banks. There are still plenty of people running their computers with low-quality sound cards with low-quality GM sound banks. So, if you want to have full control over the output of your files, you will need to reconsider the use of MIDI files and GM sound banks.

Extending the General MIDI Standard

When GM came out, some companies felt the standard didn't go far enough and was too limited in terms of sound banks. They also felt that GM didn't offer enough control over sounds themselves through MIDI. Two of those companies came out with their own versions of General MIDI—both of which offer an extended version of the GM standard. Roland called it the GS standard, and Yamaha called it the XG standard. GS and XG are supersets of the GM standard (see Figure 4.4), offering full backward compatibility with GM and offering more sounds (over 1,000 in some cases) and control over sound parameters. If you don't own any Roland GS-compatible or Yamaha XG-compatible devices, this will not be relevant to you, since these functions are usually available on Roland or Yamaha gear. However, many audio hardware manufacturers have adopted these extended parameters in order to offer both GM compatibility and added value to their product. QuickTime, for example, offers a GS sound bank rather than the basic GM sound bank when its MIDI player options are selected.

Figure 4.4   The GS and XG standards are both offering GM compatibility but propose an additional set of proprietary features.

Roland GS Standard

The GS standard developed by Roland obeys in every way the General MIDI specification and adds many extra controllers and sounds. Some of these controllers use NRPN to give macro control over a synthesizer's parameters, such as the envelope attack and decay rates. It also offers additional sound banks, which include variations on the GM sound bank and re-creations of Roland's famous MT-32 sound module.

The programs in each bank are mapped the same way as a GM instrument patch map would be: 128 sounds divided into eight families of sounds. In the GS standard, if the module receives a request for a bank or program number combination that does not exist, the module will reassign it to the master instrument in that family. Using a GS module to create a song, extra information is written in the System Exclusive (SysEx) message to specify that this file contains GS messages. System Exclusive communicates the appropriate parameter settings to MIDI devices that are not covered in other MIDI messages. SysEx messages are described in greater detail in Chapter 11. If the GM device doesn't support these extra features, it will simply ignore them and play the sequence as if it were recorded as a GM file. However, a GS module would play the file containing extra GS messages using its alternative sound banks.

Like GM modules, Roland uses a special logo to identify GS standard devices, as shown in Figure 4.5.

Figure 4.5 The Roland GS standard logo, certifying that the device is GS compatible.

Yamaha XG Standard

As with Roland GS, Yamaha came up with its own enhanced GM-compatible superset of parameters with the XG standard. What Yamaha proposes is a larger number of sound banks, more voice editing capability, integrated effects, and external inputs that connect an audio device—such as a guitar, bass, or microphone—and process the sound using the integrated effects.

The XG standard provides a minimum of 480 sounds instead of the 128 provided with GM and supports device upgrades to two million sounds. It addresses these sounds by using the control change numbers 0 and 32 (bank select MSB and LSB controllers), which enables you to choose a program and bank from this large number of sounds. The default set of sounds provided with an XG module is divided into four defined banks and a set of undefined banks for further upgrades. The four banks are as follows:

* **Melody Voices:** The default GM set of sounds and other sounds divided into sound banks.
* **SFX Voices:** A set of sound effects.
* **SFX Kits:** Two sets of sound effects, with each effect assigned to a different key on a controller keyboard.
* **Rhythm Kits:** A selection of nine drum kits and percussion. (This defaults to channel 10 as with GM. However, with XG you can have rhythm parts on other channels as well.)

The XG format also re-interprets some of the control change numbers already assigned to voice editing parameters to allow greater control over the timbre of a sound. For example, the brightness parameter (control change number 74) controls the cutoff frequency in a filter, and some NRPNs are used to control manufacturer-specific parameters (Yamaha being the manufacturer in this case). One of the XG efforts has been to give greater realism to sounds by providing control over how a sound reacts to velocity. This is achieved by using velocity

3. On multi-timbral GM-compatible devices, which MIDI channel is used by default for drum and percussion sounds?

 a) None

 b) 1

 c) 10

 d) 16

4. With GM-compatible devices, middle C below the A-440 reference will always be considered as what note number?

 a) 48

 b) 60

 c) 69

 d) 72

5. GM also provides a set of standard channel and control change messages. Which one does not belong to this list of GM-supported control change messages?

 a) Modulation wheel

 b) Channel volume

 c) Pan

 d) Data entry

6. What is the most common file extension for Standard MIDI Files?

 a) .mid

 b) .smf

 c) .gmf

 d) .wtf

7. To start a MIDI sequence at bar 1.1.0 while synchronizing to a video that begins at 9 hours, 50 minutes, 10 seconds, and 3 frames, what MIDI file parameter should be adjusted?

 a) The MIDI Time Code Quarter Frame

 b) The Time Code Offset

 c) The All Sounds Off Control Change message

 d) None of the above

8. What does the manufacturer Roland call its GM extension standard?

 a) GM Plus Standard

 b) GS Standard

 c) XG Standard

 d) XS Standard

9. Which type of Standard MIDI File is best suited for drum patterns?
    a) Type 0
    b) Type 1
    c) Type 2
    d) Type 3

10. True or False: The GM standard offers integrated effects that offer more control over the sound's timbre and presence in a GM-compatible MIDI sound module.

5 } MIDI Hardware Devices

Up until now, we discussed MIDI as a protocol and looked at how to connect different devices together using MIDI connectors. In this chapter, we look at a number of popular MIDI hardware device types currently available on the market. A musician's ability to recognize these types of MIDI devices will help in making an informed decision before a purchase and in figuring out what can and can't be done with each type of device after the purchase. This chapter will not discuss lists of features and techniques on how to use these devices. You can find this information on each manufacturer's Web site, in store brochures, magazine reviews, and user groups for any particular device. We will, however, discuss a variety of ways in which MIDI is implemented in these hardware devices and how MIDI is still being used almost a quarter of a century after it first appeared.

Here's a summary of what you will learn in this chapter:

- ※ The different types of MIDI-compatible sound generators.
- ※ The different types of MIDI controllers.
- ※ A look at patch bays and how to use them.
- ※ How to optimize a live performance MIDI setup.
- ※ How to configure a MIDI studio setup without the use of a computer.

We start by discussing different MIDI-compatible devices that make up a MIDI studio, focusing our attention on hardware in this chapter, while subsequent chapters will discuss several aspects of the software integration. However, the general principles discussed here are often mirrored in a software environment as well.

Later in the chapter, we will consider some sample MIDI configurations for specific setup situations.

MIDI Devices

MIDI devices come in all shapes, sizes, and forms. They are hardware tools offering controls over how and when MIDI information is sent from one device to another. Understanding what these devices do and what is available is important when planning your own MIDI setup or in preparation for a session in a studio where you might not be as familiar. Preparing for such sessions by deciding which type of sound generator you need, how you can control or send information to these devices using controllers, and how you can integrate these elements into a unit will save you time. Don't forget, most studios bill by the hour, so the less time you take to figure out these issues, the more time you'll have to actually create and produce the music you want.

Sound Generators

Sound generators are devices that produce sounds. That sounds pretty simple, doesn't it? That's because it is, and furthermore, without them, there would be no point in recording MIDI sequences. Among the MIDI devices, sound generators are responsible for the actual sound you hear when playing a MIDI sequence. Unlike digital audio recording, MIDI doesn't record the sound, so sound generators (or sound modules) are necessary to reproduce the audio generated by the recorded MIDI messages.

There is a variety of sound generators that produce sounds in different ways using different types of technologies to achieve the same goal: generating sounds. When building a MIDI studio or a MIDI sequence, choosing which sound generator you will use should play an important part in your planning decisions, since their costs and capabilities vary widely. One fact remains: The type of sound they generate will directly influence how your music will sound, since every sound module has its own colors and textures. Furthermore, when working with a MIDI sequence, the sound generator will need to be present until the MIDI track in a sequence is rendered as digital audio, so making sure the sound generator is there when you mix the sequence is essential. For starters, we are going to take a look at the hardware version of sound generators. We will discuss different virtual sound generators (software-based synthesizers) later in the book (see Chapter 9).

Synthesizers & Sound Modules

Synthesizers create, or synthesize, sounds in an artificial fashion, using different sound elements, such as simple and complex waveforms. Synthesizers produce their sounds through the use of oscillators, voltage-control amplifiers, and filters. Some synthesizers also make use of waveforms—digital samples of real instruments—in combination with oscillators, amplifiers, and filters. Today's synthesizers are capable of generating almost every kind of sound. Synthesizers are usually presented in two forms: as keyboard units or as rack-mounted devices that are often called sound modules. Sounds modules don't have keyboards; instead, they are controlled (i.e., triggered) only via MIDI information sent from a separate keyboard or a computer. Sound modules have the same processing power as a synthesizer with its own keyboard, but they are less expensive than full-blown synthesizers. There are many types of synthesizers on the market and even a far greater number of synthesis techniques used to create sounds. Here are the primary types of synthesizers:

* **Modular Analog Synthesizer:** Earlier types of synthesizers were not like today's synthesizers—they were not built as a single unit device but rather as individual interconnected boxes that each contained certain types of circuitry (see Figure 5.1). Boxes were

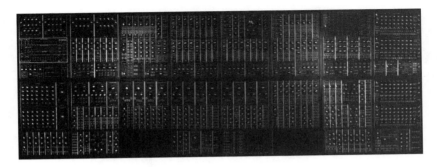

Figure 5.1 A Moog modular built for Hans Zimmer by Keith Lightner. A perfect example of the early days of modular (photo courtesy of Kevin Lightner, www.synthfool.com).

connected to one another in order to expand the circuitry's capability. One box contained a signal-creating device, such as a voltage-controlled oscillator (or VCO) or a noise generator; another box might then process the signal from the first box with voltage-controlled filters (VCF) or voltage-controlled amplifiers (VCA). These modules were often huge, and since they were built-in modules (hence the name modular synthesis), they were linked together with patch cables, acting as routing cords. Today, analog modular synthesizers are becoming popular once again because of the warmth and richness of their sound. Some even come with adapter boxes that convert MIDI into Control Voltage (CV), which lets you determine the pitch of a note. In Figure 5.2 for example, the MOTM from Synthesis Technology comes as a kit where each module is an option, including the MIDI to CV converter appearing in the bottom left corner of this module.

❋ **Self-Contained Analog Synthesizer:** These synthesizers use the same technology as modular synthesizers, with the exception that there is no needs for cables since they are pre-wired. These synthesizers will generally have an analog-style look to them, with banks of knobs that control oscillators, filters, voltage controls, and other components on their front panel. True analog synthesizers are not as common as they used to be, since many of the analog components have been replaced by digital ones, and instead of true analog oscillators (the sound-generating component), synthesizers often use digitized waveforms. But music being what it is, trends have a tendency to reappear, which is why analog-sounding instruments are making a resurgence in music stores everywhere (see Figure 5.3).

❋ **Digital Synthesizer:** In this type of synthesizer, the whole process usually stays in the digital domain. Even its source material is digital, usually digital waveforms reproduced by a sample-playback component inside the device. The end result is that a digital synth can often emulate natural timbres more realistically than its analog counterpart, although some argue that digital synthesizers sound colder or harsher than their analog counterparts. Other digital synthesizers use a strictly digital synthesis method to generate sounds rather than using samples. This is the case with the Yamaha DX-7 (shown in Chapter 1).

Figure 5.2   Dave Bradley assembled this particular MOTM (www.hotrodmotm.com) using different MOTM modules, just like building a kit car.

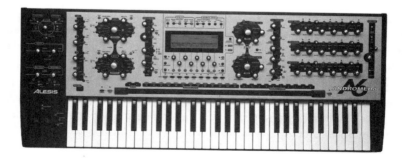

Figure 5.3   The Alesis A6 Andromeda is a good example of true analog synthesis currently on the market (picture courtesy of Alesis, www.alesis.com).

The Roland D-50, on the other hand, allows users to choose either short PCM samples (see "Sample-Playback Synthesizers" below) or digitally generated waveforms. A true digital synthesizer is one where all sound generation and manipulation happens in the digital domain and is not simply "digitally controlled" as many self-contained analog synthesizers may be (see above).

❊ **Sample-Playback Synthesizer:** This is probably the most common type of synthesizer in use today (see Figure 5.4). These synthesizers contain samples stored onboard in ROM chips in the form of PCM (Pulse Code Modulation). Many manufacturers also call these "wavetables." Wavetables may be sampled sounds originating from real instruments or synthesized tones such as sine, square, or sawtooth waves. The wavetables are then processed through various filters and envelopes to give you a whole range of sounds. This type of synthesizer has many advantages: It's versatile, cheap, usually offers a good number of sound banks (programs or presets), has a good number of polyphonic voices, and is easy to use. Many sample-playback synthesizers also include built-in sequencers and effects, which qualifies them as workstations.

Figure 5.4 Two examples of sample-playback synthesizers. On top, the EMU PK-6 synthesizer with keyboard controller, and on the bottom, the EMU Proteus 2000 rack-mounted sound module.

❊ **Physical Modeling Synthesizer:** This type of synthesizer emerged in the 90s and is becoming quite a trendsetter. Physical modeling uses software code to produce the sound instead of the usual hardware technique (see Figure 5.5). In other words, it implies that the software code is responsible for the analysis of parameter settings and the subsequent implementation of these settings while generating the actual sound. This type of synthesizer is usually very effective at emulating very complex vibrations, resonance, reflections, and other acoustic phenomena that occur in a real wind or string instrument. You

Figure 5.5 The Yamaha EX5 is an example of a synthesizer that uses physical modeling to produce its sounds.

can find this type of synthesizer design in software format as well, since it is so close to the computer in the way it approaches sound.

Samplers

Samplers are like sample-based synthesizers, with one very important difference: You can record your own sounds into them to create new programs. In this respect, a sampler is more flexible than its sample-playback counterpart. The disadvantage of a sampler over a sample-playback device is that it is, in general, more expensive and requires greater programming skills since you are the one creating sound banks. On the other hand, many companies specialize in the creation of sound banks for specific models of samplers (such as the Roland S-700 series or the Akai S series sampler, as illustrated in Figure 5.6).

What a sampler typically does is quite simple: It reproduces recorded sounds at variable frequencies corresponding to a note played on a MIDI keyboard or controller. For example, sample a guitar playing a single note, let's say a G4, and assign this note to the corresponding G4 key on the keyboard layout of the sampler. If the sampler does not have a keyboard, then a special key zone mapping window will provide the equivalent of a keyboard where notes are placed. Record other samples of other pitches, such as B4, C5, and so on, and assign them to their corresponding notes on the keyboard layout in the sampler's editing window.

Figure 5.6 The Akai S-6000 sampler—as you can see, this version of the device can be rack-mounted on a 19" rack and does not contain a keyboard controller.

After you've recorded as many samples as you need (usually, this is limited to 128 samples per program or preset), and you've mapped all these sounds to keys on your keyboard, you can play your new guitar program using your keyboard instead of the guitar used for the sampling. This technique is often referred to as multi-sampling, where an instrument is re-created by using multiple samples of its sound over the range of this instrument. This allows for a more realistic result in the end, since the sampler only has to extrapolate the audio sample over a narrow range of keys. In other words, the more samples you have, the better the end result will be, especially with acoustic instruments, since our ears are used to hearing these instruments. Furthermore, pitch-shifting a sampled sound over a wide range on a keyboard will result in unnatural artifacts appearing in the sound when played. Again taking our original sampled guitar with its recorded pitch of G4 and playing this sample by pressing a G2, the sampler will play the sample at roughly 25 percent of its original sampling rate. If you have ever tried this, you will quickly realize that the quality of a sample at 11KHz is not quite up to par with a sample at 44.1KHz.

Samplers also use loops in the sound to save on memory used to play back these sounds. Since memory is a big factor in the cost of the instrument, the more memory you use for a sound, the fewer sounds you will have. Programming loops at this point becomes very important if you want to be able to load more than one sound at a time in your sampler.

Just like other synths, samplers offer different types of sound-processing features, such as envelopes, filters, frequency oscillators, and others. All these features give you more control over the quality of the sound.

Because computers have large RAM capacities and huge hard disk capabilities and because chances are you might already own one, there is a growing number of software developers working hard to bring you a software version of what samplers do. As a result, hardware samplers have been on the decline, while software ones have increased in popularity. Many of today's samplers have adapted their features to better address the needs of live performers, most notably in the form of drum machines with loadable and customizable samples with added features such as pattern-based sequencers to save drum loops, for example. This said, using a computer as a sampler implies that a large portion of its RAM will be needed to run the sampler program and that the hard disk where the samples are stored will need to be fast enough to read the information on it quickly without disturbing other processes that might occur simultaneously inside a computer. This is especially true when using a sampler software application simultaneously with a MIDI/audio sequencer for recording and playback.

Drum Machines

This name is usually reserved for synthesizers or sample-playback devices that contain drum or percussion sounds in them. Although some drum machines expand on this definition, the purpose of this type of device is to create drum or percussion tracks. Drum machines often have internal sequencers to program and save drum songs and drum patterns (see Figure 5.7). Instead of using the typical keyboard layout, drum machines often use buttons, trigger pads, or, in some cases, electronic drum kits to control the sounds they hold. Since

Figure 5.7 The Boss DR-880 drum machine.

drum machines hold mostly drum and percussion sounds, the sequences you record in them are limited to playing rhythmic parts.

Earlier drum machines used analog synthesis to create sounds, but today most drum machines use digital samples. Certain models load sounds into memory where custom drum kits can be configured. Better drum machines (see Figure 5.10) have touch-sensitive pads so that they can transmit velocity information through MIDI cables as well as Note On messages that correspond to the different pads or controllers triggering the sounds.

Workstations

Workstations are like synthesizers or samplers (sometimes a combination of both), but besides their sound-generating abilities, they also offer built-in sequencing features to record MIDI parts on different tracks and play them back using the multi-timbral capability these workstations offer. Think of a workstation as a self-contained music production device (see Figure 5.8). Many workstations also have built-in effects that can be added to the sounds they produce. Finally, a storage device is often provided with workstations so that you can store sequences when the internal memory is full or to use these sequences later.

MIDI-Enabled Devices

MIDI-enabled devices produce MIDI data that can be played or recorded using other MIDI-enabled devices, like a link in a chain. Their main purpose is to serve as MIDI input or controller devices, not to generate sounds. Some devices included in this section are typical audio-related devices, but they all have one thing in common: They respond to and generate MIDI

Figure 5.8   The Korg Oasys is an example of a workstation that includes a sample-playback sound module, a sequencer, effects, and various controllers.

messages. Because of this, you can use these devices in a MIDI setup, and with the help of a sequencer, for example, you can control them using MIDI messages.

An example of this would be a MIDI-enabled sound effect processor, to which program change messages are sent in order to change a reverb setting. Another example is the MIDI control surface offering physical controls connected through MIDI to a software environment. The advantages of such devices over their audio counterparts are flexibility and affordability. Using a controller to automate a mix or adjust levels during recording through a series of MIDI messages over different MIDI channels makes it possible to reassign each physical control to any number of virtual controls inside a software environment. The possibilities are vast, since the range of MIDI-enabling devices is quite wide.

Keyboard Controllers

MIDI keyboard controllers are devices offering a keyboard and sometimes additional MIDI-compatible buttons, faders, or knobs that generate MIDI messages. Keyboard controllers don't come with the heavy sound-generating artillery most synthesizers offer. Any type of keyboard can be used as a controller; however, some keyboards are manufactured to do just that while others also offer sound generators. Their key action is reminiscent of a piano key action, and their keyboard have up to 88 keys. On the other end of the spectrum are small controller keyboards that hook up to a computer through a USB connection, transmitting MIDI data to a software sequencer or other software-based sound module. This type of controller usually offers a small keyboard range and no internal sounds. In any case, keyboard controllers will rarely offer anything more than a GM-compatible sound bank, which is not enough to call them synthesizers because the GM standard offers very limited sound editing capability.

For a pianist, the best keyboard controllers have more realistic piano action (see Figure 5.9), making them more sensitive to every nuance of a performance.

Other Types of MIDI Controllers

Besides keyboards, there are MIDI controllers for almost every instrument family, including strings, winds, and percussions. If you are a drummer and unaccustomed to playing a keyboard, using one to play drum parts will likely be difficult for you. Figure 5.10 shows an alternative. Drum controllers are similar to real drums, with one big difference: They are not as loud as real ones until they are plugged in. Each piece of this drum set is nothing more than

Figure 5.9   The M-Audio Keystation Pro 88 is an 88-note keyboard controller with hammer action, providing realistic piano action.

a velocity-sensitive MIDI pad that sends Note On events to a sound module (seen on the left in Figure 5.10). Using MIDI language, these events can also be transmitted to an external sequencer to record a performance just as you would with a real drummer. Only in this case, what you record is just the performance's MIDI events, not the sounds coming from the instrument itself. You could assign any number of sounds to each individual piece in the drum kit later on through the sound generator device accompanying the controllers.

Figure 5.10   The Roland V-Stage Series drum set is a sophisticated drum machine geared for drummers rather than keyboardists.

Figure 5.11 shows another example of a percussion-oriented MIDI controller. When hit with a drumstick, each portion of the pad can trigger up to eight different samples coming from a sound module. Both of these controllers offer different features that make them more than just

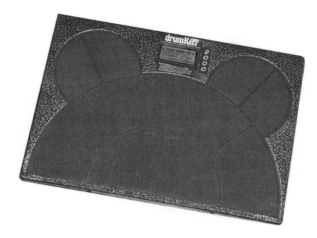

Figure 5.11 The drumKAT Turbo 2000 from Alternate Mode.

note triggers, but the principle behind both of them is the same: to allow a musician to record MIDI performances through an input device.

Another type of controller is the MIDI guitar. This presents a more complex problem, since guitar strings produce complex vibrations, and quite often the harmonics produced between the strings to create a rich guitar sound can blur the pitch, making it difficult to convert the audio signal into a Note On message with its proper note number. Different techniques have been introduced to solve this problem. One of them is to replace the actual strings with a series of string-like rubber triggers that the guitar player plucks just as if they were real strings. The position of the hand on the neck of the guitar and the trigger itself convey the proper note number to a MIDI output on the guitar controller. Another technique consists of adding a special kind of converter/pick-up on the guitar (see Figure 5.12) that analyzes the content of the audio to determine the actual pitch of the note.

The MIDI wind controller, as shown in Figure 5.13, was designed to be played like a wood-wind instrument but sound like anything that could be generated by a sound module. It will allow experienced wind players a great deal of expressive control over sounds generated by sound modules, since it uses different MIDI control change parameters in real time, just as a real woodwind instrument does. By translating the player's breath and lip pressure to MIDI data via high-resolution wind and pressure sensors, it can convert air pressure into aftertouch data to modify the tonal quality of the sound. Just as with MIDI drum or guitar controllers, MIDI wind controllers require a certain amount of familiarity with this type of instrument. For example, knowing either saxophone or flute fingering will help your performance.

Control Surfaces
MIDI control surfaces are another type of non-musical MIDI controller offering a number of programmable knobs, faders, and switch buttons. The purpose of these devices is to give

Figure 5.12   The Ztar Model Z6 (top) and Z6-S (bottom) from Starr Labs comes with either rubber strum bars (top) or string triggers (bottom) with pickups.

Figure 5.13   The Yamaha WX5 wind controller.

tactile controls virtual or software-based parameters like a track's volume, pan, or solo/mute buttons. Because these devices are programmable, the same physical control can be associated with any number of parameters inside a software application that supports it. Through MIDI messages, such as Control Change and SysEx messages, the control surface sends mixing performance information to a receiving application. For example, by associating a controller knob to a software synthesizer filter frequency, you can automate a filter sweep and record this performance as you would any Note On message from a keyboard controller using the MIDI protocol. Similarly, you can control how a mix sounds without having to rely on your mouse pointing skills (see Figures 5.14 and 5.15). Mixing multiple tracks, using only your mouse to change the volume of several MIDI instruments at once, can be difficult since you can only point and click on one virtual fader at a time on a computer screen. Using an external MIDI control surface can provide an economical solution to MIDI automation when working on mixes in collaboration with a MIDI sequencer, since you can record and program (through a software interface) what each physical controller does in your MIDI sequence as another MIDI track. We'll get more into the mixing aspect of MIDI when discussing MIDI sequencers in Chapter 8 and in the section "MIDI Enabled Mixers" later in this chapter.

Figure 5.14 The US-428 MIDI remote control surface from Tascam.

MIDI-Enabled Mixers

Since multitrack audio technology was introduced, mixing engineers have dealt with the daunting task of handling volume levels, effects, panning, groupings, equalization settings, and an ever growing number of parameters in real time. Since the majority of us humans have

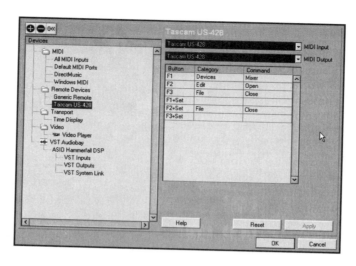

Figure 5.15   Setting up the US-428 control surface inside a sequencer software.

only two hands and 10 fingers, there's just so much we can do simultaneously. That's why mixing automation was such a welcome feature in large mixers: It gave a mixing engineer the ability to record level changes made to a mix during various "practice" passes, so that when it was time to record the final mix, the automation took over and handled all the fader level changes that had been programmed into the mixer. Mixing 24 tracks with effects had become manageable—and fun to watch, as the faders moved of their own accord during mixdown. However, motorized faders are not cheap. Eventually, though, luckily for us, MIDI turned out to be the perfect mate for the job. The main advantage of MIDI-enabled mixers over MIDI control surfaces is its ability to route audio as well as MIDI through its circuitry.

A MIDI-enabled mixer in today's world is a mixer that connects to a MIDI system using its built-in MIDI port(s), sending and receiving MIDI messages that control different mixer parameters, as discussed earlier in this chapter. To do so, the MIDI-enabled mixer, along with MIDI control surfaces, assign different control change numbers or SysEx parameters to control the manufacturer-specific parameters. Here's a look at some common MIDI controllable parameters in a typical MIDI-enabled mixer:

* Program Change messages—Can recall entire scenes or mixer setup, just as you would recall a program on a synthesizer or a reverb setting on a multi-processor device. With a single program change, you can recall volume, group, pan, effect, routing, and any other parameter included in a specific mixer device. What is recalled, however, is manufacturer specific and requires an understanding of the mixer's functions. You can usually find documentation about this with each particular device.

* Control Change parameters—Maps specific control change messages to specific parameters on the mixer or control surface. For example, Control Change number 1, normally

used for the modulation wheel, would affect the fader position on input number 1 on the mixer. Again, this is not a rule, but rather a manufacturer-specific setting.

❋ **System Exclusive parameter controls**—Allow you to save as SysEx transmissions different parameter settings such as effect, EQ, and dynamic library presets.

❋ **System Exclusive bulk dump**—Transfers an entire set of memories, settings, and parameters contained in a mixer's memory. Using this type of MIDI transfer, you can save everything your MIDI-enabled mixer or control surface has in its memory for future use. We will discuss how to do bulk dumps later, in Chapter 11. SysEx messages can also be used by control surfaces with buttons assigned to transport functions, such as play, pause, stop, record or shuttle.

❋ **MIDI Machine Control (MMC)**—A standard protocol that controls MMC-enabled tape recorders and other devices. In other words, you can control the usual Play, Stop, Rewind, Fast Forward, Record, and Pause buttons directly from assigned keys on your mixer and also save specific locations on a tape and recall these locations later from your mixer. How the transport controls are addressed and mapped on your control surface or MIDI-enabled device will vary from one device to the next.

❋ **Local Control**—Just as with synthesizers and samplers, the control surface of the mixer and the actual values held by parameters inside the mixer are separate. You can set the local control to On or Off when using your mixer in a MIDI setup. This will allow you to record automation into a sequencer, for example, and have the sequencer send the MIDI messages back to the mixer instead of having both the sequencer and the mixer controls trying to control the mixer's parameters. This would result in some MIDI data being doubled, causing the mixer to jam or stop responding since the flow of MIDI would become greater than what it can handle.

Many sequencer software developers offer tools that allow users to re-create MIDI devices such as a MIDI mixer or control surface inside their software environment. This allows you to associate virtual controls with their physical counterparts using MIDI messages while offering the advantage of showing you what values have been recorded through MIDI, since most MIDI-enabled mixers or control surfaces have very small LCD displays and cannot show all this information simultaneously. In Figure 5.16, you can find an example of this software representation in Tascam's TM-D1000 mixer. The top window shows the Cakewalk version (PC) of the Tascam TM-D1000 mixer, and the lower window shows Emagic's Logic version (Mac) of the same mixer. In most cases, you can search the sequencer's Web site to find out if your mixer setup can be downloaded and used inside your sequencer, or you can create your own mixer setup by building it from scratch using the tools provided by your preferred sequencer software.

While it is probably easier to control a mixer using physical controls, since it offers a more tactile environment than a simple mouse, a sequencer's virtual reproductions will allow you to visually monitor your mix and edit recorded MIDI data to repair or change events that aren't right. For example, if you record some mixer automation using tactile controls (through the actual mixer), but when monitoring, you find that the volume level on one of your inputs

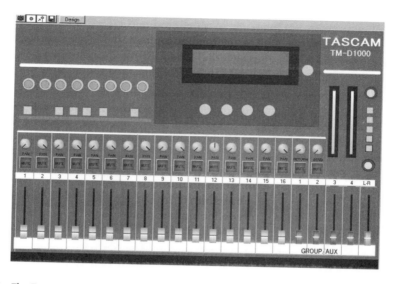

Figure 5.16 The Tascam TM-D1000 (www.tascam.com) mixer parameters reproduced in two sequencer environments.

seems to be going up and down rapidly, you might not notice this change on the mixer due to the slow response speed of the motorized fader. Or, worse yet, this might simply be a parameter that is hidden away in an LCD screen four layers deep. The software reproduction of your mixer inside the sequencer might offer a clue as to what is being controlled or what has been recorded by mistake. Using this interface to monitor the changes and then using an appropriate MIDI editing window to make the necessary changes will allow you to fix these glitches in a more effective way.

In the same line of ideas, some manufacturers offer control surfaces that look like mixers but are in fact MIDI controllers. This allows you to change mix parameters for example, using a tactile control surface rather than controlling these parameters using your mouse and software interface when connecting the MIDI control surface with your sequencer software.

For example, you could assign a MIDI fader on a control surface to control the volume level of a channel in your software's mixing window. How much control you have over parameters inside your software environment depends largely on the support your device has from the software developer of the application you are using. Since control surfaces use programmable parameters, you can assign any control to any type of MIDI messages. In other words, if you can get your sequencer or even sound module to interface with such a device, you can change different parameters in real time using MIDI to communicate messages back and forth between the control surface and another MIDI application or device. You can find examples of MIDI control surfaces by visiting the book's support site (www.wavedesigners.com) Links section. Some manufacturers are listed in the Hardware Companies category.

MIDI-Enabled Digital Effects

MIDI-enabled digital effects are similar to MIDI-enabled mixers in that they can be controlled externally via MIDI messages such as control changes and SysEx messages. Here's an example: Let's say you program an external multi-effect processor to suit certain parts of a song, assigning programs 1 through 4 as the presets used by this song. Once you program these effects, use a MIDI bulk dump to save all the device's parameters with your sequencer file so that when you load your song in the sequencer, your effect's parameters load with it. By assigning program changes for this device in the sequencer application, using a MIDI channel to identify it, you can change the program numbers you've created. Furthermore, you could use the modulation wheel to automate the reverb length of a certain program.

Digital Audio Workstations (DAW)

DAW used to be a simple acronym to identify proprietary hard disk recording systems. Today, this use is still valid, but the word proprietary does not necessarily apply. Any hard disk recording software or system using an audio hardware to transform analog signal into digital audio to record, edit, and mix is considered a DAW. You can still find the aforementioned type of DAW (see Figure 5.17). Most of today's DAWs take a more computer-integrated approach to digital audio hard disk recording by using existing audio hardware resources

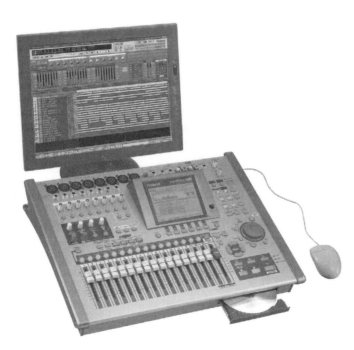

Figure 5.17 The Roland VS-2000CD V-Studio Digital Recording Workstation works as a stand-alone recording system.

combined with the computer's processing power. Finally, computer software provides the user interface that ties all these elements together.

Practically every DAW on the market today offers MIDI compatibility, ranging from simple playback control and automation to fully integrated MIDI environments such as the ones offered by sequencers—yes, sequencers. In the past decade, MIDI sequencers have been taking steps toward the digital audio realm, and the lines between pure MIDI sequencing and digital audio recording have blurred tremendously. This is why you could call software that used to be for MIDI sequencing, such as Sonar, Logic, Performer, Cubase, and more recently Reason and Live, the software version of digital audio workstations. Inversely, software such as ProTools (shown in Figure 5.18) that used to be strictly for digital audio recording have made steps toward greater integration of MIDI functions.

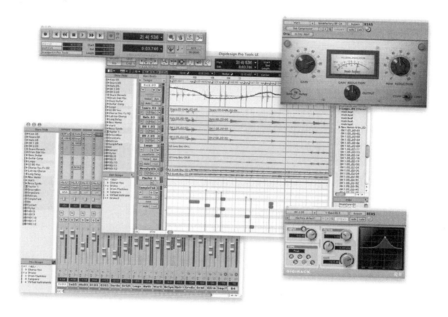

Figure 5.18 Digidesign's ProTools software now integrates both digital audio and MIDI tracks.

As with other MIDI-enabling devices, the DAW records, plays back, and saves MIDI events, and, as such, it integrates MIDI as one of its tools. However, digital audio workstations are the subject of entire books. We will discuss MIDI-related functions in later chapters, but you can find more information about digital audio in other fine books at Thomson's Web site (www.thomson.com or www.coursptr.com).

MIDI Patch Bays

As mentioned in Chapter 1, MIDI patch bays are in many ways like a MIDI matrix. They are useful to store different MIDI path settings internally for later use, especially when you're MIDI setup contains a variety of devices. They are also useful as MIDI Thru or MIDI splitter boxes—in other words, taking a signal that comes from one input and sending it to multiple outputs on the patch bay. In Figure 5.19, the signal coming from the computer's MIDI Out is received by the patch bay's MIDI In 1 and distributed or split to the patch bay's MIDI Out 2 and 3. Both MIDI devices will receive the same signal. This is also called routing a signal. In this setup, each MIDI Out on the patch bay becomes a MIDI Thru.

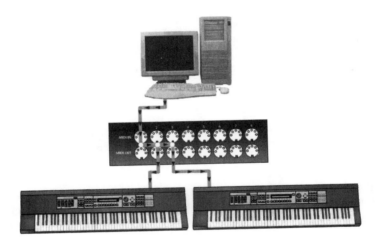

Figure 5.19 The patch bay can act as a MIDI signal splitter or Thru box.

A MIDI patch bay can also serve to merge multiple MIDI inputs into a single MIDI output. In Figure 5.20, the MIDI signal coming out of both keyboards is sent to the MIDI input of the computer. If both keyboards are sending on different MIDI channels, the computer will record both MIDI channels simultaneously. You could also use this setup to send MTC (MIDI Time Code) from one device to a sequencer while recording MIDI tracks from a controller keyboard simultaneously.

Used as a MIDI processor, MIDI patch bays can split incoming signals further into different processes: MIDI filtering, MIDI re-channelizing, MIDI transposing, MIDI delay, and MIDI range splitter. In each case, the patch bay receives a MIDI signal, and depending on the process you decide to apply, the signal will be routed just as mentioned above; i.e., by splitting and/or merging MIDI streams. However, it will also make changes to the MIDI streams as they leave the patch bay's MIDI outputs to reach their destination. Note that some MIDI patch bays do not offer processing functions. Since processing is more expensive to produce due to additional hardware components, less-expensive patch bays might not have all of the above-mentioned processes available.

Figure 5.20 The patch bay in this case acts as a MIDI signal merger box.

Here's a look at some common MIDI processes:

❈ MIDI filtering either filters out certain MIDI messages or changes one type of MIDI message to another, like transforming modulation wheel control messages on channel 1 into aftertouch control messages. Here's an example: In Figure 5.21, the keyboard sends MIDI data to the patch bay's MIDI Input 2. Let's say it is sending over MIDI channel 1, and this MIDI data is routed to the MIDI patch bay's output 6, which is hooked up to sound module A, also set to receive messages on channel 1. You could program the patch bay not to forward any program change messages from MIDI input 2 to this sound module on MIDI output 6. This could be useful to change programs on the keyboard but not on sound module A.

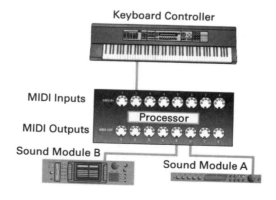

Figure 5.21 Using the patch bay in the middle of a MIDI studio setup as a MIDI processor.

❈ MIDI "rechannelizing" is an invented term that implies one thing: changing the MIDI channel information from the MIDI data coming in on one or more MIDI inputs of a patch bay. Once again, in Figure 5.21, you could take the MIDI messages from the keyboard (MIDI input 2) and route it to both MIDI outputs 5 and 6. Subsequently, you could program the patch bay to transform any MIDI channel 1 information on input 2 going to output 5 to become MIDI channel 2 information for that output and at the same time, remain on channel 1 for the MIDI output 6 (or sound module A). In other words, the keyboard and sound module A will play on MIDI channel 1, and sound module B will play on channel 2.

❈ MIDI Transposing changes the note number of a particular MIDI input on a patch bay, playing on a particular MIDI channel as it comes out of the destination output. With a computer running a sequencer, it's easier to do this through the software application. But if you don't have a software sequencer running, you might find this to be a useful tool when creating lush and thick textures. Once again, send the keyboard's output to both sound modules A and B, but this time, transpose output 5 one octave lower and output 6 one octave higher. If each instrument is set to play on the same MIDI channel, you should have a three-octave spread just by playing one note on the first keyboard.

❈ MIDI delay is another useful process if you don't have sequencer software. This feature repeats MIDI messages several times to create an echo effect. How the effect is created depends on the patch bay, but the number of times a message is repeated and the velocity at which it will be repeated (in the case of Note On messages) are two of the most common parameters for this processing.

❈ MIDI range splitter determines a note number above which each note will be sent to one output and below which each note will be sent to another output. In Figure 5.21, the keyboard could be sending note numbers above or equal to 60 (middle C) to sound module A and notes below 60 to sound module B.

Finally, patch bays can do any combinations of the above-mentioned functions as long as your patch bay supports them. To find out if it does, consult your patch bay's documentation.

The Computerless MIDI Setup

You should now have an understanding of what each type of MIDI device does, so let's look at useful ways to connect them together. Let's look at different scenarios, since there's more than one way to connect devices together, depending on the devices you are using and the purpose of your setup. For example, a live setup is different than a studio setup because you need something that is easy to set up and troubleshoot when preparing for a show. You wouldn't want to spend your sound check time finding out why you can't hear all your sounds, right?

We'll first look at some simple setups involving a minimal number of devices, so that you can understand the logic behind them. You will also understand the advantages and disadvantages related to these setups and what to expect from them. As the title of this section suggests, we will look at different setups that don't involve a computer. Setups involving computers are discussed in Chapter 6.

Obviously, we can't illustrate every possible setup scenario since there are many types of devices that serve different purposes, and keep in mind *your* goal for *your* MIDI gear since it might be different than those of the next reader. Yet, the logic of configuring a computerless MIDI studio remains the same throughout. So read this as a set of suggested setups and make the necessary modifications to fit your own scenario.

Basic Setup

Let's start with a simple three-device setup for a live performance using either one or two controller keyboards. In each example illustrated here, you will have to connect the audio outputs of your devices to a monitoring system or mixer in order to get audio feedback. Audio connections are not shown here, since our purpose is to illustrate MIDI data flow.

Out   In   Thru   In

Figure 5.22   Simple MIDI setup for live performance.

The setup found in Figure 5.22 lets the first device on the left control the second and third device on the right in the chain. Your controller doesn't have to be a keyboard. It could be a wind, guitar, or drum controller, for example. You can layer sounds from the different sound modules linked to the first controller in order to achieve a thicker sound. If you want all the devices in your chain to respond to the first controller keyboard, they will all have to be set to receive MIDI on the same channel—if the controller keyboard is sending MIDI channel 1 messages, all the other devices will need to respond to this channel.

If you would like to split your controller so that it sends MIDI messages on one channel to one device and another channel to a second device in a chain, assign different zones on your keyboard. You will need to have a controller that supports this type of keyboard, or zone split. When this feature is available, assign a MIDI channel to each individual zone on your keyboard (see Figure 5.23). Once you have programmed your controller appropriately, you will also need to configure one device to receive messages on one channel and the other device to receive messages on the second channel.

❋ **TIP**

If one of your sound modules is multi-timbral, you can set it to respond to both channels coming from a split keyboard controller. Enabling both channels causes the multi-timbral device to respond to both channels.

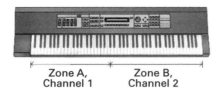

Figure 5.23 Splitting your keyboard, when this feature is supported, sends MIDI information on separate channels simultaneously.

The disadvantage in setting up MIDI devices in a chain is that you can't hook up too many devices in this chain. The problem is that each device may introduce a slight delay or cause errors in the transmission of information, which could lead to errors in the information received by devices later in the chain. If you need to hook up more devices, consider using either a MIDI merge box or a MIDI patch bay. Since this is for a live performance, there's no sequencer involved, so the flow of MIDI information goes in only one direction. In other words, you can't send MIDI from the second or third device back to the first device, since they are not connected in that direction. Connecting the third MIDI Thru connector to the input of the first device might cause a MIDI loop that would once again compromise the integrity of your MIDI information. Remember that your first keyboard is the master, and it alone will be sending information to the second and third devices in the chain; the second keyboard's output is not linked to anything, so it won't be sending MIDI events to the third device. If you wish to have more than one controller keyboard, you will need to use a patch bay or MIDI merge box (see Figure 5.24).

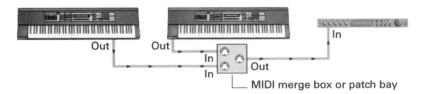

Figure 5.24 Simple MIDI setup for live performance, in which two keyboards can be used as controllers for a third sound module or MIDI device.

Using a Hardware Sequencer

When using a hardware sequencer either as an integrated part of your keyboard (workstation) or as a stand-alone unit, chances are you want to send information to this device and use it to send what's recorded back to the devices in the chain. You might also want to hook up a drum machine that holds drum patterns to this sequencer, so the order in which you place your devices will be important.

In Figure 5.25, the first device in the chain is a keyboard that acts as a sequencer, since most hardware sequencers today are integrated into a synthesizer or sampler module. This serves

Figure 5.25 Using a workstation and a drum machine in a MIDI setup.

as your controller, recorder, and playback device. The second unit in the chain is a drum machine. The output of the keyboard controller sends control commands such as play, stop, and rewind to the drum machine, so you should set the drum machine to slave to an external MIDI clock. On the other hand, since the output of the drum machine is sent to the keyboard controller/sequencer, you can also set the drum machine as the master time clock and the sequencer as slave. This gives you the flexibility of working on your drum patterns while hearing your MIDI sequence. The MIDI Thru of the drum machine forwards the information arriving from the sequencer to the other sound modules in the chain. In this scenario, the two last devices will not transmit information back to the sequencer. So, if you have SysEx information or bulk dumps that need to be recorded into your sequence, you will have to temporarily hook the MIDI out of the appropriate sound module to the MIDI In of the keyboard, unhooking the drum machine from its input.

Since a sequencer records and plays back on multiple channels at once, all multi-timbral devices in this chain react to their set MIDI channel. Just make sure to configure each device in the chain to respond to its appropriate MIDI channel. For example, the keyboard could play MIDI channel 1, the drum machine on channel 10, the first sound module could play channels 2 through 9, and the second sound module, channels 11 through 16. This is, of course, if you need all 16 MIDI channels to play simultaneously. Also, remember that two devices can play the same MIDI channel if you wish them to do so.

Using a MIDI Patch Bay

With more than three MIDI devices, it is easier to use a MIDI patch bay, especially when working without a computer hooked up to the MIDI setup. Since a patch bay merges different MIDI signals by routing the same signal to multiple outputs, every device in the chain will receive the MIDI events at the same time, rather than have a delay added by a lengthy cable linking all the devices together. When using a MIDI patch bay, it is advisable to turn the local control of the keyboard controller to off (Local Off mode), especially if you send the MIDI Out of this keyboard to the MIDI In of the patch bay and then send the MIDI Out of the patch bay to the MIDI In of the keyboard. This will prevent the creation of MIDI feedback.

In Figure 5.26, every device's MIDI outputs are connected to the MIDI inputs of the MIDI patch bay, and the MIDI patch bay's outputs are connected to their appropriate devices' MIDI inputs. By using this setup, you can create programs within the MIDI patch bay to allow for different types of MIDI paths. Here are a few useful and common setups.

When the keyboard acts as the controller and sequencer (workstation), the output of this device should be routed to all devices that need to receive MIDI messages from the

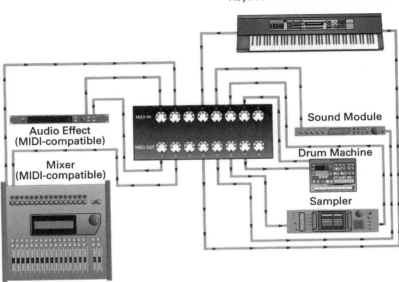

Keyboard Controller/Workstation

Audio Effect
(MIDI-compatible)

Mixer
(MIDI-compatible)

Sound Module

Drum Machine

Sampler

Figure 5.26 Linking multiple MIDI devices to a patch bay without using a computer.

sequencer; in Figure 5.26, all devices are set up to receive MIDI events from the keyboard/workstation. Each receiving device should have its own MIDI channel setting. For example, the keyboard could be channel 1, the sound module (multi-timbral) could be set to channels 2 through 9, the drum machine to channel 10, and so on. By associating devices with specific MIDI channels, you will have greater control over the messages being sent to each one of them. In this setup, the master MIDI Clock is provided by the keyboard/workstation, as it is the only one transmitting MIDI messages to other devices. So for example, the drum machine has to be slaved to an external MIDI Clock to lock its internal pattern sequencer to the tempo of an incoming workstation sequence. Now that all devices are set to respond to their own MIDI channels, set up the patch bay to take the signal coming from MIDI In 4 (in Figure 5.27) to all appropriate MIDI Outs (1 through 7 in this case). As mentioned above, if you are routing the keyboard's MIDI output back into its input, set the keyboard's Local Control to off; otherwise, you will have MIDI note doubling.

Continuing the process, to send MIDI messages back to the keyboard from another device, you could enable the patch bay's MIDI inputs of these devices to be routed back to the keyboard. For example, if you want to record MIDI automation from your mixer into a track on your sequencer (Figure 5.28), route the MIDI Out of the mixer to the MIDI In (2 in Figure 5.26) of the patch bay, and then route the signal internally so that what comes in to MIDI In 2 goes to MIDI Out 4, as in Figure 5.28.

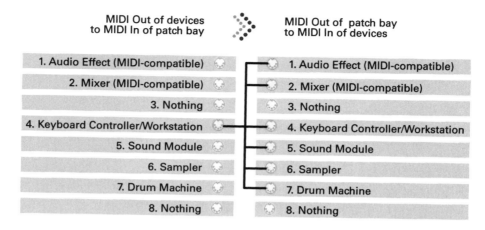

Figure 5.27 Patch bay routing example 1.

To transmit SysEx information from a device—for instance, from a sound module to a keyboard—you can create another setup in the patch bay's memory. It is wise, when doing SysEx transfers between two devices, to establish a direct link between the sender and the receiver. Otherwise, some SysEx data might be lost or cause other devices to lock or reset, especially if you have more than one device made by the same manufacturer. So, in Figure 5.29, you could assign the MIDI signal coming from the MIDI In 5 of the patch bay and send it only to MIDI Out 4 of the patch bay as well.

These are just a few examples of common MIDI setups without using a computer. Chapter 6 discusses additional setups that involve the use of a computer and MIDI connectivity, either through an integrated MIDI port on audio hardware or with a MIDI-enabled USB device.

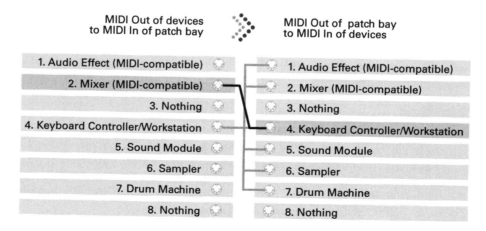

Figure 5.28 Patch bay routing example 2.

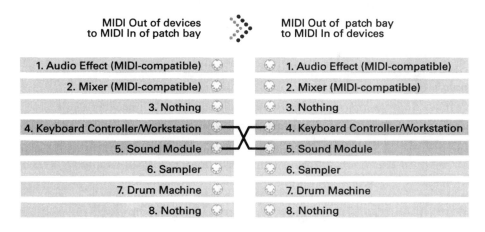

Figure 5.29 Patch bay routing example 3.

Review Questions

1. In any type of analog synthesizer, what module actually produces the sound?

   a) The Voltage-Controlled Oscillators

   b) The Voltage-Controlled Filters

   c) The Voltage-Controlled Amplifiers

   d) The Voltage-Controlled Cables

2. Which type of synthesizer is best known for its effectiveness at emulating very complex vibrations, resonance, reflections, and other acoustic phenomena?

   a) Analog Synthesizers

   b) Digital Synthesizers

   c) Sample-Playback Synthesizers

   d) Physical Modeling Synthesizers

3. What is the name of the sampling technique consisting of re-creating the sound of an acoustic instrument by using several samples over the range of this instrument?

   a) Oversampling

   b) Multisampling

   c) Legal Sampling

   d) Sample Dumping

4. What is the main difference between a keyboard synthesizer and a keyboard controller as described in this chapter?

    a) There are no differences.

    b) Keyboard controllers are always sample-playback MIDI devices, and synthesizers are always analog or digital.

    c) Keyboard synthesizers generate an audio output, and controllers don't.

    d) Keyboard controllers can generate up to 128 simultaneous notes, and synthesizers can only generate up to 64.

5. What do hardware sequencer, MIDI control surfaces, and MIDI-enabled mixers have in common?

    a) They all send and receive channel voice messages.

    b) They all have MIDI inputs and outputs.

    c) They are all MIDI controllers.

    d) All of the above.

6. To change a reverb's parameter, such as the size of the room on a MIDI-enabled digital effect, which type of MIDI message would be best suited?

    a) Note On messages

    b) SysEx messages

    c) System Realtime messages

    d) All of the above

7. What is the acronym used to identify hard disk recording systems?

    a) RAW

    b) DAW

    c) PAW

    d) LAW

8. Which of the following functions is not commonly available on MIDI patch bays?

    a) MIDI to audio conversion

    b) MIDI signal splitting

    c) MIDI signal merging

    d) MIDI signal processing

9. When connecting a MIDI workstation with a drum machine that can also hold drum patterns, how can you synchronize both together?

   a) By pressing the Start button simultaneously on both machines.

   b) By locking them together with MIDI Clock messages.

   c) By locking them together with a digital audio word clock.

   d) You can't synchronize them together unless you have SMPTE time code.

10. True or False: MIDI patch bays that can process MIDI messages use digital audio outputs to create a MIDI echo or delay effect.

6 MIDI and the Computer

Computers today are a big part of MIDI studios, since they offer both versatility and power. Musicians and manufacturers have understood this early on. The Atari ST in the mid-1980s already offered MIDI connectors on every machine. For those of you who haven't made the move to add a computer in your MIDI studio, here is your chance to learn the ups and downs of using a computer to make music with MIDI.

Choosing the right equipment for your MIDI needs can be daunting, especially when it comes to computer audio/MIDI hardware. Knowing what to look for and understanding the basic components that are available and how it can be integrated with the rest of your MIDI equipment will help you to make the right choices. Connecting the rest of your MIDI devices to a computer and getting the MIDI flowing so that you can start recording your performances is also an important step in building a creative environment that integrates MIDI, digital audio, and computer peripherals. We'll keep software applications for the next chapter since, as you will find out, there's a lot to discuss already.

Here's a summary of what you will learn in this chapter:

* What a computer MIDI interface is.
* What the different kinds of MIDI interfaces are.
* Choosing the right MIDI interface for your needs.
* Audio hardware and its MIDI implementation.
* Choosing the right audio hardware for your MIDI studio.
* The difference between wavetables, FM synthesis, and SoundFonts.
* Scenarios for the computer integration of an existing MIDI studio.
* Different solutions to using MIDI over a computer network.

MIDI Interfaces

A MIDI interface connects your external MIDI devices to your computer and vice versa. MIDI interfaces come in five basic flavors:

* As USB (Universal Serial Bus) devices connected to an available USB port on a computer. USB/MIDI interfaces come in two configurations: Either the external device connects directly to a computer through the USB connector or the USB/MIDI interface offers a breakout box that provides 5-pin MIDI connectors for external MIDI devices.

* As FireWire (also known as IEEE 1394) devices connected to an available FireWire port on a computer. Audio peripherals communicating to a computer using a FireWire connection may offer MIDI connections on a breakout box or create a virtual MIDI port inside a software environment to address the MIDI features it provides. It is unlikely that a device would use FireWire only to communicate MIDI messages to a computer since FireWire was originally developed to stream digital video content. In other words, its transmission speed would be considered "overkill" for MIDI messages.

* As PCI cards connected to a computer's motherboard. Five-pin MIDI connectors are usually provided via special cables included with the interface or purchased separately.

* As a parallel connector on older computers, providing a way to use the joystick port for MIDI as well. This solution is often found on PC-compatible systems loaded with pre-Windows 98SE operating systems.

* As a serial connection on older Macintosh computers. Recent technology developments have seen the serial bus on Macintosh computers disappear, so more and more devices use either the USB or FireWire protocol to transmit and receive MIDI to and from the computer.

MIDI interfaces can offer any number of MIDI connections, from a simple MIDI In/Out (I/O), to multiple inputs/outputs. The configuration depends on the interface itself. The number of MIDI ports (individual MIDI Ins or Outs) is part of the specification of a device and can be found anywhere these devices are sold. The more MIDI I/Os—also called MIDI ports—available, the more simultaneous MIDI channels also become available. Each MIDI port supports up to 16 MIDI channels. So, an 8-port MIDI interface will support up to 128 MIDI channels.

You should consider two questions when you get a MIDI interface:

* What type of MIDI interface best fits your computer?
* Does the number of MIDI ports offered by the interface correspond with your needs?

The type of MIDI interface you'll need relates to the kind of connector linking the MIDI device to your computer. In order to answer this question, you need to identify which technology is best suited for you and which technology you might already have on your computer. Knowing what's available on your computer might influence your choice of peripherals, since some audio hardware already offers MIDI connectivity, and others don't. For example, if your audio hardware connects to your computer through a FireWire connection and offers a breakout box with audio and MIDI connectors, you might not need an additional MIDI interface. The following sections discuss the different varieties of MIDI interfaces, both external and internal.

Using a Game Port

Much PC-compatible audio hardware developed prior to the arrival of Windows XP offers a 15-pin connector via a joystick connection. This hook-up can also be used to connect MIDI devices to a computer using a special adapter cable, which offers a male 15-pin connection jack (see Figure 6.1) at one end and a MIDI I/O at the other end. A third joystick connector makes it possible to use the same parallel port with a joystick, along with the MIDI port it provides. When such a connector is used, the MPU-401–compatible audio hardware transmits all 16 channels of information to the computer through a single MIDI port.

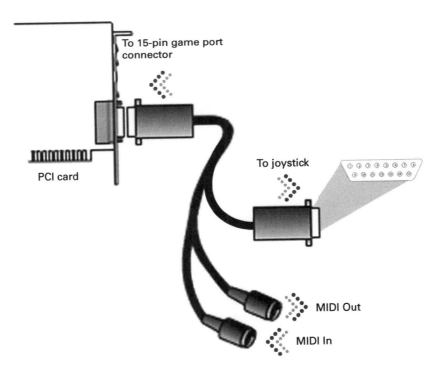

To 15-pin game port
connector

PCI card

To joystick

MIDI Out

MIDI In

Figure 6.1 The 15-pin connector hooks up to a joystick port on your audio hardware.

In Figure 6.2, you can see how each pin from the MIDI cables is routed to an individual pin on the 15-pin connector in your audio hardware's game or joystick port.

Since this type of connection is integrated to an existing audio hardware, an extra MIDI interface to connect your computer to MIDI devices is not required unless additional MIDI ports are needed on the system. Also, this type of connector is available on consumer-level

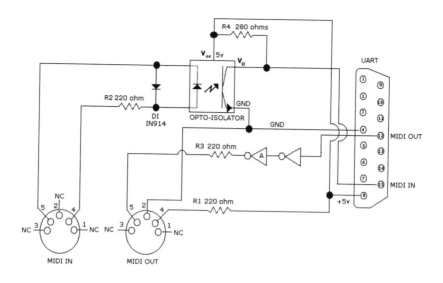

Figure 6.2 Computer audio hardware game port to standard MIDI connector configuration.

products. This type of audio hardware serves as an all-purpose device, but in most cases, it doesn't offer the high-quality components recommended for superior audio quality. As a result, they make good MIDI interfaces, are great with games, and are fairly inexpensive to purchase, but their digital audio converters used during recording and playback are adequate at best. Early Creative Labs's Sound Blaster audio hardware, for example, sports this type of adapter.

The game port MIDI connection is probably the least expensive solution, since you will kill two birds with one stone: getting an audio hardware and a MIDI interface at the same time. Most of today's PC-compatible motherboards offer integrated audio hardware with a game port if you ever run out of USB connectors for additional MIDI ports. If the MIDI to 15-pin connector cable is not included with the audio hardware, it can be purchased separately wherever computer peripherals or computer music products are sold. Many of today's virtual instruments (discussed in Chapter 9) create virtual MIDI ports when they are activated. As a result, you might only need that MIDI port to connect your computer to external MIDI devices.

Using a Serial or Parallel Port

Serial and parallel ports can be found on the back of computers. Different platforms offer different types of connectors. For example, the serial port on the back of Macintosh computers is a small rounded connector. The one on a PC is a flat, multi-pin connector, as shown in Figure 6.3. Macintosh computers made after the first generation of G3 don't even have this type of connector. As for PC users, the serial port is rarely used for MIDI, since manufacturers have adopted its game port counterpart as an alternative. This said, there is a variety of MIDI products that support either one of these connectors, and they have proven to be effective in most cases.

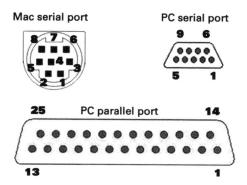

Figure 6.3   The Mac 8-pin serial port, the PC 25-pin parallel and 9-pin serial ports.

❄ The Integration of MIDI on Early Macintosh Computers

Originally, Macintosh computers had two serial ports called ADB (see Figure 6.4) and ran only one application at a time due to a problem with how the baud rate was set for MIDI use. This eventually led to a standard Mac MIDI interface that translated a serial port signal to MIDI by providing a 1MHz clock so that the Mac could divide it down to 31.25kHz. Programmers at Apple devised many workarounds to deal with this problematic situation. Eventually, due to the demands on serial ports from the growing popularity of the Internet, faxes, and networking, these two ports became oversubscribed, leaving the good people at Apple looking for other ways of connecting peripherals to their computers.

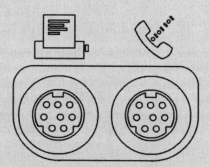

Figure 6.4   The Mac serial ports: printer port (on the left) and modem port (on the right).

In 1999, Apple decided it was time to abandon the serial ports altogether and force everyone to use USB, allowing for a greater number of peripherals to share a common port.

On PC-compatible computers, both parallel and serial ports are available on most PC motherboards, making them a viable solution for those of you who already have this type of MIDI interface. While this was and still is a viable option for MIDI communication, the number of USB and FireWire hardware devices offering MIDI functions is growing everyday. This is an indication that the standard has already changed and that future devices will be easier to use in a plug-and-play fashion, just as MIDI was always meant to be. Figure 6.5 displays examples of parallel and serial MIDI interfaces for PC computers.

Figure 6.5 The MIDIMAN's Portman in both the PC parallel version (left) and the PC serial version (right).

Using a USB Port

USB is a type of connection available on both Macintosh and a PC. The advantage USB-compliant computers and peripherals offer over serial or parallel ports is that, in theory, they are plug-and-play devices. You hook up a device to the computer, and it recognizes the device and configures itself appropriately. In reality, you sometimes have to insert an installation CD in order for the computer to recognize and configure itself appropriately. The installation procedure, however, is quite simple and rarely requires a computer restart operation.

USB data travels at a rate of 12 megabits per second (approximately 1,465Kb/sec). Compared with MIDI, at 3.8Kb/sec, USB is clearly the faster protocol. You could, in theory, connect up to 127 USB devices in a chain. Nevertheless, in practice, this number is more conservative due to the fact that some devices will reserve bandwidth speed over the particular port, making it impossible to add that many devices. USB device connectors usually sport the icon found in Figure 6.6 to identify this specific type of connection.

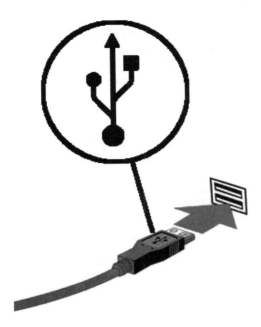

Figure 6.6 The USB icon found on USB connectors.

External USB devices need to connect to an available USB port on your computer. Your computer needs to have a recent operation system:

❈ On PCs, Windows 98SE, 2000, XP, or better is recommended.

❈ On Macs, OS 9 or better is recommended.

Most USB devices draw their power from a USB bus unless they provide independent power supplies, in which case they use the power provided by this external power supply unit. Connecting several USB devices to a USB bus without using external power supply units will consume additional battery power from laptops especially. As an alternative when a USB device does not provide its own power, you can use a powered USB hub that connects to an outlet or has its own power supply. When using several USB devices simultaneously, a powered USB hub provides sufficient power for all devices connected to it while eliminating the need for additional outlets. Because USB devices provide their own power, a USB-to-MIDI interface device doesn't require any additional circuitry, making it less expensive to have a MIDI-compatible computer setup.

Devices using USB to connect with a computer come with a built-in USB cable and an upstream connector as displayed by the letter A in Figure 6.7. If the device itself has a socket instead, the connector on the device will accommodate a downstream "B-type" connector (also represented in Figure 6.7). Because both connectors are different, it is impossible to plug USB devices the wrong way. Sockets on the back or front of computers always connect to an

"A-type" connector, while sockets on USB peripherals always connect to a "B-type" connector. A USB cable can run a maximum of 5 meters (just over 16 feet), but there can be up to 30 meters (about 96 feet) between a device and a host computer if there's a USB hub somewhere between the two. As with MIDI, extending long cables is never a good idea as it increases the risk of timing errors and data loss.

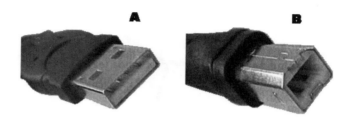

Figure 6.7   The USB connectors: (left) upstream connector, (right) downstream connector.

PCs made after 1998 will probably support USB if they are running Windows 98 or Windows 98SE. Windows 95 and Windows NT (4.0) do not support USB; however, Windows 2000 and Windows XP or higher do. Macintosh computers from the Blue & White G3 will also support USB if you have OS 9.04 or higher (USB support was introduced on OS 8.6. However, OS 9.0.4 or higher is recommended).

Once you have determined if your computer supports USB, you may opt for this type of technology (see Figure 6.8).

Figure 6.8   An example of a USB-to-MIDI interface from Edirol (www.edirol.com).

The USB protocol was not without certain problems. USB MIDI interfaces got off to a bad start due to early Macintoshes having only one port and a preliminary driver with 4ms granularity. The best results required a separate port used only for the MIDI driver and USB Manager 1.3.5 or later. Early iMacs and B/W G3s had a single USB port with a two-connector hub, so the keyboard, mouse, printer, and any other peripherals will be sharing the bus.

As with any new protocol being introduced on the market, software developers were slow to respond to issues of compatibility between certain USB devices and software applications. But this was a transition stage, and newer driver revisions are better integrated, providing good USB stability for MIDI applications. It is also good to know that most second-generation software (both driver and application software) are more reliable than the first generation. USB is no exception: In the case of Windows XP, many users have experienced problems using USB, since most of the drivers for USB devices were just starting to appear as downloadable updates on manufacturers' sites in 2001/2002. If you are not certain a USB peripheral is supported under the OS you use, consult the manufacturer's Web site to find out if the device is supported and if drivers are currently available. Make sure the USB-MIDI interface you purchase or install on your system is stable and compatible with your current system configuration. To find out if it is, simply check the hardware manufacturer's documentation online and any software documentation, as well as discussion forums related to the software you wish to use with this particular interface. Knowing ahead of time how an interface will handle itself on your system might save you some grief.

Multi-Port MIDI Interfaces

Until now, we have discussed different types of connections linking your computer to MIDI devices through stand-alone MIDI interfaces. But in the examples given above, all of these MIDI interfaces have one thing in common: They all have one MIDI In and one MIDI Out. This is fine if your setup is minimal and you don't need more than 16 MIDI channels to control MIDI devices. However, if you need to have more than 16 MIDI channels, opting for a multi-port MIDI interface might be the way to go.

Most MIDI interfaces offered on the market today can hook up to a computer using one of the connection types mentioned earlier in this chapter. Furthermore, these interfaces offer not only multiple MIDI inputs and outputs, but also multiple ports—each additional port giving you 16 MIDI channels. So, if a multi-port device connects to a computer through a serial, parallel, USB, or FireWire port, you can benefit from 32, 64, 128, or more simultaneous MIDI channels by using this interface.

When installing a multi-port MIDI interface on a computer, the different ports are accessed through a software MIDI configuration (see Figure 6.9). There are usually two levels of settings that influence how well the device will perform after its installation.

- ✳ Installing the software that comes with the device so that your OS can recognize the device and manage it. This level of settings influences most applications that interact with the MIDI interface.
- ✳ The next level is inside an application that needs to interact with the MIDI device, such as activating the MIDI ports through the MIDI setup interface inside your favorite sequencer software and then assigning a MIDI track to send or receive MIDI information on the desired MIDI port.

Figure 6.9 An example of a multi-port MIDI interface: the UM-800 from Edirol.

Audio Hardware and MIDI Integration

MIDI interfaces and audio hardware are closely related. Some audio hardware offers MIDI integration, as we already saw with the use of game ports on sound cards as a way to link your computer to external MIDI peripherals. While audio is not the main focus of this book, the following discussion looks at parameters associated with audio hardware devices and describes what's important to look for, depending on your needs. So for example, if you're using audio hardware to record vocals in a home studio and connect a keyboard controller to a computer, OS compatibility issues will be just as important as if you intend to record live bands with simultaneous inputs. However, the number of physical inputs and outputs needed will vary.

Overall Sound Quality

Above all else, your first criteria in the selection of audio hardware, if you intend to make music, should be the quality of its components: type of connectors, sample rate, and bit depth, of course, but also how the audio hardware sounds. The quality of audio hardware is often linked to its converters: analog-to-digital (or A/D) for recording and digital-to-analog (or D/A) for playback. This might seem like an obvious statement, but in the world of technical sheets and specifications, we often forget that in the end, it doesn't really matter what the specs say. If the audio hardware doesn't sound good, no matter how hard you try to sweeten the input, you won't be happy with the result. Talk to friends and professionals, read reviews, and get information before buying a product, and make sure that people using the audio hardware you've got your eye on are happy customers. If you already have audio hardware and are just looking to buy a MIDI interface, then the next point will be more important to you, since MIDI does not produce any audio output anyway. However, a well-built interface will save you the problem of bad MIDI connections due to manipulation if you need to plug and unplug your devices often.

We rarely have unlimited budgets when purchasing audio or MIDI hardware. Find different audio hardware that is in your price range and compare what they offer with your musical needs for the next 12 months. Purchasing audio hardware for things you will do two years from now is not a wise decision. By the time you're ready to use these additional features to their full capacity, the device will have gone down in price, and a better, newer model likely will be out anyway. Based on your budget, you can decide if you want to compromise features for quality or vice versa. Just remember that if music is your thing, maybe cutting down the budget for your video card or other peripherals might allow you to purchase better audio hardware. And, after all, that's what really counts.

Audio Hardware's OS Support

Any audio hardware should be supported by the operating system installed on your computer. Before purchasing audio hardware, make sure the drivers for your device exist and have been tested on the OS you are using. If the driver for the device is still being written, or the manufacturer says it will be available shortly, then it's up to you to decide if you are willing to wait for its arrival. Unfortunately, "shortly" doesn't mean "available now." If you need it immediately, then try something that already works.

Compatibility

Some audio hardware hooks up to portable computers using a PCI slot or PCMCIA connection. Other audio hardware uses a PCI host card inside the computer that connects to an external audio device. Finally, others use FireWire or USB to communicate with the computer. In order for an audio device to work, its format needs to be compatible with the computer hosting it. For example, if FireWire is not installed on your computer, you will need to purchase a FireWire PCI adapter card. When doing so, make sure the technology is compatible with the audio hardware.

If you will be making music with your audio hardware and MIDI interface, making sure that your device is compatible with the software you will be using is also essential. Visit the Web site for the software you will be using and search for tests that have been performed on audio hardware compatibility issues and reliability under their specific environment. In other words, if you are planning to work with software, make sure the manufacturer recommends the audio hardware you are also planning to use. This way, you will find out how well the audio hardware performs with this software. Sometimes, an audio hardware might perform well in a game environment, but when using virtual synthesizers, it can show its weaknesses more prominently.

Inputs Formats and Connectors

There are quite a few audio connector types and audio formats and standards available on the market. Most can be separated into two categories: analog and digital. Some computer audio hardware offers both types of connectors, while others offer only analog or digital. In the analog variety, the most popular are mini phone jacks, RCA, unbalanced or balanced quarter-inch jacks, AES/EBU, or XLR jacks. In terms of digital input, the most common types of connectors are S/PDIF, ADAT, and TDIF. S/PDIF offers a stereo pair of digital input (through a single RCA cable), while the ADAT and TDIF digital inputs offer eight digital channels. Figure 6.10 displays examples of each one of these connectors. The advantage of having multi-input audio hardware is that you will be able to record different instruments simultaneously on separate inputs. The disadvantage of having multi-input audio hardware is that the more inputs you have, the pricier the card will be. This is especially true with high-end connectors to ensure a good quality connection with your audio devices. If the audio hardware with multiple inputs and outputs is the same price as another model from a different company with only two ins and outs, chances are the trade-off will be in sound quality (A/D and D/A converters).

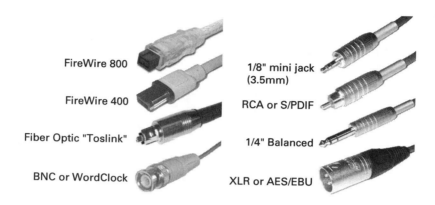

FireWire 800

FireWire 400

Fiber Optic "Toslink"

BNC or WordClock

1/8" mini jack (3.5mm)

RCA or S/PDIF

1/4" Balanced

XLR or AES/EBU

Figure 6.10 Standard analog and digital audio connectors.

Many of today's audio hardware includes at least a MIDI port, while MIDI controllers hooked up to computers through USB or FireWire create their own MIDI ports on your system after they are installed. In most situations, one physical MIDI port is enough. To separate MIDI messages from a keyboard controller from a MIDI control surface, both connected to the same computer, you still only need one MIDI port. However, control change and SysEx messages used by control surfaces might be better off on their own port. This said, control surfaces often come with their own USB or FireWire connection, creating a virtual MIDI port in your computer. While it might have been important to have multiple MIDI ports with previous generations of MIDI interfaces, the new generation of MIDI-enabled devices connecting to a computer using USB is changing this reality by providing its own port.

Outputs Formats and Connectors

Output types of connectors are identical to inputs. Outputs are used during playback to monitor something that's already been recorded or to send analog or digital audio signals to other devices. Good quality connectors are effective at reducing the introduction of noise into a signal as it is going to an external mixer, recording device, or monitoring system. If you are serious about MIDI (i.e. music or sound), avoid mini phone jack connectors (the ones similar to headphone jacks on a MP3 players, for example)—they offer poor contacts, are prone to break easily whenever manipulation is involved, and offer poor overall quality. It is also good to keep the analog-to-digital and digital-to-analog conversions to a minimum, since every time the audio signal is converted, it is modified from its original form, introducing errors. Alternatively, connecting a digital mixer to audio hardware outputs reduces the risk of errors being introduced by poor audio converters. Some consumer-level audio hardware will mark the outputs for surround sound. This is different than regular outputs, since each output is meant to feed a surround sound system in a home entertainment center. The concept behind surround sound outputs and sending outputs to a mixer is quite different, and the signal coming out of these outputs will also be different, so just make sure you have the right type of outputs for your needs.

Supported Sample Rates

The sampling rate determines how many samples per second a digital audio signal will use to reproduce the analog sound. Higher sample rates produce a wider frequency range at recording. As a result, during playback, harmonic content found in the upper frequency range associated with the crispness and sharpness of the sound provides a more defined digital audio signal. Typical sampling rates include 44.1, 48, 96, and 192 kHz.

The bit depth represents the size of the binary word used to store the amplitude value for a sample. A higher bit depth translates into more precision, a greater signal-to-noise ratio, and a greater dynamic range. Typical bit depths for audio hardware may be 8, 16, 20, 24, or 32 bits per sample. The larger the binary word, the greater the space needed to store this information, and as with the sampling rate, better quality also means more processing time and more hard disk space (fast hard drives are highly recommended for 24- or 32-bit samples). Higher sampling frequencies also require more processing time, more disk space, and faster hard disk speeds.

To use a MIDI interface or audio hardware in a post-synchronization or cross-platform environment, ensuring the timing of the audio device is accurate could save you a lot of hassle. In audio post-production work, the possibility of using either a SMPTE/MTC converter or word clock is essential to lock two or more devices together in time and to do digital audio transfers between devices. A word clock input allows your audio hardware to synchronize to an external device using its sampling rate. Inversely, audio hardware with a word clock output can be used to synchronize other devices using this device's sampling rate. A device exhibiting poor synchronization capability will leave you searching for alternatives that are usually more costly than the original audio hardware. So, once again, make sure your device supports these features if they are important to you. Also, due to the density of MTC information, it is often recommended that an entire MIDI port be dedicated to it. Avoid sending MTC, control surface MIDI messages, and other MIDI messages all on one MIDI port. MTC is timing sensitive, and the more messages a single port needs to transmit, the greater the chances are of running into timing issues.

Supported Drivers and Stability

Since we've already mentioned that it's important for audio hardware to be compatible with the OS it's running on, you should now consider which types of applications will be used to create music. Since some applications are more effective when using a certain type of driver, it is important that your audio hardware's driver matches these specifications. For example, if you intend to use Tascam's GigaStudio, make sure GigaStudio has been tested and works well with the audio hardware you intend to install. The same applies for Steinberg applications, such as Cubase or Nuendo, with their use of an ASIO driver. This type of driver is used to optimize the performance of any application that supports the ASIO protocol, such as Cubase, Nuendo, Logic Audio, Reason, and several others. Not having a compatible ASIO driver if you want to use such software might reduce your audio hardware's performance. An example of such effects would be apparent when using virtual synthesizers. In such a case, the audio hardware needs to respond quickly to the notes played on a MIDI keyboard; not having an ASIO driver would introduce a delay between the time you play a note and the time you hear it. If you've ever tried to play something with this type of delay, you probably understand that this is not a realistic creative environment. So, make sure the proper drivers for your software are available for your audio hardware.

Multi-Client Capability

In today's MIDI studio and audio-editing studios, computers are carrying an important part of the workload. You might at some point run more than one audio/MIDI application simultaneously inside a single computer, especially if you don't have the financial resources to purchase multiple computers to run all your programs in sync. Some software might take over the audio hardware's control in your computer. Having a multi-client—capable driver allows different software applications shared access to the audio hardware's resources rather than monopolizing it, rendering it useless in a second or third application you would like to run simultaneously.

MIDI Integration on Audio Hardware

Some audio hardware offers an integrated General MIDI sound bank, while others may offer more sophisticated wavetables. These sounds are appropriate for game play and may also be perfect to play most MIDI files. However, you might find inadequacies in the editing capability of those sound modules, as well as its sound quality. In general, audio hardware that is integrated to a computer system, such as Macintosh or brand name PC systems, provide such sounds, and the quality and quantity of sounds they provide vary from system to system.

In earlier models of audio hardware, FM synthesis was used to generate audio to provide MIDI support through a Yamaha OPL2 or OPL3 chip on the audio hardware adapter. This chip would synthesize sounds rather than use original samples. When you heard a cello, you heard a synthetic cello, not the real thing.

Today, wavetables are the main source of sounds for most audio hardware, and GM is the basic sound set for these wavetables. Simply put, wavetable synthesis is similar to sample playback. It uses a series of small digital audio recordings as source material to produce sounds, and then these samples are processed by the onboard synthesizer in order to manipulate different parameters of this sound, such as the envelope, the filters, and so on. It usually sounds better than an FM (frequency modulation) synthesis audio hardware, since the origin of the sound is real rather than completely synthesized.

Wavetable music synthesis should not be confused with common PCM (Pulse Code Modulation) sample buffer playback. It is similar to it but extends upon it in at least two ways: First, the waveform lookup table (the actual table of audio sample waveforms) contains samples for not just a single period of a sine function but for a single period of a more general wave shape, such as piano, violin, or brass tone. Second, a mechanism exists for dynamically changing the wave shape as the musical note evolves, thus generating a certain amount of variation in time.

In comparison to this, FM synthesis uses a first digital oscillator as a carrier, which acts as a pitch or frequency generator for the sound. Then, a second oscillator affects this first oscillator to make it modulate through time, creating variations in the sound itself. Usually, an FM synthesizer will use four to six such modulators and carriers in different combinations called algorithms.

Audio hardware using wavetables will usually have an onboard memory chip on which its samples are saved. Some of these devices will even have memory slots, expanding its memory original capability and adding additional sounds to them as you upgrade Larger wavetable memories contain more sounds. So, if you decide to go with audio hardware that offers wavetable synthesis, make sure the memory is expandable or sufficient to house a good sound library. Memory size for audio hardware that supports wavetable synthesis varies between 2MB and 64MB, allowing you to expand sound sets. The Creative Labs Sound Blaster Live, for example, comes with a 2-, 4-, or 8-MB sound set, but, depending on system RAM, can be expanded up to 64MB or more of wavetable synthesis memory.

This said, with today's faster computers and larger RAM memories, most audio hardware uses so-called "soft wavetables" instead, loading the samples into the computer's memory through special drivers provided by the operating system installed on your system. For example, Windows XP comes with WDM drivers (based on the DirectX protocol) to its users for MIDI support. On Macintosh, OSX's Core Audio components provide full support for two industry standards: DLS (Downloadable Sounds) and SoundFonts.

In each case, samples are loaded into the computer's memory when an audio or media player requires it to play a MIDI file. The operating system then uses the installed audio hardware to generate the audio output resulting from the player's MIDI playback. For example, the Roland GS standard is the default set of sounds for any media player application using Windows DirectX. QuickTime also offers its own wavetable sound bank based on the Roland GS standard.

✷ About SoundFonts

SoundFonts are to sound what TrueType fonts are to text. They represent a way to enhance your musical creations using different sounds that you may add to SoundFont-compatible audio hardware just like you can add TrueType Fonts to your computer's operating system in order to use them in your word processor or desktop publishing software to make a document look good. SoundFonts never use the audio hardware's memory to load samples but the computer's memory instead. So your computer's available memory resources are your only limit to sound set expansion.

In addition, the term "wavetable" is a more generic term used to describe an allotment of sound files one after the other, whereas SoundFonts were developed by Creative Labs and Emu Systems as a wavetable standard used on their audio hardware. This allows users to improve the sound quality of their MIDI playback by either loading a better GM wavetable sound-set or adding more sounds to their existing sound library. SoundFonts can be single sounds or complete banks, and so can wavetables. The latest revision of the SoundFont specification is 2.1 and was released in 2002.

The main intent behind the SoundFont 2 standard is to provide an "extensible, portable, universal interchange format for wavetable synthesizers." You don't need to have audio hardware that supports SoundFonts anymore, since some soft synthesizers and most samplers offer SoundFont support and editing capability.

MIDI for Gamers

If playing games is the main purpose behind your purchase of audio hardware, don't look too far and don't spend too much money—you'll need the extra cash for game controls, a good video card, and games, of course. Because audio hardware devices have been offering increased MIDI quality and performance in recent years, many games today use MIDI to generate the music soundtracks. Digital audio is still prevalent when it comes to sound effects. Game developers have exploited every aspect of audio hardware developments made in the last few years, adding real-time audio effects and soundtracks. Most games will use existing GS or GM wavetables and your audio hardware to generate the audio output, so getting audio hardware with an integrated synthesizer, preferably one that offers wavetable synthesis, will be sufficient for most of your gaming needs. Such audio hardware also plays back MIDI and audio files. Most audio hardware devices sold in computer stores along with integrated audio chips on computer motherboards should work well with computer games.

MIDI on Macintosh

Macintosh computers have provided audio and MIDI support for a long time and have proven themselves to be very efficient when it comes to handling this type of data. With changes made to OS X, the Core MIDI manages all MIDI ports and devices more efficiently than ever. Working under a pre-OS X Mac, OMS (Open MIDI System developed by Opcode) and FreeMIDI (developed by Mark Of The Unicorn) offer some MIDI functions and are better supported by certain devices than by others. Since the manufacturers that develop these MIDI managers (with the exception of OS X) also develop their own audio hardware, it is not uncommon to see that devices from one company will work better with the MIDI manager developed by the same company. The same principle applies with music software you might be running on your Mac. For example, ProTools from Digidesign and Digital Performer (from Mark Of The Unicorn) work with FreeMIDI. With OS X, however, all applications, including Cubase (from Steinberg) and Logic Audio, work well with OS X's Core Audio/MIDI. So, if you are working with a pre-OS X operating system and using Digital Performer, using MOTU (Mark Of The Unicorn) audio hardware will probably be more stable and offer better timing than if you are working with another type of audio hardware/MIDI interface. Otherwise, any MIDI interface supported by Mac OS X should work well with any application.

MIDI for Networks

MIDI in itself could be considered a way to network different devices together, but the idea of networking computers together in order to play different instruments started to interest people when software synthesizers started to appear in studios. MIDI in itself doesn't require that much processing power, since it is relatively slow when compared to other forms of communications. For example, the Internet's bandwidth using a 56K modem would be enough to transmit real-time MIDI data but wouldn't be able to send CD-quality digital audio in real time. Such a digital audio transfer from one computer to another requires communication between the two computers with much broader bandwidth.

✳ About Linear Time Base (LTB)

With the growing popularity of virtual or software synthesizers, the need for better MIDI timing within a computer is becoming increasingly important due to the nature of this type of application. Linear Time Base (LTB), which is developed by Steinberg, tries to address this issue by providing a high-speed MIDI timing protocol, offering sample-accurate timing for MIDI communications.

LTB is a MIDI time-stamping technique that bypasses the computer's operating system, in much the same way Steinberg's ASIO drivers do. As a result, transfers are more efficient, and the latency, or delays between MIDI events and the audio output of software instruments, is reduced. LTB is not a new standard but rather an enhancement to MIDI, and is only supported by a few MIDI devices developed by Steinberg.

When using a network of computers in a MIDI setting, the main advantage lies in this network's ability to share the processing of more elaborate functions, such as digital audio processes or software synthesizers running on different computers. Each processor does its portion of the work, sharing "horsepower" resources (in other words, CPU processing time). Since processing is a big part of what the computer has to do when running audio effects within a software environment or software synthesizer, more processing power is always better. MIDI itself does not require much in terms of processing power and can be easily transmitted over a local area network through specialized computer applications. Simply transmitting MIDI implies that each computer in this network produces its own digital audio output. It also implies that additional MIDI hardware devices are not required since you can play notes on a keyboard attached to one computer that triggers software synthesizers in another computer (as illustrated in Figure 6.11).

In Figure 6.12, a software application, such as MusicLab's MIDIOverLan, creates virtual MIDI ports once it's installed on a computer. You can route the MIDI signal virtually from one MIDI port to any destination port inside this network. While these applications simply transmit MIDI messages over a network, the timing, or delay between each audio hardware device installed on computers in this network, is critical. In order to synchronize more than one sequencer applications on such a network, MTC or MIDI clock messages can be used. Furthermore, the latency, or delay a computer takes to convert a MIDI message into an audio output, will be different from one computer to the next. Independent latencies imply that if one computer takes 5 milliseconds to respond and produce the audio output while the next

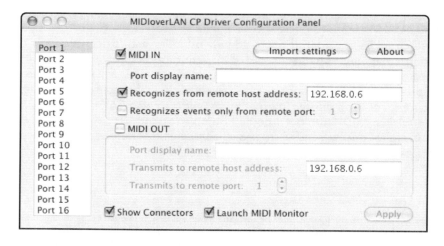

Figure 6.11 MIDI over a network (configuration A): Transmit only MIDI.

one in the network takes 500 milliseconds, the delay between both will be audible. If the MIDI messages are not transmitted effectively, the timing errors could be even more significant. The speed of the LAN adapter, the efficiency of the software application transmitting the MIDI over LAN, the audio hardware's drivers, and the sequencer/synthesizer applications will all influence how well MIDI is transmitted over a LAN.

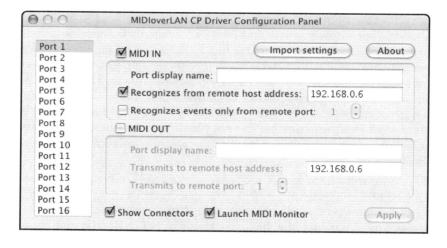

Figure 6.12 Example of application that creates virtual MIDI ports available on a cross-platform LAN.

This said, sharing processing-intensive tasks through a network, having each one running a series of software relating to a MIDI project, may help. In other words, the limit imposed by your computer on the number of virtual or software synthesizers you can simultaneously run—not to mention virtual samplers that require fast hard disk access and use up a good portion of your RAM—will no longer be dictated by the capacity of one computer but by the sum of the processing power on a network.

❄ What Does Sample-Accurate Mean?

The term sample-accurate usually refers to a synchronization mechanism that occurs between two digital audio signals, where the sampling frequency of one audio hardware or digital audio device is sent to another audio hardware or digital audio device to regulate its timing, thus synchronizing the receiving device to the sending device's sampling rate.

Since sampling rates on audio hardware occur at a very high speed, quite often at a rate of 44,100 times or more per second, this offers a very reliable and stable synchronizing signal. When two or more devices are locked to a master sampling rate, it is referred to as sample-accurate synchronization, where every sample in one device corresponds to a sample in another device.

This synchronization is usually transmitted over a special digital audio connection called Word Clock, or embedded into the existing digital audio cable using the S/PDIF, ADAT, or TDIF format.

This type of synchronization is essential when doing digital audio transfers between two digital audio devices, or it can be used to synchronize transport functions between two devices that support this type of synchronization as well.

This timing resolution far surpasses SMPTE's and MTC's resolution.

Software developers have developed a variety of ways to handle delay problems when using networks. Steinberg is one of the companies developing a technology that locks MIDI timing of different computers in a network with sample-accurate synchronization through a system called the VST System Link, which uses a single channel of a digital audio stream (such as ADAT, TDIF, or S/PDIF) to carry MIDI information over a network of computers, making it possible to run several virtual synthesizers on different machines, all controlled by a single application, thus allowing for shared processing across the entire network. Patch bay software controls the flow of information from one computer and allows for hundreds of MIDI channels to be transmitted over this single digital audio connection. For example, you could use one computer to record audio tracks, a second computer to run virtual synthesizers, and a third computer to process your audio tracks using virtual processing effects (such as reverbs, delays, and compressors). For this system to work, however, you will need compatible ASIO audio hardware and software hosts (for now, Cubase, Nuendo, and V-Stack are the only software supporting this protocol).

❄ About mLAN

Over the past decade, Yamaha developed a FireWire-based protocol that connects different mLAN-compatible (mUSIC Local Area Network) devices together in order to transmit digital audio, MIDI, and synchronization data over this network. The advantage of mLAN (see logo in Figure 6.13) over typical FireWire devices (also known as "IEEE 1394") is that mLAN can manage several devices from several manufacturers not only one device from one manufacturer. mLAN is royalty free, which means other companies can integrate mLAN-based features in their own products, just like MIDI allowed different synthesizers to talk to each ther.

Figure 6.13   The mLAN logo.

On your computer, devices connected to an mLAN port are accessed virtually at the driver level by any DAW or sequencer application that supports multi-channel ASIO drivers. If an mLAN device offers digital audio connectors and MIDI ports, all this information is transmitted through the FireWire cable and routed internally by the operating system (on XP, OSX, and eventually Linux).

mLAN runs through a FireWire cable (see examples in Figure 6.14) with a bandwidth of up to 400 megabits per second (Mbps) and with FireWire 2 up to 800Mbps. Each device in the mLAN network is equal ("peer-to-peer"), which implies that transfers can be initiated from any device in the network to any other device in the same network.

Figure 6.14   Examples of devices supporting mLAN.

Besides offering support for hundreds of digital audio channels, mLAN can support the equivalent of thousands of MIDI channels on a single network. While this is not typical, devices offering eight MIDI ports (128 MIDI channels) are not uncommon. Devices that are not mLAN enabled, such as a MIDI keyboard controller for example, can still be connected to an mLAN adapter. Its MIDI and audio are then converted into an mLAN protocol and added to the existing mLAN network. For more on mLAN, visit www.mlancentral.com.

Computer-Based MIDI Studio

In Chapter 5, we looked at different ways to connect MIDI devices together. Expanding on these examples, we now look at ways to connect computers to external MIDI devices using one or more MIDI ports on either a computer's audio hardware or MIDI interface.

Since getting MIDI in and out of your computer at this point is an important part of setting up your extended MIDI studio, let's take a look at different ways of doing so, using different commonly used devices in the configurations. Since these examples expand on the setup diagrams in Chapter 5, you should already understand the logic behind those examples.

Using a Single MIDI Port Without a Patch Bay

The example in Figure 6.15 illustrates a MIDI studio setup using a computer as a sequencer. In the absence of a patch bay, the MIDI output of the computer should connect to the MIDI input of the keyboard and vice versa (the MIDI output of the keyboard to the MIDI input of the computer). Any other MIDI devices should be connected from the MIDI Thru of the keyboard. In this case, the MIDI Thru of the keyboard feeds the drum machine's MIDI input. If you have more devices to put in the chain, follow this example. USB-driven keyboard controllers connect to the computer using USB cables, but the principle remains the same: A MIDI port will exist inside the computer, and this MIDI port can be assigned as the source and destination for MIDI messages.

To send SysEx messages from the computer to devices further in the chain, it is recommended to connect directly to the computer, temporarily disconnecting the keyboard. This is a necessary operation, albeit a disadvantage in a live concert scenario.

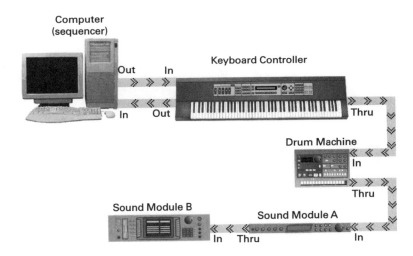

Figure 6.15 Hooking up your computer to MIDI devices without a patch bay.

Using a Single MIDI Port with a Patch Bay

When using a patch bay, your computer communicates with this device in the same way all others communicate with it—the output of the device is hooked up to a patch bay's input, and the input of the device is hooked up to the patch bay's output. In Figure 6.16, the computer is hooked up to the input and output 3 of the patch bay. Once all MIDI devices are connected, configure the patch bay appropriately and save the configurations in the patch bay's memory.

When the patch bay connects to the computer through a PCI adapter card, a USB port, or any type of connection other than a simple MIDI port, a software application provided with the patch bay will make it possible to make and save setup configurations. This also means that the patch bay offers as many ports as there are inputs on it.

On the other hand, if the patch bay connects to the computer through a MIDI cable alone, the MIDI patch bay will transmit and receive only 16 channels of MIDI data, since it is considered to be a single-port MIDI device, as shown in Figure 6.16. In this case, you still need to configure the patch bay through a front panel LCD, assigning each input to proper outputs. To take full advantage of the setup shown in Figure 6.16, create different settings for different purposes.

For example, create a main setup to use the keyboard to record events into the computer's sequencer and use the computer to echo these events back to the appropriate devices and play back any recorded MIDI messages. This includes sending SysEx messages to configure connected devices.

1. Route the signal that comes from the keyboard to the computer. In this example, PB (Patch Bay) input 4 to PB output 3.

2. Route the signal that comes from the computer to every other device in your MIDI setup, excluding the computer itself (to avoid MIDI feedback). In this example, PB input 3 should be routed to PB outputs 1, 2, 4, 5, 6, and 7.

3. To avoid MIDI doubling in the keyboard, set the keyboard's Local Control MIDI parameter to Off.

4. When using a mixer, as shown in Figure 6.16, route its MIDI output to the input of the computer—in this example, PB input 2 to PB output 3. Make sure, as with the keyboard, that the Local Control for your mixer is set to Off; otherwise, it will create a MIDI feedback loop, which can jam the MIDI device.

5. The MIDI outputs don't need to be routed to inputs, and no unwanted MIDI is sent back to the computer by these devices. That could also create an overflow of MIDI information or cause the MIDI sequencer to record unwanted events. You can always create another configuration program with a direct link to enable the communication between these devices and the computer.

6. Save this configuration to memory and recall it whenever you need it.

Another setup transmitting SysEx information directly between two devices should be created. SysEx messages are complex and can disturb the flow of MIDI events if such messages are being transmitted at the same time MIDI events are being sent across the same MIDI port. To prevent choking the MIDI port with this extra information, it's recommended that SysEx messages always travel the shortest route. With MIDI devices connected to a computer using their own dedicated MIDI port, this is not an issue anymore, but when using a MIDI patch bay, you should consider creating individual setups for SysEx MIDI dumps.

1. Create a patch (configuration program) in the patch bay for each module in the MIDI studio that needs to send SysEx to a sequencer by routing PB (Patch Bay) input to the PB

output leading to the computer. Let's take an example from Figure 6.16: Map the PB input 5 (sound module) to the PB output 3 (computer).

2. Make sure no other device is sending MIDI to the computer through the same patch bay routing. This will enable unwanted MIDI messages to be recorded at the same time.

3. Save this configuration to memory and recall it whenever you need it.

Even if you mostly work with a computer, having a patch bay used in both a studio environment and a live show environment (without a computer) would be reason enough to create a computerless setup, especially when considering the added benefit of not having to carry a laptop or computer with you if you don't need it for a live performance.

1. As with the previous setups, the idea is to connect the output of the main controller to a patch bay's input.

2. Then connect the output of the patch bay to the MIDI input of your device. You can connect as many devices as your patch bay supports.

3. Route inside the patch bay's interface the PB In to any PB Out you wish to use in your setup.

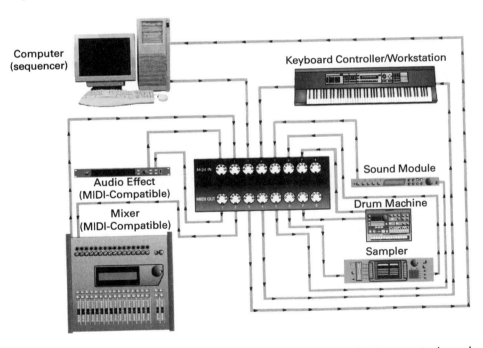

Figure 6.16 Hooking up your computer to a MIDI patch bay—in this example, the computer has only one MIDI port.

Using Multiple MIDI Ports

A MIDI multi-port system is one that offers more than one set of MIDI channels. Each additional MIDI port will give you an additional 16 MIDI channels. There are three ways of obtaining multiple MIDI ports on your computer:

1. When a multi-port MIDI interface is installed on a computer or if multiple MIDI devices connected to a computer create their own MIDI ports, as shown in Figure 6.17.

2. Having a patch bay or external MIDI controller that hooks up to a computer with a PCI, USB, or other type of connection. This lets you address each MIDI output as an independent port, as shown in Figure 6.18.

3. Having a virtual MIDI port provided by a software synthesizer, such as VST Instruments (see Figure 6.19), DX Instrument, or any other virtual type of MIDI communication with a single computer or over a network (discussed earlier in this chapter).

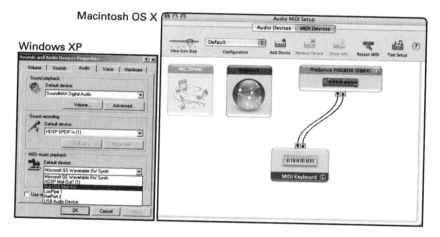

Figure 6.17 Available MIDI ports as they appear on Windows XP and on Macintosh.

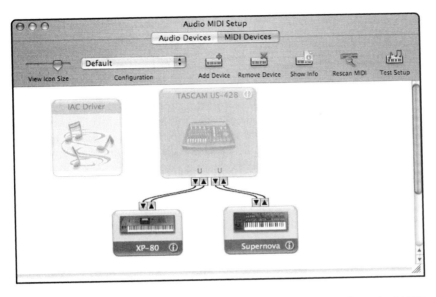

Figure 6.18 Each instrument connected to the Tascam US-428 can use up to 16 channels of MIDI to receive or send events.

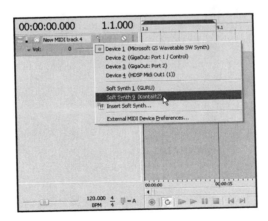

Figure 6.19 Inserting software instruments in Sony's ACID 5 Pro creates additional MIDI port destinations for MIDI tracks to play through.

In Figure 6.20, the computer is connected to a MIDI interface with four separate MIDI ports—labeled A, B, C, and D. Each port is connected to a single MIDI instrument or device. This kind of setup provides a total of 64 MIDI channels. Once inside the computer, ports are assigned to a sequencer software or MIDI application. Selecting MIDI inputs receiving MIDI messages and MIDI outputs that forward these messages to software synthesizers or external MIDI devices is also done inside a MIDI application's MIDI preferences or settings. Once these settings are done, MIDI finds its path inside the computer just as you have seen in a patch bay in a previous section in this chapter.

Multi-port MIDI interfaces may or may not support truly parallel operations. Steinberg's LTB and Emagic's AMT (Active MIDI Transmission) protocol used in their Unitor interfaces simulate parallel performance by time-stamping the data and sending it early. mLAN and some FireWire multi-port interfaces actually provide parallel channels. But mostly, you have a serial stream of data that is meta-tagged to go to the correct port, i.e. the serial bottleneck still exists and gets more clogged the more channels you have. This said, using several ports to transmit or receive several MIDI channels simultaneously is better than daisy-chaining a large number of MIDI devices to a single MIDI port.

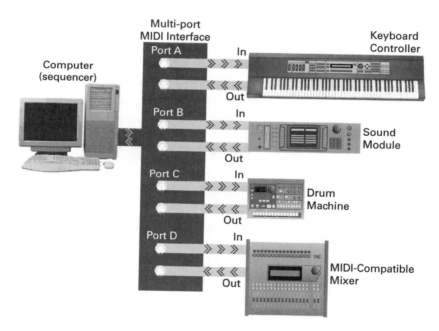

Figure 6.20 Example of a parallel connection using a 4-port MIDI interface.

If you have more MIDI devices than available MIDI ports on your computer's MIDI interface, you can always daisy-chain some devices together as described earlier in this book. There are no differences between daisy-chaining devices that are outside of a computer setup and daisy-chaining devices that are connected to a computer. As Figure 6.21 suggests, the keyboard, sampler, and sound modules are connected to the computer's MIDI port A in a daisy chain. The mixer, however, uses a MIDI port unto itself. This is an advisable practice if you are using a MIDI-enabled mixer, since quite often, the amount of controller data and information sent to and from a mixer can be important, especially during a mixdown process. You wouldn't want your MIDI to start slowing down because of a bottleneck on a MIDI port. Since many MIDI-enabled mixers will use several MIDI channels, this type of setup will allow you to take full advantage of all the controls you can have over your mixer without restricting the number of MIDI channels you can use to control other devices.

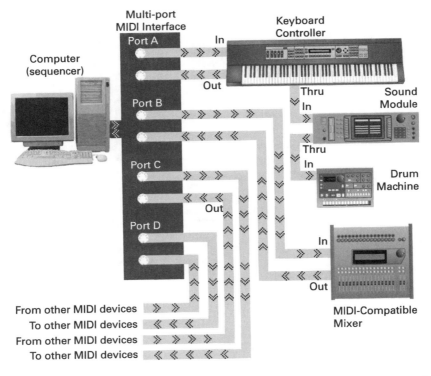

Figure 6.21 Example of daisy-chain and parallel connections using a four-port MIDI interface.

❋ About SDS and SMDI

A sample dump is an extension of the MIDI specification that transfers sample data between devices, such as a computer and a sampler, for example. Using MIDI, a sample dump transfers digital audio information back and forth using a protocol called Sampler Dump Standard (SDS). Since digital audio samples are usually quite large by nature compared to MIDI data, transferring samples to and from a sampler using this method can be quite slow due to the data rate MIDI uses, which is 31,250Hz baud, or 31,250 bits per second.

As an alternative, SCSI (Small Computer System Interface) owners can use the SCSI MIDI Device Interface (SMDI) protocol instead. This protocol uses SCSI to transmit and receive samples to and from a sampler.

This protocol is a more effective way of transmitting digital audio sample data between two devices if direct digital transfers aren't possible.

In order to use SMDI or SDS, host software is needed to configure the connection between your computer and a sampler. Sony's Sound Forge, through its Sampler Configuration option as shown in Figure 6.22, fills that purpose. You will also need a compatible external sampler and SCSI card if you wish to use the SMDI protocol. If you decide to use SDS, make sure the connection between the sampler and the computer is direct, not daisy chained or filtered in any way.

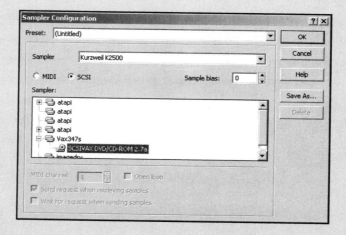

Figure 6.22 The Sampler Configuration window in Sound Forge allows you to make a connection with your sampler through MIDI or SCSI cables.

Review Questions

1. What cross-platform protocol also goes by the name of IEEE 1394?

   a) USB

   b) FireWire

   c) PCI cards

   d) None of the above

2. How many MIDI channels in total would a multi-port MIDI interface offer if it had two MIDI I/O ports?

   a) 2

   b) 16

   c) 32

   d) 64

3. Before USB, what was the most common protocol used until 1999 on Macintosh computers to transmit and receive MIDI messages?

   a) Parallel ports

   b) Serial ports

   c) FireWire ports

   d) PCI ports

4. What has replaced FM synthesis as the dominant method of offering integrated GM, GS, or XG sound banks on most audio hardware and available in most operating systems?

   a) LTB

   b) SDS

   c) Wavetables

   d) SoundFonts

5. What manufacturer was behind the development of FM synthesis and the mLAN protocol?

   a) Apple

   b) Roland

   c) Steinberg

   d) Yamaha

6. Transmitting MIDI over a network of two computers and a keyboard controller requires what?

   a) An application such as MIDIOverLan to be installed on both computers

   b) An mLAN network to be installed

   c) An application such as VST System Link and multi-port digital audio connections

   d) Any of the above

7. Digital audio using the S/PDIF format uses what type of connectors?

   a) 1/8" mini-jack

   b) RCA

   c) 1/4" balanced

   d) Fiber optic

8. What name did Steinberg give to its driver type that optimizes the performance of audio hardware by streaming the audio directly from the inputs and outputs of the hardware device when used with any compatible application?

    a) GSIF

    b) WDM

    c) ASIO

    d) RTAS

9. Among the following types of connectors, which one doesn't represent a suitable digital audio connector?

    a) 1/8" mini-jack

    b) XLR

    c) TDIF

    d) Fiber optic

10. True or False: When a MIDI patch bay with eight MIDI inputs and eight MIDI outputs communicates with an application inside a computer through a single MIDI cable, it offers a total of eight MIDI ports to this application, which results in up to 128 MIDI channels.

7 MIDI Inside Your Computer

In this chapter, we discuss the installation of peripherals such as MIDI interfaces and audio hardware with MIDI support. We also cover some optimization techniques to make sure your computer runs as smoothly as possible under audio and MIDI applications. Integrating such topics into a book about MIDI might seem like overkill, since MIDI in itself does not require that much out of a computer. After all, you could run a MIDI sequencer on a 386-compatible PC, a Mac Plus, an Atari 1040ST, or even a Commodore 64! But the reality of MIDI today is far more complex, as the lines between MIDI and digital audio are blurring with the use of virtual MIDI ports, software instruments, and integrated MIDI ports and synthesizers on audio hardware.

Don't forget that most MIDI sequencers today are offering ever more digital audio features, taking the traditional MIDI workhorses toward a completely integrated virtual studio environment. Tools like Propellerhead's Reason, for example, which integrates software instruments, as well as digital audio effects processing, mixing environment, MIDI sequencing, and parameter automation, are just a simple reminder of such environments. Understanding how to configure peripherals and set them up properly inside your computer is essential to a successful marriage between hardware and software.

Here's a summary of what you will learn in this chapter:

* How to install a MIDI or audio peripheral in a PC.
* How to install a MIDI or audio peripheral in a Macintosh.
* The importance of having updated drivers.
* How to install drivers (PC and Mac) and system extensions (Mac).
* How to optimize your computer for MIDI and audio applications.

Installing Peripherals

There are three types of peripheral installations:

❋ An external peripheral that is connected to a computer using a single cable such as a USB, serial, parallel, or FireWire connection.

❋ A PCI card that needs to be inserted inside a computer and offers different types of connectors on the back part (or visible portion) of the card.

❋ A PCI card, as with the previous type, but this time the card is connected to a breakout box using a proprietary multi-pin connector. The breakout box serves as host for all the connections, including MIDI and digital audio connectors. This type of PCI card is often referred to as a host card. The breakout box can either sit on a desk or be inserted in a standard 19-inch rack.

Installing a PCI Card

It is highly recommended to turn off a computer before connecting new external peripherals, such as a MIDI interface, MIDI sync box, or external audio interface. As for the two other types, you should not install any hardware device while the computer is running.

Here's how to install a PCI card in your computer:

1. Turn off the computer and disconnect its power supply.

2. Remove the computer's cover and position it in a way that is easy for you to access the PCI slots on the motherboard.

3. Select the empty PCI slot where you will install the card or host card. Make sure the slot is a PCI slot. PCI slots are distinguishable from ISA slots by being shorter and set back farther from the outside of the computer. If you have a motherboard that was purchased after 2000, chances are you have PCI slots, not ISA slots. Newer PC and Macintosh computers have only PCI slots.

4. Before removing the PCI card from its protective anti-static bag, touch the metal power supply case of the computer in order to dissipate any static electricity your body may have accumulated. You might want to avoid working on a synthetic or wool carpet, which are prone to accumulate static electricity.

5. Remove the metal bracket that covers the access hole on the back of the computer. This bracket is typically either fastened to the computer with a single screw or needs to be twisted off. Be careful if twisting, since you could damage motherboard components at the bottom of the bracket.

6. Position the PCI card or host card over the target PCI slot and fit the card loosely over it with the card in the upright position. Press the card gently but firmly downward into the slot until the card is completely and squarely seated in the slot. If the card seems difficult to seat, a slight rocking motion may help.

7. Screw the PCI card's metal bracket down into the screw hole on the back of the computer using the screw you removed in step 5 above.
8. Place the cover back on your computer and place it in its normal position.

NOTE

If your PCI card is a host for a breakout box, it is important that you also connect the host to the breakout box before turning on your computer again.

9. Position the rack-mount or breakout box unit appropriately in a convenient but secure location.
10. Connect one end of the supplied host cable to the appropriate connector on the rack mount unit, as described by the manufacturer.
11. Connect the other end of the host cable to the appropriate connector on the PCI host card that now resides in your computer.
12. If there are screws on each end to make the connection tighter, make sure they are tightened so that the connecting cable won't become disconnected.
13. Connect the appropriate end of the AC power supply (if your device requires AC power) into the wall outlet to supply standard house current. Plug the other end into the AC power jack behind the rack-mount unit or breakout box.

Preparing the Connection

To connect an external device to a computer through a USB, FireWire, parallel, or serial cable, you don't need to open your computer up, but you do need to make some necessary verifications in order to establish if the device you are about to install is fully compatible with your system. For example, you will have to make sure you have USB or FireWire support enabled and running or that a serial port is available. Also note that while USB and FireWire are hot-swappable interfaces (which implies that they can be plugged in and out while the computer is on), serial and parallel connections generally require the computer to be turned off before connecting anything to these ports. Even when using USB or FireWire, many audio hardware device manufacturers recommend powering up the audio/MIDI hardware before powering up the computer and avoid disconnecting a connected device once it has been powered on.

NOTE

Macintosh and newer PC-based computers come equipped with USB already enabled. If you are installing a USB device on an older model computer, make sure there is a USB port installed and enabled on the computer before continuing with the installation. From your PC desktop, right-click on the My Computer icon and select Manage from the pop-up menu. Inside the Computer Management window (under Windows XP), select the Device Manager entry under System Tools to display devices installed on your system, as shown in Figure 7.1. You should find an entry saying Universal Serial Bus Controllers. If the heading does not even exist, it means one of three things: (1) You don't have USB support, (2) You haven't enabled the USB functions in your computer's BIOS, or (3) You don't have a USB controller currently installed on your computer. If you don't have USB support on your computer, you will need to upgrade your operating system to one that supports USB or upgrade your computer to one that offers USB support. If your computer supports USB but is not yet enabled, access the computer's BIOS feature by pressing the Delete key as your computer boots up. In the BIOS feature of the computer, locate an option that enables/disables USB support; if it is set to disabled, change it to enabled, save your settings, and reboot. If it is already enabled, exit the system BIOS without saving and reboot. You should consult your computer's or motherboard's documentation in order to find out exactly how to enable USB support in your BIOS before making any changes.

If you have made changes to your BIOS, Windows should recognize any USB port present on your computer, and it will probably prompt you to enter your Windows installation disk or CD as it installs support for USB on your computer. Simply follow the on-screen instructions and installation process. Now that you have USB support, you are ready to install your USB device.

With devices connecting through a serial port, make sure a serial port is available on the computer that is not assigned to another peripheral, such as an external modem or serial mouse. On a PC, be sure the serial port is enabled, as shown in Figure 7.2. To access this window from the PC desktop, right-click on the My Computer icon and select Manage from the pop-up menu. Inside the Computer Management window, select the Device Manager entry under System Tools to display devices installed on your system, as shown in Figure 7.1. This time, expand the Ports entry and double-click on the port you want to inspect. If a COM port does not appear at all, you might have to activate it in your computer's BIOS. To activate this port in your BIOS, consult your computer's documentation or consult a computer technician if in doubt.

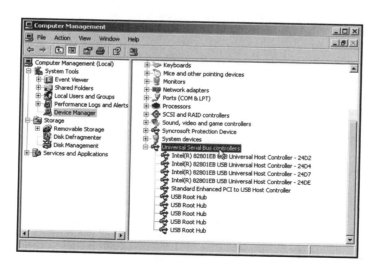

Figure 7.1 Installed USB controller support on Windows XP systems.

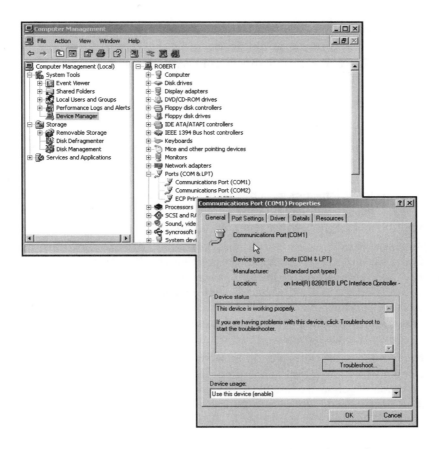

Figure 7.2 The Communications Port Properties window under Windows XP.

Serial ports are no longer available on Macintosh computers. As mentioned earlier, though, it is possible to add a serial port to a computer to remain compatible with older MIDI interfaces using serial port connections. If your Macintosh does have a serial port, it is recommended that you use the serial port labeled Modem rather than the one labeled Printer, especially if the printer system extension (the Mac's version of a printer driver) is loaded in your operating system. Finally, disconnect any device that might be connected to the Mac's modem port to install a MIDI interface on this serial port.

After completing these preliminary steps, installing an interface using a simple connection is easy. At this point, you know that your computer supports the type of connection you wish to use; its protocol communication support is installed on your computer, so you're ready to install the device's drivers (or system extensions on Macintosh computers). But before you do so:

1. Turn off your computer, USB, and FireWire devices.
2. Connect the cable to your external device.
3. Connect the other end of your cable to your computer.
4. Gather your installation disk or CD-ROM.
5. Turn on the computer and move on to the next section.

Getting the Right Driver

MIDI software communicates with MIDI interfaces or audio hardware supporting MIDI using software known as a driver. A driver is basically a dedicated program telling the operating system what the device is and how it should interact with it. The driver also gives the MIDI or audio application access to the interface itself by giving it necessary information on the card/device/ peripheral itself. Once the application knows how to address the peripheral's properties, it can display this peripheral's options in the setup dialog boxes usually found inside the application.

For example, once the application knows which peripheral you are using (through the information provided by the driver), you can choose which MIDI port you wish to activate in this application. When you purchase or install a new peripheral, such as a MIDI interface or audio hardware, you should get a CD-ROM or a diskette with appropriate drivers, or you may be able to download them from the manufacturer's Web site. In fact, it is recommended that you find out whether the driver provided with your peripheral is the latest version of this driver. If not, it is preferable to download the most recent version of the driver from the manufacturer's Web site.

You can usually the manufacturer's support Web address with the accompanying documentation. You should also know that in some cases, certain revisions of drivers work best with different combinations of environments, such as a specific software version running on a specific operating system. Reading the manufacturer's recommendations, the FAQ's (Frequently Asked Questions), user forums, and newsgroups is a great way to find out this information and make sure you have a combination that works well.

> ❋ **NOTE**
>
> In pre-OS X Macintosh operating systems, the term "driver" does not exist; instead, Macintosh refers to "system extensions," which operate in a similar way. Macintosh has adopted the term "driver" in its OS X (version 10). So, to avoid confusion, this book will always refer to "drivers," but be aware that your operating system may still call them "system extensions."

We will look at how to install a driver later in this chapter, since driver installations are OS specific. In other words, you need to install the driver that corresponds to the right device and the right operating system. For example, with a MIDI interface X model 1, you should have the driver for that specific device. Furthermore, if you are running Windows XP or OS X, have the correct version of this driver before installing it. Otherwise, you risk having a device that crashes your computer, doesn't work, prevents other devices from working properly, or simply doesn't work as well as it should. So, as you can see, making sure you have the right stuff is essential.

Most of the time, a text file called "readme" accompanies the driver files. This file usually contains precise installation procedures for your MIDI or audio device and some last minute information about your device that was added after the manufacturer printed the documentation included in its packaging. Take a moment to read this file before starting the installation procedure.

About OMS and FreeMIDI

If you are a Macintosh user with a pre-OS X system and wish to install a multi-port MIDI interface, chances are you will need to install either OMS (Open MIDI System) from Opcode or FreeMIDI from Mark Of The Unicorn (MOTU). These two applications are different versions of MIDI managers that support multiple MIDI ports and are usually required by many devices and software applications in order to address these multiple MIDI ports. If you only have a single MIDI port, you might not need to install one of these applications; however, they will provide greater control over your MIDI management on Macintosh computers. On the other hand, OS X includes its own MIDI manager called Core MIDI, so if you are running this OS, verify with your device's manufacturer documentation to find out how it is implemented in OS X.

You can get a copy of both FreeMIDI and OMS at the developers' Web sites: For FreeMIDI, visit www.motu.com, and for OMS, visit www.opcode.com. Before downloading and installing the MIDI manager, consult your device manufacturer's documentation to find out which one works best with your device. Some applications will also only work with one or the other. For example, running Cubase VST on your Mac requires OMS, not FreeMIDI (Cubase SX, a later version of Cubase, supports the MIDI manager provided with OS X).

Installing both FreeMIDI and OMS is quite simple. Depending on the number of MIDI devices you have, however, it might be a lengthy process the first time through, since you need to configure your MIDI setup before you can use the manager effectively. Once downloaded, unpack or uncompress the file and double-click the installer file. After that, all you have to do is follow onscreen instructions and then restart your computer. Note that most software applications will need OMS to run; however, if you have Performer or Digital Performer, you will need FreeMIDI.

You can run both applications at the same time, but you will need to deactivate system extensions (drivers) from one application to avoid problems.

If you are running a PC, you don't need OMS or FreeMIDI.

❋ **CONFIGURING OMS**

Here are first-time OMS configuration instructions:
Start by decompressing the OMS file you have downloaded, or locate the Opcode folder on your hard drive. Locate the OMS Applications folder, then OMS Setup. Double-click OMS Setup. OMS will inform you that it has not yet been configured. Click OK. Click OK once again in the Create a New Studio Setup

dialog box when it appears. If you have not yet installed your MIDI device driver, the OMS driver search will turn up empty. Once you have installed your device and properly configured it, run OMS and look for OMS Studio Setup. A box will appear asking you to choose the port on which you've attached your MIDI device. Do not choose a port, just click Search. OMS will then begin searching.

OMS Driver Setup shows the installed device in a list when OMS successfully finds the driver. Click OK to let OMS define (shows "Identifying") all the output ports it found on your device.

The OMS MIDI Device Setup dialog box will appear, showing the available output ports with open checkboxes to the left of each port. Check these open boxes to enable each of the output ports. Click OK. Next, My Studio Setup appears with a File Save dialog box over it. Name and save your new Studio Setup (or use the default name) before you can assign various instruments to the device's outputs and inputs. Assign your various instruments and you are done.

At this point, your MIDI device is ready for use. You may now exit OMS Setup by quitting the application. The rest is up to the configuration within your music software. Generally, this means selecting OMS Compatibility or Open Music System for your MIDI system setup.

Installing Your Driver Software

You are ready to install your peripheral once:

* ❀ The hardware components are installed.
* ❀ The proper communication ports (such as USB or serial) are enabled.
* ❀ You have downloaded the proper updated drivers.
* ❀ You have installed OMS or FreeMIDI if your hardware or software requires it.

The following instructions are standard steps that you can follow to help you understand the process of installing new MIDI-related peripherals on a specific OS running on your computer. However, it is not meant to replace the instructions provided by your device's manufacturer, since there might be some device-specific steps you have to follow.

Installing USB Port Drivers on Windows

When powering up your computer after connecting a device for the first time, the Add New Hardware Wizard window should appear, reporting that it found an unknown device. Depending on the version of Windows you have and the device you are installing, it might automatically identify which manufacturer and model you are attempting to install, especially if you are installing earlier models on a more recent version of Windows, such as Windows XP. If it does not recognize the manufacturer and model of the device, it should ask you to choose a location where it can find the proper files. Simply tell Windows where it can find the latest driver. For example, if it is on the CD provided with the device, specify the path to the CD after loading it in your CD-ROM drive. On the other hand, if you downloaded the file from the Internet, specify the location of this file on your hard disk.

❀ FILES MAY BE ZIPPED

Some downloadable files are compressed into a single file and need to be expanded into a folder or on a diskette in order for Windows to recognize these files as driver information files. If this is the case, you might have to skip the installation process for now, unpack or uncompress the files to a specific location on your disk, and then proceed to a manual installation of the drivers. This will be explained in following paragraphs.

1. Make sure your installation CD or diskette is in the computer.

2. When the Add New Hardware Wizard reports that it detected an unknown device, click Next if prompted to do so.

3. On the next screen, select Search for the Best Driver for Your Device and click Next.

4. Indicate the path to these files if the computer wasn't able to find them automatically. Select Choose Path and then type in the path or browse until you locate the appropriate files. Click OK when you are finished.

5. On the next screen, Windows should indicate it has searched for the driver files for your device and is now ready to install the driver. Click the Next button to continue. If it tells you the folder does not contain any device definition files, it might be because the path you specified is incorrect or that the file you have downloaded is compressed. Refer to the Note above if this is the case.

6. Windows will copy files and then indicate it has finished installing the software. Click the Finish button.

7. Next, you might see Windows indicating that it has found another unknown device and then see it automatically install the software for it if your device needs it. Simply let Windows install what it needs or repeat these previous steps if necessary.

At this point, the software drivers should be installed on your computer and functional.

In some cases, you might have to manually install a driver on your computer. If this is the case, follow these steps:

1. Click the Start button in the Taskbar.

2. Select Settings, Control Panel.

3. Double-click the Add/Remove Hardware icon and follow the wizard from that point on.

4. When the files have been copied, click the Finish button in the Completing the Found New Hardware Wizard dialog box.

5. At this point, Windows might need to restart in order for the driver installation to be completed. If this is the case, restart your computer when prompted to do so.

Installing USB Port Drivers on Macintosh

The first time you power up your Macintosh with the newly connected MIDI USB device, you will receive a message saying that an "unknown USB device has been detected." Click OK and proceed with the driver installation. You may also install the drivers first and then plug in the MIDI device. Just make sure your device is set to function in USB mode if it offers different modes.

For the installation, you will have to insert your CD containing the drivers in the CD-ROM drive or run the installation directly from a downloaded file from your hard disk. Find the Installer program for your device, double-click it, and follow the instructions onscreen.

Installing Serial Port Drivers on Windows

To manually install a MIDI device that uses a serial port, follow the steps below. Note that when starting your computer after connecting the device, Windows should bring you directly to the Add New Hardware Wizard. From that point on, the steps are identical.

1. From the Windows Start menu, select Settings, Control Panel, Add New Hardware.
2. Click the Next button twice. The system will now search for Plug and Play (PnP) hardware.
3. If Windows does find one or more PnP devices, select No; devices on serial ports will never show up as a PnP, so they should not appear in this list. Select Next to continue. Windows then asks if you would like it to search for the new hardware.
4. Select No, I Want to Select the Hardware from a List and press the Next button. Windows wants you to select the type of hardware you are installing.
5. Scroll down the list and highlight Sound, Video and Game Controllers. Then click Next.
6. When the next dialog appears, click the Have Disk button.
7. Insert the driver software CD or diskette in the proper drive and click OK.
8. Type in or browse until you locate the appropriate files. If you have downloaded the files from the Internet, specify the folder where these files are located.
9. When the next dialog appears, select the proper device and click OK.
10. When the next dialog appears, click Finish. Windows will copy and install the Windows driver files.

From this point on, you might need to do some additional steps, depending on the device driver and device you just installed. For additional installation setup information, consult your manufacturer's installation procedure documentation.

Installing Serial Port Drivers on Macintosh

If you have a Macintosh that supports a serial port, and its drivers are not currently installed on your system, you will need to install them prior to using this serial port. This might occur if you have added a serial port card on a G3 or G4 computer, for example. Once you have connected your serial port MIDI device to the computer, power up your device and then your computer.

1. Insert the supplied driver software CD or diskette. Have your System Folder open, with the OMS folder accessible.
2. Double-click the disk icon when it appears and open the installed device folder for Macintosh. If you downloaded the file from the Internet, open that folder. Drag the driver icon for your device into the OMS folder.
3. Within your hard drive files, find the Opcode folder. In the Opcode folder, find the OMS Applications folder, then OMS Setup. Double-click OMS Setup.

4. OMS will inform you that it has not yet been configured. Click OK.

5. The Create a New Studio Setup dialog box now appears. Click OK.

6. The OMS Driver Search box asks you to choose the port on which you've attached the installed device (either Modem or Printer). Choose a port and click Search. OMS begins searching.

7. OMS Driver Setup now shows the newly installed device (and the port to which it is attached) in a list when OMS successfully finds the driver. Click OK. OMS will now define all of the device's output ports. The OMS MIDI Device Setup dialog box will appear, showing the device's available output ports with checkboxes to the left of each port. Make sure that all of these boxes are checked to enable each of the output ports.

8. Click OK.

9. Next, My Studio Setup appears with a File Save dialog box over it. You will now need to name and save your new Studio Setup before you can assign various instruments to the device's outputs and inputs. Assign your instruments, and you are done. You may now exit OMS Setup by quitting the application.

Optimizing Your Computer for MIDI and Audio

Although MIDI is not a big consumer of computer resources, the use of MIDI-driven software instruments might require more from your computer than it can handle. Software instruments use your audio hardware to convert digital sounds it processes into analog signals that you can hear. Sometimes, your software might use samples on your hard drive to produce its sounds. When this occurs, MIDI can become a big computer resource consumer. The following tips are meant to help you optimize your system for audio—in other words, software synthesizers and samplers driven by MIDI.

Some of these tips might improve your computer's performance a little, and some might improve them a lot. It depends on your system and how it is currently configured. But, before going into the platform-specific optimization tips, here are some general tips that you might want to consider:

❈ Get as much RAM as you can. If you intend to use virtual or software synthesizers, the more RAM (random access memory) you have, the smoother your ride will be. Consider 256MB of RAM as a bare minimum. If you've noticed that your hard disk is always spinning and your computer is excessively slow, that's a good indication that more RAM is needed, as your computer is using virtual memory—a portion of your hard disk—to compensate for the lack in memory resources. This has two major effects: slowing down your system considerably and putting your hard disk under a lot of stress, which may eventually cause it to experience problems prematurely. But before you go out and buy more RAM, read some of the optimization tips suggested below—they might solve some of your problems. Also note that all RAM is not created equal, and not all motherboards take the same kind of RAM. You should refer to your computer supplier or your manufacturer's documentation to find out how you should go about updating the computer's memory. Using the identical RAM type as the one(s) already installed on your motherboard when upgrading your RAM is a good start, since the easiest way to get unpredictable behavior from your computer is to mismatch your RAM.

❅ Defragment your hard disks regularly. Hard disks are like shelves in a grocery store. People come in and grab stuff from shelves, and then employees put stuff back at the end of the day, moving misplaced products back to where they belong and cleaning up after the store closes so that the next day everything looks fresh and is easy for you to find. Now imagine if they didn't do that. Writing on a hard disk, then erasing, then writing again—eventually little bits of information are scattered everywhere on your hard disk, and your computer will have to look all over the disk to gather the information it needs to find for you. This takes time. Avoid having fragments of information spread all across a hard disk. Both Macintosh and Windows provide tools to help you do this effectively. Some recording engineers defragment their system after each recording session. Although this is commendable, it might not be necessary in your case. However, defragmenting hard disks regularly, perhaps once a week, is a good habit to cultivate if you wish a long and prosperous life for your hard disks.

❅ Update. More specifically, get the latest drivers or system extensions for your peripherals and operating system. This can help solve conflicts or improve overall performance. On the other hand, "If it ain't broke, don't fix it." If your system works fine the way it is, stick with it. You shouldn't feel the need to update for the sake of updating, but rather to solve issues that may be caused by outdated systems.

Optimizing Your PC

Most of these optimization tips will require a computer reboot before they take effect. It is recommended that you do one optimization at a time, reboot, and witness the effects of this optimization before continuing. If you don't see any changes, bring your system back to the setting it was before you applied these tips. You should always back up your system before optimizing it. If something goes wrong, at least you can go back to how it was rather than losing everything.

If it is possible, dedicate a computer to audio and MIDI applications only. This means that no other software or hardware peripherals should be connected or installed on this machine. Limiting and controlling what goes in and out will reduce the potential for conflicts, simplify the process of troubleshooting, keep your system resources open for audio/MIDI applications, and avoid all sorts of nasty problems happening while recording. So, leaving games, office applications, and especially Internet-related tools out of your computer will greatly improve your chances of having a healthy audio system.

Reduce Graphics Acceleration

This specifies the amount of acceleration you want for your graphics hardware. Full acceleration is the fastest and is recommended for most computers. When using a PCI graphics card, reducing the graphic acceleration might help, but this will not make any noticeable difference when using an AGP graphics card. In recent years, it has been found that reducing hardware acceleration in fact puts a heavier load on the CPU and uses up CPU cycles better dedicated to the music applications. Hardware acceleration should only be lowered as a troubleshooting step as it does not typically increase the overall performance of the system. When it comes to an older PCI graphics card, however, this tip may apply to you since audio and MIDI applications do not require intense graphic support. You can decrease the Hardware Acceleration slider as shown in Figure 7.3. If you don't see any changes in your audio and MIDI performance after doing this, such as drops in the audio while the screen is refreshing, set the slider back to full graphics acceleration.

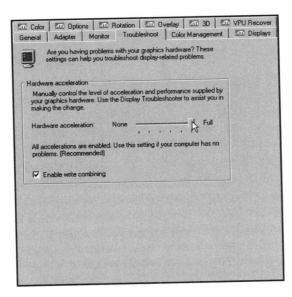

Figure 7.3 The Advanced Graphics Settings dialog box.

To adjust your graphics acceleration rate under Windows XP:

1. Right-click somewhere in the desktop and select Display Properties from the context menu.
2. Select the Settings tab and then click on the Advanced button.
3. Select the Troubleshoot tab and drag the slider to the left for no acceleration. If you find this deteriorates your graphics performance too much, bring it up a notch.
4. Click the Apply button, then OK.

Adjust for Best Performance
While Windows XP looks pretty with its rounded windows, drop shadows, and other visual enhancements, all the special features require additional processing power from the computer. Removing these enhancements can help reduce the processing load and won't affect how Windows performs, only how it looks.

To adjust Windows XP for best performances rather than greater visual effects:

1. On the computer's desktop, right-click the My Computer icon and select Properties from its context menu.
2. Click on the Advanced tab, followed by the Settings button under the Performance section.
3. By default, the Performance Options dialog box displays the Visual Effects page. When this is not the case, select the appropriate tab before continuing.
4. Select the Adjust for best performance option and click Apply, as shown in Figure 7.4.
5. Click OK twice to close all windows.

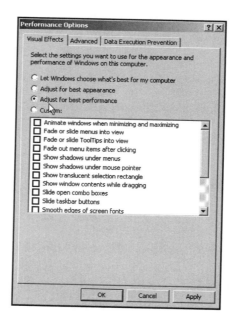

Figure 7.4   Adjusting Windows XP performance options.

Disable Unused Ports

If you don't have any USB, serial, or parallel devices hooked up to your computer, disable these unused ports since, even though they are not being used, they require additional IRQ assignments and are unnecessarily accessed by the system bus. In some cases, this might be the easiest way to resolve IRQ conflicts on older Windows 9x systems.

To disable unused ports, follow these steps:

1. Access the system's properties.
2. Select the line displaying the USB serial bus controller.

3. Select any installed component under this heading and click Remove.

4. When all entries have been removed, click Apply, and then OK. At this point you will need to reboot your computer.

5. When your computer reboots, hit the Delete key to access your system's BIOS features.

6. Locate the USB enable/disable function in the BIOS. Once located, disable it.

7. Save your BIOS settings and exit to continue with your system's rebooting process.

Disable Superfluous Startup Items

When Windows boots up, it loads a variety of programs on startup, such as anti-virus protection, system monitoring, and so on. While some of these items are essential, others will draw resources from audio/MIDI applications. Culprits include System Agent, Find Fast, Active Desktop, Office Startup, RealPlayer's StartCenter, NetMeeting, Active Movie, animated cursors and icons, and many others. They may be useful, but they use loads of memory. For example, Norton AntiVirus and Norton Utilities used together may reduce performance by up to 28%, depending on your system's resources.

To disable these items, do this:

1. Select Start, Run.

2. Type MSCONFIG and click OK.

3. Click the Startup tab.

4. Disable any startup item that you found in the list mentioned above (see Figure 7.5). You will want to leave Windows system items such as System Tray, for example.

5. Click Apply, then OK when done. If you find that you disabled some items you would like to enable again, you can simply run MSCONFIG as you just did once again and add a check next to the desired items in the list.

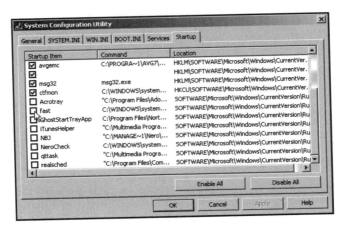

Figure 7.5 The System Configuration Utility's Startup dialog box.

Screen Savers and Power Management

This is a simple one: Don't use screen savers or power management functions unless you are using a laptop and wish to save battery power. While properly set screen savers and power management are okay, these features can consume resources at the most inopportune times. As a general rule, avoid having anything running in the background that can draw processing power away from your primary objective—recording audio and MIDI.

To disable screen savers and power management:

1. In the computer's desktop, right-click and select Properties from the context menu.
2. Select the Screen Saver tab and choose None from the dropdown menu as shown in Figure 7.6.
3. In the same page, click the Power button (this button is called Settings under Windows 98).
4. In the Power Schemes page, set the Turn Off Monitor Option to Never.
5. Repeat this selection for the Turn Off Hard Disks and System Standby options.
6. Click Apply, then OK twice to exit the Display Properties dialog box.

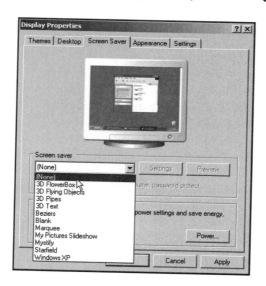

Figure 7.6   Disabling the screen saver.

Optimizing a Pre-OS X Mac

Although Apple computers are known to be easier to handle than their PC counterpart in terms of peripheral configuration, you still need to take a hand in optimizing your Macintosh for audio and MIDI applications, especially if it's running a pre-OS X operating system. Avoiding audio pops, dropouts, and clicks due to an overloaded set of system extensions (drivers) or an improperly configured OS is exactly what we are going to look at here. The only optimization tip for an OS X system would be to turn off the Energy Saver option. The remaining optimization tips found here are for pre-OS X systems.

Create a Minimal Extension Set

A good way to optimize your Mac for audio and MIDI is to reduce the number of active extensions in your system when working with this type of software.

To create a separate set of extensions containing only the extensions necessary to use with your audio and MIDI peripherals and programs:

1. Open the Extension Manager control panel found under the Apple menu.
2. Select the MacOS Base Set. This might be called MacOS x.xx Base, depending on your OS version.
3. Press the Duplicate Set button in the bottom right corner of the dialog box.
4. Rename the set with a descriptive name such as Audio, for example.
5. Enable any extensions necessary for your audio and MIDI applications and hardware, such as audio/MIDI sequencers, MIDI interfaces, and audio hardware. These extensions might include FreeMIDI power plug and system extension, OMS, preferred device, MOTU USB driver, ReWire, REX shared library, TimeBandit.shlb, USB floppy enabler, and USB OMSMIDIDriver. This is not a complete list of extensions but merely a starting point. Just make sure that you read your software and hardware manuals for a complete list of extensions that are required in such a setup.
6. Disable any extensions that do not relate to your audio or MIDI hardware and software and do not play a role in your system's operation.
7. After creating the new extensions set, close the Extensions Manager dialog box.

This new set of extensions should take effect when you reboot your Mac.

Disable Virtual Memory

Virtual memory may cause performance degradation in Apple computers, as it uses the hard disk rather than using much faster RAM. It is advisable when using audio and MIDI applications to disable it.

To disable virtual memory:

1. In the Apple menu, click the control panel and then select the Memory item.
2. Under Virtual Memory, select Off. Note that if there is over 995MB of RAM installed, virtual memory will be disabled.

The new virtual memory settings will not take effect until the computer reboots.

Set Disk Cache to Minimum

The settings for the system disk cache can affect performance. In some cases, it may help to set the Memory control panel's disk cache to 512K or lower, down to the lowest possible value. Higher settings can sometimes cause degraded performance, including audio and synchronization problems.

1. In the Apple menu, click the control panel and then select the Memory item.
2. Under Disk Cache, select the Custom setting option and then enter 512K in the appropriate box. If your computer doesn't respond well after rebooting, change this value by increments of 512K until its behavior is adequate.

The new Disk Cache settings will not take effect until the computer reboots.

When OMS is installed, Opcode recommends not running it with AppleTalk active; however, if you don't have OMS, turning this option off is still recommended, especially while running audio or MIDI applications. It is also a good idea to disconnect any network communication with other computers. This includes Internet communications as well, since these network communications might disrupt or interfere with real-time operations. The control strip can store settings for AppleTalk, File Sharing, Extension Manager, and more. You can use this as an easy way to switch between setups for audio and general purpose computing.

To disable AppleTalk:

1. Click the control strip at the bottom of your screen to expand it.
2. Locate the AppleTalk icon and select the AppleTalk Inactive option.

Disable Deep Sleep

Deep Sleep is a function that puts your entire Mac in a deep sleep state (hence the name), where not just the monitor and hard disks go to sleep, but everything else as well. Some problems might occur when a PCI device does not support this mode. For example, your Mac might not want to wake up (maybe because it's dreaming of being as popular as a PC, who knows?). In the past, MacOS systems would not attempt to enter this mode if they sensed that one or more of the installed devices did not support deep sleep. With some recent models, this appears to have changed. Support of deep sleep is a function of the PCI controller hardware and cannot be changed. However, there are settings that you can alter that should prevent you from having this problem.

To disable Deep Sleep mode:

1. Open the Energy Saver control panel.
2. Press the Show Details button or Sleep Setup tab.
3. Check the box labeled Separate Timing for Display Sleep.
4. Also, check the box labeled Separate Timing for Hard Disk Sleep.
5. Set the times for Display and Hard Disk Sleep as desired.
6. Set the top slider, labeled Put the System to Sleep Whenever... all the way to the right to Never.

This will not prevent the display and hard disk from going into Sleep mode, but it will prevent your system from going into Deep Sleep mode.

PCI Card Interaction

Digital audio PCI cards rely on being able to transfer small amounts of data across the PCI bus at regular intervals, several thousand times per second. If other PCI devices, such as video or SCSI cards, tie up the PCI bus for extended periods of time, this may prevent your audio/MIDI PCI card from completing one data transfer before the next is scheduled to begin. If this happens, the audio stream will be corrupted. Some motherboard devices may also share PCI resources, even if they do not use a PCI card. This can also affect the PCI bus as well. Here are a few troubleshooting tips you can follow to prevent this type of problem:

❋ Try lowering the colors in your display to thousands rather than millions. You can do this through the control strip.

❋ Try swapping the audio PCI with other PCI cards or simply moving the audio PCI to another PCI slot after turning off your computer. This may improve your performance.

❋ For troubleshooting purposes, you may also wish to temporarily disconnect other peripherals, including USB and FireWire devices.

Use Separate PCI Busses on Six-Slot CPUs

When experiencing PCI card interaction problems on MacOS systems with two PCI buses (all six-slot towers, including 9500, 9600, and PowerTower Pro), it is recommended that you distribute cards between the two busses so that each has the maximum PCI bandwidth available. In particular, try placing the audio PCI card on a separate bus from video (and SCSI) cards. Apple has identified and fixed a problem with certain Beige G3 Macintosh models in which the CD-ROM could cause long delays in system response while waking up, which may happen when a new CD-ROM is inserted into the drive. These delays may cause crashes with certain digital audio applications. If you have experienced this problem, you can download the G3 CD Update from Apple's Web site (www.apple.com/support/).

Review Questions

1. Which of the following type adapters is no longer present in most PC computers?

   a) PCI

   b) ISA

   c) AGP

   d) None of the above

2. What is a dedicated program telling the operating system what the device is and how it should interact with it?

   a) A sequencer

   b) A firewall

   c) A driver

   d) An editor/librarian

3. What is the name of the application developed by Opcode that allows Mac users running OS 9.x to use a multi-port MIDI interface?

   a) OMS

   b) FreeMIDI

   c) AppleTalk

   d) ProTools

4. When using a computer as a digital audio workstation, it is recommended to defragment a hard disk every:

   a) Hour

   b) Week

   c) Month

   d) Year

5. Before installing drivers for a new audio-related peripheral, you should always:

   a) Install the hardware component

   b) Ensure that the proper communication ports, such as FireWire, are enabled

   c) Download the proper updated drivers

   d) All of the above

6. What type of application uses the audio hardware to convert incoming MIDI events into digital audio sounds?

   a) Software instruments

   b) Editor/librarians

   c) FreeMIDI

   d) All of the above

7. When optimizing a computer, you should always follow each optimization step by _____ before optimizing another parameter. Complete the sentence with one of the following choices.

   a) crossing your fingers and touching wood

   b) closing all non-audio-related applications

   c) rebooting

   d) rubbing your feet on the carpet

8. Reducing graphics acceleration will not affect your computer performance much if you have this type of video adapter:

   a) PCI

   b) ISA

   c) AGP

   d) USB

9. There are three main types of audio-related peripheral installations. Which of the following items does not represent one of these types?

   a) An external peripheral connected to a computer using a single FireWire connection.

   b) A PCI card connected to a breakout box using a proprietary multi-pin connector.

   c) A PCI card inserted inside a computer, offering different types of connectors on the back of the card.

   d) A remote controller using wireless communication with the onboard network adapter.

10. True or False: On a Macintosh computer running OS X, OMS and FreeMIDI MIDI managers are replaced by Core MIDI.

✳ ✳ ✳

8 ♩ Sequencing with MIDI

This chapter takes a look at some of the basic functions of the "must have" MIDI application: the sequencer. We discuss some typical and fundamental operations you can perform with a sequencer. We also take a look at music notation software, since it often goes hand in hand with MIDI files and sequencers. In fact, many sequencers today offer extensive notation functions to produce exceptionally good printed music. I remember my days as a student when the jazz bandleader would make an arrangement for the ensemble and ask me to create individual music sheets for each part in the arrangement... if only sequencers had existed back then! I can still see myself scrambling to get those copies out without ending up with ink stains all over my hands as the night before the rehearsal got shorter and shorter.

Here's a summary of what you will learn in this chapter:

 ❈ What sequencers can do for you and what you can do with them.

 ❈ How to set up a sequencer to record MIDI from one or more MIDI inputs.

 ❈ How to use punch-ins and punch-outs to record over MIDI.

 ❈ Configuring MIDI tracks to monitor their audio output.

 ❈ What the basic MIDI editing environments found in sequencers are.

 ❈ What other editing capabilities you can expect to find in sequencers.

 ❈ How you can safely save the work you have done in a sequencer.

 ❈ How to use MIDI files to create music sheets.

 ❈ Which musical elements will appear on a music sheet and which ones won't when using a MIDI file to create a music sheet.

 ❈ What to expect when using a scanner and notation software to extract MIDI files from a piece of paper.

This chapter will not discuss specific functions or how-tos in specific software environments, since this is a subject that could fill an entire book itself. So, if you've just purchased sequencer software and wish to use it to its full potential, perhaps getting another book dedicated to your software would be a good idea. Chances are, one is available in the *Power!* series.

What Is a Sequencer?

Let's begin by defining what a sequencer is—more specifically, a MIDI sequencer. For starters, MIDI sequencers have evolved dramatically since their first appearance in the mid-80s. They are now an integral tool for the music-making hobbyist and professional composers and musicians around the world.

A MIDI sequencer is a tool that records MIDI events and plays them back as they were recorded. You can edit these events using a graphical user interface, whether via a small LCD on a hardware device or on your computer running sequencing software. Here are some things you can do with a MIDI sequencer besides just recording, editing, and playing back:

* Record MIDI at a slow tempo, then play it back at a different tempo or change the tempo as it's playing without affecting the sound quality.

* Layer different tracks containing different MIDI events assigned to specific MIDI channels so that each track can correspond to its own MIDI channel. This is like having a multi-track recording system in which each track represents an instrument or a part played by an instrument.

* Change or redirect a MIDI channel to a different channel on a sequencer track. This is very convenient to copy something you've recorded on one MIDI channel to another track and change the MIDI channel for this copied track. You end up with two instruments playing the same line you've recorded only once. Texturing a line with several sounds is a proven orchestral technique and can transform a simple yet plain musical line into a great hook.

* Adjust the performance timing through quantizing, a feature that aligns minor imperfections in your rhythmic performance to a predefined meter grid. This grid can represent any metrical subdivision—quarter notes, eighth notes, and so on. This is very useful to make musical parts tighter or to give your music a specific feel, like shuffle or swing for example, where the percentage of rhythmic correction varies to give the corresponding feel to this musical part.

* Create copies of MIDI events and repeat them over time, making the creation process a cinch, since you don't have to record everything all at once and don't have to replay every part for the length of an entire track. You can simply play a few bars, a chorus, or a verse and then copy that portion and repeat it at another location in time, instantly creating new choruses or verses, for example.

* Transpose MIDI events without changing the quality of the sound, since all you're doing is adding a value to the Note On values already recorded. Then, when the sequencer plays back, it sends the new Note On values to your MIDI device.

* Convert MIDI events recorded in a sequencer into musical notation and print it so that musicians can read it in a live studio session. How much control you have over the appearance of this musical notation depends on the notation functions built into your sequencer software.

* Create and automate mixes inside the sequencer, using MIDI controls.

MIDI sequencers have slowly integrated audio functions as computers become faster and more powerful. At this point in time, the major software developers of MIDI sequencer applications—Cakewalk's Sonar, Steinberg's Cubase SX, Apple's Logic Audio, and MOTU's Digital Performer, to name the most popular ones—all offer full digital audio support. This implies that MIDI sequencers can now handle MIDI events as well as digital audio files inside the same application.

For example, you can create MIDI tracks to record MIDI events and create audio tracks to record digital audio events. You can also use software instruments, in some cases, that use MIDI events to trigger the sounds the instruments play but use the audio hardware's outputs to generate the sounds themselves.

In fact, most of the major additions made to these applications in recent versions relate to the treatment and editing capabilities of digital audio and the integration of software instruments, as well as digital audio processing features, leaving the actual MIDI editing and recording functions pretty much unchanged. You could say MIDI sequencing has matured, and most of the MIDI functions users wanted to see in this type of application have been integrated already.

Does this mean MIDI sequencers are a thing of the past? Not at all, since the addition of software instruments (virtual synthesizers, samplers, and drum machines) as part of the sequencer toolbox gave MIDI a much-needed boost in the past few years. Using the computer as a powerful musical instrument and talking to this instrument through MIDI, just as you would with an external synthesizer, allows you to better control this instrument. For example, you don't have to purchase additional hardware, which can require changes in your studio setup. In other words, you don't have to reconfigure your studio to control this new addition. Also, since your instrument is inside your computer, accessing it is easy because you are already working inside your computer anyway. Finally, you can edit MIDI, which offers a much greater editing capability than digital audio.

Editing audio is getting easier and easier, but tasks such as pitch change, tempo changes, and even musical content changes are much easier to do with MIDI than with digital audio. Since software instruments are essentially MIDI devices, you have as much control over how they sound as you have over how the MIDI events playing through them can be edited in the sequencer.

Recording MIDI

Before starting the manipulation of MIDI information and digital audio in a sequencer, you need to record it. Before you can record, a keyboard controller needs to be connected to a MIDI port on your computer, and all your MIDI devices inside and outside of your computer need to be configured properly. This has already been discussed in earlier chapters. So let's assume you are ready to rock! You will need to activate the appropriate MIDI inputs and outputs in your sequencer's MIDI preferences or setup dialog box (see Figure 8.1). This is a way of telling your sequencer which MIDI port(s) will be receiving the MIDI events and which MIDI port(s) are used to send MIDI events to external devices and software instruments.

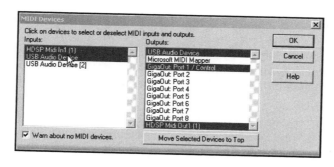

Figure 8.1   Sonar's MIDI Devices setup dialog box.

This is usually done through the MIDI preferences settings inside your sequencer application. Enabling MIDI ports in the application's preferences will make these ports available for use when recording or assigning MIDI events to outputs.

Setting Up Your Track

A track in a sequencer is like a track on a multi-track recorder. You can use it to record events from one or more MIDI inputs, depending on your MIDI studio setup and the application itself. However, you don't need to specify whether a track will be mono or stereo, since MIDI events are neither. However, the audio output of a MIDI sound module or software instrument may be mono, stereo, or surround. Quite often, to record on a track, you will need to select it, make it active, and arm it for recording. Let's take a look at how the MIDI signal flows from the input of your computer to the track's output:

1. Playing MIDI on a controller sends MIDI events to the computer (when it's hooked up properly, obviously). All events are sent using the MIDI channel assignment on the controller itself. For example, if the keyboard uses MIDI channel 1, all messages entering the application (in this case, the sequencer) will have channel 1 as their channel information.

2. Activating or assigning the MIDI input port inside a sequencer application tells it to accept incoming MIDI events on this port. When the track is armed for recording, MIDI events coming on this MIDI port will be recorded and placed inside this track.

3. Routing the MIDI events to the appropriate destination makes it possible to monitor these events. For example, to hear events sent by a keyboard playing back through the sound module of this keyboard, assign the MIDI track's output to the corresponding MIDI port hooked up to the keyboard. If you are using a MIDI port called A, then the track should be assigned to send the MIDI events back to MIDI port A. On the other hand, if you would like to send the MIDI coming on port A to another MIDI port, such as a virtual MIDI port created by a software instrument, you can select this as the outgoing MIDI port.

4. Your MIDI events are coming in with MIDI channel 1 as the input channel (in this example), but ultimately, it is the track's MIDI channel assignment that determines which MIDI channel plays back. So, to play the events on MIDI channel 2, select the new channel from the track's channel setting. This re-maps the events from channel 1 to channel 2 when they come out from MIDI port A (as set in step 3 of this example).

5. Then, the information comes out from MIDI port A on channel 2 and is sent to whatever device is hooked up to this MIDI port. In other words, you can take any MIDI event coming from any port on any channel and send it to any other port on any other channel.

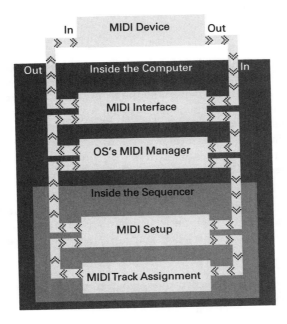

Figure 8.2   The path taken by a MIDI signal from your MIDI device to a sequencer and back out to a MIDI device.

As you can see in Figure 8.2, a MIDI device sends MIDI events to the input of a MIDI interface. Your OS's MIDI manager then makes the link with your software application, forwarding the MIDI events. For your software application to open the door for this information, it needs to be configured properly, as mentioned above. Then, the sequencer's MIDI track assignment will reroute the information accordingly and send the MIDI data back to the MIDI interface or forward it internally to a virtual MIDI port, such as a software instrument.

To find out if you have successfully configured a track, try playing on a keyboard and listen to the result as you hit the notes. After setting the audio monitoring system properly, if you can hear what's coming out of the desired sound module or virtual instrument, then you have configured your track properly and should be able to record MIDI events on this track.

To record in a sequencer is quite simple. Usually, the process begins by arming a track for recording and hitting a Record button, which sometimes needs to be followed by a Play button. Setting up the sequencer to generate a click track or metronome tick helps keep your performance in sync with the bars and beats found in the MIDI sequence.

Recording from Multiple MIDI Sources

Many of you will be using a sequencer in a music creation environment, using a keyboard or single controller device to input MIDI events into the sequencer. This type of setup is simple and described above. However, you might want to record multiple MIDI sources at once in the sequencer. This can be done in different ways, depending on your software and its configuration.

Recording from multiple MIDI sources on multiple tracks can be useful when you want to record more than one musician simultaneously, rather than having each musician play one line, record it, and then pass to the next musician. Another use for this application might be for sequencer-to-sequencer transfers, where all the tracks from one sequencer are recorded onto their own tracks in a receiving sequencer. In order to achieve multi-input or multi-channel recording, you need to set each source instrument to a different MIDI channel and arm multiple MIDI tracks for recording in the destination sequencer, assigning each track to its corresponding MIDI input port and input channel, if this option is available. You might also want to read up on your sequencer's documentation to find out if there are some specific steps you need to take in order to perform this kind of recording operation.

If a sequencer does not support multi-track recording, simply assign each instrument its own MIDI channel, if not its own MIDI port, and use editing tools inside the sequencer to extract each MIDI channel recorded onto one track, splitting it into multiple tracks.

Punching In and Out

In the good old days of analog tape recording, when a mistake was made while recording, you had to roll back the tape, start the playback, and just before you wanted to record over what sounded bad, you "punched in" the Record button to enable the Record function. When you arrived at the point on the tape where you wanted to keep what was there, you "punched out" the Record button, reverting to the playback function for that track.

MIDI sequencers can be easily programmed to automatically punch in and punch out at specific time locations. This technique is useful when most of a recorded track is good, with the exception of a few bars here and there. Punching in replaces the mistakes without erasing and re-recording the whole track.

In fact, you will find that punching in a MIDI sequencer is particularly simple. That's because you can manipulate MIDI events easily and program your sequencer to punch in at a specific bar and beat and do the same for the punch out point.

You can also select the MIDI events in an appropriate MIDI editor and delete them. Then you can record over this track. Since MIDI only records played events, whenever and whatever you play will be recorded at the time and in the track you have selected. Sometimes, however, it might be easier to simply cut out the MIDI events that were bad and add new ones on another MIDI track.

The punch process usually consists of a few simple steps:

1. Set a punch-in time. This marks the beginning point at which the existing MIDI events on the track will be replaced by the newly recorded events.

2. Set a punch-out time. This is the point at which the recording will automatically stop on this track.

3. Set a pre-roll and post-roll time. Pre-roll is a lead-in time before the punch in, and post-roll is how long the track will play after the punch-out point. The purpose of this is to give the performer a couple of bars to hear the sequence before and after recording begins and ends. Pre- and post-roll functions are not be implemented in all sequencers; read your sequencer's documentation to find out exactly how yours works.

4. Set a loop region if needed. Sometimes repeating a looped portion of a song is useful to create multiple takes of this area. Each take can be stored on a separate track in your sequencer.

As you can see in Figure 8.3, Steinberg's Cubase Transport bar has a function that lets you set the punch-in and punch-out times; in this figure, the punch-in is set to bar 3-beat 1, and the punch-out is set to bar 5-beat 1. The cycle mode is also enabled and will loop between bars 1 and 7.

Figure 8.3 Cubase's Transport panel.

MIDI Playback Configuration

MIDI sequencers generally record MIDI events on tracks using the MIDI channel they receive from the input, as mentioned in the "Setting Up Your Track" section earlier in this chapter. These MIDI events are then sent to the output port and MIDI channel assigned for the track. To properly play back a track, you need to configure this track to send the recorded events to the appropriate MIDI output port and MIDI channel. Take Figure 8.4, for example. In this case, the keyboard sends MIDI events on channel 1, MIDI port A. By assigning the output of the MIDI track to MIDI port B, channel 5, the destination sound module responding to this port and MIDI channel reproduces these events. You can change the port and channel settings at any time during playback/recording or once the sequencer is stopped. This allows you to play MIDI events and monitor them through different instruments, ports, or channels without affecting the original MIDI performance. So, what was originally a piano sound could become a string sound, a clarinet sound, or even a drum sound, simply by changing the MIDI playback configuration of your recorded track.

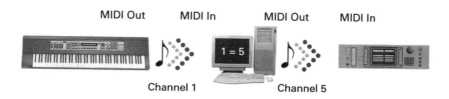

Figure 8.4 The sequencer's track setting can change the track's MIDI output configuration during playback.

Editing MIDI: Typical Editing Windows

MIDI sequencers offer a number of editing environments. Each editing window in a sequencer is designed to emphasize certain types of MIDI events and make its editing easier. For example, to create copies of certain sections of an arrangement, you work in one editing window. To tweak a few notes in a string part, you have another window. To add a cowbell and tighten your snare drum, you guessed it, there's an editing window for that as well. So, let's take a look at the most common MIDI editing windows.

The Main Project Window

The main project window typically offers a global view of a song, arrangement, or project (see Figure 8.5) where all MIDI and audio tracks are laid out in rows on one side of the screen (often on the left hand side), and your MIDI events held in boxes on the right. These boxes have different names, depending on the application itself, but they usually serve a similar

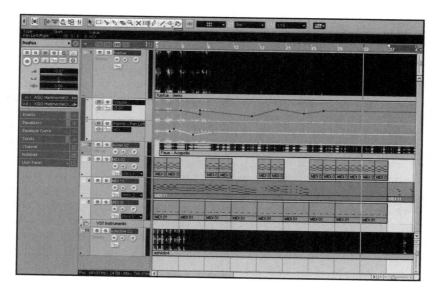

Figure 8.5 Cubase SX project window.

purpose. You can think of them as building blocks containing MIDI or audio events that can be copied, moved, transposed, muted, stretched, or grouped together.

While the look and feel of most sequencer applications may be different, there are many similarities among them. If you break down each application, you can find common areas. Once you understand these common areas, you will be able to quickly find your way around any sequencing application. Here's a breakdown of these common areas.

Menus and Toolbars Area

Menus and toolbars are where most of the tools and options available in the software are located. If the menu is not attached to the project window, it is usually in the top part of the window, which is the case with Digital Performer and Sonar. When you are looking for a function like creating markers, copying events, or inserting a track, menus are usually where you find what you need. Toolbars are meant as shortcuts to most common tasks, like opening another window, changing the tool you are currently using, and so on.

Figure 8.6 Sonar's menus and toolbar area; buttons inside the toolbar can be rearranged.

Track List and Track Details Area

This is where detailed information for each track is located, such as the name of a track, the type of information contained in a track such as audio, midi, and automation, and so on. You can also find information that relates to track settings for output assignment, such as MIDI ports, MIDI channels, instrument names used by a MIDI device for this track, and digital audio outputs or inputs used by the software if you are in record mode. You may also switch between different modes for a track, like muting a track, soloing it, or enabling the record-ready state for this track if the software requires it. In some cases, you can even view the track automation in this area. You will want to get familiar with the information displayed in this area because it is crucial to the rest of your sequencer functions.

Time Display or Ruler Area

This is where you will find a horizontal ruler with both the bars and beats of your sequence and the time information for your project. By looking at the ruler, you can quickly spot where you are in the project. You may also find regions and markers in this area as well. Markers are used to identify specific points in your project. You can give the markers a name and quickly navigate between them. Regions are similar to markers in the sense that they serve as reference points; however, they identify a beginning and an end of a section in a project. You can use regions to identify different sections of a song such as a chorus, verse, bridge, and so on.

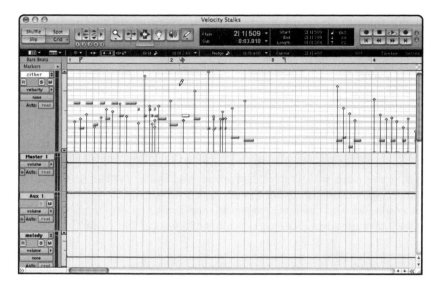

Figure 8.7 ProTools track list area displays current settings for each track in a project.

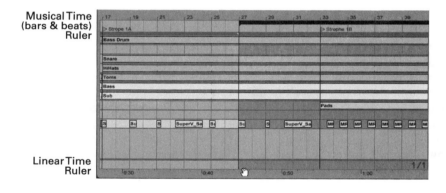

Figure 8.8 Live's Time display area.

Track View Area

This is where you will find the actual events on each track. An event can usually be one of three things: MIDI data, audio data, or automation data. How these events are called in a sequencer depends on the sequencer itself. You can think of the blocks represented in a track view area as containers of events. Double-clicking on a container usually opens the associated event type editor window. For example, double-clicking on a MIDI container or clip will open a MIDI editor. On the other hand, if you double-click on an audio clip or container, it will open an audio editor. You can usually copy these containers, move them around, delete them, and so on. When you do so, you copy, move, or delete any information that pertains to that specific series of events found inside the container. When you record MIDI events, a container is created automatically. If you stop the recording and then start recording again, another container will appear over or merged with the previous container if you were record-ing over an already recorded series of events. The behavior of the sequencer in this case, whether it replaces or adds to the previous recording, is usually determined by the sequencer's recording options.

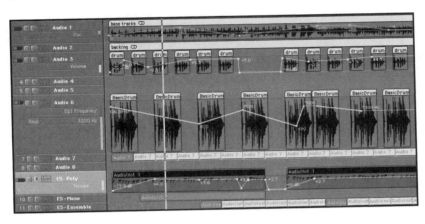

Figure 8.9   Logic Audio's track view area.

Zoom and Scroll Areas
Moving around in your project, viewing certain details for certain tracks, or going from bar 1 to bar 500 requires that you sometimes change your magnification level to view more information at once or zoom into a specific detail on screen. The same applies for scrolling. As with any other application, the scrollbars and zoom functions allow you to move your point of view and change your focus within your project. Note that, quite often, you will find quick keyboard shortcuts and even special keyboard combinations to quickly recall a zoom level or a previously stored window setup.

The Piano Roll Editor
The piano roll analogy is often used to describe how MIDI performances are recorded be-cause it provides a simple yet visual representation of this recording. A real piano roll is a long piece of paper rolled over a cylinder, with holes punched through the paper along its vertical length. The paper cylinder is mounted and fed inside the mechanical piano through an intricate set of gears, making its way to an empty cylinder. As the player presses on pedals, the cylinder starts rolling, advancing from one cylinder to the next, passing in front of rods that move as they encounter holes in the paper, thus activating the piano mechanism to play the corresponding note.

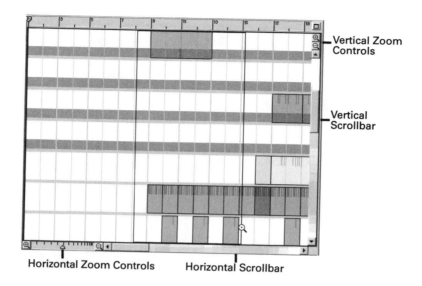

Figure 8.10   Reason's horizontal and vertical zoom and scrollbar controls.

The metaphor seems like a good one for describing the MIDI editing environment. The piano roll editing environment is, simply put, a virtual piano roll, where MIDI events appear, passing from right to left—from beginning to end. The lower notes appear at the bottom of the display, while higher notes appear at the top. In Figure 8.11, you can see a keyboard displayed in

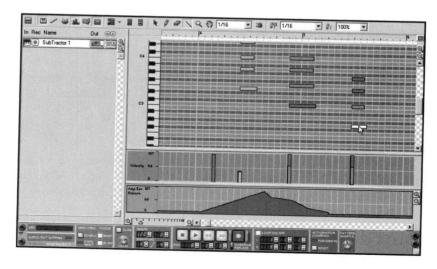

Figure 8.11   Reason's Edit mode uses a piano roll editing window.

the left portion of the window. This represents the MIDI keyboard with its octaves numbered for easy reference. To the right of the keyboard, you can see horizontal rectangles, each one representing a MIDI Note On message. The rectangle's left edge represents the starting point—when the note was played along the timeline—and the right edge represents the end point—when the note was released. The ruler on top identifies the bars and beats when these events occurred, and a colored grid helps users to quickly tell whether notes are recorded properly according to a rhythmic grid and piano keyboard (displayed on the left). In this figure, you can also see that each note is color coded to display its velocity value, which is also represented below the piano roll in the display.

Besides a simple Note On message, the piano roll view can also displays other information, such as control changes, velocity information, and other selectable MIDI events.

In this type of window, you can edit MIDI events that are part of a container present in the main project window. It is the representation of the contents of this container. You may select an event by clicking on its representation in the piano roll view, move it, copy it, delete it, and change its length, velocity, or any other recorded MIDI parameter for that matter.

Since this type of editing environment represents a good graphical interface, it is the ideal place to edit MIDI events that are harmonic, melodic, or even rhythmic in nature. As you will see in the next section, drum tracks can be edited in both the piano roll editor and a specific drum editing window.

The Drum Editor

MIDI events intended for drum parts, unlike other musical instruments recorded with MIDI, don't normally have length associated with them, since what counts in a drum partition is the moment of attack, or attack time. That's why MIDI drums often have their own editing environment. Another particularity with drum tracks is that, although each instrument in a drum kit is mapped to a specific key on the keyboard, these keys do not refer to actual pitch values on a keyboard. That's why in a drum editor, key names or note numbers are associated with instrument name rather than the usual keyboard layout on the left hand side, as was the case in the piano roll editor. For example, C1 on your keyboard triggers the kick drum; D1, the snare; E1, the floor tom; and so on. Representing these instruments makes more sense than representing the keyboard used to play these instruments, since C1 in a drum map or drum part, for example, doesn't really play a C1 pitch.

That's why, as shown in Figure 8.12, instead of a keyboard, drum kit–specific information is found in the left portion of the window. You can also notice that each MIDI Note On event is represented by a single triangle in a grid rather than horizontal rectangles with a length value for sustained notes. This doesn't mean that notes can't be sustained but rather that it is not represented in a MIDI drum part.

As with the piano roll editor, you can edit MIDI events in this window. The lower portion of the editor usually displays other channel voice messages such as velocity or control changes. If your sequencer allows you to define a track as being percussion or drum content rather

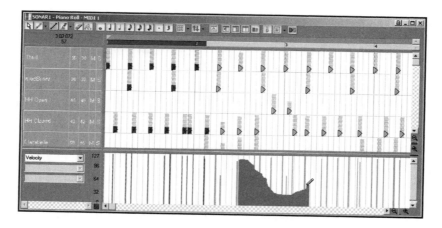

Figure 8.12 The piano roll view of Sonar when a MIDI track is associated with a drum map.

than simply MIDI content, then chances are, double-clicking on the clips contained on these tracks will open up the drum editing window automatically.

The List Editor

The list editor offers a spreadsheet-like view of all events that were recorded for a selected track(s) or part(s) in a track. This is not an editing environment where you fine-tune melodies or cut and paste notes. You may, however, use this environment to find mistakes or pinpoint the source of problems you can't find in other editors or, if they are present there, not as easily editable. Examples include program changes, aftertouch values, and so on. Since MIDI events appear in a list, you can see them in column form, sorted by the order in which they occur. Here's another example: When a track changes its program number every time you start the playback, and this is something you want to fix, the list editor is the place to view and make changes to this type of event. The list editor is a last resort editing environment because it offers a lot of information on each event and is not represented in a music-friendly fashion. In other words, you can use this when you are troubleshooting a track or a project and can't find something in other windows, or to add specific information at a specific location on a track and just want to do this by entering its corresponding values in a table, such as the one found in this window. The list editor is ideal to change the bank select value in a list, to change the velocity of a note from 55 to 90, or to add a MIDI mode change message that will be sent out to the device connected to the track containing these events.

As you can see in Figure 8.13, each column represents a category of information. In this case, the first column represents the type of MIDI event, which also corresponds to the Status byte in a MIDI message, so changing the value in the Data 1 column for the Program Change event at the top of the list would change the patch played by the MIDI destination device. Changing Start and End times of Note events affects when and how long these events are.

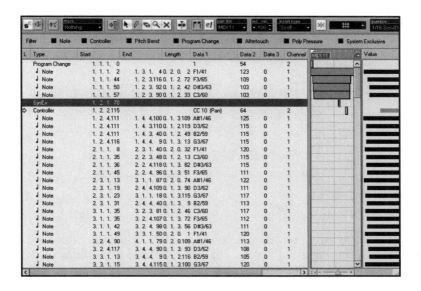

Figure 8.13 Cubase's list editor.

Other Editing Windows

Sequencers offer many other editing environments—some more common than others. Here's a look at some of these other editing windows.

The Score Editor

If you are preparing music for musicians, you will need to create a MIDI recording. Then, using it as the basis for your score layout, you can create individual music sheets for each musician. You could also add notes one by one in notation software, as you will see later, but the information will still remain a MIDI event that you lay out and print, not audio.

As you can see in Figure 8.14, MIDI events become music sheets in the score editor. Obviously, this type of editor will not serve any purpose if you can't read music. But then again, you might use it to learn how to read your own music!

The Tempo and Meter Editor

MIDI sequencers can also store musical information that is needed to reproduce a performance accurately but that has no direct impact on the recording of the performance itself. Among this musical information are tempo changes, time signatures, and meter changes, all of which need to be included in a MIDI sequencer file but are not recorded when the performer plays or records a part.

When playing an intro, finishing a song, or changing the mood anywhere within a song, chances are you might slow down, speed up, or do both. Your song might also start in a 4/4 time signature, later on changing to 6/8. Unless you have programmed these tempo and

Figure 8.14 Cubase's score editor.

meter changes prior to your recording, you will need to add them afterward. This is when a tempo and meter editor comes in handy. The ability to add these changes in a sequencer is important because you want your sequencer to follow these changes so that when you add other parts to this recording, they all fall into place at the appropriate bar and beat. The place to do this is usually a special track that controls the playback of all other tracks. What this special track is called depends on the software you are using, but usually it has its own editing environment. In Figure 8.15, the window displays tempos on the left hand side, a graphical representation in the center, and a list display in the right pane. The tools in the upper portion

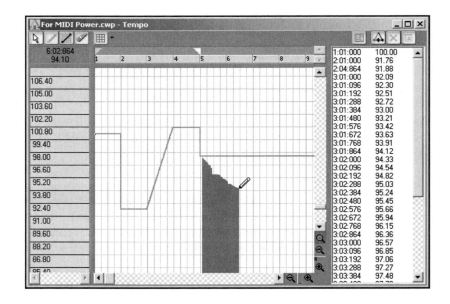

Figure 8.15 Sonar's tempo editor.

of the window allow you to add or erase information through the graphical display or simply enter new values, modify, or erase existing ones in the list display.

Time signatures are also an important part of MIDI sequences. They represent how the music is organized in bars and beats. For example, a 4/4 time signature means that a bar will be made up of four quarter notes, hence the 4/4. The ability to change time signature values in order to reflect the proper bar count in a sequence is crucial. As with the tempo, this also can be found in a control or master track and have its own editing environment.

The Audio Editor

MIDI isn't the only type of data you can record and edit in sequencers. Audio editing is becoming a must-have feature in today's MIDI sequencers. Since audio is very different from MIDI in many ways, editing it is also handled through specific editing environments. Audio editing comes in two basic flavors.

The first type is called non-destructive editing. Non-destructive editing chops up, moves, copies, and edits digital audio without modifying the original digital audio file—hence the name. Non-destructive editing creates references that identify regions and markers in an audio file, pointing to portions of audio used in your sequencer (see Figure 8.16). These references are kept in a separate file and are needed by your sequencer to properly display the audio segments it uses in its project window. Those segments are what you see represented in the clips in this window.

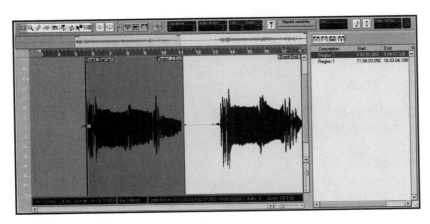

Figure 8.16   Logic's audio editor.

When you delete a clip or segment in the sequencer, you are removing the visual reference to the clip from your project but not the actual digital audio file on the hard disk. This allows greater flexibility when arranging a song or organizing audio on tracks. You can reuse certain audio information over and over again without copying the actual audio file over and over.

The second type of digital audio editing in sequencers is called destructive editing. In destructive editing, the content of the original digital audio file is modified. This type of editing can serve different purposes. You can remove unnecessary portions of audio data to save disk space, normalize the digital audio recording to get a better output level, and remove noise directly in the file rather than have processing applied in real time. This saves processing power for other essential tasks. Another useful application for destructive editing consists in adding tempo and original key information inside the audio file so that sequencers will know how to loop this audio file and keep it in sync with the rest of your project's tempo and key (see Figure 8.17).

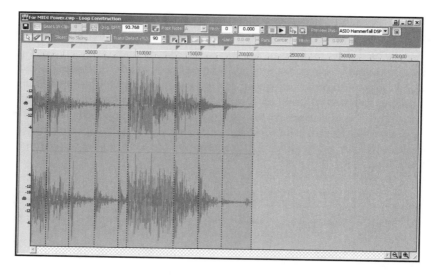

Figure 8.17 The Sonar loop construction editor adds slicing markers in an audio file in order for this file to follow the sequencer's tempo—pitch information can also be added to the audio file.

The Pattern Editor

The term sequencer was coined in reference to hardware sequencing devices when this technology was introduced in the early days of synthesizers. At the time, the idea was that a machine could put in sequence a series of notes and then loop that sequence over and over again. Today, sequencers do much more than that, but the concept of looping a sequence is now referred to as pattern sequencing, or step recording. Because the old school sounds and techniques are back in style, so are the old ways of building songs. Today, however, the way software developers go about it is much more sophisticated and much more flexible, since it uses software programs to emulate what hardware devices could and couldn't do back then. In fact, today you can "sequence" sequences—in other words, create patterns of melodic, harmonic, or rhythmic content that change over time through pattern sequencing. Reason, a software application developed by Propellerhead, offers a self-contained MIDI studio with different virtual synthesizers and an integrated multi-function sequencer. One of those sequencers is called a pattern sequencer. You can create patterns that are saved in banks and program numbers. For example, you may have eight patterns in bank A, eight patterns in bank B, and so on. Then, in your sequence, you can automate these pattern changes through time, going from pattern D8 to A2 to A3 and to A1 (as shown in Figure 8.18). Each pattern corresponds to its own musical element, in this case, a drum pattern played by the Redrum virtual drum machine inside Reason.

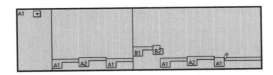

Figure 8.18   Reason's Redrum pattern sequencer.

The Controller Editor

MIDI controllers, as you saw in Chapters 2 and 3, are plentiful. Some sequencers will display them in the same window as the Note On events through the piano roll editor or in the list editor, as seen above. However, some sequencers will also provide a distinct editing environment in which you can view all the MIDI controllers that have been recorded in your project. With the appearance of MIDI remote control devices, controllers are more and more associated with mix automation data. When this is the case, MIDI messages associated with mix automation parameters in an application will appear as individual automation lines associated with their respective parameters.

In Figure 8.19, the first bass track in Ableton's Live software displays track volume automation, which was recorded using an external MIDI remote control device by associating a fader from this device with the track's volume fader. Editing this automation is often done directly along the automation line, wherever it may appear in the corresponding editor.

Saving MIDI Files

As with any other computer application, when you are done working on a project or after you've worked on it for a while, you have to save it. But saving your project file in the sequencer's default format does not mean saving it as a MIDI file. When saving a file, you are saving all kinds of information that is not MIDI related, such as audio mix automation, effects settings, digital audio files location on audio tracks, and much more. If you want to save your project file as a Standard MIDI File, you need to tell the sequencer application that this is how you want to save it. When saving as a Standard MIDI File, only the relevant MIDI events are saved.

So why would you want to save as a MIDI file after working in your sequencer? Here are some reasons that warrant such an operation:

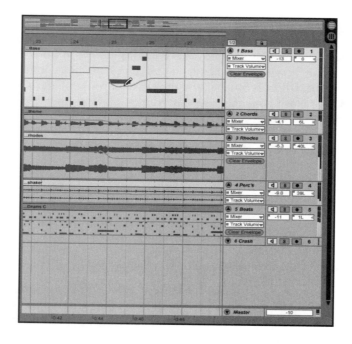

Figure 8.19   Live's Arrangement view displays associated MIDI controller-based automation.

❋ To export this MIDI recording in music notation software if your sequencer does not have notation options. The MIDI file will hold all the notes and track information that will later be used by notation software. It will then be able to convert this MIDI data into music sheets.

❋ Cross application and cross platform compatibility. You will be able to take the MIDI tracks of a project into other applications that may not support the proprietary file format used by your sequencer. Let's say you prepare a song in your own studio. After saving all your tracks in a sequence and exporting the MIDI content to a Standard MIDI File, you can take this MIDI file to another studio and use the equipment they have there, which might sound better than what you have at home. Preparing the tracks in your own studio will save extra studio time, and saving in a Standard MIDI File makes your work compatible with any sequencer application so you won't have to redo the work.

❋ Preparing a file for the Web. You will have to save sequences in a standard MIDI format for online browsers to understand the content of the file when preparing MIDI files for the Internet.

Remember that sequencers will save all the MIDI events, audio events, project settings, automation, loaded software instruments, and software processing settings (such as reverbs, delays, compressors, and other effects in a file) with the sequencer's extension at the end of the filename. You might not see this extension, depending on your computer's configuration, but it will still be part of the file. Save your file in this format if you want to be able to retrieve this non-standard MIDI information later. Most sequencers will not include the digital audio files in this saved project file. However, your project file will contain links to these audio files, so it is important that you remember where the files are or make a copy of them in a safe place. You might want to use a utility in your sequencer to save all the files (including the audio files) used in your project in a single folder on your computer. This makes it easy to back up the information on a CD-R, CD-RW, DVD+R, or any other removable media for safekeeping.

❀ **TIP**

There are two types of computer users: those who have lost information and those who will lose information! This said, making regular backup copies of your work and saving them in a safe location, preferably outside of your working environment, will not only help you retrieve the information in case your computer crashes but will also provide you with a copy of your work in case something really bad happens to your studio, like a flood, fire, or burglary. We often take these things lightly until something happens, and then we freak out because all our work is gone. Replacing your music is as hard as replacing family pictures; once it is gone, it's just about impossible to get it back. So be wise about this.

Other MIDI Programming Options

Some MIDI sequencers add to the set of tools provided by the software through a set of customizable functions using a proprietary programming language included in the software. For example, Sonar uses a language called CAL (Cakewalk Application Language). You can use predefined CAL scripts that act like macro commands inside Sonar to do different tasks, such as adding a dominant seventh chord to existing notes on a track, as shown in Figure 8.20. Another tool similar to this is the Interactive Phrase Synthesizer, or IPS, found in Cubase VST, which generates accompaniment using the MIDI input as source material for its MIDI output.

These tools are meant to extend the possibilities of sequencers and add functionality. Getting to know them might open up new creative possibilities for you.

Notation: From MIDI to Paper

This next section is for those who know how long it takes to transcribe music to paper by hand and wish there was a better way of doing it—especially if your music calls for a complete band with brass, wind, and string sections!

When recording a musical performance, you might not realize it, but you are doing what musicians have been doing for ages, with one exception: You don't have to write everything down on paper as you work because the sequencer remembers what you have just played and lets you edit it. This has spawned new ways of creating music simply because it makes hearing layers of musical events instantaneous. Fifty years ago, musicians had to understand

```
; DOUBLE.CAL
;
; This adds addition octaves above or below the selection of notes.
; An example of use would be to octave a string riff or bass line to make
; it thicker.
;
; Note: Does the same as:
;
;    1. Copy
;    2. Paste to blank track
;    3. Transpose the temporary track by an octave
;    4. Cut the temporary track
;    5. Paste onto the original track
;
; To create more than one octave, the number of steps increases signifigantly.
;
; To use DOUBLE.CAL
;
; Enter how many extra octaves you would like.  (enter a positive number
; To place the octaves above, or a negative to place it below)
;
; Next Enter how much each octave will raise or lower its velocity.
; (A negative number will make the additional octaves softer)
(do
    (int octaves 1)
    (int current 0)
    (int veldrop 0)
    (int direction 1)
    (getInt octaves "How many octaves would you like?" -7 7)
    (getInt veldrop
            "How much velocity should be added to each additional octave?"
            -127
            127)

        (if ( < octaves 0) ; if make octaves below...
                (do
                        (= octaves (- 0 octaves)) ; make # octaves positive
                        (= direction -1))         ; set the direction negative
                (= direction 1))            ; else make the direction positive


    (message "Making " octaves "octaves.  Droping vel. by " veldrop
            "each octave")
)

; body
(if (== Event.Kind NOTE)
    (do
        (= current 0)
            (while (< current octaves) ; while still making octaves for this
note...
                    (do
                        (+= current 1)
                        (insert Event.Time
                                    Event.Chan
                                    NOTE
                                    (+ Note.Key (* (* 12  direction)
current))
                                    (+ Note.Vel (* current veldrop))
                                    Note.Dur)
                    )
                )
    )
)
```

Figure 8.20   An example of a CAL script—the text beginning with a semicolon at the top of the script tells you what the script that follows will do.

music harmony, counterpoint, melodic construction, and rhythmic patterns. They had to hear it all in their minds, play the basic elements on their instrument, write it down on paper, and then bring these sheets of handwritten music to musicians in order to actually hear the end result, making last-minute changes once in the studio. This was very time consuming.

Thankfully, you don't have to deal with this anymore. Now, you can record everything inside a sequencer, assign different instruments to tracks, listen to the result, make changes to the parts that don't work well, and when everything is just like you want it, you can convert your MIDI file into musical notation. The fact that you can record your music in a MIDI environment won't make you come up with better ideas, but being able to hear what you wrote does help you to make things better in the long run.

There are two basic software application types that allow you to make the transition between recorded music to musical notation: music notation applications such as Finale (see Figure 8.21) and sequencer applications that have integrated notation features. Both types of applications will transform MIDI into musical notation or add musical notation symbols directly onto staves on a score.

Figure 8.21 An example of a jazz lead sheet in Finale.

Limitations: MIDI to Notation Conversion

Music transcription is like writing a foreign language. It is filled with scripting rules and exceptions. One of these rules relates to the appearance of notes within bars, where each subdivision of a beat has its space and place in this bar. Since music is a mathematical language, making everything fall in where it should rhythmically is very important when writing down this language. Imagine for a second that you needed to speak Russian, Chinese, Greek, or Arabic. Not only would you need to learn how to speak the language and make sentences, you would also have to learn how to write the language using a completely different set of characters.

Now, let's imagine again that your best friend is Chinese. He has taught you a few words, and you are now able to say a few sentences in this language. That's your first step; now, you may want to write it down. Music notation is just like a foreign language. You can hear it, and you can write it down so that other people can read it and play it. When you play a MIDI instrument and record it, it is like learning how to speak a foreign language. When you want to write it down, it is like learning how to write this language. You may be able to do one, but not necessarily the other. This is where notation software can help you. However, as you will see, there are some limitations to what notation software can do on its own.

First of all, as we've seen, if you want to convert your music into sheet music, it has to be in MIDI format. If you've been working with audio loops and samples, you are out of luck—audio files don't convert well into the MIDI files necessary for conversion into musical notation. Some applications attempt to do this, but they work well only on simple monophonic events and are prone to result in more work to fix things than simply transcribing the original part to begin with.

Another such limitation is the difficulty met when trying to convert freely recorded performances into musical notation. When you record a freestyle improvisation using your MIDI keyboard, for example, you are, as suggested previously, speaking the language. If you want to have this printed out, you will also have to know how to write the language and express it as simply as possible, so the tools provided by the notation software can interpret the meaning of your expression as it tries to follow the music scripting rules.

Finally, converting MIDI into music notation is like converting English to French or vice versa; software is always limited by its programming, and thus it will only interpret what it is programmed to understand. When working with MIDI files, it is important to review the final notation output before printing it. There might be many little details you'll want to correct.

About Musical Notation

Music notation can be broken down into different musical elements. These elements represent different aspects of the music notation, some of which are handled automatically when using a MIDI file to generate the notes for a music score. Others need to be added manually using the tools at your disposal. When you are working on a specific aspect of a score layout, all the related musical elements can be found in one tool palette or one menu. For example, if you want to enter lyrics to a MIDI song file, a lyric tool might be available in a text tool palette or menu, depending on the options available in your software.

The next two sections discuss both the musical elements that may be imported directly from the MIDI file and other musical notation elements that have to be added manually. Examples include slurs between notes, special articulation settings, or dynamic indications such as p, mf, f (piano, mezzo forte, forte). Note that with imported elements from MIDI, your software will use default settings in handling the automatic layout. You might want to customize these settings in order to get better results or to match the settings with the type of music you wish to print.

Musical Elements Automatically Imported from MIDI Files

When converting MIDI events into musical notation, a staff—the place where notes are placed—will be created for each track in the MIDI file. If all the MIDI events are on one track, they will all appear on one staff. To prevent this from happening, separate each instrument (i.e., give each one its own track) beforehand. You read a staff as you would read text, going from left to right. Most staves use five lines when relating melodic or harmonic content that is meant to be played by a tone-based instrument (i.e. an instrument that plays pitched notes, such as a keyboard, violin, or marimba). Placing notes on a staff's line determines its note value in terms of height in a scale, for example, a C, D# (D sharp), or Bb (B flat). The clef at the beginning of the staff will determine exactly which line corresponds to which note.

Typically, monophonic instruments (capable of playing only one note at a time) will use one staff. Polyphonic instruments (capable of playing two or more notes simultaneously, such as a piano) often use two staves to accommodate notes for this part, since their note range will most likely span across these staves.

A clef tells the musician what each note on a staff represents. For example, in Figure 8.22, the first clef in the upper left corner shows a treble clef, telling the musician that the second line from the bottom in the staff represents a G. From that reference point, a musician will know how to read every other note on the staff. In the second row of clefs, the center position of the clef indicates where the C is in the staff. A bass clef tells the musician where the F key is, and so on.

Clefs will be added automatically to each staff. Your musical notation will attempt to assign a clef corresponding to the note range content of the instrument. However, you can change

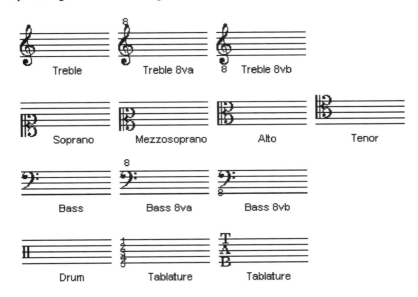

Figure 8.22 Different musical clefs.

the default assignment for a clef if it makes it difficult to read the notes. In Figure 8.23, both staves are playing an identical bass line, but the top staff uses a treble clef, which was assigned by default. Because the notes are lower than the five lines provided by the staff with this clef, additional lines are added. This makes it difficult to read, and a bass player would not be accustomed to this notation. That's why it is better to change to a bass clef for this part as shown in the lower staff of this figure. Notes will appear in the center of the staff, making it easier to read.

Figure 8.23 The top staff shows notes displayed using the treble clef, while the bottom staff shows the same notes displayed with the bass clef.

The MIDI event lengths determine the notes' length values. When playing a part, you might not play precisely on a beat's subdivision, or you might not hold the notes for as long as they should be held. For example, you might anticipate the third beat slightly and hold the note for just under a half-note value. But in reality, you would like this to be represented by a half-note occurring on the third beat of this bar. This may not be a bad thing when you want to add feel to your music. However, when converting your performance to music notation, avoid having unnecessary information that makes it harder to read. In Figure 8.24, both staves play the same line, but the top one hasn't been quantized, and no measures were taken to tell the notation software how to optimize the display of events. The lower staff's events have been quantized, and some optimization options were selected to tell the application how to create a cleaner display of MIDI events.

Figure 8.24 A before (top staff) and after (bottom staff) MIDI quantize view.

Notes are the graphic representations of MIDI Note On events. Usually, in a staff, when no notes are played, silences are inserted to tell the musician to count while waiting for new notes to be played. Figure 8.25 shows the most common types of note length values, their musical representation when a note is played, their silence representation when no notes are played, and in the last column, how many notes of this length are needed to fill a 4/4 bar.

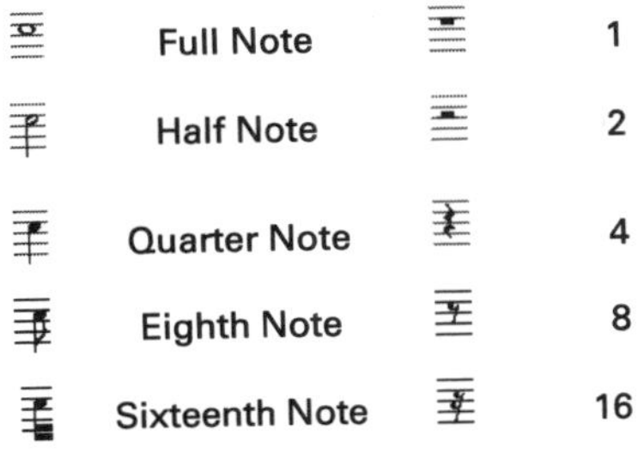

𝄻	Full Note	𝄻	1
𝄼	Half Note	𝄼	2
𝄽	Quarter Note	𝄽	4
𝄾	Eighth Note	𝄾	8
𝄿	Sixteenth Note	𝄿	16

Figure 8.25 Most common note length names with their musical representation, which includes how these values are represented when no notes are played.

The MIDI file's time signature is always added automatically at the beginning of a song. If the time signature changes during the song, a new time signature is added automatically at the appropriate location.

Time signatures represent the metric division of music. It is usually displayed as a fraction over an integer. The integer represents the value of the beat subdivision, and the fraction represents the number of beats in the bar. For example, a 4/4 bar has four quarter notes per bar, 6/8 has six eighth notes per bar, 2/2 has two half-notes per bar, and so on. This influences how you count the music and how notes will be divided in bars.

When more than two eighth notes or shorter are played in a row, usually the notation application will create a beam that ties these notes together. This notation rule makes it more obvious to see the beat definition when many notes appear in a single bar. This is done automatically, but you can also change the way notes are beamed together, as displayed in Figure 8.26. In the first bar of the top staff, the beats are grouped automatically, but on the first bar of the second staff, the sixteenth-notes have custom beams. Customizing beams can be used to emphasize certain rhythmical phrases or patterns as you see appropriate.

Figure 8.26 Example of how you can beam different groups of notes together.

A key signature indicates the scale or key used in a song or a portion of a song. When a note is played outside this key, an "accidental" note tells the musician that a note doesn't belong to this key. It is important to identify the key at the beginning of each staff for each instrument; otherwise, the notation application might add an unnecessary number of accidental notes in the staff, making it more difficult to read. In Figure 8.27, the top staff displays a key signature, since this melody is played in the key of F sharp (F#). By adding a key signature, you make the notes easier to read in the staff. Otherwise, you would have to add accidentals, as shown in the lower staff in the same figure. In both cases, the end result remains the same, but these additional accidentals are not as easy to read. In some cases, accidentals are unavoidable; however, assigning the right key signature to a staff will minimize their use.

Figure 8.27 An example of accidental notes combined with key signatures.

Page and measure or bar numbers are important for musicians because they serve as reference points. For example, when practicing a song, a musician might refer to page 4, bar 22. This helps other musicians to quickly pinpoint the location of a musical event in a part. Usually, this is added automatically by the notation application. You may also add other custom reference points such as section names.

Musical Elements Added Manually

The following elements are part of the musical layout but are not elements that can be converted from the MIDI events directly because they relate to layout features that are not recorded through MIDI. You will need to consult your notation software documentation in order to use most of these features. An application, depending on its notation-editing capabilities, might not support some of these elements.

At the beginning of a song, an incomplete bar is called a pickup bar, which leads in to the first full bar of the song. You will need to tell the notation software how to handle this, since pickup bars are usually not counted in the bar counts. As you can see in Figure 8.28, the first bar is incomplete, showing only three eighth notes out of a possible eight.

Figure 8.28 An example of a pickup bar at the beginning of a song.

When creating a MIDI file, you set the sequencer to play at a specific tempo setting. However, this tempo setting might not appear by default on a printed page. It is important to tell the musician at what tempo this song should be played. You can add tempo settings at the beginning of the file, as shown in Figure 8.28 at the top of the first staff.

Bar lines are used to define the boundaries of a bar. Normal bar lines are added automatically in a score at the end of each bar. You can, however, use special bar lines that will indicate a change of section or the end of a piece or tell the musician to go back to a specific bar and repeat the content found between specially marked bars, as displayed in Figure 8.29.

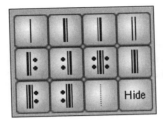

Figure 8.29 Selecting the proper bar lines tells a musician which bars should be repeated.

Special non-standard shapes for note heads (Figure 8.30) are used to represent percussion instruments or spoken words. You can use special note heads included in a notation application to create this effect manually.

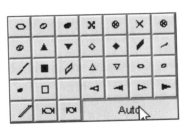

Figure 8.30 Non-standard note heads.

Guitar chords, tablatures, and chord names are other aspects of musical writing that can be incorporated into a score to give additional information to musicians. In fact, if you are preparing a jazz or improvisational piece, giving a chord structure along with a melodic line and some rhythmic indications might be all you need.

When playing music, you don't always play the notes the same way. Sometimes notes are hit hard, and other times you gently stroke the keys. You might also want to slur between two notes to give it a distinct color. Although this information might be recorded in your MIDI file, it is unlikely to translate well into musical notation. Ties, slurs, and other interpretation markings are also useful to give the musician indications on how to play melodic, rhythmic, or harmonic content. Notation software usually provides tools to add different types of indications, as shown in Figure 8.31.

Figure 8.31   Adding articulation, ties, and slurs to indicate how certain notes should be played.

Lyrics are not, by nature, musical events. However, they are part of songs, and as such can be included on musical sheets. As you can see in Figure 8.32, you can type lyrics below or above your notes and have the text follow the note spacing so that if you add more notes or more text, the layout will be adjusted appropriately.

Figure 8.32   Adding lyrics to your music.

These are only a few aspects of musical notation in relation to MIDI file conversion. You will find that creating scores using MIDI and notation software can be quite engaging. Who knows, you might even want to go into the music publication business once you're done exploring the possibilities these tools offer.

Scanning Musical Scores

Some notation software may provide tools to convert already written sheet music into MIDI files, although this requires a scanner and a good printed version of the music you wish to scan. This is, by all means, not an exact science. So, the more information besides notes, staves, bar lines, key signature, and clefs there is, the more difficult it will be for the computer. It is as complex to convert a graphic file into MIDI information as it is to scan a graphic file and have software understand what the picture is about.

Score Sequence and Performance Sequence

Chances are, when creating music using a sequencer, you most likely will work on this music until you get everything just right. This can mean spending time recording the perfect interpretation of all your parts, tweaking each one of them until they sound just right to your ears. If you want to create music sheets for musicians, then stop, save your file, make a copy of this file, and rename it. By using the renamed copy of your file, you can now make changes to the MIDI parts that are not well suited for an audio rendering but are well suited for a musical transcription.

For example, you could quantize all your musical events so that they appear correctly in your score. The idea is to optimize your file for score, not for sound. Since what might sound good to your ears might not be well suited for MIDI notation conversion, it is better to not touch the original version of your MIDI file. When working in the music notation part of your sequencer or in a notation application, you will end up with a MIDI recording that might not sound as "musical" as your original copy, since it is meant to look better than it sounds. Having a copy of your work offers the best of both worlds.

Review Questions

1. What is the appropriate question for the following statement: An application that records MIDI events and plays them back as they were recorded.
   a) What is a software instrument?
   b) What is an audio multi-track recorder?
   c) What is a sequencer?
   d) What is an operating system?

2. What is the appropriate question for the following statement: Adjusts the performance timing by aligning minor rhythmic imperfections in a performance to a predefined meter grid.
   a) What is quantizing?
   b) What is transposing?
   c) What is automation?
   d) What is buffering?

3. Which of the following editing procedures can be applied to both MIDI and audio events but do not affect the audio quality when applied to digital audio?
   a) Transposing
   b) Changing the tempo
   c) Cutting, copying, or moving
   d) All of the above

4. Select the appropriate ending for this statement: MIDI recorded in a sequencer always plays_____.
   a) on the same MIDI channel coming from the track's MIDI input.
   b) on the same MIDI channel assigned to the track's MIDI output.
   c) on the same MIDI channel found on the hardware device connected to the MIDI track.
   d) on the MIDI channel set by the MIDI interface.

5. Select the appropriate ending for this statement: To simultaneously record MIDI from more than one source on two separate MIDI tracks, you will need _____.

   a) more than one software instrument.

   b) more than one sequencer.

   c) more than one musician.

   d) more than one available MIDI channel or MIDI port.

6. In a sequencer, what does the punch-in time represent?

   a) It marks the beginning point at which the existing MIDI events on the track will be replaced by the newly recorded events.

   b) It marks the end point at which the existing MIDI events on the track will stop being replaced by the newly recorded events.

   c) It marks the beginning point at which new MIDI events will appear after they have been pasted from a clipboard.

   d) It marks the beginning of a song or project inside a MIDI sequencer.

7. What does the following sentence describe: An editing environment where MIDI events appear, passing from right to left or from beginning to end, and the lower notes appear at the bottom of the display while higher notes appear at the top.

   a) The main window of a MIDI editor

   b) A list editor inside a MIDI sequencer

   c) A piano roll editor inside a MIDI sequencer

   d) A score editor inside a MIDI sequencer

8. I am a MIDI editor displaying the pitch of Note On events as individual instruments rather than actual pitches and only display the start time, not the lengths of these events. What am I?

   a) A piano roll editor

   b) A drum editor

   c) A list editor

   d) A score editor

9. Which of the following type of MIDI events can't be recorded in a MIDI track while recording other MIDI performance events?

   a) Control change messages

   b) Channel voice messages

   c) Tempo and meter changes

   d) None of the above

10. True or False: You can't convert audio loops imported in a sequencer project into musical notation without converting the loops into MIDI events first.

9 MIDI Software: A Sound Creation Environment

In the past five years, MIDI has taken somewhat of a back seat to progressions in digital audio. The fact that computers are now capable of handling so much information with such great speed and reliability changed the world of sound creation by integrating big studio technology in small studio setups—and those developments had many wondering what would happen with MIDI.

In reality, the arrival of software instruments not only proved that MIDI isn't dead but has given it a second wind, influencing how musicians around the globe create music. Software instruments are providing an alternative to MIDI hardware device setups, just as digital audio workstations have given multi-track recording artists the tools they needed to produce better quality material in the comfort of their own home studios.

Getting rid of MIDI hardware altogether is an option but not a recommended one—MIDI sound modules still offer much in the way of processing power, sound quality, and the much-desired tactile surface to control its parameters. However, software sound modules offer even more flexibility, and computers are now capable of handling an even greater number of tasks, making them the perfect hosts for these applications.

Here's what you will learn in this chapter:

* What software instruments are.

* How software instruments integrate into your computer environment.

* The difference between plug-ins and stand-alone software instruments.

* The best plug-in standard for you.

* The advantages and disadvantages of software instruments.

* How audio hardware drivers affect software instrument behavior.

* What virtual MIDI ports are.

* How to use a software instrument with your sequencer.

* How to automate your software instrument's parameters in your sequencer.

❋ Editor/librarian: Why you need one.

❋ How to work with an editor/librarian software application.

❋ How you can convert MIDI tracks into audio tracks.

❋ How you can use MIDI to automate your mix using a sequencer.

Software Instruments

There are many types of sound modules—analog and digital synthesizers, samplers, sample playback synthesizers, and drum machines. All of these devices serve a purpose in a MIDI studio. Imagine having the sound creation potential of these machines inside your computer. You can stop imagining now because that's what software instruments are. With the exception of true analog synthesis, software instruments emulate the creative power behind these devices. The buttons, knobs, and controls you would find on a real synthesizer are reproduced on your computer screen in great detail in some cases. Other software instrument developers use the fact that they are not tied to a hardware device to push the design envelope one step further, offering very funky-looking interfaces. In the end, it all comes down to the sound these software instruments produce, and in many cases, they will offer you more control over the sound than their hardware counterparts were ever capable of delivering.

So, if you can't afford a $3,000 hardware sound module, you might just find what you need in a $300 software application!

What Is a Software Instrument?

A software instrument, also called soft synth or virtual instrument, is an application written to emulate a hardware MIDI device. It has the same types of controls as its hardware counterpart (see Figure 9.1), and in some cases, the developers will pitch in a few extra features that are usually not included in the traditional hardware device. In other cases, software instruments approach sound creation in a way that has only been seen in computer environments. So, in this respect, they are a breed of their own.

The idea can be brought down to a simple concept: A software instrument uses a computer's processing power to emulate synthesizers, samplers, and drum machines, and the audio hardware's outputs serve as the audio outputs to monitor the signal or record it as a digital audio signal.

Currently, there are three categories of software instruments:

❋ Stand-alone applications

❋ Standard plug-in formats

❋ Proprietary applications

The stand-alone category is a software application just like any other that runs on its own. It uses a MIDI interface or MIDI port to receive MIDI events and the computer's audio hardware to monitor the audio output. Stand-alone versions do not load inside another application, unlike the plug-in instruments discussed next. When working with stand-alone software

❋❋❋

Figure 9.1 Examples of software instruments.

instruments, virtual audio and MIDI connections between a sequencer and the software instrument must exist in order to use the instrument with the sequencer. This said, using a sequencer is not required, and a stand-alone software instrument can certainly act as a hardware synth, where the computer serves as the brain for the processing taking place in an actual hardware synthesizer.

The plug-in category comes in different formats. For example, plug-ins written in DirectX are supported by Cakewalk through its DXi format (DirectX Instruments). The VST or VSTi format (Virtual Studio Technology Instruments) developed by Steinberg is supported by an ever-growing number of software developers. For example, Ableton's Live 5 and up support VST instruments, and so does Sony's ACID Pro 4. AU, or Audio Units, is another plug-in format developed by Apple that adds functionality to audio applications. Along with the VST format, AU is probably the most popular plug-in format on the OS X platform. HTDM (Host Time Division Multiplexing) is a format developed by Digidesign and meant to add software instrument capability to its line of software (ProTools being the most famous one). HTDM is a combination of TDM and RTAS (Real-Time AudioSuite), which gives the ProTools family access to software instruments just as the VST and DirectX standards do.

Note that Digidesign now provides a VST wrapper, making it possible to use VST instruments within the ProTools environment. Wrappers are small programs that convert one format into the next, acting as a "go for," fetching instructions for the host application. For Digital Performer (from MOTU) users, the MAS (MOTU Audio System) format is supported as well as VST plug-ins if you have the VST Wrapper application, which allows VST plug-ins to be used in Digital Performer. You can find more information on the VST Wrapper at this Web address: www.audioease.com. The software developer FXPansion also provides a VST-AU adapter that translates, or "wraps," VST plug-ins into AU-compatible plug-ins for Mac OS X users. This type of adapter makes it possible to use VST plug-ins you already own in Apple's Logic Audio 6 software.

The proprietary category works in specific sequencer host applications, such as Apple's line of software instruments for Logic Audio or even Creamware's selection of software/hardware solutions (see Figure 9.2). Creamware offers software instruments that work only with its audio hardware but can be integrated or controlled by other MIDI sequencers. Contrary to plug-ins and stand-alone versions, proprietary versions require their own hardware or software host. For example, without a Creamware audio hardware supporting the software instrument made for it, the software instrument won't run at all, as it will be looking for a device on the computer that does not exist.

Which technology to use depends on your needs and your current setup. For example, if you are already using Cubase as your sequencer, chances are you will want to continue using the VST standard. On the other hand, nothing prevents you from using any number of standards in your computer. In fact, Cubase is compatible with DirectX plug-ins; however, it's not compatible with the DXi standard, as it has been developed by a direct competitor (Cakewalk).

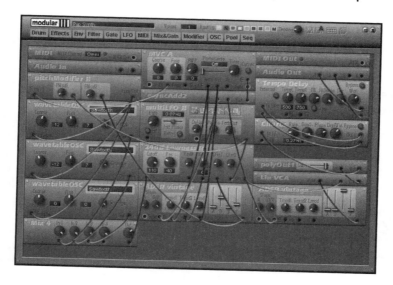

Figure 9.2 The Modular III is an example of a proprietary software instrument.

Also, while the DXi standard is based on the DirectX standard, its implementation inside Cakewalk does not allow it to function inside Cubase, but it is supported by a number of other DirectX-compatible applications, such as FL Studio, Celemony's Melodyne, and many more.

As for proprietary solutions such as the ones proposed by Creamware, some of them may offer cross-application compatibility. You will, however, need to find out what works and what doesn't before you purchase any software instrument—to avoid getting an application that does not work with your current creative environment. As technology moves quickly in this area, the best way to keep up to date with standards is through the developers' online Web sites. Make sure to visit the support Web site for links to these resources.

✳ WHAT IS A PLUG-IN?

A plug-in is a software application that runs within a host application, adding functionality to the application. For example, a software synthesizer plug-in adds the function of a synthesizer to sequencer software; a reverb plug-in adds algorithms with adjustable parameters to create a reverb effect in multi-track hard disk audio recording software. Each host application is compatible with one or more plug-in application formats. On a PC, the most common plug-in standards are DirectX and VST. On a Macintosh computer, the most common plug-in standards are VST, AU, TDM, and MAS. Plug-ins are installed separately in their own folder or in a folder that is common to all host applications, depending on the plug-in format. For example, it is recommended to install all VST plug-ins in a common folder that all VST-compatible hosts can share. Because all VST plug-ins share this common folder, the host applications can all point to this common location, reducing the space required by additional installations of the same plug-in. With DirectX plug-ins, you need to install DirectX support if it is not already installed.

Once DirectX support is installed, install the plug-in in an appropriate folder. As the DirectX plug-in is installed, an entry is made in the DirectX library database found in the DirectX folder. All host applications supporting DirectX plug-ins will be able to recognize a DirectX plug-in installed anywhere on your computer. When you load the host application to memory, it scans the library database to find any compatible plug-ins it can use and loads them in the appropriate plug-in menu inside the application. You can download the latest DirectX support file from this URL: www.microsoft.com/windows/directx.

There are a few advantages to using software instruments:

* ✳ Diversity—They can create sounds using a diverse set of controls, which are not limited to the hardware wiring of a real synth. In some applications, you can create your own signal path to create new ways of producing sounds.

* ✳ Economy—Because everything depends on your computer and not an external device, you don't have to pay for the additional hardware components. Program development is not cheap, but when you compare it to the cost of developing and producing an actual synthesizer or sampler, it is clear that a CD in a box will cost less than a 25Kg keyboard with all its parts.

* ✳ Flexibility—Software applications, by nature, are flexible tools. When you want an application to do something, you simply program it. When you work with a hardware sampler, the only upgrades come in the form of a newer model. But flexibility is also about being able to use multiple instances of the software, loading the soft synth more

than once in the same song, giving you the equivalent of two or more synthesizers. Have you ever dreamed of having a rack filled with synths to work with? Now it's possible. Furthermore, because most software instruments are routed through a virtual mixer (provided in any DAW or software sequencer), you can apply a number of audio processes to its audio output and keep each output separate. With hardware devices, the outputs are often limited, and unless you record the audio outputs of these MIDI devices, processing is limited to what is included inside the device itself.

While these are advantages, you should be aware that software instruments also come with some disadvantages:

⁂ Processing power limitations—A hardware MIDI device provides its own processing power, while software instruments do not. When using soft synths, a computer must handle all required processing power for the application. Not only does the computer have to run the sequencer application, read audio tracks, and record audio tracks to and from a hard disk, it also has to process any software instrument applications. Chances are, the more flexible and powerful those instruments are, the more processor intensive they will be. While software coding is made more efficient and less processing intensive with each new revision of the application, the combined number of processes running on a single computer can quickly turn a workhorse in to a stubborn mule that doesn't want to move.

⁂ Memory limitations—Software synthesizers are loaded in your computer's memory. The more RAM (random access memory) you have, the more applications you will be able to run and the more smoothly they will run. Software samplers might also use your RAM to load a portion of their sounds. If you have limited RAM, you will be limited in the number of sounds you can load simultaneously.

⁂ Hard disk speed limitations—When working with software samplers, not only are you using RAM, but you are also using your hard disk as an audio streaming device. If you are running this application along with an audio multi-track or sequencer application, you are putting your hard disk in overdrive, accessing a lot of information simultaneously. Having a fast hard disk will help postpone clicks, pops, crackles, dropouts, and other nasty little side effects caused by reading errors when the disk access requests become overwhelming. It is recommended that your hard disk be no slower than 7,200 RPM and have an access time averaging around 10 ms or better. Even at these speeds, there will be a moment when the hard disk will no longer be able to respond to all disk access demands if the quantity of samples loaded into a software sampler, combined with a large number of audio tracks, surpasses its capacity.

⁂ Sound quality—Since your audio hardware ultimately produces the sound, the quality of its digital-to-analog converters will be an important factor in the quality of the output signal as well. Getting audio hardware that sounds good becomes increasingly important as you rely on it more than ever with this type of tool.

Audio Hardware Drivers and Software Instruments

Since software instruments use your audio hardware for their audio outputs, good audio hardware providing low noise outputs and well-written drivers is essential. How quickly the sound can be generated and converted from digital to analog will make all the difference in the world when playing with the software instrument. In fact, if you don't have audio hardware that supports the standards required by these software instruments, or if your audio hardware doesn't have the proper drivers, you can almost forget about using software instruments altogether. It's that simple.

If you don't have proper drivers, this is what happens: When you are playing on a keyboard, the MIDI information travels to the sequencer and then to the software instrument, which processes the information and sends the digital audio information to your operating system. The OS takes the data and forwards it to the audio hardware's digital-to-analog audio converters. That's when you hear the sound. Most likely, at this point, there is a delay that occurs between the time you presses on the key and the time you hear the sound. This delay is called latency: the delay between the input and the output.

To avoid latency problems, you need to bypass the operating system and stream the information directly from the software instrument to the audio hardware. To do this, you need a specially designed driver. There are a few standards out there that may help:

❋ The ASIO (Audio Stream Input/Output) and ASIO2 drivers have been developed by Steinberg to optimize the stream of audio information inside your computer. If you use any Steinberg, you should make sure the audio hardware has an ASIO driver if you want to enjoy your soft synth experience on PC-compatible computers and pre-OS X Macintosh users. Macintosh users with OS X use Core Audio drivers provided with the OS or through a more recent version found on the audio hardware manufacturer's Web site.

❋ The GSIF (GigaStudio InterFace) driver developed by Tascam will greatly improve the stream of digital audio information inside your computer, as with the ASIO drivers. If you use any Giga products (GigaStudio or GigaSampler), having an audio hardware with GSIF support will reduce the chances of having bad experiences with software instruments.

❋ DirectX, WDM (Windows Driver Model), and E-WDM (Enhanced Windows Driver Model) support for any DirectX or (E-)WDM-compatible software instrument is essential. This means having the latest driver versions installed on your PC-compatible computer. Both drivers are developed around Microsoft technology to provide better data processing and compatibility within the Windows environment.

❋ The EASI (Enhanced Audio Streaming Interface) driver, developed by Apple (formerly developed by Emagic), is similar to Steinberg's ASIO driver in the sense that it optimizes the audio stream by bypassing the OS. Although pre-OS X Macintosh computers supported ASIO and ASIO 2 drivers, if your main working environment is made up of Logic products, you might want to find audio hardware with a driver written in this format.

Once again, if your Macintosh operates under OS X, EASI is replaced by the Core Audio drivers.

❋ It is possible that by the time you read this, there will be new driver technology out there that provides even better audio hardware access for software instruments. Stay alert on this topic by visiting manufacturers' and software developers' Web sites, as well as appropriate newsgroups, since using the best driver technology available to address your audio hardware will help you get better results from your software instrument.

You can get an audio hardware compatibility list to find out which audio hardware supports which standard and also find out how particular audio hardware performs in a specific hardware/software combination. To get this list, you may visit your sequencer or software instrument's Web site and search for tested audio hardware. Visit the support site (www.wavedesigners.com) for this book and navigate in the Links section to find additional updated links to these resources.

Additional MIDI Ports

When using a software instrument, you are basically loading a virtual synthesizer in your computer. You access this virtual synthesizer or control its functions through its graphical interface. To send MIDI messages to this software instrument, you configure the instrument to receive MIDI messages through one of the MIDI input ports installed on your computer. When you want to use your software instrument in a sequencer environment as a plug-in or as stand-alone software controlled by the sequencer, you need to tell your sequencer application to send MIDI events it receives to this software instrument. That's where virtual MIDI ports come in.

A virtual MIDI port is, for all intents and purposes, identical to a hardware MIDI port. It sends and receives MIDI events over a maximum of 16 different MIDI channels. It also contains its own name when used inside of a sequencer application. For example, if you are using the GigaStudio sampler, this application will create a number of virtual MIDI ports in your computer, as shown in Figure 9.3, each of which is given a separate name. You can then decide to make a "virtual" MIDI connection to or from this port by selecting it inside your sequencer, just as you would any other port. The same applies for DXi, VSTi, or any other software instrument. Because these ports are, by definition, "virtual," you don't need to make a physical connection. However, you do need to make a virtual connection by assigning the output of a MIDI track to such a port, as discussed in Chapter 8.

All currently available software instruments create their own MIDI ports when they are loaded, both as stand-alone instruments and as plug-ins. In some cases, a software instrument will create permanent MIDI ports that will stay on your computer even when the instrument is not loaded into memory. These ports can be accessed directly from a sequencer when selecting which MIDI Out port to use for a specific track. By selecting this port in a sequencer, you are routing the MIDI messages to the application's MIDI input, as displayed in Figure 9.4. As you can see in this figure, it is the stand-alone software instrument that sends the digital audio information to your audio hardware in order to monitor the software's audio output.

❋ ❋ ❋

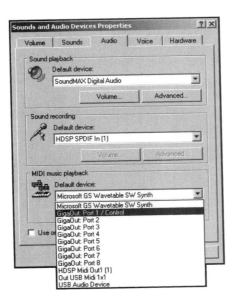

Figure 9.3 GigaStudio creates permanent virtual MIDI ports in an XP system's Sounds and Audio Devices Properties configuration.

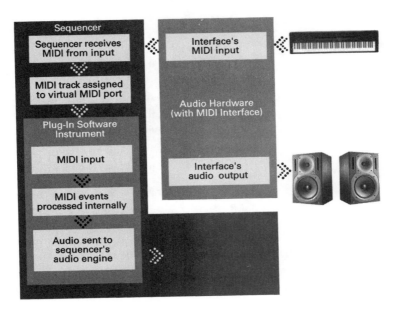

Figure 9.4 Routing of a MIDI signal from its MIDI interface input to a stand-alone software instrument, while passing through a MIDI sequencer.

When the software instrument application is a plug-in within a host application, the routing is similar. Instead of routing the MIDI signal to an external application, however, the MIDI will be routed internally to the plug-in, as shown in Figure 9.5.

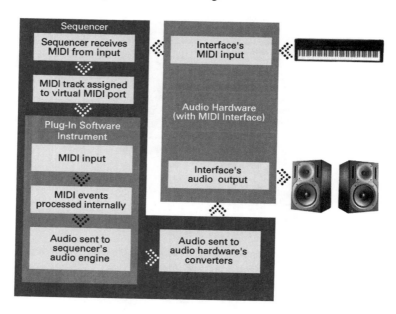

Figure 9.5 Routing of a MIDI signal from its MIDI interface input to a plug-in software instrument while passing through a MIDI sequencer.

When loading a plug-in software instrument inside a sequencer, a virtual MIDI port is created to accommodate this plug-in. Selecting this virtual port as the destination for MIDI events makes it possible to monitor the audio output of this virtual device through the audio outputs of the installed audio hardware.

Stand-Alone Software Instruments

Stand-alone software instruments offer working environments that do not require the use of additional software to host the application, so they are not plug-ins to this host application. In other words, you can run the application on its own and trigger the instrument using an external controller keyboard or through a representation of a keyboard onscreen. It is recommended to use an external keyboard controller to play these software instruments as you would any hardware sound module.

When installing a stand-alone software instrument, you can configure the application to respond to a MIDI input, just as you would configure your sequencer to respond to incoming MIDI input from one of your MIDI interface's MIDI ports. In all other aspects, it is a software application that works on its own, just like a word processor or graphics editing software.

Figure 9.6 GigaStudio from Tascam is an example of a stand-alone software sampler.

Inside the application environment, you may use the editing tools that are at your disposal to edit sounds, save sounds, and create sound banks. In Figure 9.6, you can see Tascam's GigaStudio interface. This and other applications in the same category take sampling to a new level of editing flexibility and overall sampling process, since it allows you to edit sample programs directly in the computer through a graphic interface. Once the sample programs are saved, you can load them into memory and assign them to specific MIDI channels. After you have configured the application to receive MIDI messages, you can play it just as you would a hardware sampler. GigaStudio also offers a mixing environment to route samples through effects (the effect can be seen in the lower right corner of Figure 9.6), allowing you to further process each sound before it is sent to the audio hardware's outputs.

To use this stand-alone sampler application with your favorite sequencer, you can configure GigaStudio to launch your sequencer from its interface (see Figure 9.7). This will allow you to use the sounds loaded in the sampler in your sequencer.

Once in your sequencer, you will need to choose the appropriate MIDI port so that the MIDI messages are routed to the sampler application. In this case, the MIDI ports that will appear in your sequencer will be labeled appropriately to identify this application, as shown in Figure 9.8.

With some stand-alone applications, you will need to launch the sequencer before you can call it from within the other application. Once the sequencer is loaded, you can load the

Figure 9.7 Launching an external sequencer from a stand-alone application.

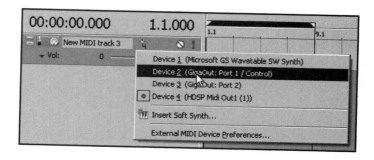

Figure 9.8 Selecting the Tascam GigaStudio MIDI port in your sequencer application.

software instrument to activate its virtual ports inside the sequencer. Read the documentation from your sequencer and software instrument to find out exactly how to proceed and in which order the software has to be loaded.

What Is ReWire?

ReWire is a technology developed by Steinberg and Propellerhead Software. It connects different software applications together using virtual audio and MIDI cables. In fact, by activating ReWire channels in the host application, you are patching the virtual audio outputs of other ReWire-compatible software into the host's mixing environment. By allowing the audio to stream between applications, it also provides a sample accurate synchronization between the two applications. Furthermore, you can lock transport controls such as playback, stop, rewind, and record functions from any connected ReWire applications. In other words, when you press Play in one application, all the connected ReWire applications will start playback in sync with the master application's MIDI tempo. ReWire can create up to 64 audio channels in your sequencer's mixer window.

Ableton Live, Adobe Audion, Cakewalk Sonar, Digidesign ProTools, Apple Logic Pro, MOTU Digital Performer, Sony ACID, Steinberg Cubase, and Nuendo are all ReWire-compatible host applications.

Some stand-alone software instruments will offer interconnectivity between applications through internal audio connections made between these applications. ReWire, as described in the Previous Note, represents one way of connecting a stand-alone software application to a sequencer. Propellerhead's Reason software (see Figure 9.9) is a stand-alone application that incorporates a variety of software instruments and a sequencer application bundled together—among those instruments, you will find a synthesizer, two types of samplers, a drum machine, and a variety of effects and other modules to process these instruments.

Figure 9.9 An example of a ReWire 2-compatible application: Reason.

For example, if you are using Cubase with an application such as Reason, which is a ReWire 2-compatible application, you would load Cubase into memory, activate ReWire channels (see bullet 1 in Figure 9.10), and then launch Reason. In Figure 9.10, you can see that Reason has been loaded and, in bullet 2, the Audio Out of Reason shows that ReWire is active. Therefore, all audio is being patched through ReWire, slaving Reason to the ReWire host. Reason is considered stand-alone software, since it runs independently from any other software. Once you have loaded software instruments inside Reason, they will become available as MIDI port destinations in the host application. Any ReWire2 application offering software instruments can be triggered and controlled from the sequencer's interface. In bullet 3 of Figure 9.10, all instruments that are loaded in Reason appear as additional MIDI output ports in the MIDI port output selection in Cubase's MIDI track options.

Figure 9.10 Activating ReWire channels to access additional software instruments.

Plug-In Software Instruments

A plug-in software instrument can offer the same benefits as a stand-alone version. In fact, many such plug-ins are offered as stand-alone versions as well. However, when using plug-ins, you must install the appropriate plug-in version that corresponds to the host's supported format, as mentioned at the beginning of this chapter. Once you have installed a plug-in software instrument, you are ready to use it as a MIDI-controllable instrument inside compatible host-sequencer software.

In Figure 9.11, the MIDI track's output (bullet 1 in this figure) is assigned to the Stylus RMX (bullet 2 in this figure) software instrument. Events played on this track will be relayed to the

Figure 9.11   Example of a VST Instrument plug-in and its MIDI track output assignment in Cubase.

instrument and will be routed to one of the eight stereo audio channels the instrument provides (bullet 3 in this figure).

In Cubase, to assign a VST instrument to a track:

1. Select the VST Instrument panel from the Panels menu.
2. In the VST Instrument panel, select an installed VST instrument from the drop-down menu (see Figure 9.12).
3. Select the track you wish to use to control the VST instrument.
4. In the selected track, choose the appropriate MIDI port corresponding to this VST instrument (see Figure 9.13).
5. Now, select a MIDI channel for this instrument.
6. Finally, choose a program number or name from the instrument's program list and start playing.

In Sonar, to assign a DX instrument to a track:

1. Right-click in the track area and create a MIDI track.
2. Right-click again in the track area and create an audio track.
3. Expand both tracks so that you can see their properties.

Figure 9.12   Choosing an instrument from the VST instrument's drop-down menu.

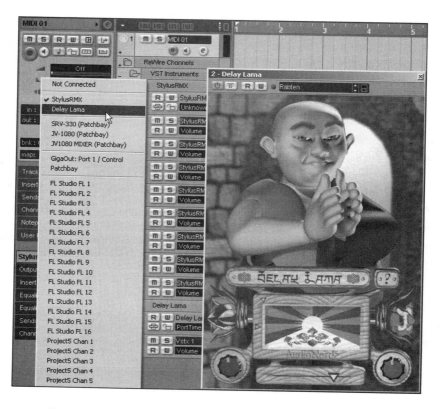

Figure 9.13   Assigning the loaded VST instrument's virtual MIDI port.

4. Right-click in the FX section of the audio track and choose the DX Instruments from the context menu, then choose the appropriate DX instrument you wish to use (see Figure 9.14).

5. Now, go back to the MIDI track you just created and choose the DXi's virtual MIDI port from the MIDI output's menu, as shown in Figure 9.15.

6. Choose a MIDI channel for this virtual instrument.

7. Choose a program name or number for the instrument's presets and start playing.

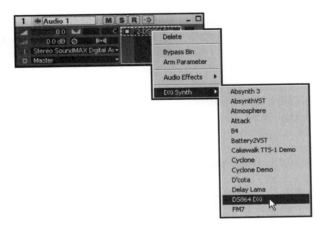

Figure 9.14 In Sonar, the software instrument is assigned to the audio track as an audio FX.

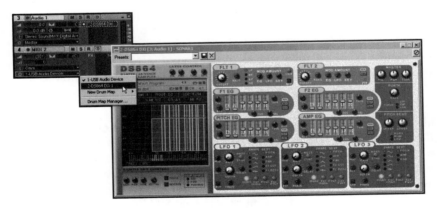

Figure 9.15 Assigning the MIDI track to play on the newly created virtual MIDI port corresponding to the DXi instrument.

These are only two examples where software instruments are loaded inside a sequencer environment. In both cases, the MIDI setup makes sure the MIDI events are routed from an external keyboard controller to the software instrument itself. In both cases again, the audio output of the software instrument appears as an audio channel in the application's mixing environment where it can be further processed. Logic, Digital Performer, Live, and most other applications that support proprietary instruments, standardized plug-ins, or stand-alone connections will need to be set up appropriately in order to be used in a creative session.

Mix Automation with MIDI

Using a sequencer to automate your mix is not only easy but also very versatile. Mixing is part of the final stages of your creative process. Once all the tracks are down, recorded in MIDI or audio, depending on your project, you can add life to your creation by placing instruments in their own space, adjusting their levels, panning them, and adding effects.

Creating an audio mix inside a sequencer is usually provided through an audio mixer panel or window in the software itself. MIDI mixing may be done in the same mixing window or a different mixing window. How exactly this is done depends greatly on the software you use. However, when controlling MIDI automation, you are basically sending MIDI messages to MIDI devices. As mentioned earlier in this book, there are specific controller numbers for volume, pan, and other MIDI parameters. Using a sequencer's built-in MIDI mixer gives you a graphic interface to control these parameters and save changes you make to these values to a special mixing track. You can also embed the automation directly into the actual MIDI track you are mixing simply by adding control changes to the events already recorded on the track.

MIDI-enabled mixers or control surfaces can also be used to add automation to MIDI tracks. In this case, the mixer maps the set of control changes and other MIDI messages to its automatable parameters. Automatable parameters are any parameters that your mixer will let you control or will use to record automation. For example, moving a fader on your mixer might create a series of volume control messages for the specific fader channel you move. When you record the MIDI events generated by your mixer to a sequencer, you will notice that it does not generate any MIDI note messages, but rather control change messages. When it is played back, depending on your mixer and its configuration, you might see the fader moving on its own.

Most MIDI-enabled and automatable mixers will use more than one MIDI channel to transmit their MIDI data because they might have many automatable parameters. The volume faders on mixer inputs are a simple example. However, you might also want to control the EQ, the compression level, the solo and mute assignments, recall entire sets, or change integrated effects to a different patch. All these parameters require many MIDI messages, since each parameter needs to be associated with an existing MIDI message. Mixers use proprietary mapping systems, where each MIDI channel and each control change message is assigned a parameter inside the mixer. The exact mapping is pretty complex, and since it is proprietary (each mixer uses its own MIDI event mapping system), all you really need to do is make sure your mixer can send and receive MIDI events.

The bottom line is that you need to make sure that the MIDI channels your mixer uses are not used by any other MIDI devices. This is why it is recommended that a MIDI-enabled hardware mixer be assigned to its own MIDI port, provided you have a MIDI port to spare. This will allow you to have a tactile mixing interface that sends MIDI messages to your sequencer and receives these messages from the sequencer during playback.

If you recall correctly (if not, you can always go back to Chapter 2 to refresh your memory), some control change messages have an LSB and an MSB equivalent, giving you fine and coarse tuning. This is handy when mixing with a MIDI mixer if the mixer uses the fine values. This would mean smooth fades and changes when mixing. Although this is not a common feature in consumer-priced mixers, you might find it in high-end devices. In any case, using your mixer's automation capability alongside your MIDI sequencer can definitely be a time saver at mixing time.

Software Instrument Automation with MIDI

You can control certain parameters of an external MIDI device through control change MIDI messages. You can automate these changes by recording them inside your sequencer. Stand-alone and plug-in software instruments, like their hardware counterparts, have the same control possibilities. When you use the sequencer's MIDI mixing environment to send different MIDI messages to the hardware or software MIDI device, you are remote-controlling these parameters from the sequencer. In the same way, when you change these parameters from the front end of your instrument (software or hardware), the changes can be recorded in the sequencer and played back in real time. This automation can add more dynamics to your music performance.

How your sequencer handles what you automate depends on the sequencer itself, what you are trying to automate, and how the software instrument, in this case, communicates these changes to your sequencer. If you are trying to automate common controllers, chances are you can do this through a MIDI mixer in your sequencer or by adding values to the control change area of the piano roll editor in your sequencer. Here's a list of the most common controllers handled and identified within your sequencer:

- ✳ Channel Voice Messages: Velocity, polyphonic key pressure and aftertouch, program changes, and pitch bend.
- ✳ Control Changes (also Channel Voice Messages): Modulation, breath controller, foot controller, volume, balance, pan, expression, and sustain.

Since you can use your controller keyboard to automate these common parameters, you will also control these parameters for any instrument assigned to echo the events through the MIDI track's output port setting in your sequencer, provided you have not filtered any of these messages inside your sequencer's MIDI preferences. To verify if these events are filtered from what the sequencer records or not, you can look in your sequencer's MIDI options or preferences. You will find an option corresponding to different filters that are applied to your recording. Unfilter any type of MIDI message you wish to record before starting your automation.

You might also want to automate other parameters in real time through MIDI, such as the cutoff frequency, a resonance filter, or the LFO rate of a software instrument. All these parameters can be, in most cases, automated through your sequencer. Furthermore, by associating a MIDI control surface with the parameters of a software instrument, the controls available on this control surface will have the same effect as hardware controls on a hardware synthesizer. Where a hardware synth uses SysEx to transmit parameter changes to the sequencer in order to automate the changes, MIDI control surfaces send change voice messages such as control change (also known as continuous controllers in some more recent documents) and Note On messages to change the software parameters associated with the software instrument.

In order to properly configure both the MIDI control surface and a sequencer, you must understand the following concepts surrounding MIDI control surfaces:

Each control, which might be a button, a slider/fader, a key, a rotary knob, or something else, sends a MIDI value. What value this control sends is, in most cases, programmable. In many cases, such devices will come with preset parameter settings, where for example a specific knob will send a CC10 (Pan control) message. Because this knob is programmable, it could send anything on one of 16 channels. A button could be programmed to send an Omni Off message to all receiving MIDI devices or applications. How a MIDI value is assigned or associated with a control varies from one device to the next, so you will have to consult your hardware documentation for that part of the programming process. Start by finding out if there are preset settings already programmed and see which MIDI messages are associated with each control.

Once each control on the MIDI control surface is programmed, it can be associated with almost any virtual or MIDI hardware-based parameter, making it easier to edit a session, record and automate parameter changes inside a sequence, for example.

With some applications, associating incoming MIDI messages to virtual controls is done through a MIDI learning process. This process basically goes as follows:

Begin by configuring the application's MIDI preferences properly. For example, make sure the MIDI port associated with the control surface is enabled for both the inputs and outputs. Some applications will offer MIDI filtering options. Use them to filter out specific messages if ever you run into problems with SysEx messages, for example. Otherwise, make sure the application is not filtering messages it will need to receive in order to have the physical MIDI controls affect the virtual controls in the application.

When a software application offers a learning mode, you can select a virtual parameter with the mouse pointer and move the hardware control to associate both of them together. Once the learning mode has been enabled, programming the software application to respond appropriately to physical controls from a device is as easy as clicking on an onscreen control, then moving the control you want to use to change that parameter's value.

Once again, there may be some preset or pre-programmed setups made available by the software developer or the hardware manufacturer, making associating a large number of

Figure 9.16 Associating MIDI remote control parameters with Live.

controls quite simple. When this is not the case, save your setups in case you need to use the same preferences later.

Figure 9.16 displays the four steps involved in setting up a MIDI remote control surface in Ableton's Live software, starting with the MIDI Preferences in bullet 1, followed by the selection of the Edit MIDI Map function under the Options menu (bullet 2). As a result, the automatable parameters appear highlighted, as in bullet 3. The third step consists of selecting the desired parameter with the mouse. Notice the small corner frames around the fader display for the second audio track. Finally, after moving the corresponding parameter on the MIDI remote control, the corresponding MIDI message, in this case, a volume control change message (CC07) on channel 2, is associated with its virtual counterpart in Live (see bullet 4).

Other applications, such as Cubase in Figure 9.17, offer a greater set of programming flexibility by letting you add names to controllers and set up each MIDI parameter individually, which is displayed in the top table of this figure. The bottom table displays how these settings are interpreted by the software in this particular project.

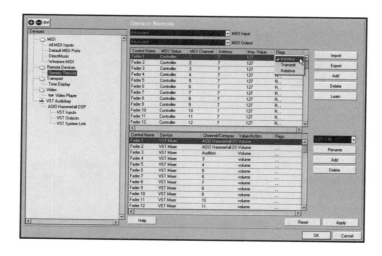

Figure 9.17 MIDI device settings for a generic remote control in Cubase.

The Learn button in this figure can also be used to automatically configure the MIDI parameters in the upper table by applying the message parameters the control sends to the selected row in the table. As you can see, the environments are different, but the principles behind MIDI control surface programming remain the same.

Editors and Librarians

When working with MIDI devices such as synthesizers and samplers, editing sounds, saving the ones you like, and recalling banks of sounds are all considered common tasks. If you are satisfied with the sounds that come with your device and have never edited a sound in it, this section will not apply to you. On the other hand, if you never did it for lack of understanding, this section just might put a smile on your face.

There are a great number of synthesizers, samplers, and drum machines currently available on the market. Most of them offer parameters to control how they sound. Usually, this is done through pages on your instrument's LCD panel. How much control you have over each sound depends on each device itself. However, computers provide two tools that give you a better grip on what you are editing and also over how you manage these programs: editor and librarian applications.

Editor software displays the parameters of a MIDI device through a graphic user interface, makes it possible to change to these parameters and hear the result, and finally, can save these changes to a file on the computer or send them back to the device. It connects to a device using the MIDI protocol; more specifically, SysEx messages. SysEx coming from the MIDI device updates the information in the software. Once edited, the corresponding SysEx is sent back out to the MIDI device to update its parameters.

Librarian software keeps computer file records of patches, banks, performances, and other specific information related to an external device. When you want to load these sounds or, more precisely, parameter settings associated with each sound/preset, you can load the file and transfer the settings to an external device using the MIDI connection between your computer and the device.

It is common to find both editing and librarian functions in the same application, making it possible to edit and save the settings in a large database of patch, bank, or performance setups. You can even create specific settings for songs, creating a performance in which a set of custom program settings is loaded for your song.

When you load editor/librarian software for the first time, it will ask you to define which instrument is in your setup or, more specifically, which instrument you would like to manage using the software. When defining the instruments, create a connection inside the software and between the computer and the external devices. SysEx information should be flowing in both directions.

In Figure 9.18, the window on the left displays devices recognized by the editor/librarian. Each window inside the application displays a specific setting from one of the installed devices. Changing parameters here will send SysEx messages to this device, changing its parameters as a result. All the editable parameters for a patch from this device are represented in this scrollable window. You can even change the name of a program from your computer's screen, and this name will be updated automatically. You may also use a virtual onscreen keyboard to trigger different notes to audition the changes you make to the MIDI device's parameters.

The need for such tools is limited to controlling external hardware devices. In other words, you don't really need an editor/librarian for software instruments, since all the parameters are already inside your computer and are easily accessible. You can see this type of editing environment as an extension of your external MIDI device. This makes it easy to keep these devices in another room even, controlling them from a distance using your computer's MIDI interface to talk with them.

Because this communication is done through SysEx, and every device needs to be configured in your software before you start editing, making changes to one device should not affect any other device. SysEx, after all, is talking to a single device through manufacturer identification codes found in its messages. If SysEx is still a mystery to you, and you are not sure you want to start dealing with this right now, don't worry. The messages you send from the editor/librarian's interface will be transparent to you—transparent in the sense that you will change a knob or a value that corresponds to a parameter displayed onscreen, not the hexadecimal values that these changes really send to your device.

Converting MIDI to Audio

MIDI is not audio. Really? Yes, really. I know this must sound like a stupid statement at this point, but it remains one of the most common misconceptions in audio today. Many people often confuse MIDI and digital audio and wonder how they make an audio CD from MIDI files, or why MIDI files don't play without at least a synthesizer plugged at its output (virtual

Figure 9.18 MIDIQuest is an example of an editor/librarian application.

or not). The answer is simple: You have to record the audio output of a MIDI performance in order to create a digital audio file beforehand. By now, you probably understand the difference between MIDI and audio because you have been wise and have been reading this book to find out all about MIDI. Congratulations!

How do you convert MIDI into audio? It all depends on the software you are using and what you use to play the MIDI events. There are three possible situations:

* You are using an external MIDI device with a sequencer.

* You are using a third-party MIDI software synthesizer with a sequencer. This could be software loaded outside of your sequencer but controlled by your sequencer or a wavetable synthesizer chip on your audio hardware used to generate sounds triggered by your sequencer.

* You have software synthesizers loaded as plug-ins inside your software sequencer.

In all three situations, let's assume your sequencer is capable of recording audio while it's playing back MIDI tracks. If not, you will need to find another way to record the audio output from a MIDI performance—in other words, a way of recording the sounds coming through your MIDI device's audio outputs.

To convert MIDI tracks into an audio track when using an external MIDI device (see diagram in Figure 9.19), you must:

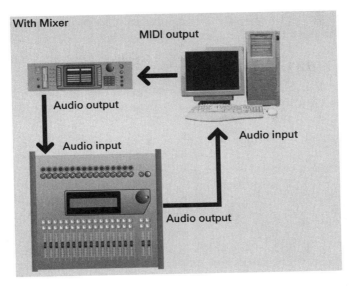

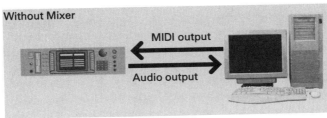

Figure 9.19 Converting MIDI into audio using an external MIDI device—in the top portion, using a mixer, and in the bottom portion, without the use of a mixer.

1. Start by turning the MIDI metronome off, especially if the same device you are using to record generates a metronome tick.
2. Mute all audio tracks already created and all the MIDI tracks you don't want to include in the audio file you are about to create.
3. Create an empty audio track, either mono or stereo, depending on the MIDI sound you want to convert.
4. Assign the audio output of your MIDI device to the appropriate audio input on your audio hardware. If you are using a mixer, send your mixer's output to the appropriate recording device.
5A. When using a mixer that receives the audio signal from the output of your audio hardware while it is sending the audio signal of your MIDI device you are recording, mute the output of your audio hardware. Otherwise, you will have a feedback loop. This will

occur if the signal coming from the computer's audio output is sent back into its audio input after passing through the mixer.

5B. When not using a mixer, connect the audio output of your MIDI device into the audio input of your audio hardware.

6. Activate or enable the audio track in your sequencer for recording. It is also possible to record into an external recording device, such as a multi-track recorder or DAT recorder. In both cases, don't start recording yet.

7. Start playback and monitor the levels of the audio coming into the recording device from either the sequencer's audio mixer or the recording device's input indicator. Adjust the levels so that they are always close but under the 0 dB digital limit, without going over it. This will provide the best result.

8. Set appropriate input levels and assure there are no feedback loops. If you notice feedback somewhere or a slight phase difference in the sound caused by the monitoring of both the source of the MIDI device and the audio output of the audio hardware, mute the output of the audio hardware to prevent it from being recorded back into the audio input.

9. Position the playback cursor at the beginning of the appropriate part and start recording the MIDI device's audio output.

10. When done, save the recording and position the newly recorded file, if the sequencer hasn't already done so, at the appropriate location in your project. Usually, this is done automatically. If you have recorded onto another device, such as a DAT recorder, you will need to transfer back into the sequencer or lock the sequencer through a synchronization function (explained in Chapter 10).

11. Mute the MIDI track you have just recorded and un-mute all the other tracks to hear the result.

12. Repeat this operation for every MIDI track you wish to record as an individual audio track in your sequencer.

To convert MIDI tracks into an audio track using internal MIDI software, you have two possibilities: First, if your software has a built-in recording tool, it might record the MIDI it receives from the sequencer directly to a digital audio file. This is the case with GigaStudio from Tascam (see Figure 9.20).

More frequently, plug-software instruments are loaded as plug-ins inside a host. When this is the case, the host application usually provides a method to render the audio result of MIDI events passing through the software instrument without having to play the whole sequence back. There are two common types of plug-ins: DXi (DirectX Instrument) developed by Cakewalk and VST (Virtual Studio Technology) Instruments developed by Steinberg (also compatible with many other applications). The specific steps involved vary from one application to the next, but in many applications, the rendering process is similar to the recording process described above. You will have to read your software's documentation to find out exactly how to do this, but let's look at a typical example of this. The virtual instrument (DXi or VSTi), when loaded, uses your audio hardware's audio output to generate the sounds it produces.

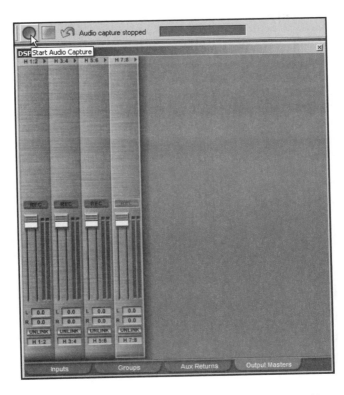

Figure 9.20 Tascam's GigaStudio captures its audio output directly to a file on a computer.

While inside your sequencer, MIDI events played by an external keyboard or a recorded sequence trigger the audio output of the instrument, producing its audio output. When you convert the MIDI data into audio, the sequencer uses a built-in function that renders the audio file internally, taking the notes it has to record from the MIDI information recorded in the associated MIDI track. You can later import the rendered audio tracks and mute the original MIDI tracks in order to mix all the audio content in your project to a final two-track stereo mix.

In Cubase, once a range is selected for a MIDI track routed through a VST instrument, the Audio Mixdown function's dialog box offers users the possibility of rendering specific audio outputs. In Figure 9.21, the Waldorf Attack's output 1 will be exported as a Broadcast Wave file in a stereo interleaved, 24-bit, 48KHz digital audio file. Once exported, the audio file will be added to the project's media pool, and a new audio track will be created where the audio rendering of the original MIDI events is placed.

However, if your software does capture its audio output directly to hard disk, you will have to proceed exactly as you did with the external MIDI device. Instead of sending the MIDI to an external device, you are sending it to another internal MIDI application. The audio output of this internal MIDI synthesizer or sampler software can be recorded internally if you have

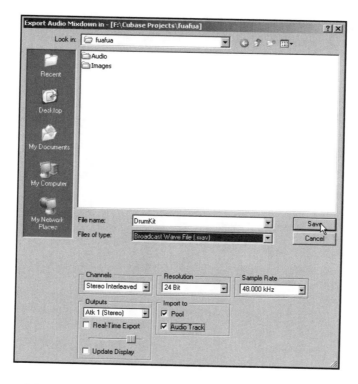

Figure 9.21 Exporting MIDI tracks routed to software instruments in Cubase.

full duplex audio hardware. Full duplex is a term that refers to the audio hardware's ability to play and record at the same time. If you don't have full duplex capability, you will have to record the audio output of your software synthesizer to an external audio recording device and then record back into the sequencer.

Review Questions

1. Which category of software instrument always requires a host application in order to use it?

   a) Stand-alone

   b) Plug-in

   c) Proprietary

   d) Hardware

2. Which of the following pairs matches the appropriate plug-in format with its developer?

   a) HTDM = Mark Of The Unicorn
   b) RTAS = Apple/Emagic
   c) VST = Steinberg
   d) MAS = Digidesign

3. Which of the following items could potentially limit the usability of software instruments?

   a) Processing power
   b) Memory (RAM)
   c) Hard disk speed
   d) All of the above

4. Software instruments depend on which computer peripheral to generate their output?

   a) The MIDI keyboard controller
   b) The audio hardware
   c) The external mixer
   d) The drivers

5. It was developed by Steinberg to optimize the stream of audio information inside your computer. What is it?

   a) An ASIO driver
   b) A GSIF driver
   c) An E-WDM driver
   d) An EASI driver

6. Which of the following software instrument plug-in formats needs DirectX installed on your computer in order to work and is not compatible with Macintosh computers?

   a) RTAS
   b) VST
   c) DXi
   d) All of the above

7. Which of the following statements is accurate?

   a) When using stand-alone software instruments along with a sequencer, the order in which you launch applications is important.
   b) When using stand-alone software instruments along with a sequencer, the order in which you launch applications is not important.
   c) When using stand-alone software instruments, you can't use a sequencer simultaneously.
   d) Stand-alone software instruments always include sequencing functions.

8. I am a protocol developed by Steinberg and Propellerhead that connects different compatible software applications together using virtual audio cables. What am I called?

   a) Sonar

   b) Reason

   c) ReWire

   d) FireWire

9. MIDI remote control surfaces use which type of MIDI messages to communicate mix automation information to a sequencer?

   a) MIDI control change messages

   b) MIDI channel voice messages

   c) MIDI SysEx messages

   d) All of the above

10. True or False: You always need to use a physical MIDI port's output to forward MIDI events to a software instrument.

10 MIDI Software Applications

A number of MIDI applications allow just about anyone to use MIDI in ways that were not possible before the integration of computers into the MIDI world. MIDI players allow computer users to hear MIDI files through audio hardware's synthesizer chip or software's integrated wavetable. MIDI monitors allow a user to monitor MIDI going into or coming out of the computer. These and other applications represent a new breed of MIDI tools for non-musicians.

Other MIDI programs are designed to support special functions not necessarily found in more general MIDI editing software. For example, your sequencer might not provide any MIDI effects such as MIDI delays or MIDI arpeggios, or you might find a stand-alone utility that converts sample-based sounds from one sampler format to another sampler format handy and useful. MIDI programmers have also given us new tools to create, edit, convert, and publish our MIDI files on the Web. MIDI, after all, was also meant to link hardware devices through a common communications protocol, right?

Here's a summary of what you will learn in this chapter:

* What MIDI players are.
* Examples of MIDI utilities and related applications.
* Sample format conversion tools.
* Getting applications to share MIDI and audio resources inside a computer.
* What the downloadable sound format is and why it was developed.
* What the eXtensible Music Format is and how you can use it to publish your MIDI files on the Web.
* How to publish MIDI files on a Web page.

MIDI Players

A MIDI player is a software application that plays back MIDI files. They exist as Internet browser plug-ins and as stand-alone applications. You can't edit MIDI files with a MIDI player. However, if you don't have a software sequencer, MIDI players will allow you to listen to MIDI files on your computer. MIDI players can, in some cases, include sound banks, which are usually GM, GS, or XG compatible.

For Macintosh users, the easiest way to listen to MIDI files is either through QuickTime or by using the Finder's playback transport controls if you are using OS X.

For both Windows and Macintosh users, your OS provides some built-in MIDI players, such as Windows Media Player on Windows or QuickTime for Macintosh. However, you can also use one of the following alternatives:

* QuickTime also offers a PC version, which provides you with its own GS sound bank: www.apple.com/quicktime.

* Winamp is a popular MP3 player (see Figure 10.1), but it also handles MIDI files: www.winamp.com.

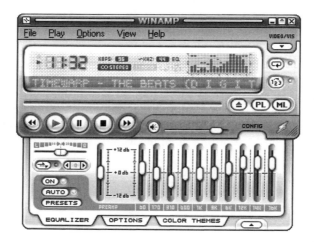

Figure 10.1   Winamp not only plays audio files but also supports MIDI files.

Utilities

By now you understand the difference between MIDI and audio. You also know how to convert MIDI into audio. But what about converting audio to MIDI or converting sound patches used in one sampler software into patches for use in another sampler application? Maybe you're having some MIDI problems, and you'd like to monitor the MIDI activity going into or coming out of your computer. How about a tool to organize your MIDI files into a database to find them quickly? These are only a few examples of available MIDI utilities. In fact, if there's something you want to do with MIDI, there is probably a software tool available on the Web that will help you do it. One of the great aspects of MIDI is its versatility and its capacity to be easily manipulated.

Let's take a look at some of the software tools that are available to enhance your MIDI experience and make your life easier. These examples are merely starting points, offering an overview of what's available. You will find additional information about software manufacturers in the support Web site accompanying this book under the MIDI Resources category in the Links section of the site (www.wavedesigners.com).

MIDI to Guitar Chords Utility

If your software sequencer doesn't handle guitar chords well, or if its guitar chord detection is limited, there is a little application that might be useful. It recognizes chords and converts them into useful guitar fingering notation so that you can add this fingering information to a score (see Figure 10.2).

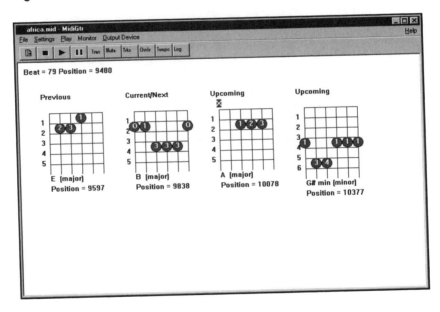

Figure 10.2   The MIDI guitar chord finder is PC freeware.

MIDI Message Monitoring

Remember when we were discussing MIDI messages? All those values in Status bytes and Data bytes? Well, using a MIDI monitor utility allows you to see these messages in action and helps you to understand what's really happening in the MIDI message passing through. For example, Figure 10.3 monitors MIDI messages in different formats. This might be useful if you are trying to troubleshoot your MIDI setup, searching for filters or modifiers along the way.

A modifier is a parameter that is set to transform your MIDI message in some way and can be found in a MIDI sequencer or a MIDI patch bay, for example. If you are unaware that such a modifier is being applied, you might have varying results, and a MIDI monitor like this one could help you determine if such a modifier is being applied to MIDI messages. You can also use a tool like this to better understand the content of MIDI messages, as it shows you all the values that are passed in the message. With the Midi Monitor application found in Figure 10.3, the top portion displays the different values in a MIDI message in a variety of formats (binary, hexadecimal, decimal, explicit, and event value, to be exact).

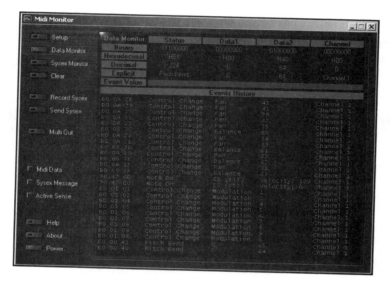

Figure 10.3 An example of a MIDI monitor application.

From Digital Audio to MIDI

You've created a great guitar line with your guitar and recorded the audio track, but you can't remember what notes you played. You would like to find a way to convert your audio file into MIDI data so that you can play this part on another instrument. This type of conversion is not usually very precise, due to the inherent difficulties of converting polyphonic instruments recorded as audio into MIDI events. However, some software attempts to do just that. You can use this as a starting point and then work on the MIDI events in a sequencer to extrapolate the rest of the MIDI events needed to reproduce the guitar line or to print a score of this line using appropriate music notation software.

In Figure 10.4, there are three file path references appearing in the window. The middle path refers to the digital audio input file used as the source material to be converted into MIDI. To work effectively, this file should contain clear recognizable tones and pitches. In other words, the more instruments and the more reverb or noisy artifacts there are in the audio

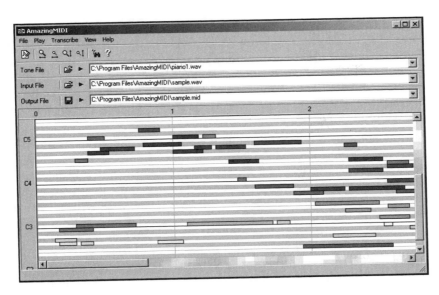

Figure 10.4 AmazingMIDI's interface converts digital audio into MIDI parts.

source material, the less likely you will be satisfied with the resulting MIDI file. This said, you should use an audio editor to remove background noises and possibly normalize the audio content—which boosts the audio signal to its maximum value without clipping. Once the audio file has been optimized, the software requires a tone file. A tone file is an audio reference with which the software compares the input file. For example, if you've recorded a guitar line as your input file, you might want to also record a single guitar note as a reference. This will increase the software's effectiveness in detecting the actual notes played in the input file. Once both these files are selected, as shown in Figure 10.4, you are ready to start the transcription setup process.

The transcription setup process determines how the audio content should be analyzed. The documentation provided with the software helps to understand what exactly each parameter in this window does. Once you have set the proper parameters for the transcription of digital audio into MIDI, you can proceed to the conversion. The MIDI result appears at the bottom of this figure and can be saved as a MIDI file and imported in your sequencer for further editing. This said, don't expect a perfect match all the time. This is an estimation of what was played, and some notes might appear that were never played. That's why you will need to edit the MIDI events in your sequencer; however, it is a good starting point and may reduce your transcription time when done properly.

Format Conversion Tools

With the popularity and development of sampler software instruments comes a new challenge for MIDI musicians: how to keep using sound programs from your old AKAI S-1000 sampler library in your new GigaStudio, HALion, or Sample Tank software. Thousands of sounds have been programmed in one format or another, and you might also have gathered a good collection of your own sounds, spending many hours tweaking loop points and envelopes and assigning each sample to specific keys to get the end result. In light of all that work, changing your sampler might not seem so appealing after all, particularly if it means having to redo all that work! Rest assured, you won't have to start over from scratch; this is something that software developers have caught up with.

There are already many tools converting sounds from one format to another. For example, converting a wave or AIFF file into an MP3 file is now easier than ever. However, the challenge when it comes to samplers is the inherent programming that goes into creating an instrument. For example, sampler instruments start with sampled sounds that might be layered across a velocity range. You might have a hard hit snare drum when the MIDI velocity is between 100 and 127, a medium hit snare when the velocity is between 64 and 100, and a low or soft snare hit when the velocity is between 0 and 64. When you play the note to which your snare is assigned on a keyboard or another controller, the velocity at which you play will determine which sample is played in the sampler. Then, you might add an envelope to this setting, pan it a bit off center, and so on. Note that you have to assign a good number of samples to different keys on a range of notes in order to reproduce an acoustic instrument realistically. Looping sounds at a specific point in an audio file is also very time consuming but necessary when programming sounds. All these elements that go into the creation of a sampled sound need to be reproduced, or translated, from one sampler format to another if you want to be able to use your sample library in a different sampler. That's what format conversion tools are used for. Many software samplers already support a number of formats and can convert formats when importing them. If the format you need is not supported by your sampler, using third-party sample conversion software might offer an alternative solution.

In Figure 10.5, you can see the Chicken Systems Translator, which lets you browse the contents of different sampler formats in an Explorer fashion. You can listen to the samples selected before converting them and manage sounds from this interface.

Figure 10.6 shows another example of a sampler format conversion tool that lets you see the structure of each sound as it was originally programmed. Again, converting your sounds will preserve most of the programming information involved in the sound's setup, saving you many hours of programming time. For example, in this figure the sound format used was for an EMU 4 disc. This can then be exported to a GigaStudio, Pulsar STS, or HALion sampler format, not to mention the usual AKAI S6000 series or plain old MP3, to name a few.

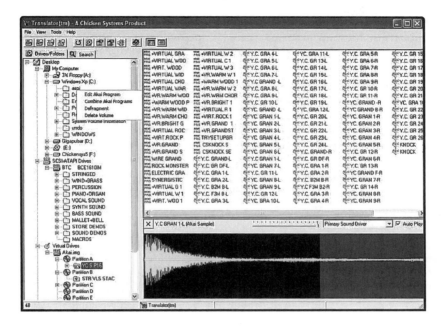

Figure 10.5 Chicken Systems Translator converts any sampler format to any other sampler format.

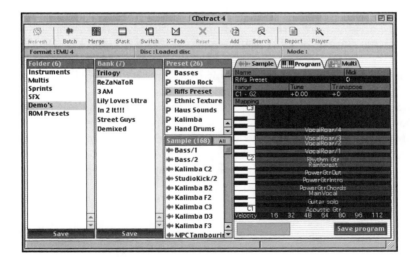

Figure 10.6 CDxtract is another conversion tool for sampler formats—this is the OS X version.

Both these applications will map the proper samples and parameters to their appropriate MIDI note numbers so that, for instance, a C3 sample will correspond to a C3 sample in the converted format.

Samples to SoundFonts

It is also possible to use individual samples present in your computer as a base for a SoundFont set. To use SoundFonts, you will need a compatible audio hardware, sequencer, or software synthesizer. Once sounds are loaded into a SoundFont-compatible audio hardware or software instrument, you can use them as you would a sampler—reading samples from the hard disk through this application's interface. Here's an example: With a Sound Blaster AWE64 audio hardware (a SoundFont-compatible card) and Cubase, you can assign the AWE64's synth as the MIDI track's output. Then, you choose the SoundFont instrument from Cubase's Instrument menu in the Inspector area. This will give you access to the SoundFont banks installed on your audio hardware.

In order to use SoundFonts with your compatible audio hardware, the SoundFont Management System provided by the audio hardware manufacturer needs to be installed on your system. Note that audio hardware that supports SoundFonts was originally developed for PC computers, but since Creative Labs opened the SF2 format to the public domain, more and more support, acceptance, and development has been seen on Macintosh computers. For example, OS X 10.3 from Apple now supports SoundFont through QuickTime, and many third-party software samplers using VST instrument or DirectX (PC only) standards also support this sample format.

Since SoundFonts are organized banks of programs (patches), you should know a little bit about how to create banks from samples. In Figure 10.7, the material for the banks is samples that are recorded on your hard disk or found on a sampling CD. These samples are the sound sources for the programs assigned in your sequencer. Each sample is assigned to individual keys or key ranges, which is called the multi-sample level. Each sample can also be assigned a specific velocity range. If, for example, you wish to have a different sample play when you play harder, you can assign a different sample for higher velocities. Once the multi-samples are mapped to your keyboard, you can assign them to a program and add different playback parameters to them, such as an envelope, a filter, or effects. This mapping of sampled and multi-sampled audio files along with the envelope, filter, and effect settings represents the program itself that you can select using a program change number. The program and all its settings, including the key mapping and referred samples, will be saved in a SoundFont bank, which is then loaded into your sequencer. Once it is loaded, you can call a program in a bank.

To create such banks, you will need a SoundFont bank editor (see Figure 10.8) to convert digital audio samples into a SoundFont-compatible format. The Alive window, for example, creates program banks and saves them as SoundFonts and imports SoundFonts already made and plays them through your audio hardware as a software instrument.

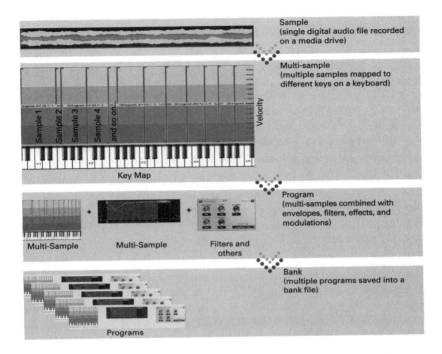

Figure 10.7   Example of a SoundFont bank structure.

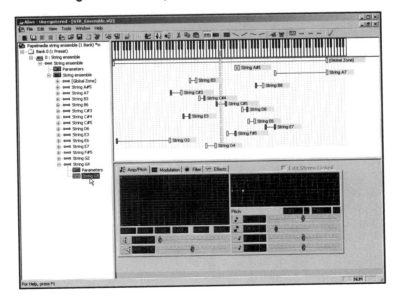

Figure 10.8   The Alive SoundFont editor window.

Sharing Resources Inside Your Computer

When using MIDI, sharing resources inside your computer may imply sharing a MIDI port and audio hardware access. To make sure your resources are spread around adequately, you'll need to plan ahead. Since the main issues discussed in this book are the MIDI ports and how they are used and the software applications that use the audio hardware's audio outputs in both audio- and MIDI-related tasks, knowing what your software requires and the workaround might help you get over some of these issues. This said, some software is less fussy in terms of shared audio resources, while others might take over your audio hardware completely, leaving it useless if you load a second application that requires it.

Certain software applications don't talk to each other internally. For example, if you are running a stand-alone version of a software instrument, Cakewalk's Sonar won't talk to it. By installing a virtual MIDI port, you can create inter-application communication, or bridge, between applications when no other method is already provided by the applications themselves.

Figure 10.9 shows that configuring one application to send MIDI to another (applications that don't normally share a virtual connection) is quite similar to using software instruments within a single application or setting up MIDI communication between two applications that are already sharing resources. In this example, you need to set the first application (the one on the left in the figure) to send MIDI to the installed virtual MIDI port's output and set the second application (the one on the right) to receive MIDI from this virtual MIDI port. Hubi's MIDI Loopback offers such connection for Windows 3.1 and 95 users. This very small application (it takes 5KB of memory inside your computer while running) creates up to four additional MIDI ports inside your computer. Once they are installed, you will find these

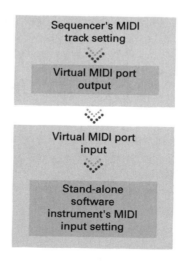

Figure 10.9 Diagram of a virtual MIDI port being used between two applications.

additional ports in your MIDI setup options. Once activated, you can then send MIDI events through these new ports so that your applications can share the MIDI data. You can download a free copy of this application. Visit www.wavedesigners.com to access the Links area.

On a pre-OS X Mac, you can enable inter-software communication of MIDI events through MOTU's FreeMIDI. To activate this function under FreeMIDI, you first need to have this installed on your system. Then, you open FreeMIDI and select the Preferences option in the File menu. In the Preferences window, enable Inter-application MIDI and click OK. You can then exit FreeMIDI and launch the application, which should receive MIDI from your sequencer and select the FreeMIDI input from its MIDI options. You should note that OMS does not support inter-application configuration. On a Mac running OS X, all inter-application connectivity is handled by the Core MIDI and Audio settings.

In terms of audio resources, there are two aspects to consider:

✳ The capacity your audio hardware's driver has to share its access between two or more applications. Your audio hardware needs to have a multi-client driver. This type of driver will allow more than one client (software application) to access its resources at a time. You will need to consult your audio hardware's manufacturer documentation or Web site to find out if the audio hardware is multi-client or not. You can also find out what limitations it has in this regard, or tips and tricks on configuring your applications to work well with this audio hardware.

✳ The capacity your software application has to share its access to the audio hardware resources with others. Certain applications will not share audio hardware access. It also implies that in some cases, you will need to load a certain application before another. Consult your application documentation to find out what the proper procedures are and what kind of restriction this resource sharing will add to your setup.

Once you have resolved these two issues, there is not much more you can do. If you find that you can't share your audio hardware resources for one of the reasons mentioned above, you will need to revise your strategy. To avoid this, it is always good to plan ahead: ask questions on compatibility and resource sharing issues, check for updated drivers that might improve your audio hardware's functionality, or get another computer to add overall horsepower to your setup.

MIDI Web Solutions

The Internet is a great way to find information and promote your work to others. One of the ways you can do this is by creating a Web site with samples of your work, along with some information about you, your band, or any other information you deem interesting. When it comes to putting your music on the Web, there are two options: posting either audio files or MIDI files.

Posting audio files offers the advantage of assuring your sound quality; it will be the same for every person who visits your Web site. The disadvantage is that the user will have to wait for the file to download to his computer in order to listen to it. You could choose to stream your audio content, which diminishes the download time, since streamed audio starts playing as it is being transferred. However, this method requires quite a bit of knowledge and still requires a large bandwidth from the user's perspective in order to avoid dropouts in the sound as it is being downloaded or streamed.

The alternative is MIDI, which offers the advantage of being much smaller than its digital audio counterpart. The disadvantage is that you don't control the final output of the MIDI file on the user's system, and since each system is different, the sound quality (as well as the sounds themselves) might vary widely from system to system. There are options, described below, that may help limit this uncertainty. Among those are downloadable sounds (DLS) and eXtensible Music Format (XMF) files.

Once you've decided whether to use audio or MIDI when publishing your music on the Web, you will need to know how to include these files in your Web pages. Here again, you have two options: You can add a link to your file or embed your file in the Web page itself. Both methods are described later in this chapter.

Downloadable Sounds (DLS)

In the past decade, wavetable synthesis has become increasingly prevalent, and so has the need for a standard wavetable-based format that defines musical instruments. Although the GM specification defines a set of 128 instruments, it lacks enough depth and breadth to deliver a truly consistent playback experience across a wide range of platforms. This is due in part to the wide variety of devices used to play these GM sounds. Some GM devices will use FM synthesis or wavetables, while others will use SoundFonts. The result is a wide range of sound quality. The need for a musical instrument standard that allows composers to define exactly how each musical instrument sounds on a wide variety of playback devices is finally met with the downloadable sounds (DLS) format.

When authoring for MIDI, a composer faces two limitations: the limited set of instruments that GM provides, and the lack of consistency in the quality of GM sound banks, ranging from good to outright ridiculous. Other media do not suffer from these problems. For example, a graphic designer or an audio engineer can rely on consistent results on multiple hardware solutions. MIDI, unfortunately, does not offer such consistency, so content developers such as you might opt for digital audio rather than MIDI. However, digital audio is not as flexible and interactive as MIDI, not to mention the additional storage and transmission bandwidth requirements of this medium. These two points are of particular significance on the Web.

DLS (Level 2.1) enables the author to define and create an instrument by combining a recorded waveform or set of waveforms with articulation information. An instrument designed this way can be downloaded and then played like any standard MIDI synthesizer through a compatible DLS application or a plug-in supporting DLS sound banks. This will give the MIDI author a common playback experience and an unlimited sound palette for both instruments and sound effects, unlike GM. It also offers audio interactivity and MIDI storage compression, unlike digital audio. However, the DLS standard does not contain MIDI events themselves but rather the instrument definitions (sound banks) needed by a MIDI file to play correctly.

If you look at Figure 10.10, you can see that there are three components required for DLS to work. First, the MIDI file is the source material that triggers the sounds, just as it would trigger your usual external or software MIDI instruments. It is, for all intents and purposes, a regular SMF file. What is special about it is that it refers to a bank of DLS sounds. It does this by using a DLS-compatible software instrument such as the DLS software synthesizer included with Sony's ACID 5 (as shown in Figure 10.11).

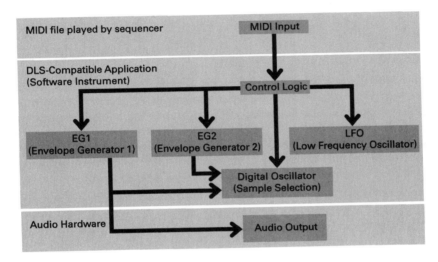

Figure 10.10 How DLS works in your computer.

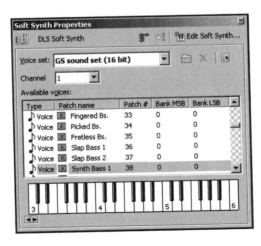

Figure 10.11 An example of a DLS-based software instrument.

The DLS-compatible instrument or sound bank reader processes the samples found in this bank by applying the DLS architecture to them. This architecture is not uncommon; however, the parameters defined by this architecture must meet a specific DLS standard. In Figure 10.10, the MIDI fed into the instrument passes through the control logic of the DLS-compatible instrument. On the left, envelope generators define the shape of the sound, such as modifying the attack time, decay, sustain, and release times. The information also passes through an LFO to adjust the different pitch of samples to the notes that might be played in a MIDI file. The frequency of the LFO (Low Frequency Oscillator) in this case determines the playback frequency of the sample, not the vibrato or filter sweep frequency as is usually associated with LFOs. This information is combined with the actual samples found in the sound bank and sent to the audio hardware for audio playback.

The extended RMID file is a format based on the RIFF (Resource Interchange File Format) developed by Microsoft and used for file types such as WAV and AIFF (Audio Interchange File Format). When used to house MIDI and DLS information, the RMID file contains a single SMF data image, a single DLS data image, plus supplemental data such as a version stamp, copyright notice, and other descriptive information. In this sense, an extended RMID file can be used for portability of music, just like a standard MIDI file, with the exception that authors can define their own instruments rather than using only GM instruments.

To find out more about DLS and RMID, visit the MMA's Web site at www.midi.org.

eXtensible Music Format (XMF)

In recent years, the MMA has developed a new format called eXtensible Music Format (XMF). This file format is actually a meta format—a container file that points to other types of files, in this case, MIDI files, RMF (Rich Media Files), DLS (Downloadable Sounds) files, and digital audio files. Its purpose is to serve as a standard format for transmitting MIDI files and sample bank information used by this MIDI file to a MIDI player over the Internet, between applications that support the XMF standard, or to mobile devices such as cellular phones, just as the RMID described earlier in this chapter.

The concept of an XMF file is similar to other types of metafiles, such as those found with MP3 files (M3U), RealMedia content (RAM—real audio and real video), and Windows Media Format through its WAX metafiles: They all contain links to media file content.

Musicians can create a MIDI file using downloadable sounds (DLS) or GM as the sound bank for this MIDI file, then through the Web or even on cordless communication devices, the music can be transmitted using very little bandwidth, since MIDI is small. The quality of the sounds will be guaranteed by the DLS provided or through the user's pre-downloaded set of DLS.

Here's an example of how this might work. In Figure 10.12, an HTML file on a Web site holds a link to an XMF file. When a user clicks on the link, the XMF file transfers to the user's computer. Remember, the XMF file only contains links to other media files, but since it is small, it loads quickly and prompts the associated plug-in player (such as a QuickTime, Windows Media Player, or other XMF plug-ins you might have on your computer) to load in the user's

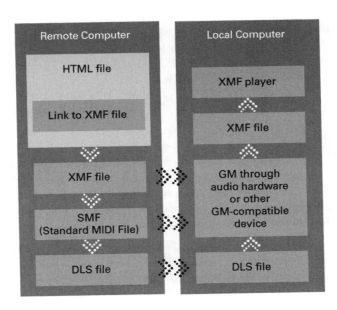

Figure 10.12 How XMF connects MIDI files, sounds, and Web pages together.

memory. Once the plug-in is active in the user's memory, this plug-in starts downloading the actual media files referred to in the XMF file.

This is the same process used when creating streaming content on the Web using RealAudio, Windows Media Format, or MP3 playlists. The fact that the metafile itself is small allows the computer to quickly load the player needed to reproduce the content of this XMF file. When it finds links to the media files, it starts downloading them to the computer. When it has downloaded enough information to start playback, it begins to play the content. In this context, XMF files usually call a MIDI file with its associated files: DLS or RMF sound banks.

For example, you could include along with the MIDI file a downloadable sample file that would contain the custom sound banks you used to create your MIDI file. If the MIDI file only refers to sounds from the GM sound bank through program changes, the XMF player plug-in may use the existing GM sound bank found with your associated player. Or, you can also include your own GM sound bank if you want to make sure the sounds are exactly as you intended them. Production notes can also be included in different languages. The XMF file recognizes the user's regional setting and downloads only the appropriate language for this user. Once these files are downloaded, the MIDI playback will begin. In most cases, this should not be long, since MIDI requires very little space and DLSs are, when programmed properly, very space efficient as well.

The applications of XMF are still being defined, since this standard has just been accepted by the MMA. At this time, wireless communications applications seem likely to benefit the most from this standard.

Integrating MIDI Files in Web Pages

As mentioned earlier in this chapter, there are two ways you can include MIDI files in your Web page: by embedding the content into your page or by creating a link to a file inside your HTML page. Both are quite easy to implement.

The first method consists of adding a link to the MIDI file from within an HTML document (Web page). The second method consists of embedding the MIDI file in the page; it will start loading on the user's computer just as a graphic file loads automatically in a Web browser. The link provides the user with the option of downloading the MIDI file or not, whereas the embedded MIDI file doesn't give the user this option. If your MIDI file is more than 40KB, you should consider giving the user the option of downloading it. Otherwise, visitors to your Web page will be forced to wait for the file to download before everything appears clearly on the page. There are, however, workarounds to this. For example, adding an embedded file at the bottom of the page rather than at the top will help since browsers read HTML and load pages from top to bottom.

Here's the HTML code for adding a link to a MIDI file:

```
<A HREF="MyMIDIFile.MID">Example Of My MIDI Work</A>
```

The opening HTML tag tells the browser that this is the referenced file of a link: <A HREF= " ">. The name inside the quotation marks represents the actual MIDI file being referenced: "MyMIDIFile.MID." The filename must be written between double quotation marks. The text that follows is the text that will appear as the hyperlink in your HTML document. By default, hyperlinked text is underlined, but this is not always the case when using customized Cascading Style Sheets or more elaborate Web programming tools. The last tag indicates the end of the hyperlinked text: </A>. When the referenced MIDI file is not in the same folder as your HTML page, add the relative path to the filename. For example, if your file is in a subfolder called "MIDIFILES," add the following information in your file reference description: <A HREF= "MIDIFILES/MyMIDIFile.MID">. Some Web servers are case sensitive, so making sure you standardize your naming convention will help avoid errors. The other method consists of embedding a MIDI file in your Web page. This method, as mentioned above, will download the file automatically on the user's computer as the page loads. When the file plays, how it looks on your page depends on the player that will load in the user's computer. There isn't much you can do about that, since you can't know for sure what player the user associated with the MIDI file extension. You can, however, provide a link to your favorite MIDI player plug-in in case the user does not have such a MIDI player installed on his computer. This said, most computers running Windows XP or Macintosh will have built-in players that support MIDI files. How it starts playing or how many times it plays are parameters that you can adjust.

Here's the HTML code for adding an embedded MIDI file to a Web page:

```
<EMBED SRC="MyMIDIFile.MID" WIDTH="144" HEIGHT="25" AUTOSTART="TRUE"
REPEAT="TRUE"></EMBED>
```

The HTML tag in this case is <EMBED SRC>. This tag is compatible with both Internet Explorer and Netscape browsers, so you should not have to write different HTML codes for different browsers, as is the case for some HTML tags (such as <BGSOUND>).

The filename represents the file you wish to load automatically in the page's browser. If the file is not in the same folder as the HTML file, as with links described earlier, you will need to specify the relative path to this file. The parameters that follow the filename will vary, depending on your needs. The WIDTH and HEIGHT parameters represent pixel values you wish the player to use. The actual look of the player associated with MIDI will vary, depending on the user's installed player, which will be invoked by the HTML page. A larger amount will create a larger space for your player to be embedded in, while a width equal to and a height equal to will hide the player from the user's view, making it impossible for the user to use the player's controls. This might be useful if you don't want the user to stop the music.

The AUTOSTART parameter can be set to TRUE or FALSE. If it is set to TRUE, the player will start playing the MIDI file as soon as it is loaded automatically. If it is set to FALSE, the user will have to press the Play button of the player in order to start the playback. Note that if you set your player to be invisible (WIDTH and HEIGHT set to 0 and 2, respectively, as mentioned above), you will have to set the AUTOSTART parameter to TRUE. Otherwise, the user won't know there is a MIDI file there and will not hear anything, nor will it be possible to start the playback.

The REPEAT parameter can be set to TRUE FALSE. If it is set to TRUE, the player will start playing the MIDI file according to the AUTOSTART parameter's setting but then will keep on repeating until the user presses the player's Stop button. If it is set to FALSE, the MIDI file will play once and stop when it reaches the end of the file.

The </EMBED> tag marks the end of the embedding information. However, it is not required by your browser in order for the tag to work, unlike the </A> tag in the link. You might find that certain Web page authoring environments, such as FrontPage or Dreamweaver, will report an error in the script if you omit it.

You may combine the linking and embedding methods in the same Web page. Just be sure to set the AUTOSTART parameter to FALSE, or you might have all the player's instances playing at once, which could cause the page to lock up. Figure 10.13 shows an example of both embedded MIDI files and a linked MIDI file. The player itself may be different on your computer, since the MIDI player associated with your browser and OS will influence the layout of the information.

Figure 10.14 displays the sample code used to create this page. You will note in this figure that the text is in lowercase, not in uppercase as in the examples above. HTML code is not case sensitive; however, sticking with one convention will make your life easier when sifting through pages of code. Some HTML editors will color code information as well to help you identify quickly normal text and HTML coding.

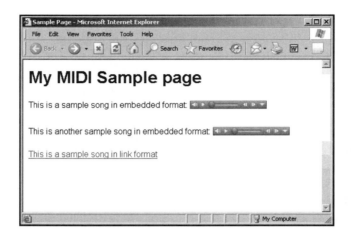

Figure 10.13 HTML sample page as displayed in the browser window.

```
1  <!DOCTYPE HTML PUBLIC "-//W3C//DTD HTML 4.01 Transitional//EN"
2  "http://www.w3.org/TR/html4/loose.dtd">
3  <html>
4  <head>
5  <title>Sample Page</title>
6  <meta http-equiv="Content-Type" content="text/html; charset=iso-8859-1">
7  </head>
8
9  <body>
10 <h1>My MIDI Sample  page</h1>
11 <p>This is a sample song in embedded format:
12     <embed src="ChordStructure1.mid" width="144" height="32" autostart="false" align="absmiddle"></embed>
13 </p>
14 <p>This is another sample song in embedded format:
15     <embed src="ChordStructure2.mid" width="144" height="32" autostart="false" align="absmiddle"></embed>
16 </p>
17 <p><a href="ChordStructure3.mid">This is a sample song in link format</a></p>
18 </body>
19 </html>
20
```

Figure 10.14 Sample code that was used to create the page in the previous figure.

This is a very simple example using no graphical elements or tables to position your MIDI player and text in the page. However, no matter how complex your pages become, the information needed to actually add a MIDI file, embedded or linked, remains the same.

The examples just given will use any installed MIDI plug-in on a user's computer. If you would like to force the user to use a specific plug-in, though, you will need to add additional code in your page. This is not advisable, since it might deter users from hearing your material—nobody likes to add plug-ins they will use only a few times. However, to do so, consult the documentation on the site that developed the plug-in you want the visitors to use. This would include in most cases a plug-in Class ID parameter, which identifies the plug-in to the browser, and a location from which the user can download the plug-in if the browser doesn't recognize it. In other words, the browser would tell the user that he needs to download a plug-in in order to hear the content of this site and point the user to the proper location from which the plug-in can be downloaded.

Review Questions

1. Select the question matching this statement: A software application that plays back MIDI files using a GS-compatible wavetable sound bank.

    a) What is a software synthesizer?

    b) What is a utility?

    c) What is a driver?

    d) What is QuickTime?

2. Digital audio to MIDI conversion works best when:

    a) The audio contains monophonic content.

    b) The audio contains polyphonic content.

    c) The audio contains rhythmic content.

    d) The audio contains harmonic content.

3. Select the question matching this statement: An application that maps the proper samples and parameters to their appropriate MIDI note numbers so that, for instance, a C3 sample will correspond to a C3 pitch when porting patches from one sampler to the next.

    a) What are SoundFonts?

    b) What is digital audio to MIDI conversion tool?

    c) What is a sample format conversion tool?

    d) What are wavetables?

4. There are two major issues associated with sharing resources between two audio applications inside a computer. What are they?

    a) The number of video monitors and audio hardware devices connected to the computer.

    b) The number of simultaneous tracks and the format these tracks support.

    c) The number of MIDI ports and number of MIDI channels available.

    d) The audio hardware and software application's capacity to share these resources.

5. DLS is the acronym for:

   a) Digital Line System

   b) Direct Link Software

   c) Downloadable Sounds

   d) Digital Level Sounds

6. Find the correct question that matches this statement: A container file that points to other types of files, such as MIDI files, RMF (Rich Media Files), and digital audio files.

   a) What is the Resource Interchange File Format?

   b) What is the eXtensible Music Format?

   c) What is the MPEG Layer 3 Format?

   d) What is MIDI?

7. When embedding a MIDI file in an HTML Web page, what can you do to make sure all the images load in the page before the MIDI file starts downloading?

   a) You place the MIDI file at the bottom of the page.

   b) You can't control this.

   c) You only use images smaller than the MIDI file.

   d) All of the above.

8. When embedding a MIDI file in an HTML Web page, which player will appear to play the MIDI file?

   a) QuickTime

   b) Windows Media Player

   c) Winamp

   d) It depends on the player installed on the person's computer.

9. When programming patches for samplers, mapping samples to different note numbers, it is also possible to have different samples triggered, depending on the speed at which you strike a key. What is the name of the MIDI parameter that makes this possible?

   a) Attack

   b) Velocity

   c) Aftertouch

   d) Modulation

10. True or False: It is not possible to send MIDI events from one application inside a computer to another application inside the same computer unless they are compatible applications.

11 } Deeper into MIDI: System Exclusive and Synchronization

System Exclusive (SysEx) messages and synchronization are probably two of the most misunderstood aspects of the MIDI protocol. Synchronization locks multiple devices together using time code or MIDI clock, while SysEx lets users control and automate MIDI device parameters in real time.

SysEx defines and records MIDI events and parameters that are not defined or recorded in other MIDI messages, such as an envelope for a specific sound or a cutoff frequency in a device's filter. SysEx is supposed to be transparent to the user. But even when you notice these messages, you may not see the values, such as a note number that corresponds to a key on your keyboard or a velocity value for that key when it passes. SysEx passes values in much the same way that values in a control change or a Channel Voice message are passed; what's different is what it affects when it passes these values. In addition, a large portion of SysEx is manufacturer specific. And by the way, SysEx is only relevant for hardware devices, not software instruments, as you will discover later in this chapter.

Synchronization is not a tool you will use in a typical setup, since your sequencer is, by default, the driving force behind the timing of a song or project. On the other hand, working with video, external multi-track recorders, or multiple sequencers, synchronization is essential for the timing to remain consistent among the various components. Synchronization is an essential part of music composition for film. Starting video playback while monitoring the audio playback and operating transport controls are all part of what synchronization makes possible.

Here's a summary of what you will learn in this chapter:

* What SysEx is and what it's for.
* Why use SysEx.
* How SysEx messages are constructed.
* The difference between manufacturer-specific SysEx and universal SysEx messages.
* How to send and receive SysEx messages.
* How to record SysEx in your software for later use.

* Editing SysEx... not! Why?
* Synchronization options.
* The difference between MIDI clock and time code.
* The precision of ASIO 2 synchronization.
* What MIDI Machine Control is.
* What MIDI Show Control is.

What Is SysEx?

SysEx messages transmit information that is not included in any other MIDI messages. These transmissions fall under two categories: manufacturer-specific SysEx messages and universal SysEx messages. Manufacturer-specific SysEx messages are used to send data that is specific to a particular manufacturer's device, such as a dump of its patch memory, sequencer data, waveform data, or information that is particular to a device. None of these messages are defined in non-SysEx MIDI messages.

In the case of universal SysEx messages, they transmit information to any MIDI device, but like their manufacturer-specific counterpart, none of the information they contain is part of the regular non-SysEx MIDI messages. For example, this could be a message telling the receiving device to disable its GM mode or set its master volume parameter to a specific value. The master volume parameter is different than the channel volume level value, since it affects the general volume level of a multi-timbral device. For example, one multi-timbral device could have channel 1's volume set at 64, channel 2's volume set at 96, channel 3's volume set at 45, and its master volume set at 100. Raising the master level volume for this device to 127 would effectively raise the overall volume level of all the channels at the output of this device, but the actual channel volume level values would remain the same (i.e. 64, 96, and 45).

In other words, SysEx is used to change MIDI device parameters that are not identified or addressed by MIDI messages described earlier in this book. Using SysEx represents the only method of retrieving, sending, or saving these parameter values through a MIDI connection. SysEx messages do not contain any regular MIDI messages. SysEx messages are, to a large extent, what makes MIDI control surfaces possible.

You could say that SysEx controls parameters determining how sounds are produced outside the defined MIDI message parameters—such as control change events—while other MIDI events control what sounds are produced and when to produce them. Here's an example: To change and automate the filter envelope of a sound playing on channel 1 through time, SysEx is the only way to achieve this. Once the sequencer is set to not filter out SysEx messages, you can change the value of this parameter (the filter envelope) on your MIDI device and record it as a series of SysEx MIDI values. When you play it back, the parameter will change through time, just as any other MIDI event—except, in this case, it's called a SysEx MIDI event.

To better understand the beast that is SysEx, let us look at how it is constructed. Hopefully, by the end of this discussion, you will realize that the beast was only the shadow of a small harmless creature that can easily be tamed. Once you understand what SysEx is about, you will be amazed at how much control you can have over your MIDI device and realize that this control can easily be translated into new creative musical directions.

Anatomy of a SysEx Message

A SysEx message can be as small as 10 bytes or as large as 10,000 bytes. Each SysEx message contains eight parts (nine in the case of Roland), each one playing a specific role. These parts are laid out in Table 11.1.

In the first column, you will find the part number, sorted in order of its appearance in the SysEx message. Each part inside a SysEx message plays its own role, which is identified in this table.

The second column displays the number of bytes used to send this part and whether this part is conveying a status or data portion of the SysEx message. A Status byte in a MIDI message identifies to the MIDI device what to do with the following Data bytes. You saw that a Note On message, for example, had one Status byte telling the device that this is a Note On for a specific MIDI channel. It also tells the receiving device that the two following Data bytes represent the MIDI note number and the velocity of this note. SysEx messages, in this respect, are identical, as they also contain Status and Data bytes.

The third column indicates whether this part is defined by the MIDI specification or not—whether the part (portion of the SysEx message) is common to all devices or specific to a manufacturer and model. When the information is common to all devices and all SysEx messages and is defined by the MIDI specification, the word *Common* appears in this column. For example, manufacturer ID numbers are common to all SysEx messages. Although their value is specific to a manufacturer, all manufacturer ID numbers are identified in the MIDI specification. When the part is specific to a MIDI device, the word *Specific* appears in this column. Looking for a meaning to these values without your manufacturer's documentation would be useless, since the values contained here are meant only for a specific device made by a specific manufacturer. You will need to consult the manufacturer's documentation to find the meaning these values represent for a specific device. This is definitely not something I suggest you do. Sitting down and trying to figure out what value is passed by which parameter and how it is represented in a SysEx message is much more complicated than simply using SysEx in the context of the songwriting process.

The fourth column indicates the content of each part. This content takes the number of bytes indicated in the second column. Finally, below each part, you'll find a description of what each part does.

Table 11.1 SysEx Messages Parts Explained

Parts	# of bytes (byte type)	Common or specific	Content of byte
1	1 byte (Status)	Common	Start SysEx message
Description:	Tells the device that the following data is a SysEx message.		
2	1 or 3 bytes (Data)	Common	Manufacturer ID number
Description:	Identifies the manufacturer to the receiving device. For example, if you have a Korg synth and a Yamaha synth, the Korg synth will ignore the SysEx message when it sees that the manufacturer ID does not correspond to its ID.		
3	1 byte (Data)	Common	Device ID number
Description:	This value is only relevant when you have more than one device from the same manufacturer in a daisy chain. Each device should be set to its own device ID number. This is usually done in your device's system options or system MIDI settings. By having a device ID that identifies each device in your chain, you can address each device with its own set of SysEx messages.		
4	1 byte (Data)	Common	Model ID number
Description:	This identifies the model number of the device. Once again, if you have more than one device from the same manufacturer, the model ID will tell the device if this message applies to it or not. In other words, your Roland JV-1080 will ignore this message if it is identified with the Roland D-50 model ID number.		
5	1 byte (Data)	Common	Send or receive command
Description:	This tells the device if the SysEx message is sending information to it or requesting information from it. For example, an editor/librarian might be requesting parameter settings from your device. When you edit the settings in the editor, you are sending SysEx to the device to update its parameter to correspond to the changes you made in the software.		
6	3 bytes (Data)	Specific	Start address
Description:	This is the first address on which the SysEx intends to act. The actual meaning of this address is defined in your MIDI device's manual in the address map table (usually found at the end of the manual, since nobody usually pays it much attention). Your device will put the values found in the next part, starting at the value in this part. Let's say you have tickets with numbers on them. Each number corresponds to a specific task. The start address is like if I were to say: "Look at these people in line, walk up to the fifth person, and start giving every one in that line a draw ticket, and continue doing so until you run out of tickets." The fifth person in the line-up represents		

Parts	# of bytes (byte type)	Common or specific	Content of byte
	the start address. In this example, imagine that every person in line represents a parameter in your device. It is from this start address that you will either put values to or retrieve values from, depending on whether you are sending or receiving a SysEx, as defined in part 5 of the SysEx message.		
7	Variable (Data)	Specific	Data values

Description: When part 5 tells the device at the receiving end of a SysEx message that it should be *sending* rather than *receiving* values, the values it sends are found here, starting at the address identified in part 6. When part 5 tells the device to go in receiving mode instead—in other words, requesting data from a device—it retrieves the data and applies it to the parameters starting at the specified address in part 6. The string of values will correspond to the number of bytes it should be retrieving. In this case, there will always be 3 Data bytes (by default) to identify the length of data it needs to retrieve from your device.

8	1 byte (Data)	Roland only	Roland checksum value

Description: This part is found only in Roland devices and serves as a verification mechanism, using a simple mathematical formula to check the integrity of the SysEx data. This value is compared to the result of the mathematical formula, and if both match, the Roland device will accept the SysEx message as being valid. If the result of the mathematical calculation does not match the content of this byte, it will discard the SysEx message, since it interprets it as being corrupted.

9	1 byte (Status)	Common	End SysEx message

Description: Tells the device that the end of the SysEx message has arrived. The device receiving information will then cease to expect SysEx data, and the device sending will stop sending information.

Like all MIDI messages, SysEx messages use binary information to communicate its information. The MIDI specification usually represents this information in the form of hexadecimal values rather than in decimal or binary values. You will find in Appendix A, Table A.1 a table with decimal, binary, and hexadecimal equivalences. This should help you to understand the values that are sent; however, the meaning of these values will be explained here. You might also want to take a look at other tables found in this appendix if you feel the need to do so as you are reading this section.

SysEx messages always start with the F0 value. When the device finds this value in a Status byte (such as the one found in part 1 of a SysEx message), it knows that what follows is a SysEx message. All SysEx messages end with the F7 value. F0 represents the Start SysEx message, and F7 represents the End SysEx value. In Table 11.1, F0 is found in part 1, and

F7 is found in part 9 (part 8 is found only in Roland devices). Here's an example of a typical SysEx message using a hexadecimal string.

Table 11.2 A SysEx Message String, Example 1

Values sent:	F0	41	10	6A	12	01 00 00 28	06	51	F7
Message part:	1	2	3	4	5	6	7	8	9

In Table 11.2, The message would set the reverb type of a Roland JV-1080 performance to Delay. Here's how it breaks down:

Table 11.3 Explanation of Values Found in Example 1

Part	Value	What this means
1	F0	Status byte's start SysEx message.
2	41	This is the manufacturer ID number for Roland.
3	10	This is the device ID number, which in this example corresponds to the JV-1080 Unit number value, converted into hexadecimal. Once again, in this example the unit would be set to 17. To get the device ID, Roland uses the system common parameter minus one, so 17 − 1=16; 16 in hexadecimal is 10. This identifies a specific Roland device in a chain if more than one Roland device was daisy chained.
4	6A	This is the model ID number corresponding to the JV-1080. Each device has its own model ID number.
5	12	This is the command ID: 12 represents a Send command or Dump. If it were 11, it would be a Receive command or Dump Request. There can be other manufacturer-specific commands, such as sequencer dump request or global data dump; however, these will allow your device to send or receive specific sets of values (part 7) for the parameter defined in part 6 of the SysEx message.
6	01 00 00 28	The first set of two values, 01 00, represents the start address for the JV-1080's temporary performance parameters. To find out which address corresponds to which parameter, you will have to look at your device's manual in the parameter base address table found at the end of the documentation. The third value, 00, points to the performance common parameter, telling the JV-1080 that this is not a performance part parameter but rather a parameter that will affect all parts in a performance, since it is common to all. The last value, 28, refers to the reverb type of this common performance parameter. So, the target for the value found

Part	Value	What this means
		in part 7 is the reverb type for the common temporary performance parameter. You could call this the start parameter ID address. If more values were sent in part 7, all subsequent values (in part 7) would be inserted from this point on in your device's address map. It goes without saying that this example, with these values, only represents the reverb type for the JV-1080. In another MIDI device, though, these values could represent something completely different.
7	06	This represents the value that will be sent to the reverb type for the common temporary performance of the JV-1080. In this device, 06 represents the Delay.
8	51	This is the Roland checksum byte. The error-checking process uses a checksum formula that is quite simple. In essence, it involves adding all the values of parts 6 and 7 together, converting to decimal, dividing by 128, and subtracting the remainder from 128. In this case: 1+0+0+40 (28 in hexadecimal)+6=47; since 47 is less than 128, you don't need to divide it to get the remainder. Finally, 128 −47=81; 81 in hexadecimal is 51. If the values in parts 6 and 7 don't match up to the one in part 8, the SysEx message is discarded. This said, there are as many ways of calculating checksums as there are manufacturers. You shouldn't worry too much about it, since this is always transparent to users anyway.
9	F7	This identifies the end of the SysEx message.

Universal SysEx

Most System Exclusive messages are manufacturer specific. However, there is another kind of SysEx, one that's common to all manufacturers, called the universal SysEx message. It is considered a SysEx message because its header (always F0, or Start SysEx) and footers (always F7 or End SysEx) are identical to those in the manufacturer-specific SysEx. Universal System Exclusive messages are used for extensions to the MIDI standard. They are not reserved for any particular manufacturer and may be used by any suitable MIDI device.

Universal SysEx is used for the following types of messages:

✳ To enable or disable GM mode in a GM-compatible sound module. Some devices have built-in GM modules or GM patch sets in addition to non-GM patch sets or non-GM modes of operation. When GM is enabled, it replaces any non-GM patch set or non-GM mode with a GM mode/patch set. This allows a device to have modes or patch sets that go beyond the limits of GM and yet still have the capability to be switched into a GM-compliant mode when desired.

❋ In a multi-timbral instrument, volume settings for each part are handled by the control change number 7 (volume). However, you can also control the master volume of your device using a universal SysEx message.

❋ Occasionally, a device may want to know what other devices are connected to it. For example, editor/librarian software running on a computer may need to know what devices are connected to the computer's MIDI port so that the software can configure itself to accept dumps from those devices. To do so, it may perform an Identity Request by sending this type of SysEx message. In return, the devices will send an Identity Reply message containing information about who they are. Knock, knock. Who's there? It's me Karma, Korg Karma!

❋ MIDI samplers use digital audio waveforms as their audio source. A sub-protocol was implemented within MIDI in which devices can exchange this digital audio waveform data. In other words, it's a protocol that exchanges digital audio data over MIDI cables within the parameters of MIDI. Because of the nature of digital audio, these transfers are usually substantial. The only way to do this is with universal SysEx messages, and so several specific SysEx messages were defined in order to implement Sample Dump Standard (SDS). Many samplers support this protocol. This was discussed earlier in this book (see Chapter 6).

❋ When working with video, it is possible to lock a MIDI sequencer with the videotape playback device using MTC (MIDI Time Code). Although MTC quarter frames are system-common messages, a full frame information—a single hour, minute, second, frame, and sub-frame information—can be sent using the universal SysEx message to cue a slave device to a specific point in time. This full frame message sends the complete SMPTE time address in hours, minutes, seconds, and frames in a single message. The slave (SMPTE recipient) doesn't actually start running until it starts receiving quarter frame messages. This implies that the slave is stopped when receiving this type of message. During shuttle modes (fast-forward or rewind), the master should not continuously send quarter frame messages but, rather, send full-frame messages at regular intervals.

There are two categories of universal SysEx messages: real-time and non-real-time. A real-time universal SysEx message occurs at the moment in time it should be sent in order to achieve the desired effect. One example would be to send a MIDI Machine Control (MMC) message to start the playback of a tape recorder using a real-time universal SysEx message at the beginning of a song as the sequencer starts playing the sequence. A non-real-time universal SysEx message can occur at any time, and its timing is not critical to the sequence of events. A bulk dump of program settings from a hardware device to an editor/librarian application is a good example of non-real-time universal SysEx messages at work. You will find more on this in the paragraphs that follow. Every function mentioned in the list above will fall within one of these two categories. This is identified in the first Data byte following the SysEx Status byte. Looking at Table 11.1, in a manufacturer-specific SysEx message, you would find the manufacturer ID; however, in a universal SysEx, you would find either the value 7E to identify a non-real-time message or 7F to identify a real-time message, since no manufacturer ID is required for universal messages. Let's take a look at each part of a universal SysEx message in Table 11.4.

Table 11.4   The Content of a Universal SysEx Message

Part	Value (or range)	Content
1	F0	SysEx Start (Status byte)

Description:

This tells the device that the following bytes consist of SysEx information.

| 2 | 7E or 7F | Non-real-time or real-time |

Description:

This tells the device if the universal SysEx is of real-time (7F) or non-real-time (7E) nature.

| 3 | 00 to 7F | Channel |

Description:

This range of values is meant to identify a device or a channel. Usually, SysEx messages do not have channels; however, it is possible with universal SysEx to specify a channel. This allows a musician to set various devices to ignore certain universal SysEx messages. For example, if the device has a base channel set to 1, it could filter out any universal SysEx messages sent on another channel. This range of values provides up to 128 different channels. However, the last value, 7F, would tell the device to disregard any channel information and respond to any channels

| 4 | 00 to 7F | Sub ID 1 |

Description:

This defines the category of the SysEx's function. For example, when you wish to use the GM mode, the value would be 09. This would activate the GM enable/disable mode. However, whether it is active or not would be defined by a second byte found in part 5. Another example of a sub ID would be to identify a device control, such as a master volume or a pitch bend. The sub ID for a device control would be represented by the hex value 04. The specific device control would then be identified in part 5 as well. In some cases, however, only one ID is needed to identify the function, such as when you wish to do a sample dump or a generic handshake between two devices to confirm that the information was sent properly to the right device. You will find a list of all sub IDs in Table 11.5.

| 5 | 00 to 7F | Sub ID 2 |

Description:

This value adds precision to the function defined in part 4 of this message. As mentioned above, this could represent the value set by the GM mode; for example, 00 would be disabled and 01 enabled.

Part	Value (or range)	Content

It could also identify a device control, such as the master volume or the pitch bend for the device. The actual values for these parameters will be found in the following part.

6	Any value	Data

Description:

This part represents the actual data sent by the parameter defined in parts 4 and 5. This could contain any number of bytes. A sample data dump would be quite large, for example. Another example of data could be the MTC full frame SMPTE time code address.

7	F7	End of SysEx

Description:

This identifies the end of the SysEx message.

Here's a list of all the defined universal SysEx functions, as found in Sub ID 1 described in part 4 of Table 11.4:

Table 11.5   Real-Time and Non-Real-Time Functions as Defined by Sub ID1, with Their Associated Hexadecimal Values

Non-real-time Sub ID 1	Function name	Real-time Sub ID 1	Function name
01	Sample dump header	01	MIDI Time Code (MTC) full message and user bit
02	Sample data packet	02	MIDI Show Control
03	Sample dump request	03	Notation information
04	MIDI Time Code (MTC) for cueing purposes	04	Device control
05	Sample dump extensions	05	Real-time MTC cueing
06	General information	06	MIDI Machine Control (MMC) commands
07	File dump	07	MMC responses
08	MIDI tuning standard	08	MIDI tuning standard
09	General MIDI		
7B	End of file		
7C	Wait		

Non-real-time Sub ID 1	Function name	Real-time Sub ID 1	Function name
7D	Cancel		
7E	NAK (last data packet not received correctly)		
7F	ACK (last data packet received correctly)		

Sending SysEx

Now that you know what you can find in a SysEx message, how can you make a device send SysEx? Fortunately, that's the easy part. As mentioned previously when discussing patch bay configurations and editor/librarian applications, it is important that a direct MIDI connection between the sender and the receiver be made. You can work with SysEx messages even with devices in a daisy chain. This, however, requires extra precautions, such as assigning a different device ID number for each device in the chain and making sure the base MIDI channel is also different. These precautions will help ensure that the MIDI device you meant to communicate with processes only the SysEx messages.

Usually, there is a function or utility button on the front panel of MIDI devices to send a bulk dump. This means that you will be sending SysEx messages. From that point, you can choose what kind of information you want to send. For example, you might send user patches, performances, or system settings. If there are no such buttons on your device, there are two workaround solutions:

- Get an editor/librarian application that will identify your device, and initiate a SysEx bulk dump request from this application. This allows the software to receive the appropriate SysEx information from any external MIDI device.
- Find out what message makes the device dump its settings via its MIDI Out. Use the SysEx editor in a sequencer to insert that message in a track. Writing such a SysEx string can be fairly complicated and requires an extensive study of the fine print in the operation manual. So, if in doubt, stick with the first method and get an editor/librarian, as it'll save you a lot of headaches.

As you can see in Figure 11.1, the Info section of this dialog box displays the instrument information and the data type of the bulk dump being transferred, along with the device ID number (Comm Ch) and the MIDI ports over which the information is being transferred.

Recording SysEx

There are two reasons you would record SysEx: to save all the values that make up one program or to save all programs in the instrument or device so that when you play a song, it remembers the external device's setup. This will allow you to recall the device's parameters

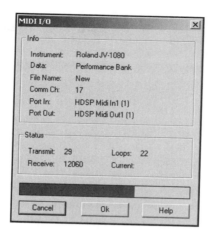

Figure 11.1   A bulk dump transfer of performance banks in the Roland JV-1080.

as they were when you saved the song. The next time you load the song, you won't have to change anything on your device when you load the song, since the parameters were stored with the sequence using SysEx. This is called a bulk dump.

The second reason would be to store codes that instruct the instrument to change one of its settings, such as the cutoff frequency of a filter, or the decay of a reverb during playback or at the beginning of the song. System Exclusive can be used as a last resort for things that can't be done with regular MIDI messages. This is done through SysEx parameter changes.

Since your MIDI device stores values for its parameter in its memory, changing these values will result in changing the parameter's settings as well. Usually, your MIDI device can send all or some of these parameters to your computer or a sequencer using what is called a bulk dump. This action is performed using SysEx messages, as described earlier. You can use a bulk dump to make a copy of your MIDI device's settings, or you can allow editor/librarian software to gather information about your current device settings.

Once a device's SysEx has been dumped into the computer's memory, it can be sent back to the device later to reset all the parameters to the way they were when you saved them. When using an editor/librarian application, you can make changes to these parameters and transmit the changes back to your device. In this case, your computer (through the use of the editor/librarian) becomes a remote control application for your MIDI device.

Most hardware MIDI devices send a bulk dump of all or some of the device's parameters. Consult your device's documentation. Once you've identified where the bulk dumping function is and how to proceed, here's what you'll do to record a bulk dump in your sequencer:

1. Connect the MIDI Out of your device to the MIDI In of your computer or sequencer.
2. Disable any SysEx filters from your sequencer's MIDI filter options if necessary, as shown in Figure 11.2. As the name implies, filters will prevent SysEx messages from being recorded by the sequencer.

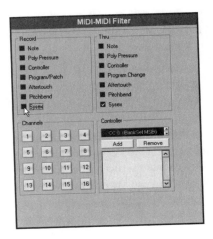

Figure 11.2 The MIDI Filtering option.

3. Create a MIDI track in your sequencer in which to record the SysEx.
4. Click on the Record button in your sequencer to initiate the recording process. Mute all other tracks while recording SysEx. Performing a SysEx bulk dump will require a large portion of the MIDI bandwidth, and it is recommended that you create a MIDI file with just this information.
5. Press the appropriate buttons on your MIDI device to initiate the bulk dump. Some devices display a special message to confirm the SysEx is being transmitted. When the device is done with its transmission, you should see a message such as "Done" or "Completed."
6. Stop the recording.
7. Save the information. To avoid recording more SysEx messages by mistake, you may re-enable the SysEx filtering option if you are done recording the bulk dump at this point.

Proceed similarly to record parameter automation in a sequencer. For example, this would be useful if you would like to change the reverb type of your MIDI device's reverb at bar 15. Because MIDI is transmitted over a serial cable, pieces of information are sent one after the other, not side by side. With SysEx, the entire message is transmitted before the rest of the MIDI messages can resume their course. So if you wish to record SysEx parameter changes as you are playing notes, the more SysEx messages you are sending, the longer it will take for the other events to be transmitted. So, keep your SysEx events as short as possible or, if you can, make sure not to overload the MIDI port with this type of message. To record parameter changes to your sequencer during playback:

1. Connect the MIDI Out of your device to the MIDI In of a computer or sequencer.
2. Disable any SysEx filters from the sequencer's MIDI filter options if necessary.
3. Create a MIDI track in the sequencer where you wish to record the SysEx.
4. Chances are if you want to update parameters during playback, you probably already have a MIDI track with recorded events. To hear any previously recorded information, such as an existing reverb setting in our example, unmute the track.
5. Begin the record process in your MIDI sequencer.
6. Make the changes to your external MIDI device's parameters when it is appropriate in the song.
7. Stop the recording process when done.
8. Rewind and start playback to hear the result. Let's assume the same example: If you've recorded a reverb type change from a plate to a hall reverb, this parameter should now change automatically every time your device receives this SysEx message.

Since you recorded the SysEx events on another track, if you are not satisfied with the result, you can always erase these events and start over without affecting the other types of events recorded for this part. For example, to change the cutoff frequency of a synth line playing on MIDI port A, channel 1, you would have one track containing the notes played by the synth and another track that performs the change in the cutoff frequency using SysEx. Erasing the SysEx events will not affect the notes, since they are on separate tracks.

Most software synthesizers can also be automated, but since they are integrated to the software environment, automating their parameters does not require SysEx messages, but rather, automation is recorded on special automation tracks. The most common methods of creating such automation is by using the computer mouse or by associating MIDI control surface knobs, faders, and buttons to parameters available inside the software. Once this association is created, changes made to the MIDI surface's controls can be recorded, just as with SysEx, to create parameter automation inside a MIDI sequence.

Here are some tips to keep in mind when recording SysEx:

✳ Record just the parameters you need to record. If you're performing a bulk dump, your MIDI device will likely offer different options. This will save space in your sequencer and speed up the SysEx transfer back to your MIDI device. In a live performance, you don't want to have to wait too long between songs for SysEx to be uploaded to your MIDI devices, so keeping things to a minimum is necessary.

✳ To send parameter information and patch information from a sequencer to an external MIDI device only before a song starts to play, put the SysEx information before the first bar, if possible, or before the occurrence of MIDI events in the MIDI sequence. This prevents lags caused by long SysEx messages being sent simultaneously with other MIDI events.

❋ To only change the sound settings (program) during playback, you might be better off creating two different programs and using a program change during playback rather than using a SysEx message. Program changes are more efficient in this case and will take less time to update your external MIDI device. On the other hand, if you want your sound to change dynamically throughout the song—let's say changing the LFO rate when the chorus arrives—you will be better off using SysEx parameter controls for this change.

❋ Avoid sending a SysEx bulk dump from your sequencer to several external MIDI devices simultaneously.

❋ Make sure when you record a bulk dump that you are using the same device ID number as you will be using when sending this bulk dump back to the MIDI device. Otherwise, the device might not accept the SysEx bulk dump.

❋ Certain sequencers will allow you to send a SysEx bulk dump automatically whenever you load a MIDI file. Use this feature to configure your devices appropriately for each song, but keep the previous tips in mind.

Transmitting SysEx

Once your bulk dump or SysEx parameters have been recorded in a sequencer, it can be sent back to the MIDI device whenever needed. This is fairly easy to do, since you already know how to do a bulk dump in one direction. Here's how to transmit the information back to your external MIDI device:

1. Connect the MIDI Out of your sequencer to the MIDI In of the external MIDI device.

2. Disable any filters that would prevent your sequencer from playing back the SysEx information.

3. If your MIDI device can deactivate its SysEx reception, make sure this option is disabled. In other words, you want your MIDI device to respond to incoming SysEx information.

4. Solo the track containing the SysEx data. This might not always be necessary, but it's a good precaution to take, since you might have more than one SysEx data track or other events that will cause the transfer to interrupt abruptly.

5. Play back the data from your sequencer. The display on your external MIDI device should indicate that it is receiving SysEx.

You should take the same precautions when sending SysEx to your MIDI device as you do when your sequencer is receiving SysEx. For example, try not to send more data than required. If all you need to recall is a single program, avoid sending full bulk dumps to your machine. If the bulk dump serves to set up your device for a song, try putting your SysEx in the count-in bars before the actual song starts.

Editing SysEx!?

We've seen what a SysEx message contains and looked at some examples at the beginning of this chapter. If you are a real masochist or need to edit a corrupt SysEx instruction manually, you may do so using a SysEx editor if your sequencer provides one. Though it's possible, editing SysEx is not everyone's cup of tea. It requires a profound understanding of your device's parameter map and hexadecimal conversion skills, since each SysEx dump contains several strings of hexadecimal SysEx messages. In other words, it's best to leave the handling of SysEx messages to your software applications, such as sequencers and editor/librarians.

MIDI Synchronizing Options

MIDI, as you know by now, serves as a communication mechanism between two MIDI-compatible devices. It also serves as a synchronization tool between different time-based devices. This could be a sequencer and a drum machine, two sequencers, a sequencer and a video playback device, or even a sequencer and a multi-track tape recorder with intelligent MIDI capability. In this last example, the tape recorder would control the playback of your sequencer through time code (SMPTE converted into MTC), and then your sequencer would send playback control commands to this device through MIDI. This is called MIDI Machine Control (MMC). A more recent addition to MIDI synchronization has been the development of ASIO 2 and other such drivers (ReWire 2 for example), which synchronize effects to a MIDI tempo. For example, you can use a delay effect in which each occurrence of the delay will be in sync with 16th notes in a sequence. Changing the tempo of the song also changes the corresponding timing values inside the delay. Traditionally, to have such timing synchronicity, you'd have to manually calculate delay times and then recalculate them if you changed the tempo setting.

Before we take an in-depth look at synchronization, it is important to understand the different types of synchronization, its terminology, and basic concepts. There's always a master/slave relationship between the source of the synchronization and the recipient of this source. There can be only one master, but there can be many slaves to this master. There are three basic synchronizing methods here: time code, MIDI clock, and word clock.

Time Code

Time code is an electronic signal used to identify a precise location on time-based media such as audio, videotape, or digital systems that support time code. This location represents a time address in hours, minutes, seconds, and frames, and some more advanced synchronization devices will even display the usually hidden sub-frame information. The electronic signal is sent along with the media to allow other devices to synchronize with this signal. A locking mechanism in the receiving device is used to make sure the time location of the sending device is matched by the time location of the receiving device's time location.

For example, a videotape containing time code information is sent to a sequencer in order for the sequencer to lock and follow the video's time location. Imagine that a postal worker delivering mail is the locking mechanism, the houses on the street are location addresses on the time code, and the letters have matching addresses. The postal worker reads the letters and makes sure they get to the correct address, just as a synchronizing device will compare the time code from a source and a destination, bring the two (or more) devices into simultaneous operation, and make sure, as the postal worker does with letters, that events are happening when they should along the time line. This time code is also known as SMPTE (Society of Motion Picture and Television Engineers) time code, and it comes in three flavors:

- ✻ MTC (MIDI Time Code) is the MIDI version of SMPTE time code and is normally used to synchronize audio or video devices to MIDI devices such as sequencers.
- ✻ VITC (Vertical Interval Time Code) is normally used by video machines to send or receive synchronization information to and from any type of VITC-compatible device. VITC may be recorded as part of the video signal in an unused line, which is part of the vertical interval. It has the advantage of being readable when the playback video deck is paused.
- ✻ LTC (Longitudinal Time Code) is also used to synchronize video machines. Unlike VITC, however, it is also used to synchronize audio-only information, such as a transfer between a tape recorder and a sequencer. LTC usually takes the form of an audio signal that is recorded on one of the tracks of the tape. Since LTC is an audio signal, it is silent if the tape is not moving.

Each one of these time codes uses an hours:minutes:seconds:frames format.

WHAT ARE FRAME RATES?

As the name implies, a frame rate is the number of frames a film or video signal displays in one second. Locking frame rates with MIDI through MTC might seem challenging at first, but once you understand which frame rate your video project uses, you'll figure it out quickly.
The acronym for frame rate is "fps" for Frames Per Second.

There are several possible frame rates to choose from. Here's a look at common frame rates and when they are most likely to appear or be used:

- ✻ 24fps—Used by motion picture film or some professional digital video (DV) streams, you will likely not encounter this fps standard, since chances are you do not have a film projector hooked up to a computer running a sequencer to synchronize sound.
- ✻ 25fps—Refers to the PAL (Phase Alternate Line) video standard used mostly in Asia and SECAM/EBU (Sequential Color And Memory/European Broadcast Union) video standard used mostly in Europe. If you live in those areas, this is the format your VCR uses. A single frame in this format is made up of 625 horizontal lines.
- ✻ 29.97fps—Also known as 29.97 Non-Drop. This refers to the NTSC (National Television Standards Committee) video standard used mostly in North America. If you live in this area, this is the format your VCR uses. A single frame in this format is made up of 525 horizontal lines. On some devices using only two digits to represent the time code format, you might see this time code represented as 30fps. However, you should not think of it as the actual 30fps time code, which represents the NTSC black and white standard. This latter format is quite rare, and unless there is another way used by your time code

reader to identify properly the difference between 29.97 Non-Drop and 29.97 Drop Frame, when it is written "30," you may assume it refers to 29.97 Non-Drop.

* 29.97fps DF—Also known as 29.97 Drop Frame (hence the DF at the end). This can also be referred to as 30 DF on older video time code machines. This is probably the trickiest time code of all to understand since there is a lot of confusion about the drop frame. In order to accommodate the extra information needed for color when this format was first introduced, the black and white's 30fps was slowed to 29.97fps for color. Though this is probably not an issue for you, in broadcast, the small difference between real time (also known as the wall or house clock) and the time registered on the video can be problematic. Over a period of one SMPTE hour, the video will be 3.6 seconds or 108 extra frames longer in relation to the wall clock. To overcome this discrepancy, drop frames are used. This is calculated as follows: Every frame 00 and 01 is dropped for each minute change, except for minutes with 0s (like 00, 10, 20, 30, 40, and 50). Therefore, two frames skipped every minute is 120 frames per hour, except for the minutes ending with zero, so 120 − 12 = 108 frames. Setting your frame rate to 29.97 DF when it's not—in other words, if it's 29.97 (Non-Drop)—will cause your synchronization to be off by 3.6 seconds per hour.

* 30fps—Used with the first black and white NTSC standard. It is still used sometimes in music or sound applications where no video reference is required.

* 30fps DF—This is not a standard time code protocol and usually refers to older time code devices that were unable to display the decimal points when the 29.97 Drop Frame time code was used. Try to avoid this time code frame rate setting when synchronizing to video, since it might introduce errors in your synchronization. SMPTE does not support this time code anyway.

As stated above, in any synchronization situation, there is always a master/slave relationship. The master's time code controls any slaved device set to follow it. When you want to synchronize different devices, you need to set the sending device as the master and the receiving devices as slaves in order for these devices to follow the master's timing.

Sequencers have special synchronization options that allow you to set up your software to either control other connected devices or slave to an incoming time code or synchronization clock. In order for synchronization to occur, you need to make sure that the following components are set up properly:

* Physical connections: This will vary, depending on the type of synchronization you are using. For example, if you are using MIDI clock, connect the master and slaves using a MIDI connection. Since your master is sending the MIDI clock, the MIDI Out of the master should be connected to the MIDI In of the slave device(s). On the other hand, if you are using an SMPTE time code such as a VITC or LTC, you will need to convert this to MTC (in most cases) in order for your sequencer to recognize the time, since most sequencers are MTC compatible.

* Virtual connection: It's important to tell the software where the time code is coming from or going to once the physical connections have been established. For example, when

using a multi-port MIDI interface with a built-in SMPTE-to-MTC converter, select the appropriate port on the interface that corresponds to the incoming sync signal. When echoing the MTC to another device from a sequencer, configure the appropriate port connected to the external MIDI device expecting a sync signal.

※ Master (internal)/slave (external) relations: You will then need to configure your sequencer to a master or slave setting. This will allow the sequencer to either send out synchronization information generated internally or wait for it to arrive on a designated MIDI port or other synchronization connection from an external source.

※ Sync format: Telling the software which type of time code you are using is important if you want it to stay synchronized. Choosing one of the aforementioned time codes in your sync dialog box will ensure this. Typically, when a sequencer is in slave mode or following an external time code, it is the incoming time code format that dictates the sequencer's sync setting.

MIDI Clock

MIDI clock is a tempo-based synchronization signal used to synchronize two or more MIDI devices together with beats-per-minute (BPM) for a guide track. This is different than time code, since it does not refer to a real time address in hours, minutes, seconds, and frames. MIDI clock sends 24 evenly spaced MIDI clocks per quarter note. So, at a speed of 60 BPM, it sends 1,440 MIDI clocks per minute (one every 41.67 milliseconds), whereas at a speed of 120 BPM, it will send double that amount (one every 20.83 milliseconds). Because it is tempo based, the MIDI clock rate changes to follow the tempo of the master tempo source. You don't have to do anything when changing the tempo; the MIDI clock rate follows automatically.

When a master sends a MIDI clock signal, it sends a MIDI Start message to tell its slave to start playing a sequence at the speed or tempo set in the master's sequence. When the master sends a MIDI End message, it tells the slave to stop playing a sequence. Up until this point, all the slave can do is start and stop playing MIDI when it receives these messages. If you want to tell the slave sequence where to start, the MIDI clock has to send what is called a Song Position Pointer message. This is a system common MIDI message and was discussed in Chapter 2. For example, to lock a software sequencer to a hardware sequencer, the song position pointer message tells the slave device (the software sequencer) the location of the master device's song position (the hardware sequencer). It uses the MIDI data to count the position where the MIDI Start message is in relation to the master. The Song Position Pointer message would tell the software sequencer the bar and beat position of the hardware sequence.

Using MIDI clock should be reserved for use between MIDI devices only, not for audio or video. Most high-end sequencers, such as Logic or Cubase for example, no longer slave to MIDI clock. Since it's a tempo-based system, it is not well suited for use with audio or video. While MIDI clock keeps good synchronization between similar MIDI devices, audio requires much greater precision. Video, on the other hand, works with time-based events, which do not translate well when you change the tempo's BPM speed.

Another type of MIDI-related synchronization is MIDI Machine Control (MMC). The MMC protocol uses System Exclusive messages over a MIDI cable to remotely control hard disk recording systems and other machines used for record or playback. Many older MIDI-enabled devices support this protocol, which is described later in this chapter.

MIDI Time Code (MTC)

MTC messages are an alternative to using MIDI clocks and Song Position Pointer messages (telling a device where it is in relation to a song). MTC is essentially SMPTE (time based) mutated for transmission over MIDI.

On a soundtrack of a movie, there are six categories of sounds: music, sound effects, room tones or ambiances, Foley, ADR (Automatic Dialog Replacement), and lastly, but most importantly, dialog. All of these categories, with the exception of music, refer to non-musical time references, such as seconds and frames rather than bars and beats. As you could imagine, a car explosion doesn't really have to be on bar 5, beat 2, but rather at 45 seconds and three frames past the scene's beginning. Such references are known as absolute time-based references, and it is the way these non-musical elements are referred to when working on a film/video project. In contrast, musical elements are often referred to as relative music-based locations. They are relative to a bar and beat, and changing the tempo of the song will change when a music-based time reference occurs along an absolute time-based reference.

This said, when working on music for a film or video project, you will have to deal with both relative (music-based) and absolute (time-based) references because the film itself sends time code information that represents the absolute time, and your MIDI sequencer works in relative time against this absolute time reference.

ASIO 2

Steinberg developed a cross-platform, multi-channel audio transfer protocol called ASIO (Audio Stream Input/Output). Many manufacturers of audio/MIDI hardware and software are adopting this protocol. It gives software access to the multi-channel capabilities of a wide range of audio hardware. It also expands on the basic capabilities of a standard audio hardware, allowing more than two audio channels at once. For example, by using audio hardware with eight inputs and eight outputs, you could record on these eight inputs simultaneously and also play back on the eight outputs simultaneously.

The ASIO 2 specification defines the interface that manufacturers of professional audio hardware must use to create an ASIO driver for their hardware. The driver allows the host application (audio/MIDI) to see all of the inputs and outputs available on the audio hardware. This allows the users to record more than two tracks simultaneously. This is not a very radical departure from other types of drivers. However, ASIO 2 shines by providing the user with a way to bypass the operating system while making the link between the audio hardware and the host application more efficient. This translates into smaller delays between the input of audio hardware and its output. A long delay would make it very difficult to record audio and monitor what you're playing through headphones as you are playing other recorded tracks in your project. This delay is called latency, and ASIO drivers reduce this latency factor to very small amounts—in some cases, as low as 1 millisecond. When playing with software instruments, the shorter the delay between the time you press on a MIDI note on a keyboard and the time you hear the actual note generated by the instrument, the better or more realistic the feel of playing a real instrument will be.

With ASIO 2 drivers comes a new feature called ASIO positioning protocol. This is a technology that ensures that audio in the host application (such as Cubase or Nuendo) is in sample accurate sync with external devices. Sample accurate implies that for each sample being sent out, there will be a corresponding sample received. In other words, imagine a time code with as many time location addresses as your project's sampling rate. This is part of the ASIO 2 feature specification. In order to take advantage of the ASIO positioning protocol, your audio hardware must have an ASIO 2 driver written for it. ASIO 2 can read an external word clock, which is a digital clock provided by the sample rate of an external device, and lock to it. This will give a sync that is accurate to one forty-four thousandth (1/44,000th) of a second, or approximately 0.02 milliseconds. To find out if you can use ASIO drivers, you will need a compatible host application and audio hardware that offers ASIO support. You will have to consult your software and hardware documentation to find out if they do. Currently, Steinberg, Apple, Propellerhead, Ableton, Sony, Digidesign, and other companies offer software products that support ASIO drivers.

MIDI Machine Control (MMC)

MIDI Machine Control (MMC) was added to the MIDI protocol in 1992 and serves as a transport control mechanism between various machine types. At the time it was developed, it was thought that MMC could be used to connect different transport controls between audio tape recorders, video, CD players and recorders, and other digital audio recording systems. However, in today's practical applications, MMC is used as a way to control the transport controls of an audio tape recorder or digital audio multi-track using an MMC-compatible sequencer.

MMC sends MIDI to a device, giving it commands such as play, stop, rewind, go to a specific location, punch-in, and punch-out on a specific track. Although MMC is quite extensive with its 100-page-long official documentation, its use in the music world has not been extended to its full potential. This is because the market has adopted a more integrated approach, using computers as a way to record audio rather than an external analog tape recorder, while external digital audio multi-track recorders use other technologies to lock up to other devices such as time code and word clock sync.

In order to make use of MMC in a setup where you are using a multi-track tape recorder and a sequencer, you need to have a SMPTE time code track sending time code to a SMPTE/MTC converter (see Figure 11.3). Then, you would send the converted MTC to your sequencer so that your sequencer can stay in sync with the multi-track recorder. Both devices are also connected through MIDI cables. It is the multi-track that controls the sequencer's timing, not vice versa. The sequencer, in return, can transmit MMC messages through its MIDI connection with the multi-track, which is equipped with a MIDI interface. These MMC messages tell the multi-track to rewind, fast-forward, and so on. Hitting Play in the sequencer tells the multi-track

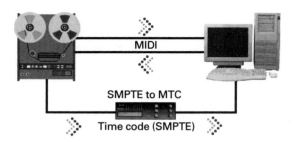

Figure 11.3 Signal path of an MMC-enabled setup.

to go to the position where playback in the sequencer begins. When the multi-track reaches this position, it starts playing the tape back. Once it starts playing, it then sends time code to the sequencer, to which it then syncs.

MIDI Show Control (MSC)

MIDI Show Control (MSC) is intended to provide MIDI control of lighting and other theatre equipment such as smoke machines, elevators, and lighting automation of a play (see Figure 11.4). It can also be used at amusement parks and other similar venues for synchronizing purposes, as well as for controlling various equipment via MIDI remote control.

MSC differs from anything else within MIDI since, first of all, the chances of a lighting MSC setup and a MIDI music setup being hooked together are remote at best. One of the reasons for this is that there are very rigorous safety protocols built into MSC due to the safety hazard that automating a light or an elevator movement implies. These safety protocols are not implemented in music-oriented MIDI. Imagine for a second that a crane starts moving as someone is on it; this could be a bit more catastrophic than if you send the wrong control change to your MIDI device, for example. In short, if you wish to use MIDI and MSC together, you can synchronize them using MTC, MIDI clock sync, or time code when you need to have lighting controlled by musical events that occur in time. However, hooking both setups together would probably be counterproductive, since MIDI messages tend to lose their effectiveness when a large number of devices are receiving and sending information simultaneously. This is why it is suggested to use multiple MIDI ports rather than daisy-chaining multiple MIDI devices together. For the same reason, it is more efficient to separate the two systems, since they do not control the same type of equipment and their purposes are different. It just happens that the communication system they use is derived from the same protocol: MIDI.

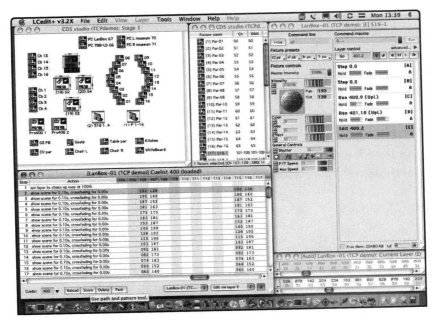

Figure 11.4 The LCEdit+ is software that is used with hardware components that allow you to control a lighting setup–this software goes with the LanBox-LC hardware interface (www.cds.nl).

Review Questions

1. Select the question matching this statement: It controls parameters determining how sounds are produced that are outside the defined MIDI message parameters.

   a) What is the Data Entry controller?

   b) What is the General Purpose controller?

   c) What is LTB?

   d) What is SysEx?

2. How many parts does a SysEx message for a non-Roland device have?

   a) 1

   b) 8

   c) 9

   d) 16

3. Select the question matching this statement: Tells a device that the following data is a SysEx message.

   a) What is the Start SysEx message?

   b) What is the Manufacturer ID number?

   c) What is the Device ID number?

   d) What is the Start Address message?

4. If all SysEx messages begin with the F0 hexadecimal value, how do they always end?

   a) It depends on the device.

   b) It depends on the values being sent.

   c) The FF hex value

   d) The F7 hex value

5. Complete the following sentence: There are two categories of SysEx messages: One is called universal SysEx, while the other is called _____.

   a) Manufacturer Specific SysEx

   b) Roland Checksum

   c) GM Specific SysEx

   d) None of the above

6. Select the non-real-time universal SysEx message from the following list:

   a) MMC Start Command message

   b) MMC Response message

   c) File dump message

   d) Device Control message

7. Complete the following sentence: MIDI's equivalent of SMPTE is called _____.

   a) MMC

   b) MTC

   c) LTC

   d) VITC

8. Complete the following sentence: The North American (NTSC) standard frame rate for video is _____.

   a) 25fps

   b) 29.97fps

   c) 29.97 DF fps

   d) 30fps

9. Select the question matching this statement: A tempo-based synchronization signal used to synchronize two or more MIDI devices together with beats-per-minute (BPM) for a guide track.

    a) What is a digital clock?

    b) What is time code?

    c) What is MIDI clock?

    d) What is word clock?

10. True or False: To change a device's parameter using SysEx, it is not necessary to do a bulk dump SysEx transfer to this device; you can transfer the value for this single parameter if needed.

12 The Standard MIDI File Format

This chapter is meant for those of you who would like to understand how a Standard MIDI File saves recorded MIDI events into a file format and then reproduces this content through MIDI sequencer applications. You do not need to read through only to use SMF, since most of what is explained here is automatically interpreted by a MIDI player or sequencer application anyway. On the other hand, to understand how MIDI is recorded into a file, this chapter is meant just for you. This is, after all, a book called *MIDI Power!* So dig in.

The Standard MIDI File (SMF) format was designed to record and play back musical performances through a MIDI sequencer. This format saves MIDI messages and a time stamp associated with each message. The time stamp represents clock durations—in other words, how many clock pulses to wait before playing the event.

Here's a summary of what you will learn in this chapter and a look at the content of a SMF:

* MIDI messages: all types of messages, including SysEx.

* Time stamps for each message.

* Tempo settings for the song.

* Pulse Per Quarter Note (PPQN) resolution information or resolution expressed in time code format (SMPTE).

* Why time signatures are associated with a song.

* Where key signatures appear for each track.

* How track names are associated with musical parts.

* Using pattern names to represent all parts or tracks in a song or all parts for a portion of a song.

The information contained in an SMF represents the common elements that all players and sequencers understand. The SMF format also supports sequencer-proprietary information. This allows sequencers to save additional information to the file without making it unreadable by other sequencers. It works a bit like the manufacturer ID number in a SysEx message. In this case, however, the sequencer ID is attached to parts of the information that are sequencer specific and can be found anywhere in the file, not just at the beginning of the file where manufacturer ID numbers are located.

For example, a sequencer can save a file with the metronome clock set to On by attaching specific information to the SMF. Another sequencer will simply ignore this information if it doesn't understand it. In other words, SMF can always be backward compatible because of these ID messages. If the application doesn't understand them, it simply skips them. These ID messages are sent in what is called a MIDI chunk.

SMF is most often used in sequencer or MIDI player applications. But it can also be used in other MIDI applications such as editor/librarian applications, since SMF can hold SysEx information that can store or load instrument settings used by these latter applications. The most common application of SMF, though, is to record and play back MIDI songs.

MIDI Chunks

A MIDI chunk is a group of related bytes MIDI uses to save or transmit information to and from a SMF. It is the building block of MIDI files and is comparable in structure to a MIDI message, in the sense that it is made up of a Status byte and followed by a series of Data bytes. Each chunk can contain many bytes of information, depending on its content. There are two types of chunks: header chunks and track chunks. Both have a similar structure but serve different purposes. The header chunk is found only once, at the beginning of the SMF. It defines the information that follows as a MIDI file. There will always be only one header chunk in a MIDI file, since its only purpose is to define the MIDI file itself.

This could be compared to the SysEx's Start SysEx message. A series of variable length track chunks containing MIDI messages follow the header chunk, which are found in the MIDI file's tracks. A track in a MIDI file represents the same thing as a track in a sequencer. So, if you have 10 tracks in your sequencer and you save it as a MIDI file format, this file will contain 10 track chunks under its header chunk. Each track chunk is structured as follows:

  * Four bytes that define what type of chunk this is; those four bytes are called the chunk ID. This will be referred to as the MThd chunk (MIDI Track, header chunk) or MTrk chunk (MIDI Track, track chunk). These four bytes will represent ASCII characters, as opposed to binary values. ASCII stands for American Standard Code for Information Interchange. Computers can only understand numbers, so an ASCII code is the numerical representation of a character such as "a" or "@" or an action of some sort. So in hex, this could be either 4D 54 68 64, which represents the four letters M, T, h, and d in ASCII; or 4D 54 72 6B, which represents the four letters M, T, r, and k.

  * Four bytes (32-binary bits in this case, not ASCII) that represent the total length of the chunk's data portion. This excludes the eight bytes needed to identify the chunk's type and length. In other words, it tells the receiving device how long the information that follows this header will be.

  * The data holds a variable amount of binary bytes representing information specific to the chunk type (MThd or MTrk). This is explained later in this chapter.

In Figure 12.1, you can see a typical chunk structure in a standard MIDI file. This represents the meta-structure of the MIDI file, where chunks are defined as being either MThd or MTrk, and their respective data length. It also shows what type of data appears for each type of chunk.

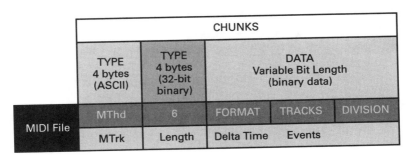

Figure 12.1   The SMF chunk structure.

MThd Chunk

The MThd chunk identifies the format of the MIDI file, the number of tracks it holds, and how it is divided in terms of time base or clock base. There is only one MThd chunk per SMF. Since each event in a MIDI file occurs in time, the header chunk defines how much time it should wait between each event. This time base or clock base represents the default value that applies throughout the file. In other words, it uses this value as a time grid value that will serve as a reference to align all the events found in the file. A MThd chunk will always hold six Data bytes of information (see Figure 12.2):

❋ Two bytes for the format.

❋ Two bytes for the number of tracks. When the MIDI format 0 is used, this will always be set to 1, otherwise, it can be any number of tracks found in your MIDI sequence or pattern.

❋ Two bytes for the division, which defines the default unit of delta time for this MIDI file. A delta time can be either the number of time units in each quarter note or the frame rate and ticks for each frame. What type of time metering system it uses (MIDI clock or SMPTE time) depends on the setting used when the file is saved or the setting used by the device using the MIDI file.

In a MIDI file, an event's time precedes the Data bytes that make up that event. In other words, the bytes that make up the event's time-stamp come first. A given event's time-stamp is referenced from the previous event. For example, if the first event occurs 8 clocks after the start of play, then its delta time is 08. If the next event occurs simultaneously with that first event, its time is 00. So, a delta time is the duration (in clocks) between an event and the preceding event. A delta time is stored as a variable length quantity set of bytes. A variable length quantity is a method MIDI uses to optimize the information needed to transmit values in a

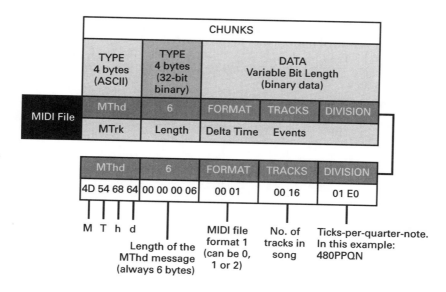

Figure 12.2 The content of a MThd chunk (header chunk).

MIDI file. Because each 7-bit message MIDI transmits can have values ranging from 0 to 127; using variable length quantities to store the delta time associated with each event makes it possible to have larger values to represent a longer delta time between events. Each 7-bit byte reserves the last bit (on the right, or LSB) to indicate the last variable length quantity byte representing this delta time, with a maximum value of 0F FF FF FF. In other words, variable length quantities break up large values into a series of bytes (up to four bytes) and then reassemble them to re-create a long delta time when needed.

Format

The two format bytes indicate the file format of this SMF. File format is designated by one of three values that corresponds to the MIDI formats discussed earlier in this book:

* MIDI format 0 contains one single track containing MIDI data on possibly all 16 MIDI channels.

* MIDI format 1 contains one or more simultaneous tracks starting at an assumed position of zero. Each track can hold one or more MIDI channels. The sum of these tracks is considered as one sequence or pattern. The first track of a format 1 file is special and is also known as the tempo map. It should contain all meta-events such as time signatures, tempo settings, and so on. This is probably the most common MIDI format.

* MIDI format 2 contains one or more sequentially independent single-track patterns. If your sequencer separates its MIDI data into different blocks of memory but plays only one block at a time, then it will read or write this type. In this case, each block is

considered a different sequence or pattern. Drum machine patterns are a good example of this pattern sequence use.

Division

The last two bytes in the MThd chunk indicate how many pulses, or clocks per quarter note (referred to as PPQN) resolution, the time stamps are based upon. For example, if your sequencer resolution is set to 480 PPQN, as shown in Figure 12.3, the value in hexadecimal for this field would be 01 E0. This is referred to as the delta time. In other words, a time stamp called delta time occurs at intervals determined by the PPQN value and saved with the file.

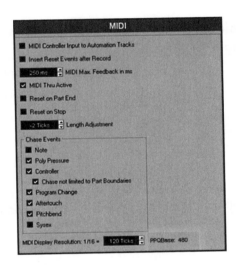

Figure 12.3   The system resolution for this sequence is set at 480 PPQN.

This division value, as shown in Figure 12.2, can also represent SMPTE values rather than PPQN as discussed in the previous paragraph. This will be the case when the first byte is one of the four following values: −24, −25, −29 (for the 29.97 drop frame standard), or −30 (for the 29.97 non-drop standard), which correspond to the four SMPTE standard frame rates.

If bit 15 (when counting from right to left from 0 to 15, for a total of 16 bits) is a 0 (in binary), then it means the division represents ticks per quarter note. If it is a 1, then bits 0 to 7 represent the number of delta time units per SMTPE frame, and bits 8 to 14 represent the SMPTE frame rate mentioned above.

Tables 12.1 and 12.2 represent the possible values found for this division.

Table 12.1   Samples of Typical PPQN Values Converted into Hex Value Found in the MThd Division Data Field

HEX	PPQN
00 60	96
00 C0	192
01 80	384
07 80	1920

Table 12.2   SMPTE Values Expressed in the MThd Division Data Field (Bits 8 to 14) to Identify the Frame Rate

HEX	Value	Description	Bit 15	Bits 14-8	Bits 7-0
E2	−30	29.97 frames per second (non-drop)	1	110 0010	See Table 12.3
E3	−29	29,97 frames per second (drop frame)	1	110 0011	See Table 12.3
E7	−25	25 frames per second	1	110 0111	See Table 12.3
E8	−24	24 frames per second	1	110 1000	See Table 12.3

Notice that all the binary values in Table 12.2 begin with the value which implies an SMPTE ticks per frame division rather than a ticks per quarter-note division format (when word begins with a 0 instead).

Table 12.3   Ticks per Frame Resolution Values Expressed in the MThd Division Data Field (Bits 0 to 7) when Using SMPTE Format

HEX	Value	Description	Binary
04	4	MIDI Time Code (MTC) resolution (or ticks per frame)	00000100
08	8	SMPTE bit resolution (or ticks per frame)	00001000
0A	10	SMPTE bit resolution (or ticks per frame)	00001010
28	40	Millisecond resolution when combined with 25fps SMPTE	00101000
50	80	SMPTE bit resolution (or ticks per frame)	01010000
64	100	SMPTE bit resolution (or ticks per frame)	01100100

MTrk Chunk

The MThd chunk is usually followed by a series of MTrk chunks. Any other types of chunks would be proprietary and would be ignored by a device reading the MIDI file if it does not recognize it. In other words, if the MThd chunk is followed by something other than an MTrk chunk, all devices with the exception of the device for which this chunk type was meant will ignore it.

Like the MThd chunk, the MTrk chunk contains three parts: the type, which identifies it as being an MTrk chunk; the length, which represents the total number of bits it contains in its data portion; and the data itself. The data for an MTrk chunk contains all of the MIDI event data and timing bytes for these MIDI events, along with non-MIDI data for one track. You can have as many MTrk chunks as there are tracks in your MIDI file, as defined in the MThd chunk's tracks field mentioned above. For example, if the MThd chunk indicates that this is a format 0 MIDI file with one MIDI track, there will be only one MTrk chunk following the MThd chunk. On the other hand, if this is a format 1 MIDI file and it has 16 tracks, the MThd chunk should be followed by at least 16 MTrk chunks (see Figure 12.4).

In a single MTrk chunk, you can have three types of events:

❋ **MIDI events** represent the core of the MIDI file, since it represents all channel voice messages and channel mode messages as defined in this book. Running status (see the following Note) is applicable within MIDI files. Running status is cancelled by any SysEx or meta event.

❋ **SysEx events**, both manufacturer-specific and universal system exclusive event messages, are saved in a MIDI file.

❋ **Meta data events** are used for things like track names, lyrics, and cue points, which don't result in MIDI messages being sent but are still useful components of a MIDI file.

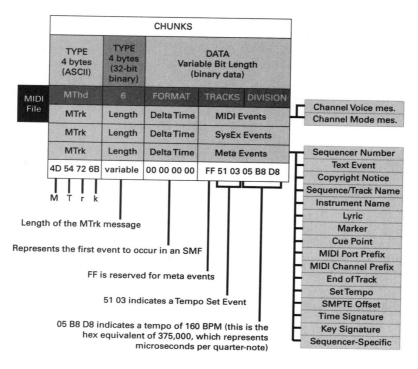

Figure 12.4 The MTrk chunk and its different types of events.

figure, shows that the Status byte is only found at the beginning of the set of MIDI events that carries the same Status byte. When a running status occurs, no additional information is added to the MIDI message or string of messages, but rather, the sequencer will omit saving the redundant information in its MIDI stream. Similarly, MIDI devices will understand that a running status is in effect when receiving only a series of Data bytes. For this to work, certain rules apply:

❋ A running status can only be used as long as the same Status byte still applies, as shown in Figure 12.5. It will stay active until a new Status byte is received; in other words, there are no time limits to running Status bytes.

❋ It only applies to channel voice and channel mode messages. Furthermore, it is not affected by system real-time messages.

❋ Any SysEx or system common message as well as a device power on will cancel the running status. If a running status is cancelled, subsequent Data bytes are ignored until the next Status byte arrives.

Using a running status will reduce the MIDI data needed to communicate information, thus making the communication more efficient. This is particularly important when large amounts of data are transmitted over a single MIDI port. Sequencers and MIDI files will usually use a running status.

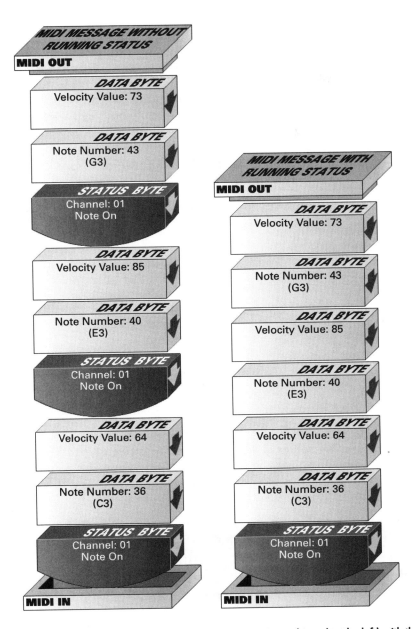

Figure 12.5 Comparing normal MIDI messages without running Status bytes (on the left) with the same MIDI message with a running Status byte (on the right).

MIDI Events

MIDI events such as channel voice and channel common messages are transmitted (or saved) in the same way they are transmitted through MIDI, with the exception that they have a delta time stamp attached to each of them. Looking at the example in Table 12.4, the MIDI data would contain the subsequent information in the MTrk chunk data field. Note that the delta time is equal to zero because all events are played simultaneously rather than one after the other. Therefore, there are no delays between each event.

Table 12.4   Content of the MTrk Data Field for a C Major Chord MIDI Event with Running Status

Delta time (in variable-length quantity)	Status byte	Status value in Hex	First Data byte	Hex value	Second Data byte	Hex value
00	Note On, Channel 1	90	Note number	24	64	40
00	(running status)	N/A	Note number	28	85	55
00	(running status)	N/A	Note number	2B	73	49

The complete MTrk data in hex format for this event would look like this:

4D 54 72 6B **0A** <u>00</u> 90 24 40 00 28 55 00 73 49

In the example above, the values in italic represent the chunk's type, the value in bold represents the length of the data field, the underlined value represents the delta time value, and the normal text represents the MIDI events themselves.

SysEx Events

The only difference with SysEx sent over MIDI in real time and SysEx found in an SMF is the addition of the delta time value after the Start SysEx Status byte. For example, if you had this SysEx message sent in real time:

F0 41 10 6A 12 01 00 00 28 06 51 F7

It would look like this in an SMF (notice the second value, which represents the delta time in variable length quantity format):

F0 <u>07</u> 41 10 6A 12 01 00 00 28 06 51 F7

Meta Events

Meta data events are used to store special non-MIDI-related information that is relevant to a Standard MIDI File. All meta events begin with the reserved Status byte value FF, which identifies it appropriately as a meta event. This is followed by the type's identification byte and acts like a second Status byte, since it defines the values that follow it. Following the identification is the data's length value in variable length quantity format, which includes only the actual length of the data for this event, not the type and the length byte itself.

Meta events are not mandatory unless otherwise specified, and certain sequencers might not support some meta events. In this case, they would simply be ignored. You can also find more than one meta event per MTrk chunk. When this happens, meta events are separated by their respective delta time values to indicate the time at which they should occur following the previous event. This implies that MIDI events and meta events can coexist in the same MTrk chunk.

There are 16 defined meta event types that can hold information such as track names, MIDI port information, time signatures, tempo settings, and so on. The next section describes them using a common number of parameters, such as when they are used, how these events are represented in hex, and so on.

Sequence Number

- ❉ When: This is an optional event that must occur before any non-zero delta time events and before any MIDI events of a MTrk chunk.
- ❉ Common identifying value: FF 00 02
- ❉ Number of Data bytes: 2 bytes
- ❉ Complete message representation in hex: FF 00 02 XX XX, where XX are variable value bytes.
- ❉ Represents: In a MIDI file format 0 or 1, this event is placed in the first MTrk chunk and represents the sequence number. If there were several MIDI files, this would represent the song collection's number; in other words, each file would contain its own sequence number for the whole file. In a MIDI file format 2, this number represents each pattern or MTrk chunk. If the XX XX value is omitted in the SMF, then the first MTrk chunk is the first pattern. There can be one sequence number per MTrk chunk.

Text Event

- ❉ When: This is an optional meta event but usually this is found at the beginning of an MTrk chunk.
- ❉ Common identifying value: FF 01
- ❉ Number of Data bytes: Variable
- ❉ Complete message representation in hex: FF 01 LL LL XX XX XX..., where LL represents the length of this event in bytes and XX represents the actual text in 8-bit ASCII or 8-bit binary format. The length is expressed in variable length quantity format and can use as many bytes as it needs.
- ❉ Represents: Any amount of text for any purpose, such as adding comments on the song or MIDI setup instructions.

Copyright

- ❋ When: This is an optional meta event but usually is found at the beginning of an MTrk chunk.
- ❋ Common identifying value: FF 02
- ❋ Number of Data bytes: Variable
- ❋ Complete message representation in hex: FF 02 LL LL XX XX XX..., where LL represents the length of this event in bytes and XX represents the actual text in 8-bit ASCII or 8-bit binary format. The length is expressed in variable length quantity format and can use as many bytes as it needs.
- ❋ Represents: A copyright text message.

Sequence Track Name Event

- ❋ When: This is an optional meta event, but usually this is found at the beginning of an MTrk chunk.
- ❋ Common identifying value: FF 03
- ❋ Number of Data bytes: Variable
- ❋ Complete message representation in hex: FF 03 LL LL XX XX XX..., where LL represents the length of this event in bytes and XX represents the actual text in 8-bit ASCII or 8-bit binary format. The length is expressed in variable length quantity format and can use as many bytes as it needs.
- ❋ Represents: The text representing the name of the sequence or track.

Instrument Name

- ❋ When: This is an optional meta event but usually is found at the beginning of an MTrk chunk.
- ❋ Common identifying value: FF 04
- ❋ Number of Data bytes: Variable
- ❋ Complete message representation in hex: FF 04 LL LL XX XX XX..., where LL represents the length of this event in bytes and XX represents the actual text in 8-bit ASCII or 8-bit binary format. The length is expressed in variable length quantity format and can use as many bytes as it needs.
- ❋ Represents: The name of a track as found in most sequencers. This could represent the actual instrument's name or something else, since you could have a track playing a guitar instrument but choose to call this track "Rhythm Guit." Usually, the actual instruments are set by the MIDI device's program change event within the MTrk chunk if these program changes have been saved with the MIDI file. This is especially true when it comes to GM sound module program changes. This is a visual aid to identify a track.

Lyric Event

* ❋ When: This is an optional meta event and can occur anywhere in the MTrk chunk.

* ❋ Common identifying value: FF 05

* ❋ Number of Data bytes: Variable

* ❋ Complete message representation in hex: FF 05 LL LL XX XX XX..., where LL represents the length of this event in byte and XX represents the actual text in 8-bit ASCII or 8-bit binary format. The length is expressed in variable length quantity format and can use as many bytes as it needs.

* ❋ Represents: Text for a song's lyrics, which occur on a given beat. A single lyric meta event should contain only one syllable.

Marker

* ❋ When: This is an optional meta event and can occur anywhere in the MTrk chunk.

* ❋ Common identifying value: FF 06

* ❋ Number of Data bytes: Variable

* ❋ Complete message representation in hex: FF 06 LL LL XX XX XX..., where LL represents the length of this event in bytes and XX represents the actual text in 8-bit ASCII or 8-bit binary format. The length is expressed in variable length quantity format and can use as many bytes as it needs.

* ❋ Represents: Text that represents a marker occurring on a given beat. Marker events might be used to denote a loop start and loop end (i.e., where the sequence loops back to a previous event).

Cue Point

* ❋ When: This is an optional meta event and can occur anywhere in the MTrk chunk.

* ❋ Common identifying value: FF 07

* ❋ Number of Data bytes: Variable

* ❋ Complete message representation in hex: FF 07 LL LL XX XX XX..., where LL represents the length of this event in bytes and XX represents the actual text in 8-bit ASCII or 8-bit binary format. The length is expressed in variable length quantity format and can use as many bytes as it needs.

* ❋ Represents: Text representing a cue point that occurs on a given beat. A cue point might be used to denote where an audio file or sampled sound starts playing. The text in this case would represent the file's name.

MIDI Channel Prefix

* ❋ When: This is an optional meta event but usually this is found at the beginning of an MTrk chunk before any meta event but after the sequence number meta event.

* ❋ Common identifying value: FF 20 01

* ❋ Number of Data bytes: 1 byte

* Complete message representation in hex: FF 20 01 XX, where XX represents the MIDI channel. A value of 0 represents the first MIDI channel.
* Represents: Since MIDI file format 0 saves all parts in one track—therefore one MTrk chunk—you can assign MIDI channel meta data to associate a channel with subsequent meta events or MIDI voice messages, since both would be in the same track. For example, you could have the rhythm guitar playing on MIDI channel 1 and the melodic guitar playing on MIDI channel 2, therefore naming these two parts through the instrument meta event and then assigning a MIDI channel to these parts. It is also possible to have more than one MIDI channel event in a given track, if that track needs to associate various events with various channels.

MIDI Port (Channel Prefix)

* When: This is an optional meta event but usually is found at the beginning of an MTrk chunk before any MIDI events.
* Common identifying value: FF 21 01
* Number of Data bytes: 1 byte
* Complete message representation in hex: FF 21 01 XX, where XX represents the MIDI port number. A value of 0 represents the first MIDI port in the system.
* Represents: This is used to identify a specific MIDI port on your system while saving a MIDI file. This allows you to use more than 16 MIDI channels (16 per port).

End of Track Event

* When: This is not an optional meta event, and it should be found at the end of every MTrk chunk in a MIDI file.
* Common identifying value: FF 2F 00
* Number of Data bytes: none
* Complete message representation in hex: FF 2F 00
* Represents: This is used to identify the end of an MTrk chunk. There will be only one end of each track meta event per MTrk chunk.

Tempo Event

* When: This is an optional meta event and can occur anywhere in the MTrk chunk. If there are no Tempo Meta events in the MTrk chunk, the default tempo setting assumed will be 120 BPM.
* Common identifying value: FF 51 03
* Number of Data bytes: 3 bytes
* Complete message representation in hex: FF 51 03 XX XX XX, where XX represents the value in microseconds per quarter note of the tempo—in other words, how long each quarter note in the sequencer will be.

✳ Represents: Indicates a tempo change in microsecond per quarter note format. For example, a tempo of 160 BPM would be converted into microseconds (375,000 microseconds) and then into hex (05 B8 D8). This represents the number of microseconds for each quarter note.

SMPTE Offset

✳ When: This is an optional meta event. If the file is in MIDI format 1, it should be stored with the tempo map in the first MTrk chunk and will have no meaning in any other MTrk chunk. It also has to appear, when it does, at the beginning of the MTrk chunk before any MIDI events.

✳ Common identifying value: FF 54 05

✳ Number of Data bytes: 5 bytes

✳ Complete message representation in hex: FF 54 05 HH MM SS FF BB, where HH represents the hour value of the SMPTE, MM the minute value, SS the second value, FF the frame value, and BB the subframe value in one-hundredths of a frame divisions, even if MThd division settings specifies a different subframe division setting.

✳ Represents: This is the SMPTE start time in hour, minute, second, frame, and subframe format for the MTrk chunk. A SMPTE offset refers to the SMPTE time at which the sequence should start. For example, you might have an SMPTE offset at 09:59:45:00:00, which implies that bar one, beat one of the MIDI file will only start when it receives this SMPTE (converted into MTC) time stamp.

Time Signature Event

✳ When: This is an optional meta event and can occur anywhere in the MTrk chunk. If there are no time signature meta events in the MTrk chunk, the default time signature setting assumed will be 4/4.

✳ Common identifying value: FF 58 04

✳ Number of Data bytes: 4 bytes

✳ Complete message representation in hex: FF 54 05 NN DD MM CC, where NN represents the numerator value of the time signature. DD represents the denominator value and is a negative power of two, where 2 is equal to a quarter note, 3 to an eighth note, and so on. MM represents the number of MIDI clocks in a metronome click, and CC represents the number of notated 32nd notes in a MIDI quarter note (or the 24 MIDI clocks). The standard is usually eight since there are normally eight 32nd notes per quarter note.

✳ Represents: This allows a program to relate what MIDI thinks of as a quarter note, or if it is something different. For example, if you have a 4/4 time signature, the event would read as follows: (FF 58 04) 04 02 18 08, where the first 04 represents four values defined by the next DD byte, 02 (which represents quarter notes, or 2 to the power of 2 is equal to 4). This means that there are four quarter notes per bar. The value of 18 in hex is 24 in decimal, which implies that there are 24 MIDI clocks in one quarter note, and 08 means that there are eight 32nd notes per quarter note. Here's another example: If you have a 9/8 time signature, the event would read as follows: (FF 58 04) 09 03 24 08, where 09 represents how many values will be defined by the denominator byte, 03 in this case (2 to the power of 3 is equal to 8). Each dotted quarter note value holds 36 MIDI clocks (24 in hex) and there are eight 32nd notes per quarter note (by default).

Key Signature Event

* When: This is an optional meta event and can occur anywhere in the MTrk chunk.

* Common identifying value: FF 59 02

* Number of Data bytes: 2 bytes

* Complete message representation in hex: FF 59 02 AA MM, where AA represents the number of accidentals in the key signature. A value of –7 would mean seven flats, –6 would mean six flats, and so on. Zero would represent the key of C (no flats and default key if meta event is not present). Positive values represent the number of sharps, up to seven sharps. The MM value represents the key mode. A value of zero represents a major mode and one a minor mode.

* Represents: This allows you to set a particular key signature to an MTrk chunk.

Proprietary (Sequencer Specific Meta) Event

* When: This is an optional meta event and can occur anywhere in the MTrk chunk.

* Common identifying value: FF 7F

* Number of Data bytes: variable

* Complete message representation in hex: FF 7F LL LL XX XX, where LL represents the length of this event in bytes and XX represents the actual text in 8-bit ASCII or 8-bit binary format. The length is expressed in variable length quantity format and can use as many bytes as it needs.

* Represents: A program to store proprietary data can use this. The first bytes should be a unique ID that identifies the program using these proprietary events or some other program that might recognize it. A four ASCII character ID is recommended for this.

Review Questions

1. An SMF begins by identifying the MIDI track. The first four bytes is always either a header chunk or what?

   a) The delta time
   b) The track chunk
   c) The ASCII value representing the letters "MThd"
   d) None of the above

2. How many MThd (header chunks) are there in a single standard MIDI file?

   a) 1
   b) 6
   c) 16
   d) It depends on the number of tracks found in the file.

3. Which of the following choices does not represent one of the three types of MTrk chunk?

   a) Format event
   b) MIDI events
   c) SysEx events
   d) Meta data events

4. Select the appropriate question for the following statement: Since many messages share the same Status byte information, all subsequent MIDI messages sent with the same Status byte information will omit this similar Status byte from the message and only transmit the Data bytes.

   a) What is delta time?
   b) What is pulse per quarter note (PPQN)?
   c) What is a running status?
   d) What is a MIDI message?

5. What difference is there between a SysEx message sent over MIDI in real time and the same message in an SMF?

   a) There is no difference.
   b) In an SMF, SysEx messages always start with an MTrk chunk.
   c) In an SMF, a delta time value is added to the SysEx message.
   d) An SMF does not support SysEx messages.

6. All Meta Event messages in an SMF begin with a reserved Status byte hex value. What is this value?

   a) F0
   b) FF
   c) F7
   d) None of the above

7. What happens when a Meta Event is not recognized by a particular sequencer or MIDI player?

   a) It is ignored.

   b) It is interpreted as an error.

   c) The application will prompt a warning asking what it should do with this value.

   d) It is assigned to the next Meta Event value.

8. How many defined Meta Event types are there in an SMF?

   a) 2

   b) 8

   c) 16

   d) Unlimited

9. When there are no more MIDI events on a track, a specific meta event is added to the MTrk chunk in the SMF. What is this message?

   a) Sequence Track Name event

   b) Cue Point

   c) MIDI Channel Prefix

   d) End of Track event

10. True or False: The Sequence Name Meta Event is obligatory and usually found at the end of a MThd chunk.

Appendix A }

Understanding Binary, Decimal, and Hexadecimal

Since MIDI is a binary "language" often represented as hexadecimal values, understanding how to convert binary numbers to decimal values or to hexadecimal values is essential. This is especially true if you are trying to find out why a MIDI file has errors, or simply to understand how the MIDI language works. MIDI is also expressed in hexadecimal values because of its simple two-digit approach, which is sufficient to express all the values included in the MIDI specification. Because it is most likely expressed in hex, chances are, if you want to edit a specific value in a SysEx message, converting hex to its decimal value can become a handy tool.

You don't need to know how to use hex or how to convert it to use MIDI. This protocol is meant to be pretty transparent, and the values passing through a MIDI connection are usually converted into something easy to understand once they appear in a sequencer. Since many examples and descriptions of how MIDI works refer to hex values, this appendix will give you the necessary tools to make the conversion an easier one.

Decimal Numbering System

In our day-to-day lives, we count and number things based on the decimal system. This numbering system is so named because it is based on 10 values, which can be combined to give us every possible combination of numerical values. These 10 values are 0, 1, 2, 3, 4, 5, 6, 7, 8, and 9. Adding a second digit in front of the first one, so 10 follows 9, forms the next value in this series. This added digit represents multiples of 10; therefore, (1 × 10) + 0 = 10. With two digits, you can express values of up to 99. After this, you need to add a third digit in front, which represents multiples of 100 (or 10 × 10 × 1). The pattern repeats when you reach 999—a fourth digit is added, which represents multiples of 1,000 (or 10 × 10 × 10 × 1), and so on. So, the value 4,568 can be interpreted as [(4 × 1000) + (5 × 100) + (6 × 10) + (8 × 1)], all of which are multiples of 10 because this is how the "decimal" system works. The decimal numbering system is referred to as "base 10" because of it.

Binary Numbering System

Computers use a different numbering system, called the binary system. It is so named because it is based on two values, which can be combined to give us every possible combination of numerical values. The two binary values are 0 and 1.

The binary system makes great sense in the computing environment, where the two binary values of 0 and 1 can correspond to the on and off states of an electrical switch. Counting simple switches is a relatively straightforward task for a computer. If you have only one digit in your system, you can have two different values (0 or 1). For this reason, the binary system is also referred to as "base 2." When you want to represent a value higher than 1, you need to add another digit in front of it, to have 4 different values: 0, 1, 10, 11 (00 and 01 are the same as 0 and 1).

To have more than four different values, you can add a third digit in front, which will give you eight values: 0, 1, 10, 11, 100, 101, 110, and 111. Notice that every time you add a digit, it multiplies the possible values by the base value. So, one digit is 2, two digits is (2 × 2 = 4), three digits is (2 × 2 × 2 = 8), and so on, just like in the decimal (base 10) numbering system. So, the value 255 in decimal is represented by 1111 1111 in binary, the value 17 in decimal is represented by 1 0001, and so on.

Hexadecimal Numbering System

The hexadecimal numbering system uses 16 different values, which are a combination of the first 10 decimal values and letters from A to F to represent values 11 through 16: 0, 1, 2, 3, 4, 5, 6, 7, 8, 9, A (10), B (11), C (12), D (13), E (14), and F (15). Because hexadecimal numbering uses 16 values, every subsequent digit added in front of the first adds a multiple of 16 (because this is a "base 16" numbering system). So, after F would come 10, 11, and so on, until FF is reached. In fact, you express 256 different values when using only two digits in this system (16 × 16 = 256). We look at hexadecimal values because, although MIDI uses binary language, binary is more difficult to calculate because of the high number of digits it uses. If you take the same examples given above, the value 255 in decimal becomes 1111 1111 in binary and FF in hexadecimal, which is much shorter than its binary representation. Imagine trying to represent the value 65,535 in decimal; this would take 16 characters, while its hexadecimal value is represented by only four— FF FF. Since MIDI messages are sent over a binary system, converting these binary numbers into hex values makes it easier to understand their meaning due to the smaller number of characters hex uses to represent these messages. Most MIDI documentation does not refer to binary values but rather to hexadecimal representation, and here lies the real reason why understanding this numbering system is important.

In Table A.1, you can compare decimal, binary, and hexadecimal numbering values.

Table A.1   Equivalents Between Decimal, Binary, and Hexadecimal Numbering

Decimal	Binary	Hexadecimal	Decimal	Binary	Hexadecimal
0	00000000	00	27	00011011	1B
1	00000001	01	28	00011100	1C
2	00000010	02	29	00011101	1D
3	00000011	03	30	00011110	1E
4	00000100	04	31	00011111	1F
5	00000101	05	32	00100000	20
6	00000110	06	33	00100001	21
7	00000111	07	34	00100010	22
8	00001000	08	35	00100011	23
9	00001001	09	36	00100100	24
10	00001010	0A	37	00100101	25
11	00001011	0B	38	00100110	26
12	00001100	0C	39	00100111	27
13	00001101	0D	40	00101000	28
14	00001110	0E	41	00101001	29
15	00001111	0F	42	00101010	2A
16	00010000	10	43	00101011	2B
17	00010001	11	44	00101100	2C
18	00010010	12	45	00101101	2D
19	00010011	13	46	00101110	2E
20	00010100	14	47	00101111	2F
21	00010101	15	48	00110000	30
22	00010110	16	49	00110001	31
23	00010111	17	50	00110010	32
24	00011000	18	51	00110011	33
25	00011001	19	52	00110100	34
26	00011010	1A	53	00110101	35

Decimal	Binary	Hexadecimal
54	00110110	36
55	00110111	37
56	00111000	38
57	00111001	39
58	00111010	3A
59	00111011	3B
60	00111100	3C
61	00111101	3D
62	00111110	3E
63	00111111	3F
64	01000000	40
65	01000001	41
66	01000010	42
67	01000011	43
68	01000100	44
69	01000101	45
70	01000110	46
71	01000111	47
72	01001000	48
73	01001001	49
74	01001010	4A
75	01001011	4B
76	01001100	4C
77	01001101	4D
78	01001110	4E
79	01001111	4F
80	01010000	50
81	01010001	51
82	01010010	52
83	01010011	53
84	01010100	54
85	01010101	55
86	01010110	56

Decimal	Binary	Hexadecimal
87	01010111	57
88	01011000	58
89	01011001	59
90	01011010	5A
91	01011011	5B
92	01011100	5C
93	01011101	5D
94	01011110	5E
95	01011111	5F
96	01100000	60
97	01100001	61
98	01100010	62
99	01100011	63
100	01100100	64
101	01100101	65
102	01100110	66
103	01100111	67
104	01101000	68
105	01101001	69
106	01101010	6A
107	01101011	6B
108	01101100	6C
109	01101101	6D
110	01101110	6E
111	01101111	6F
112	01110000	70
113	01110001	71
114	01110010	72
115	01110011	73
116	01110100	74
117	01110101	75
118	01110110	76
119	01110111	77

Decimal	Binary	Hexadecimal	Decimal	Binary	Hexadecimal
120	01111000	78	153	10011001	99
121	01111001	79	154	10011010	9A
122	01111010	7A	155	10011011	9B
123	01111011	7B	156	10011100	9C
124	01111100	7C	157	10011101	9D
125	01111101	7D	158	10011110	9E
126	01111110	7E	159	10011111	9F
127	01111111	7F	160	10100000	A0
128	10000000	80	161	10100001	A1
129	10000001	81	162	10100010	A2
130	10000010	82	163	10100011	A3
131	10000011	83	164	10100100	A4
132	10000100	84	165	10100101	A5
133	10000101	85	166	10100110	A6
134	10000110	86	167	10100111	A7
135	10000111	87	168	10101000	A8
136	10001000	88	169	10101001	A9
137	10001001	89	170	10101010	AA
138	10001010	8A	171	10101011	AB
139	10001011	8B	172	10101100	AC
140	10001100	8C	173	10101101	AD
141	10001101	8D	174	10101110	AE
142	10001110	8E	175	10101111	AF
143	10001111	8F	176	10110000	B0
144	10010000	90	177	10110001	B1
145	10010001	91	178	10110010	B2
146	10010010	92	179	10110011	B3
147	10010011	93	180	10110100	B4
148	10010100	94	181	10110101	B5
149	10010101	95	182	10110110	B6
150	10010110	96	183	10110111	B7
151	10010111	97	184	10111000	B8
152	10011000	98	185	10111001	B9

Decimal	Binary	Hexadecimal	Decimal	Binary	Hexadecimal
186	10111010	BA	219	11011011	DB
187	10111011	BB	220	11011100	DC
188	10111100	BC	221	11011101	DD
189	10111101	BD	222	11011110	DE
190	10111110	BE	223	11011111	DF
191	10111111	BF	224	11100000	E0
192	11000000	C0	225	11100001	E1
193	11000001	C1	226	11100010	E2
194	11000010	C2	227	11100011	E3
195	11000011	C3	228	11100100	E4
196	11000100	C4	229	11100101	E5
197	11000101	C5	230	11100110	E6
198	11000110	C6	231	11100111	E7
199	11000111	C7	232	11101000	E8
200	11001000	C8	233	11101001	E9
201	11001001	C9	234	11101010	EA
202	11001010	CA	235	11101011	EB
203	11001011	CB	236	11101100	EC
204	11001100	CC	237	11101101	ED
205	11001101	CD	238	11101110	EE
206	11001110	CE	239	11101111	EF
207	11001111	CF	240	11110000	F0
208	11010000	D0	241	11110001	F1
209	11010001	D1	242	11110010	F2
210	11010010	D2	243	11110011	F3
211	11010011	D3	244	11110100	F4
212	11010100	D4	245	11110101	F5
213	11010101	D5	246	11110110	F6
214	11010110	D6	247	11110111	F7
215	11010111	D7	248	11111000	F8
216	11011000	D8	249	11111001	F9
217	11011001	D9	250	11111010	FA
218	11011010	DA	251	11111011	FB

Decimal	Binary	Hexadecimal		Decimal	Binary	Hexadecimal
252	11111100	FC		254	11111110	FE
253	11111101	FD		255	11111111	FF

Converting Values

The following table displays the number of values displayed when using different numbering systems. The first row indicates the number (quantity) of digits in the number, and the first column on the left displays the numbering system used. The hexadecimal system displays a greater number of values with the fewest number of digits. Displaying the decimal value 256 takes three digits in decimals but will take eight digits in binary (1111 1111) and two digits in hexadecimal (FF).

Table A.2 Possible Values in a Numbering System Displayed by Digit Increments

Digits:	8	7	6	5	4	3	2	1
Decimal	100,000,000	10,000,000	1,000,000	100,000	10,000	1,000	100	10
Binary	256	128	64	32	16	8	4	2
Hex	4,294,967,296	268,435,456	16,777,216	1,048,576	65,536	4,096	256	16

The above table can also be used as a reference point when converting values from one format to another. As you can see in this table, you can express a far greater number of values using hexadecimal numbering than with decimal or binary numbering systems. Here are a couple of examples of how this works.

First, let's take the value 11010110 in binary. How can you find out what value this has in decimal or hex?

To convert a binary value into a decimal value, you multiply each digit by its multiple, starting with 1 for the smallest value (digit number 1), then 2, then 4, then 8, and so on, as shown in Table A.3.

Table A.3 Converting a Binary Value into a Decimal Value

Digit's Multiple	128	64	32	16	8	4	2	1
Binary Value	1	1	0	1	0	1	1	0
Total	128	64	0	16	0	4	2	0

You then add up the totals: 128 + 64 + 0 + 16 + 0 + 4 + 2 + 0 = 214. So 11010110 is the binary equivalent of 214 in decimal.

To convert this same binary value (11010110) into a hexadecimal value, the process is similar, but you need to divide each cluster of four digits into two separate calculations.

Why divide it in two? Because it takes four binary digits to represent as many values as one hexadecimal digit (16 values). The first four digits of the binary word will give you the second hexadecimal digit, and the last four digits in the binary word will give you the first hex digit, as shown in Table A.4.

Table A.4   Converting a Binary Value into a Hexadecimal Value

Digit's Multiple	8	4	2	1	8	4	2	1
Binary Value	1	1	0	1	0	1	1	0
Total in Decimal	8	4	0	1	0	4	2	0

If you add up the first four digits, you get 13 as a decimal value, or D in hex. The next set of four digits added up gives you a total of 6 in decimal values or 6 in hex. So, the hex equivalent to 11010110 in binary and 214 in decimal is D6.

To reverse this calculation, you can multiply the digits in a hex value to extrapolate their decimal equivalent as follows: D6 = (D × 16) + (6 × 1) = (13 × 16) + (6 × 1) = (208 + 6) = 214.

If you have a three-digit hex number, for example, you would multiply this third digit by 256, the fourth digit by 4,096, and so on, as Table A.2 suggests.

The choice is yours here. You can try to understand what eight binary digits represent, since every MIDI message comes in 8-bit words, or you can simply use a set of two hex digits representing the same value. Table A.5 provides an example of this conversion as it applies to a MIDI message.

Table A.5   A Single MIDI Message Displayed in Binary, Hex, Decimal, and Its MIDI Equivalent for the Musician

Type of Byte	Status Byte	Data Byte	Data Byte
In Binary	100101T11	00111100	01101110
In Hex	97	3C	6E
In Decimal	151	60	110
What it means in MIDI	Channel 8	Note On Middle C (number 60)	Velocity of 110 out of 127

Appendix B

MIDI 1.0 Specification

The following tables represent the MMA's (MIDI Manufacturers Association) 1995 update of the MIDI 1.0 specification, which defines the MIDI protocol. You should use this appendix as a reference guide and a summary of the information explained in Chapters 2 and 3.

Expanded Status Bytes List

In the following tables, you will find a list for each category of Status bytes found in a MIDI message. Remember that each MIDI message starts with a Status byte and is then followed by its appropriate number of Data bytes. This section lists all possible Status byte values sorted in binary order and what they represent.

Table B.1 Expanded Status Bytes List for the Note Off Function

STATUS BYTE				DATA BYTES	
1st Byte Value: Binary	1st Byte Value: Hex	1st Byte Value: Dec	Note Off Function	2nd Byte	3rd Byte
10000000	80	128	Chan 1	Note Number (0-127)	Note Velocity (0-127)
10000001	81	129	Chan 2	"	"
10000010	82	130	Chan 3	"	"
10000011	83	131	Chan 4	"	"
10000100	84	132	Chan 5	"	"
10000101	85	133	Chan 6	"	"
10000110	86	134	Chan 7	"	"
10000111	87	135	Chan 8	"	"
10001000	88	136	Chan 9	"	"
10001001	89	137	Chan 10	"	"
10001010	8A	138	Chan 11	"	"
10001011	8B	139	Chan 12	"	"
10001100	8C	140	Chan 13	"	"
10001101	8D	141	Chan 14	"	"
10001110	8E	142	Chan 15	"	"
10001111	8F	143	Chan 16	"	"

Table B.2   Expanded Status Bytes List for the Note On Function

STATUS BYTE				DATA BYTES	
1st Byte Value: Binary	1st Byte Value: Hex	1st Byte Value: Dec	Note On Function	2nd Byte	3rd Byte
10010000	90	144	Chan 1	Note Number (0-127)	Note Velocity (0-127)
10010001	91	145	Chan 2	"	"
10010010	92	146	Chan 3	"	"
10010011	93	147	Chan 4	"	"
10010100	94	148	Chan 5	"	"
10010101	95	149	Chan 6	"	"
10010110	96	150	Chan 7	"	"
10010111	97	151	Chan 8	"	"
10011000	98	152	Chan 9	"	"
10011001	99	153	Chan 10	"	"
10011010	9A	154	Chan 11	"	"
10011011	9B	155	Chan 12	"	"
10011100	9C	156	Chan 13	"	"
10011101	9D	157	Chan 14	"	"
10011110	9E	158	Chan 15	"	"
10011111	9F	159	Chan 16	"	"

Table B.3   Expanded Status Bytes List for the Polyphonic Aftertouch Function

STATUS BYTE				DATA BYTES	
1st Byte Value: Binary	1st Byte Value: Hex	1st Byte Value: Dec	Polyphonic Aftertouch Function	2nd Byte	3rd Byte
10100000	A0	160	Chan 1	Note Number (0-127)	Aftertouch Amount (0-127)
10100001	A1	161	Chan 2	"	"
10100010	A2	162	Chan 3	"	"
10100011	A3	163	Chan 4	"	"
10100100	A4	164	Chan 5	"	"
10100101	A5	165	Chan 6	"	"
10100110	A6	166	Chan 7	"	"
10100111	A7	167	Chan 8	"	"
10101000	A8	168	Chan 9	"	"
10101001	A9	169	Chan 10	"	"
10101010	AA	170	Chan 11	"	"
10101011	AB	171	Chan 12	"	"
10101100	AC	172	Chan 13	"	"
10101101	AD	173	Chan 14	"	"
10101110	AE	174	Chan 15	"	"
10101111	AF	175	Chan 16	"	"

Table B.4 Expanded Status Bytes List for Control Change and Channel Mode Messages

STATUS BYTE				DATA BYTES	
1st Byte Value: Binary	1st Byte Value: Hex	1st Byte Value: Dec	Control/Mode Change Function	2nd Byte	3rd Byte
10110000	B0	176	Chan 1	See Table B.10	See Table B.10
10110001	B1	177	Chan 2	"	"
10110010	B2	178	Chan 3	"	"
10110011	B3	179	Chan 4	"	"
10110100	B4	180	Chan 5	"	"
10110101	B5	181	Chan 6	"	"
10110110	B6	182	Chan 7	"	"
10110111	B7	183	Chan 8	"	"
10111000	B8	184	Chan 9	"	"
10111001	B9	185	Chan 10	"	"
10111010	BA	186	Chan 11	"	"
10111011	BB	187	Chan 12	"	"
10111100	BC	188	Chan 13	"	"
10111101	BD	189	Chan 14	"	"
10111110	BE	190	Chan 15	"	"
10111111	BF	191	Chan 16	"	"

Table B.5   Expanded Status Bytes List for the Program Change Function

STATUS BYTE				DATA BYTES	
1st Byte Value: Binary	1st Byte Value: Hex	1st Byte Value: Dec	Program Change Function	2nd Byte	3rd Byte
11000000	C0	192	Chan 1	Program # (0-127)	None
11000001	C1	193	Chan 2	"	"
11000010	C2	194	Chan 3	"	"
11000011	C3	195	Chan 4	"	"
11000100	C4	196	Chan 5	"	"
11000101	C5	197	Chan 6	"	"
11000110	C6	198	Chan 7	"	"
11000111	C7	199	Chan 8	"	"
11001000	C8	200	Chan 9	"	"
11001001	C9	201	Chan 10	"	"
11001010	CA	202	Chan 11	"	"
11001011	CB	203	Chan 12	"	"
11001100	CC	204	Chan 13	"	"
11001101	CD	205	Chan 14	"	"
11001110	CE	206	Chan 15	"	"
11001111	CF	207	Chan 16	"	"

Table B.6   Expanded Status Bytes List for the Channel Aftertouch Function

STATUS BYTE				DATA BYTES	
1st Byte Value: Binary	1st Byte Value: Hex	1st Byte Value: Dec	Channel Aftertouch Function	2nd Byte	3rd Byte
11010000	D0	208	Chan 1	Aftertouch amount (0-127)	None
11010001	D1	209	Chan 2	"	"
11010010	D2	210	Chan 3	"	"
11010011	D3	211	Chan 4	"	"
11010100	D4	212	Chan 5	"	"
11010101	D5	213	Chan 6	"	"
11010110	D6	214	Chan 7	"	"
11010111	D7	215	Chan 8	"	"
11011000	D8	216	Chan 9	"	"
11011001	D9	217	Chan 10	"	"
11011010	DA	218	Chan 11	"	"
11011011	DB	219	Chan 12	"	"
11011100	DC	220	Chan 13	"	"
11011101	DD	221	Chan 14	"	"
11011110	DE	222	Chan 15	"	"
11011111	DF	223	Chan 16	"	"

Table B.7   Expanded Status Bytes List for the Pitch Wheel Control Function

	STATUS BYTE			DATA BYTES	
1st Byte Value: Binary	1st Byte Value: Hex	1st Byte Value: Dec	Pitch Wheel Control	2nd Byte	3rd Byte
11100000	E0	224	Chan 1	Pitch wheel LSB (0-127)	Pitch wheel MSB (0-127)
11100001	E1	225	Chan 2	"	"
11100010	E2	226	Chan 3	"	"
11100011	E3	227	Chan 4	"	"
11100100	E4	228	Chan 5	"	"
11100101	E5	229	Chan 6	"	"
11100110	E6	230	Chan 7	"	"
11100111	E7	231	Chan 8	"	"
11101000	E8	232	Chan 9	"	"
11101001	E9	233	Chan 10	"	"
11101010	EA	234	Chan 11	"	"
11101011	EB	235	Chan 12	"	"
11101100	EC	236	Chan 13	"	"
11101101	ED	237	Chan 14	"	"
11101110	EE	238	Chan 15	"	"
11101111	EF	239	Chan 16	"	"

Table B.8   Expanded Status Bytes List for the System Common, Realtime, and Exclusive Functions

STATUS BYTE				DATA BYTES	
1st Byte Value: Binary	1st Byte Value: Hex	1st Byte Value: Dec	Message Function	2nd Byte	3rd Byte
11110000	F0	240	System Exclusive	Actual SysEx message	Actual SysEx message
11110001	F1	241	MIDI Time Code Qtr. Frame	Actual time address	Actual time address
11110010	F2	242	Song Position Pointer	LSB	MSB
11110011	F3	243	Song Select (Song #)	values 0-127	None
11110100	F4	244	Undefined	N/A	N/A
11110101	F5	245	Undefined	N/A	N/A
11110110	F6	246	Tune Request	None	None
11110111	F7	247	End of SysEx (EOX)	"	"
11111000	F8	248	Timing Clock	"	"
11111001	F9	249	Undefined	"	"
11111010	FA	250	Start	"	"
11111011	FB	251	Continue	"	"
11111100	FC	252	Stop	"	"
11111101	FD	253	Undefined	"	"
11111110	FE	254	Active Sensing	"	"
11111111	FF	255	System Reset	"	"

MIDI Note Numbers

The following table lists all the MIDI notes and their corresponding note numbers according to the MIDI specification.

Table B.9   MIDI Note Numbers

Octave #/Pitch	C	C#/ Db	D	D#/ Eb	E	F	F#/ Gb	G	G#/ Ab	A	A#/ Bb	B
-1	0	1	2	3	4	5	6	7	8	9	10	11
0	12	13	14	15	16	17	18	19	20	21	22	23
1	24	25	26	27	28	29	30	31	32	33	34	35
2	36	37	38	39	40	41	42	43	44	45	46	47
3	48	49	50	51	52	53	54	55	56	57	58	59
4	60	61	62	63	64	65	66	67	68	69	70	71
5	72	73	74	75	76	77	78	79	80	81	82	83
6	84	85	86	87	88	89	90	91	92	93	94	95
7	96	97	98	99	100	101	102	103	104	105	106	107
8	108	109	110	111	112	113	114	115	116	117	118	119
9	120	121	122	123	124	125	126	127				

Controller Messages (Data Bytes)

The following table is a summary of controller messages in numerical (binary) order. This table is intended as a quick reference to all controller and channel mode messages. Since all control change messages contain the same first Status byte (identifying it as a control change event), this table only represents the second and third bytes of each message.

Note that in this table, the abbreviation MSB refers to Most Significant Byte, and LSB refers to Least Significant Byte.

Table B.10   Control Change and Channel Mode Messages (Status Bytes 176-191)

2nd Byte Value: Binary	2nd Byte Value: Hex	2nd Byte Value: Dec	Function	3rd Byte Value	3rd Byte Use
0000000	00	0	Bank Select	0-127	LSB
0000001	01	1	Modulation wheel	0-127	LSB
0000010	02	2	Breath control	0-127	LSB
0000011	03	3	Undefined	0-127	LSB
0000100	04	4	Foot controller	0-127	LSB
0000101	05	5	Portamento time	0-127	LSB
0000110	06	6	Data Entry	0-127	LSB

2nd Byte Value: Binary	2nd Byte Value: Hex	2nd Byte Value: Dec	Function	3rd Byte Value	3rd Byte Use
0000111	07	7	Channel Volume (formerly Main Volume)	0-127	LSB
0001000	08	8	Balance	0-127	LSB
0001001	09	9	Undefined	0-127	LSB
0001010	0A	10	Pan	0-127	LSB
0001011	0B	11	Expression Controller	0-127	LSB
0001100	0C	12	Effect control 1	0-127	LSB
0001101	0D	13	Effect control 2	0-127	LSB
0001110	0E	14	Undefined	0-127	LSB
0001111	0F	15	Undefined	0-127	LSB
0010000	10	16	General Purpose Controller 1	0-127	LSB
0010001	11	17	General Purpose Controller 2	0-127	LSB
0010010	12	18	General Purpose Controller 3	0-127	LSB
0010011	13	19	General Purpose Controller 4	0-127	LSB
0010100	14	20	Undefined	0-127	LSB
0010101	15	21	Undefined	0-127	LSB
0010110	16	22	Undefined	0-127	LSB
0010111	17	23	Undefined	0-127	LSB
0011000	18	24	Undefined	0-127	LSB
0011001	19	25	Undefined	0-127	LSB
0011010	1A	26	Undefined	0-127	LSB
0011011	1B	27	Undefined	0-127	LSB
0011100	1C	28	Undefined	0-127	LSB
0011101	1D	29	Undefined	0-127	LSB
0011110	1E	30	Undefined	0-127	LSB
0011111	1F	31	Undefined	0-127	LSB

2nd Byte Value: Binary	2nd Byte Value: Hex	2nd Byte Value: Dec	Function	3rd Byte Value	3rd Byte Use
0100000	20	32	Bank Select	0-127	LSB
0100001	21	33	Modulation wheel	0-127	LSB
0100010	22	34	Breath control	0-127	LSB
0100011	23	35	Undefined	0-127	LSB
0100100	24	36	Foot controller	0-127	LSB
0100101	25	37	Portamento time	0-127	LSB
0100110	26	38	Data entry	0-127	LSB
0100111	27	39	Channel Volume	0-127	LSB
0101000	28	40	Balance	0-127	LSB
0101001	29	41	Undefined	0-127	LSB
0101010	2A	42	Pan	0-127	LSB
0101011	2B	43	Expression Controller	0-127	LSB
0101100	2C	44	Effect control 1	0-127	LSB
0101101	2D	45	Effect control 2	0-127	LSB
0101110	2E	46	Undefined	0-127	LSB
0101111	2F	47	Undefined	0-127	LSB
0110000	30	48	General Purpose Controller 1	0-127	LSB
0110001	31	49	General Purpose Controller 2	0-127	LSB
0110010	32	50	General Purpose Controller 3	0-127	LSB
0110011	33	51	General Purpose Controller 4	0-127	LSB
0110100	34	52	Undefined	0-127	LSB
0110101	35	53	Undefined	0-127	LSB
0110110	36	54	Undefined	0-127	LSB
0110111	37	55	Undefined	0-127	LSB
0111000	38	56	Undefined	0-127	LSB
0111001	39	57	Undefined	0-127	LSB
0111010	3A	58	Undefined	0-127	LSB

2nd Byte Value: Binary	2nd Byte Value: Hex	2nd Byte Value: Dec	Function	3rd Byte Value	3rd Byte Use
0111011	3B	59	Undefined	0-127	LSB
0111100	3C	60	Undefined	0-127	LSB
0111101	3D	61	Undefined	0-127	LSB
0111110	3E	62	Undefined	0-127	LSB
0111111	3F	63	Undefined	0-127	LSB
1000000	40	64	Damper pedal on/off (Sustain)	0-127	LSB
1000001	41	65	Portamento on/off	< 63 = Off	≥ 64 = On
1000010	42	66	Sustenuto on/off	< 63 = Off	≥ 64 = On
1000011	43	67	Soft pedal on/off	< 63 = Off	≥ 64 = On
1000100	44	68	Legato Footswitch	< 63 = Off	≥ 64 = On
1000101	45	69	Hold 2	< 63 = Off	≥ 64 = On
1000110	46	70	Sound Controller 1 (Sound Variation)	0-127	LSB
1000111	47	71	Sound Controller 2 (Timbre)	0-127	LSB
1001000	48	72	Sound Controller 3 (Release Time)	0-127	LSB
1001001	49	73	Sound Controller 4 (Attack Time)	0-127	LSB
1001010	4A	74	Sound Controller 5 (Brightness)	0-127	LSB
1001011	4B	75	Sound Controller 6	0-127	LSB
1001100	4C	76	Sound Controller 7	0-127	LSB
1001101	4D	77	Sound Controller 8	0-127	LSB
1001110	4E	78	Sound Controller 9	0-127	LSB
1001111	4F	79	Sound Controller 10	0-127	LSB
1010000	50	80	General Purpose Controller #5	0-127	LSB
1010001	51	81	General Purpose Controller #6	0-127	LSB

2nd Byte Value: Binary	2nd Byte Value: Hex	2nd Byte Value: Dec	Function	3rd Byte Value	3rd Byte Use
1010010	52	82	General Purpose Controller #7	0-127	LSB
1010011	53	83	General Purpose Controller #8	0-127	LSB
1010100	54	84	Portamento Control	0-127	Source Note
1010101	55	85	Undefined	0-127	LSB
1010110	56	86	Undefined	0-127	LSB
1010111	57	87	Undefined	0-127	LSB
1011000	58	88	Undefined	0-127	LSB
1011001	59	89	Undefined	0-127	LSB
1011010	5A	90	Undefined	0-127	LSB
1011011	5B	91	Reverb Send Level	0-127	LSB
1011100	5C	92	Effects 2 Depth	0-127	LSB
1011101	5D	93	Chorus Send Level	0-127	LSB
1011110	5E	94	Effects 4 Depth	0-127	LSB
1011111	5F	95	Effects 5 Depth	0-127	LSB
1100000	60	96	Data entry +1	N/A	N/A
1100001	61	97	Data entry −1	N/A	N/A
1100010	62	98	Non-Registered Parameter Number LSB	0-127	LSB
1100011	63	99	Non-Registered Parameter Number MSB	0-127	MSB
1100100	64	100	Registered Parameter Number LSB	0-127	LSB
1100101	65	101	Registered Parameter Number MSB	0-127	MSB
1100110	66	102	Undefined	N/A	N/A
1100111	67	103	Undefined	N/A	N/A

2nd Byte Value: Binary	2nd Byte Value: Hex	2nd Byte Value: Dec	Function	3rd Byte Value	3rd Byte Use
1101000	68	104	Undefined	N/A	N/A
1101001	69	105	Undefined	N/A	N/A
1101010	6A	106	Undefined	N/A	N/A
1101011	6B	107	Undefined	N/A	N/A
1101100	6C	108	Undefined	N/A	N/A
1101101	6D	109	Undefined	N/A	N/A
1101110	6E	110	Undefined	N/A	N/A
1101111	6F	111	Undefined	N/A	N/A
1110000	70	112	Undefined	N/A	N/A
1110001	71	113	Undefined	N/A	N/A
1110010	72	114	Undefined	N/A	N/A
1110011	73	115	Undefined	N/A	N/A
1110100	74	116	Undefined	N/A	N/A
1110101	75	117	Undefined	N/A	N/A
1110110	76	118	Undefined	N/A	N/A
1110111	77	119	Undefined	N/A	N/A
1111000	78	120	All Sound Off	0	0
1111001	79	121	Reset All Controllers	0	0
1111010	7A	122	Local control on/off	0 = Off	127 = On
1111011	7B	123	All notes off	0	0
1111100	7C	124	Omni mode off (+ all notes off)	0	0
1111101	7D	125	Omni mode on (+ all notes off)	0	0
1111110	7E	126	Poly mode on/off (+ all notes off)	N/A	N/A
1111111	7F	127	Poly mode on (incl mono=off+all notes off)	0	0

MIDI Messages

The following tables are a summary of the channel voice messages, mode messages, system common messages, and system real-time messages.

Before you take a look at these tables, take a look at the legend below, which offers a description for values you will find in this section's tables. Each value in this legend represents a series of variables grouped under one value. For example, cccc is used to represent the channel numbers in a message, but since there can be 16 different MIDI channels, each "c" represents a bit that will be replaced by its corresponding MIDI channel value in the binary word. In other words, a Note Off event always begins with 1000 and is followed by its channel number, which can be any value between 0000 and 1111, corresponding to the 16 MIDI channels. The number of times a character is repeated in the legend represents the number of bits that can change, depending on the value it represents. That's why the note number is represented in this legend by seven "n" letters, since there can be 128 different note numbers.

- ✳ cccc: represents the channel number.
- ✳ nnnnnnn: represents the note number.
- ✳ vvvvvvv: represents the velocity value.
- ✳ #######: represents the control change number.
- ✳ VVVVVVV: represents the value for the control change.
- ✳ ppppppp: represents the program number value.
- ✳ PPPPPPP: represents the pressure value.
- ✳ mmmmmmm: represents the Most Significant Bit value.
- ✳ lllllll: represents the Least Significant Bit value.
- ✳ iiiiiii: represents the manufacturer ID number.
- ✳ ddddddd: represents SysEx data values.
- ✳ sssssss: represents the song selection value.

Table B.11   Summary of Channel Voice Messages

Status Byte	Data (2nd Byte)	Data (3rd Byte)	Description
1000cccc	0nnnnnnn	0vvvvvvv	Note Off event: This message is sent when a note is released (ended).
1001cccc	0nnnnnnn	0vvvvvvv	Note On event: This message is sent when a note is depressed (started).
1010cccc	0nnnnnnn	0vvvvvvv	Polyphonic Key Pressure (Aftertouch): This message is sent when the pressure (velocity) of a previously triggered note changes.

Status Byte	Data (2nd Byte)	Data (3rd Byte)	Description
1011cccc	0#######	0VVVVVVV	Control Change: This message is sent when a controller value changes. Controllers include devices such as pedals and levers. Certain controller numbers are reserved for specific purposes. See Channel Mode Messages.
1100cccc	0ppppppp		Program Change: This message is sent when the patch number changes.
1101cccc	0PPPPPPP		Channel Pressure (Aftertouch): This message is sent when the channel pressure changes. Some velocity-sensing keyboards do not support polyphonic aftertouch. Use this message to send the single greatest velocity (of all the current depressed keys).
1110cccc	0lllllll	0mmmmmmm	Pitch Wheel Change: This message is sent to indicate a change in the pitch wheel. The pitch wheel is measured by a 14-bit value. Center (no pitch change) is 2000H. Sensitivity is a function of the transmitter.

Table B.12   Channel Mode Messages (See Also Control Change in Table B.11)

Status Byte	Data (2nd Byte)	Data (3rd Byte)	Description
1011cccc	0#######	0VVVVVVV	Channel Mode Messages: This is the same code as the Control Change (Table B.11) but implements Mode control by using reserved controller numbers. The numbers are:
1011cccc	01111010	00000000	Local Control Off: When Local Control is Off, all devices on a given channel will respond only to data received over MIDI. Played data, etc., will be ignored. 2nd Data byte = 122, 3rd Data byte at 0 = Local Control Off
1011cccc	01111010	01111111	Local Control On: This restores the functions of the normal controllers. 2nd Data byte = 122, 3rd Data byte at 127 = Local Control On

Status Byte	Data (2nd Byte)	Data (3rd Byte)	Description
1011cccc	01111011	00000000	All Notes Off: When an All Notes Off is received, all oscillators will turn off. 2nd Data byte = 123, 0 = causes All Notes Off. (See text for description of actual mode commands.)
1011cccc	01111100	00000000	Omni Mode Off: 2nd Data byte = 124, 0 = causes All Notes Off.
1011cccc	01111101	00000000	Omni Mode On: 2nd Data byte = 125, 0 = causes All Notes Off.
1011cccc	01111110	00000000	Mono Mode On (Poly Off): This is where M is the number of channels: 2nd Data byte = 126, v = M (also causes All Notes Off).
1011cccc	01111111	00000000	Poly Mode On (Mono Off): 2nd Data byte = 127, 0 = also causes All Notes Off.

Table B.13   System Common Messages

Status Byte	Data (2nd Byte)	Data (3rd Byte)	Description
11110000	0iiiiiii	0ddddddd	System Exclusive: This message makes up for all that MIDI doesn't support. If the synthesizer recognizes the I.D. code as its own, it will listen to the rest of the message (ddddddd). Otherwise, the message will be ignored. System Exclusive is used to send bulk dumps such as patch parameters and other non-spec data. (Note: real-time messages may be interleaved ONLY with a System Exclusive.)
...	...	0ddddddd	11110111
11110001			Undefined.
11110010	0lllllll	0mmmmmmm	Song Position Pointer: This is an internal 14-bit register that holds the number of MIDI beats (1 beat = six MIDI clocks) from the start of the song.
11110011	0sssssss		Song Select: The Song Select specifies which sequence or song is to be played.
11110100			Undefined.

Status Byte	Data (2nd Byte)	Data (3rd Byte)	Description
11110101			Undefined.
11110110			Tune Request: Upon receiving a Tune Request, all analog synthesizers should tune their oscillators.
11110111			End of Exclusive: Used to terminate a System Exclusive dump (see above).

Table B.14 System Real-Time messages

Status Byte	Data (2nd Byte)	Data (3rd Byte)	Description
11111000			Timing Clock: Sent 24 times per quarter note when synchronization is required (see text below).
11111001			Undefined.
11111010			Start: Start the current sequence playing. (This message will be followed with timing clocks.)
11111011			Continue: Continue at the point the sequence was stopped.
11111100			Stop: Stop the current sequence.
11111101			Undefined.
11111110			Active Sensing: Use of this message is optional. When initially sent, the receiver will expect to receive another Active Sensing message each 300 ms (max), or it will assume that the connection has been terminated. At termination, the receiver will turn off all voices and return to normal (non-active sensing) operation.
11111111			Reset: Reset all receivers in the system to power-up status. This should be used sparingly, preferably under manual control. In particular, it should not be sent on power-up.

System Exclusive Messages

The following tables display the manufacturer ID numbers associated with SysEx messages. The MIDI protocol provides a way of letting a device know if the SysEx string it's receiving should be executed or not. When the device compares its manufacturer ID with the incoming

SysEx, for example, and finds a match, it assigns and executes whatever parameter's value change the SysEx message contains.

While this list reflects the current list made available by the MMA at the time this book went to press, some changes may have occurred since its publication. Furthermore, this list displays manufacturers in Byte order and doesn't reveal the manufacturer's current status.

Table B.15   System Exclusive Single Byte Manufacturer ID Numbers (North American Manufacturer's Group)

Byte 1	Byte 2	Byte 3	Company Name
00H	00H	74H	Ta Horng Musical Instrument
00H	00H	75H	e-Tek Labs (Forte Tech)
00H	00H	76H	Electro-Voice
00H	00H	77H	Midisoft Corporation
00H	00H	78H	Q-Sound Labs
00H	00H	79H	Westrex
00H	00H	7AH	Nvidia
00H	00H	7BH	ESS Technology
00H	00H	7CH	MediaTrix Peripherals
00H	00H	7DH	Brooktree Corp
00H	00H	7EH	Otari Corp
00H	00H	7FH	Key Electronics, Inc.
00H	01H	00H	Shure Incorporated
00H	01H	01H	AuraSound
00H	01H	02H	Crystal Semiconductor
00H	01H	03H	Conexant (Rockwell)
00H	01H	04H	Silicon Graphics
00H	01H	05H	M-Audio (Midiman)
00H	01H	06H	PreSonus
00H	01H	08H	Topaz Enterprises
00H	01H	09H	Cast Lighting
00H	01H	0AH	Microsoft (Consumer Division)
00H	01H	0BH	Sonic Foundry
00H	01H	0CH	Line 6 (Fast Forward)
00H	01H	0DH	Beatnik Inc.
00H	01H	0EH	Van Koevering Company

Byte 1	Byte 2	Byte 3	Company Name
00H	01H	0FH	Altech Systems
00H	01H	10H	S & S Research
00H	01H	11H	VLSI Technology
00H	01H	12H	Chromatic Research
00H	01H	13H	Sapphire
00H	01H	14H	IDRC
00H	01H	15H	Justonic Tuning
00H	01H	16H	TorComp Research Inc.
00H	01H	17H	Newtek Inc.
00H	01H	18H	Sound Sculpture
00H	01H	19H	Walker Technical
00H	01H	1AH	Digital Harmony (PAVO)
00H	01H	1BH	InVision Interactive
00H	01H	1CH	T-Square Design
00H	01H	1DH	Nemesys Music Technology
00H	01H	1EH	DBX Professional (Harman Intl.)
00H	01H	1FH	Syndyne Corporation
00H	01H	20H	Bitheadz
00H	01H	21H	Cakewalk Music Software
00H	01H	22H	Analog Devices (Staccato Systems)
00H	01H	23H	National Semiconductor
00H	01H	24H	Boom Theory Adinolfi Alternative Percussion
00H	01H	25H	Virtual DSP Corporation
00H	01H	26H	Antares Systems
00H	01H	27H	Angel Software
00H	01H	28H	St Louis Music
00H	01H	29H	Lyrrus dba G-VOX
00H	01H	2AH	Ashley Audio Inc.
00H	01H	2BH	Vari-Lite Inc.
00H	01H	2CH	Summit Audio Inc.
00H	01H	2DH	Aureal Semiconductor Inc.
00H	01H	2EH	SeaSound LLC
00H	01H	2FH	U. S. Robotics

Byte 1	Byte 2	Byte 3	Company Name
00H	01H	30H	Aurisis Research
00H	01H	31H	Nearfield Multimedia
00H	01H	32H	FM7 Inc.
00H	01H	33H	Swivel Systems
00H	01H	34H	Hyperactive Audio Systems
00H	01H	35H	MidiLite (Castle Studios Productions)
00H	01H	36H	Radikal Technologies
00H	01H	37H	Roger Linn Design
00H	01H	38H	TC-Helicon Vocal Technologies
00H	01H	39H	Event Electronics
00H	01H	3AH	Sonic Network Inc.
00H	01H	3BH	Realtime Music Solutions
00H	01H	3CH	Apogee Digital
00H	01H	3DH	Classical Organs, Inc.
00H	01H	3EH	Microtools Inc.
00H	01H	3FH	Numark Industries
00H	01H	40H	Frontier Design Group LLC
00H	01H	41H	Recordare LLC
00H	01H	42H	Starr Labs
00H	01H	43H	Voyager Sound Inc.
00H	01H	44H	Manifold Labs
00H	01H	45H	Aviom Inc.
00H	01H	46H	Mixmeister Technology
00H	01H	47H	Notation Software
00H	01H	48H	Mercurial Communications
00H	01H	49H	Wave Arts
00H	01H	4AH	Logic Sequencing Devices
00H	01H	4BH	Axess Electronics
00H	01H	4CH	Muse Research
00H	01H	4DH	Open Labs
00H	01H	4EH	Guillemot R&D Inc.
00H	01H	4FH	Samson Technologies
0H	01H	50H	Electronic Theatre Controls

Byte 1	Byte 2	Byte 3	Company Name
00H	01H	51H	Research In Motion
00H	01H	52H	Mobileer

Table B.16 System Exclusive Single Byte Manufacturer ID Numbers (European Manufacturer's Group)

Byte 1	Byte 2	Byte 3	Company Name
00H	20H	2BH	Medeli Electronics Co.
00H	20H	2CH	Charlie Lab SRL
00H	20H	2DH	Blue Chip Music Technology
00H	20H	2EH	BEE OH Corp.
00H	20H	2FH	LG Semicon America
00H	20H	30H	TESI
00H	20H	31H	EMAGIC
00H	20H	32H	Behringer GmbH
00H	20H	33H	Access Music Electronics
00H	20H	34H	Synoptic
00H	20H	35H	Hanmesoft Corp.
00H	20H	36H	Terratec Electronic GmbH
00H	20H	37H	Proel SpA
00H	20H	38H	IBK MIDI
00H	20H	39H	IRCAM
00H	20H	3AH	Propellerhead Software
00H	20H	3BH	Red Sound Systems Ltd.
00H	20H	3CH	Elektron ESI AB
00H	20H	3DH	Sintefex Audio
00H	20H	3EH	MAM (Music and More)
00H	20H	3FH	Amsaro GmbH
00H	20H	40H	CDS Advanced Technology BV
00H	20H	41H	Touched By Sound GmbH
00H	20H	42H	DSP Arts
00H	20H	43H	Phil Rees Music Tech
00H	20H	44H	Stamer Musikanlagen GmbH

Byte 1	Byte 2	Byte 3	Company Name
00H	20H	45H	Musical Muntaner S.A. dba Soundart
00H	20H	46H	C-Mexx Software
00H	20H	47H	Klavis Technologies
00H	20H	48H	Noteheads AB
00H	20H	49H	Algorithmix
00H	20H	4AH	Skrydstrup R&D
00H	20H	4BH	Professional Audio Company
00H	20H	4CH	DBTECH/MadWaves
00H	20H	4DH	Vermona
00H	20H	4EH	Nokia
00H	20H	4FH	Wave Idea
00H	20H	50H	Hartmann GmbH
00H	20H	51H	Lion's Tracs
00H	20H	52H	Analogue Systems
00H	20H	53H	Focal-JMlab
00H	20H	54H	Ringway Electronics (Chang-Zhou) Co. Ltd.
00H	20H	55H	Faith Technologies (Digiplug)
00H	20H	56H	Showworks
00H	20H	57H	Manikin Electronic
00H	20H	58H	1 Come Tech
00H	20H	59H	Phonic Corp.
00H	20H	5AH	Lake Technology
00H	20H	5BH	Silansys Technologies
00H	20H	5CH	Winbond Electronics
00H	20H	5DH	Cinetix Medien und Interface GmbH
00H	20H	5EH	A&G Soluzioni Digitali
00H	20H	5FH	Sequentix Music Systems
00H	20H	60H	Oram Pro Audio
00H	20H	61H	Be4 Ltd.
00H	20H	62H	Infection Music
00H	20H	63H	Central Music Co. (CME)

Table B.17 System Exclusive Single Byte Manufacturer ID Numbers (Japanese Manufacturer's Group)

Byte 1	Byte 2	Byte 3	Company Name
40H	---	---	Kawai Musical Instruments Mfg. Co., Ltd.
41H	---	---	Roland Corporation
42H	---	---	Korg Inc.
43H	---	---	Yamaha Corporation
44H	---	---	Casio Computer Co., Ltd.
46H	---	---	Kamiya Studio Co., Ltd.
47H	---	---	Akai Electric Co., Ltd.
48H	---	---	Victor Company of Japan, Ltd.
4BH	---	---	Fujitsu Limited
4CH	---	---	Sony Corporation
4EH	---	---	Teac Corporation
50H	---	---	Matsushita Electric Industrial Co., Ltd.
51H	---	---	Fostex Corporation
52H	---	---	Zoom Corporation
54H	---	---	Matsushita Communication Industrial Co., Ltd.
55H	---	---	Suzuki Musical Instruments Mfg. Co., Ltd.
56H	---	---	Fuji Sound Corporation Ltd.
57H	---	---	Acoustic Technical Laboratory, Inc.
59H	---	---	Faith, Inc.
5AH	---	---	Internet Corporation
5CH	---	---	Seekers Co., Ltd.
5FH	---	---	Sd Card Association
00H	40H	00H	Crimson Technology Inc.

Appendix C

Understanding Timing Concepts

As a musician, you are probably familiar with the concept of beats per minute (or BPM) when working with sequences. This usually determines the speed at which the song will play. However, sequencers use other timing mechanisms, such as sequence resolution, which determines the precision of each quarter note. Then there are the synchronization concepts inherent to any type of work where two or more devices need to be locked together. This is the case with MIDI clock, mainly used to synchronize two or more MIDI devices, and SMPTE, which is used when working with video or time-based projects.

Since MIDI files save information regarding these timing concepts, it might be useful to understand how they can relate to one another. This might help you to identify problems that might occur with timing or synchronization.

Beats Per Minute (BPM)

Since this is probably the most common way to express the speed of a musical project, let's start here. BPM expresses the tempo of a song by defining how many quarter notes are found in each minute. MIDI files, however, use the opposite of this to express timing. BPM expresses the number of quarter notes per time, whereas MIDI files use time per quarter notes. This makes it easier to specify more precise tempo divisions than with BPM.

A quarter note always refers to a single beat, no matter what the tempo is or the time signature division. This value is not the most precise way to count information in the computer or sequencer world, however, since a beat may be shorter in some cases and longer in others, depending on both the time signature and tempo setting of the song. It's also possible that both of these values might change along the way in the song.

For a musician, a tempo of 60 BPM means that there will be 60 evenly spaced beats in every minute. This determines the speed of the song. To convert this tempo into a MIDI File format's tempo, using the three bytes of data in the MThd chunk, you need to convert the value of a quarter note into the number of microseconds each quarter note takes to play back.

One microsecond is the equivalent of one one-millionth of a second (1/1,000,000). So, in one minute, there are 60,000,000 microseconds. If you want to know how many microseconds each quarter note lasts, you need to divide 60,000,000 by the BPM value. For example, at 60 BPM, 60,000,000 / 60 = 1,000,000 microseconds (in hex: 0F 42 40), or 1 second, since 60 BPM is the equivalent of one beat every second. At a tempo of 160 BPM, 60,000,000 / 160 = 375,000 microseconds (in hex: 05 B8 D8) for each beat or quarter note. A more precise application of this would be with a finer resolution tempo, such as 120.56 BPM, which would be 497,677 microseconds to the quarter note. By using time per quarter note instead of quarter notes per time, a greater resolution is provided without the use of fractions.

Later, if you need to lock MIDI with time code, using the time per quarter note will become increasingly useful, since SMPTE also uses a time scale, based on hours, minutes, seconds, and frames. Having a reference to time will help resolve the differences between BPM and SMPTE.

Pulses Per Quarter Note (PPQN)

Sequencers use an internal timing resolution to synchronize events known as Pulses Per Quarter Note (PPQN). This division is also called "ticks." In other words, a tick is the smallest unit in your sequencer's resolution. Your sequencer will then use the PPQN resolution to represent the location in time of a MIDI event, rather than using a microsecond value. For example, you might see that an event occurs at 1.1.48. This implies that an event occurred at bar one, beat one and a half if the sequencer's PPQN or resolution is set to 96 PPQN, where 48 represents the eighth note value. Today's sequencers typically offer much higher PPQN resolution, going from 96 PPQN to 1,920 PPQN. Sequencers using such a high resolution will usually subdivide each beat into sixteenth notes, adding the PPQN after this. For example, 1.1.48 would then become 1.1.2.0000, where the value 2 represents the second sixteenth note value.

Using the BPM's microsecond value, you can then determine how long each pulse in a PPQN resolution lasts. Do this by dividing the value of microseconds per quarter note by the PPQN value. For example, each pulse (or tick) in a song playing at 160 BPM with a 96 PPQN resolution would last 3,906.25 microseconds.

Here's the formula:

* (microseconds per minute) divided by (beats per minute) = 60,000,000 / 160 = 375,000 microseconds per quarter note.

❋ (microseconds per quarter note) divided by (pulses per quarter note) = 375,000 / 96 = 3,906.25 microseconds per pulse.

In other words, to have a resolution of 96 PPQN at a tempo of 160 BPM, each pulse will last 3,906.25 microseconds, or 3.9025 milliseconds, or 0.0039062 seconds.

Both BPM and PPQN values are independent of each other, since you can change the sequencer's resolution without affecting its BPM setting. However, a higher resolution will yield a greater precision in the timing of MIDI events in relation to the performance itself. With more precision in resolution, you get more accurate MIDI timing in your recording of a MIDI performance. And that's where all the subtleties of interpretation come into play.

A faster BPM will result in shorter pulse times, and a slower BPM will result in longer pulse times.

MIDI Clock

The MIDI clock, as mentioned earlier, serves mostly to keep two MIDI playback devices in sync by generating a MIDI clock signal every one twenty-fourth of a quarter note. In other words, you always have 24 MIDI clocks per quarter note. This clock is tempo dependent, as with the PPQN resolution. However, it is far less precise than its PPQN counterpart, since it divides each quarter note into only 24 values. This value is interpreted as a tempo-based timing clock.

To relate a MIDI clock with the tempo's microsecond value, you need to divide the quarter note's microsecond value by the number of MIDI clock it holds, which is always set to 24. Keeping our previous example of 160 BPM, where each quarter note lasts 375,000 microseconds, you would divide this value by 24. Here's the formula to do this:

❋ (microseconds per minute) divided by (beats per minute) = 60,000,000 / 160 = 375,000 microseconds per quarter note.

❋ (microseconds per quarter note) divided by (MIDI clock per quarter note) = 375,000 / 24 = 15,625 microseconds per MIDI clock tick.

In relation to the PPQN, if you are using a resolution of 1,920 PPQN, each MIDI clock will represent 80 PPQN clocks. At 96 PPQN, each MIDI clock will represent 4 PPQN.

SMPTE

SMPTE keeps track of time, not tempo. It is a time-based synchronizing mechanism rather than a tempo-based mechanism, such as BPM, PPQN, and MIDI clock. There are four types of SMPTE time codes: 24 frames per seconds, 25 frames per seconds, 29 frames per second (which is actually 29.97 frames per second with drop frame; see Chapter 11 for more details), and 30 frames per second (which is actually 29.97 frames per second without drop frame). Further subdivision of time breaks up each one of these frames into sub-frames.

To better understand the concept of time-based timing in relation to tempo-based timing, compare audio to MIDI. For example, if you look at Figure C.1, you will notice on the left side

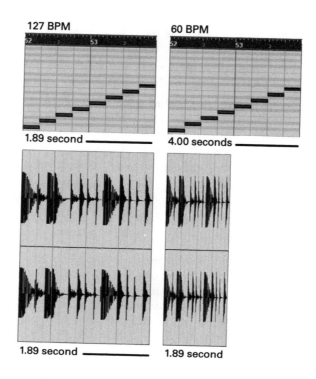

Figure C.1 Comparing MIDI and audio events.

that a series of notes is played at 127 BPM. At this speed, the entire series of events, or entire bar, fits into 1.89 seconds. The audio event also plays at the same beat and also fits into 1.89 seconds. However, if you change the tempo to 60 BPM, the MIDI events within the same bar will take 4 seconds to play, whereas the audio file still plays within 1.89 seconds. This is one example of how relative tempo timing differs from absolute time-based timing.

Furthermore, if you look at Figure C.2, you will find the SMPTE time line at the bottom. This represents time in hours, minutes, seconds, and frames (no sub-frames are included in this example). In the center of the figure, you can see the first frame of a scene, which starts at the SMPTE time stamp of 01:00:04:00 (or one hour, four seconds). At the top, you can also see two tempo time lines. The one right above the video frame is set to play at 120 BPM, while the time line above that is set to play at 60 BPM. Notice that if the song plays at 120 BPM, the bar and beat location corresponding to the first frame in the video is bar 3, beat 1. On the other hand, if the sequence plays at 60 BPM, the same first frame will correspond to bar 2, beat 1.

If you consider the end of the frame to be the end of the video sequence, then at 120 BPM, the video sequence will play over eight complete bars, whereas if the MIDI file plays at 60 BPM, the same video will play over four bars.

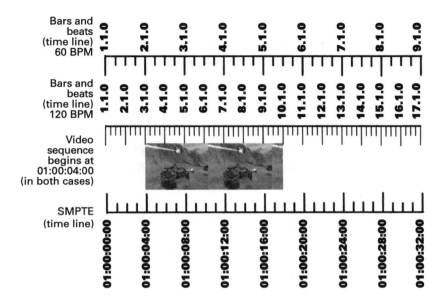

Figure C.2 Comparing MIDI tempo scale with SMPTE time-based scale.

In order for a MIDI file to lock to a time code such as SMPTE, the microsecond-measuring units are once again invoked.

Many MIDI devices will use an MTC-converted SMPTE time code to synchronize with video players, for example. In other words, the SMPTE is converted into a format that is supported by MIDI files, such as MTC. Internally, your sequence will still have to keep a PPQN resolution and a BPM tempo. By converting the passing of sub-frames and frames into microseconds, you can find a match for each pulse. Let's take an easy example to illustrate this. If you have a frame rate of 25 fps (frames per second) and 40 sfps (sub-frames per second), you would have a total of 1,000 sub-frames in one second. Each sub-frame would last 1 millisecond, or 1,000 microseconds (1,000 microseconds = 1 millisecond, 1,000 milliseconds = 1 second).

Let's go back to our example of a sequence playing at 160 BPM with a 96 PPQN resolution. We had found that each quarter note takes 375,000 microseconds. If you divide this by 1,000 sub-frames, you will end up with the value representing the number of sub-frames actually fitting into one quarter note. So 375,000 / 1,000 = 375 sub-frames per quarter note. Now, since you have 96 pulses in each quarter note, you need to divide the number of sub-frames per quarter note in order to have completed the circle back to the value in milliseconds of sub-frames. In this case, 375 sub-frames / 96 PPQN = 3.90625 sub-frames will pass in every pulse. Since this value is in milliseconds, multiplying it by 1,000 should give you the exact same microsecond per pulse value, which is 3,906.25 at this speed and PPQN resolution.

Formulas

Here is a recap of these and other useful formulas:

* Getting the microseconds per beat value (MSPB): 60,000,000 / BPM

* Getting the microseconds per pulse value (MSPP): MSPB / PPQN

* Getting the microseconds per clock value (MSPC): MSPB / 24

* Extracting the BPM from the MSPB value: 60,000,000 / MSPB

* Getting the number of PPQN per MIDI clock: PPQN / 24

* Getting the number of sub-frames per quarter note (SFPQN): MSPB / (frames per second × sub-frames per second)

* Getting the number of sub-frames per pulse (SFPP): SFPQN / PPQN

* Getting the number of microseconds per sub-frame (MSPSF): 1,000,000 × frames × sub-frames

* Getting the number of microseconds per pulse (MSPP) using frames and sub-frames: (SFPQN/PPQN) × frames per second × sub-frames per second

Appendix D

The MIDI Troubleshooting Checklist

If you find yourself perplexed or facing a problem you just can't seem to resolve, this appendix offers a checklist of questions and procedures that can help. Usually, things get complicated when we don't know where to start, and then we circle around the problem, sometimes never finding a solution. These questions may help you find something you overlooked in your setup—perhaps the one missing piece that's causing you a headache.

Each section covers a specific type of problem. When troubleshooting, go through the questions that pertain to your specific issue. The questions are meant to direct your attention to a particular aspect that could affect the problem. Once you checked and answered the question, test if the problem still exists or not. If it's still there, go to the next question and repeat until you resolve the issue. If you get to the bottom of the list and still experience a problem, try a Web search. Visit manufacturer or software developer Web sites. Remember to always keep your applications, drivers, and BIOS current with the latest versions available.

I Can't Hear Any Sound

When trying to access sounds from a MIDI keyboard controller:

* Is the device supposed to generate sounds?
* Is the volume turned up high enough?

* Is your audio output connected to a sound-monitoring device such as an amplifier and speakers or a pair of headphones? If so, are those powered up and ready to receive the audio signal? Is the level on those devices set so that you can hear something?

* Is your keyboard's Local MIDI setting set to the On position? If not, change it.

* If your keyboard is a sampler, perhaps you need to load sounds into its memory before continuing. Are there any sounds currently loaded into your memory?

* Are you in the device's Play mode? Some devices, such as workstations, will have different modes, and some of them will not allow you to hear the sounds as you play unless you are in the proper mode.

When trying to access sounds from a sound module while triggering events from a controller keyboard:

* Make sure you've checked the previous list of questions before you continue.

* Is the MIDI Out of your keyboard connected to the MIDI In of your sound module?

* Are you sure the MIDI cable is securely connected at both ends? Has this MIDI cable been tested in a successful setup before? Sometimes we assume the problem is with the way things are connected. Though that's often the case, faulty MIDI cables may also be the cause of bad MIDI transmissions.

* Is your controller keyboard sending MIDI events over the same MIDI channel as set in the sound module?

* Are there any intermediary devices between the MIDI device sending the information and the one receiving it? If so, are the MIDI connections appropriate for this setup (MIDI Out of device 1 to MIDI In of device 2, then MIDI Thru of device 2 to MIDI In of device 3, and so on)?

When sending MIDI from a controller keyboard to a MIDI sequencer:

* Make sure you've checked the two previous lists of questions before you continue. It is always easier to troubleshoot a problem when you've got the bases covered. The previous questions help ensure that everything outside of your computer setup is hooked up properly and is functional.

* Is your keyboard's MIDI Out connected to the computer's MIDI In? If there's a device between the controller and the computer, is the MIDI connection set up properly?

* Is the MIDI interface to which your keyboard hooks up installed properly on your computer? In other words, have you been able to send MIDI successfully using this MIDI interface? If you are not certain, verify that your MIDI interface is installed and functional before continuing.

* If you are using a Mac, is either FreeMIDI or OMS installed on your computer? This is especially important in two instances: If you are not running on OS X, and if you are using a multi-port MIDI interface.

* Did you configure your software to receive from the proper MIDI input port?

- Did you set the MIDI track to play on the proper MIDI channel? In other words, does the track MIDI channel assignment correspond to the device's MIDI channel, and is this MIDI channel active on your MIDI device?

- Multi-timbral MIDI devices can set parts to play certain MIDI channels and not others. You can also set a multi-timbral device to respond—or not—to a specific MIDI channel. Are you sure your MIDI device is set to respond to the channel setting in your sequencer's track?

- Is your MIDI sequencer at least receiving MIDI from its input? Most MIDI sequencers have a MIDI activity display that lets you see if a signal is received or not. If you don't see any activity from the MIDI input monitor window, you might want to go back and verify the previous links in your chain (by making sure you've checked the previous questions in this appendix).

- If there is MIDI activity entering the MIDI sequencer but nothing happens at this point, try re-routing the MIDI coming into your sequencer to another device or another MIDI channel to see if your MIDI output is working. Are other instruments (software or hardware) responding to MIDI events being sent by your keyboard controller?

- Have you looked at your MIDI configurations inside your software application to find out if it is not filtering a specific type of MIDI event? Usually, SysEx events are filtered, which, unless you are doing SysEx transfers, is fine.

- If you are trying to access the built-in sounds on your audio hardware, you will need to use a sequencer or other type of MIDI application to connect the MIDI In of your computer to the audio hardware's onboard synthesizer. In other words, your audio hardware's MIDI input will not automatically receive the MIDI from this input unless you "echo" it back to the sound module on this audio hardware; you do this through a MIDI Thru switch found in a MIDI application such as a sequencer.

When sending MIDI from one software to another inside your computer:

- Have you connected both applications through a virtual MIDI port that would allow these two applications to exchange MIDI messages?

- Does your audio hardware have multi-client support? In some cases, when software takes over the control of the audio hardware, any other application that attempts to access the audio hardware will be denied access. If this second application is a software instrument, chances are you won't hear anything. Consult your audio hardware and software documentation to find out how to deal with this issue.

I Have a MIDI Feedback Loop

A MIDI feedback loop occurs when a MIDI message is sent back to the device that initially sent it and plays again then sends it back into the same MIDI cable and...well, you get the point. It's a loop and it's nasty. To avoid loops, here's what you can do:

* Use the MIDI Out connector only on the device you will be using as a controller. Typically, if you are using a keyboard and some sound modules, use the MIDI Thru from all the other devices if they are used in a chain.

* Unless your keyboard is used on its own or in a live setup without a patch bay or a computer, you should make a habit of setting it to Local Off mode in order to prevent it from playing its own sounds twice. Normally, in a computer setup or in a patch bay setup, you can set the output of the computer or patch bay to send MIDI messages back to the keyboard. That way, you can hear the audio result of these MIDI messages.

* Avoid configurations in which all the outputs of all MIDI devices are connected to all inputs of all MIDI devices when using a MIDI patch bay or a multi-port MIDI interface. This type of setting will surely be susceptible to MIDI feedback loops. Create different settings for different needs.

* You might also want to check some typical MIDI setups found earlier in this book to figure out the best way to hook up your equipment.

* A virtual MIDI port might cause a MIDI feedback loop between two applications. Make sure the virtual MIDI doesn't echo the MIDI messages back to the source of the MIDI events being sent.

I'm Having MIDI Sync Problems

Synchronizing two MIDI devices together can be a bit tricky. In some cases, especially when older MIDI devices are part of your setup, the MIDI sync capabilities might be limited. However, understanding the basic principle of synchronization will help you establish a successful sync between two devices. This basic principle reads as follows: There should be only one master sending its synchronizing signal to one or more other devices. Once you've got this down, all you need to figure out is what kind of sync this device can output and how to set every other device in the chain to lock to this signal.

Following are some common sync options.

When using MIDI clock to sync two MIDI devices such as a drum machine and a MIDI sequencer:

* Make sure the master device is set to send the sync signal.

* Make sure the MIDI connection between the two devices is set appropriately, both in terms of hardware connection (through MIDI cables) and through software setup (assigning a specific MIDI port through which you are sending the MIDI clock, and a MIDI port through which you are receiving a MIDI clock).

* Set the receiving device to slave to the external MIDI clock.

* Make sure the type of sync signal, in this case a MIDI clock, is the same on both devices. Having one device set to receive a MIDI clock while the master is sending an MTC will not work.

When using MTC to sync two MIDI devices or a MIDI device to a video playback device:

- ❄ Most video playback devices with time code on them will not have MIDI Time Code (MTC) but rather SMPTE time code. To use SMPTE with a sequencer, for example, you will need to convert it to MTC first, so you will need to have an SMPTE-to-MTC converter somewhere in your setup.
- ❄ Once you've determined that you do indeed have an SMPTE-to-MTC converter, you will need to set this converter to send out the MTC signal it converted from the SMPTE master to any other device it should control. Sending a converted SMPTE-to-MTC time code to a slave device implies that you will control the MIDI playback from the video playback. Make sure your MIDI device is set to receive (or slave to) the MTC.
- ❄ Set your synchronization options properly in your receiving device. If you are transmitting 24fps time code, then this device should be set accordingly.
- ❄ Make sure your device—your sequencer, for example—is also looking for a sync signal on the correct MIDI port. Then, activate the sync option in your application to start only when it is locked with the incoming MTC signal.
- ❄ If you are using two MIDI devices, and one generates MTC while the other slaves to it, make sure, once again, that the master/slave relationship is observed and that all MIDI ports used to transmit and receive the MTC signal are configured properly in the appropriate setup windows.

Appendix E

MIDI Arrangements: Tips & Tricks

Working with sequencers is a great way to create and edit your music. Getting around in your sequencer's environment is one thing, but knowing how to get the best results from it depends greatly on the sequencer application you will be using. However, there are some tricks that can help you get more out of your musical arrangement. Remember: The tools you are using to create music will not necessarily make your music better. How you write and arrange your music, however, will make all the difference.

This appendix will focus on ideas for making your MIDI sequences sound better, no matter which sequencer application you are using. After all, a sequencer is only a tool that lets you organize and edit your musical ideas; it won't make the music for you.

Getting a Thicker Sound

To many ears, getting a thicker sound often means adding musical parts. While this can be a good way to add more depth to your musical arrangement, it might also lead to an over-crowded and muddled arrangement, where the important musical parts get lost in a sea of notes and rhythmic patterns.

Quite often, the desire for a thicker-sounding arrangement comes from the fact that the sounds used in the current arrangement are not thick enough to convey the depth you had hoped for. This is often the case when using low-quality sound modules or GM sound banks alone. The following tips will help you thicken your sound without adding musical parts to your arrangement.

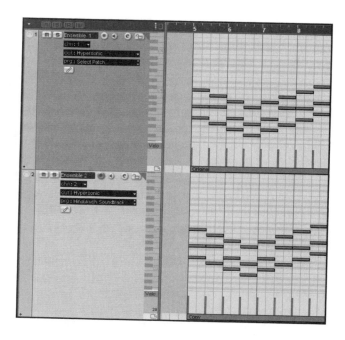

Figure E.1 The same part is copied onto another track, playing simultaneously, but with a different patch.

Doubling Parts

Sometimes, all your part needs is a bigger sound. To achieve this using a GM device, you can create a copy of a part onto another track and assign it a second, similar patch. For example, try using two piano sounds or two string ensemble sounds.

Once you've doubled your part, you can pan the first hard left and the second hard right. The drawback to this technique is that you will now be using twice as many voices in your sound module. In other words, if you were playing a three-note harmony part in which each note uses two voices in your sound module, instead of taking up six voices it will now take up 12. If your sound module is limited to 24 voices, you will need to make sure not to use too many doubled parts. An alternative is to bounce completed MIDI parts to audio if your sequencer supports both audio and MIDI sequencing.

In Figure E.1, you can see that the events playing on both tracks are the same, but they play on different MIDI channels. Furthermore, one track is panned hard left, and the other (the one selected in the figure) is panned hard right (found to the left of the pointer in the figure).

Adding Delay

To increase the effect of the previous technique, you can add a very slight delay between the two tracks by shifting all the events in one track forward or backward a couple of ticks. You may want to use the instrument with the more noticeable attack as the original and

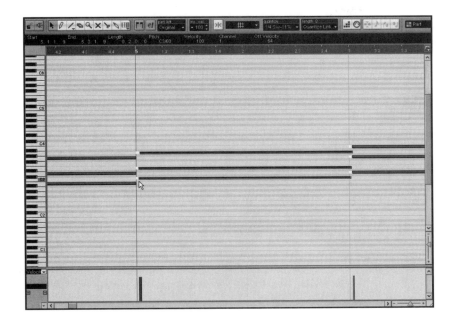

Figure E.2 The delayed notes appear in a darker shade over the original part that's in a lighter shade—you can notice this mostly at the bar 5 mark.

the instrument with the less noticeable attack as the delayed part. Don't add too much delay, or you will hear both instruments as separate entities, and that will only muddy your arrangement.

If your sequencer uses a quantization grid when you are editing the events, make sure this grid is turned off. Otherwise, you will not be able to move over these events in small increments. You should also make sure that you select all the events in a part before using this method, to avoid having some notes farther apart than others.

This technique basically simulates what happens in the real world when more than one musician plays the same part, as when 20 violinists play the same notes. These 20 players will play in sync, but there will always be very small variations in their attack time. These variations blur the attack a bit, making it sound thicker.

In Figure E.2, you can see the same part played on two channels and displayed in a single piano roll editing window. Here, the first part plays on the beat and appears in a lighter shade. The second part, played on another channel, appears on top with a darker shade. As you can see, the delay between the two parts is very small, making the attack difference barely noticeable.

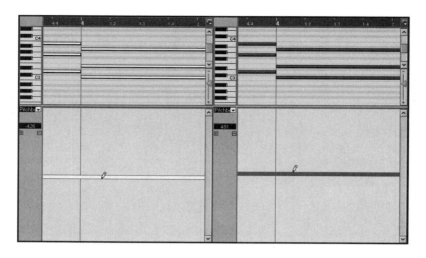

Figure E.3 The left window shows that the instrument's pitch bend level is set down, while the right window shows the pitch bend level is up, creating a slight detune effect.

Detuning

You may also want to slightly detune a set of doubled parts. For example, by setting the first part a few cents off, using either the fine-tune parameter on your device or adding one pitch bend event at the beginning of each track (see Figure E.3), you can increase the width of the sound. For a better result, you should tune one instrument sharp and the second instrument flat by the same amount, so that the ear centers the end pitch, as it should be. Note that you should use this in conjunction with the doubling part technique, in which a musical part is doubled up on two different MIDI channels and panned hard left and hard right.

Orchestrate

One of the philosophies behind orchestration is to double an existing musical line at a different pitch or different volume level using different instruments, rather than making every instrument in the orchestra play a different musical part. For example, the flute might play a line, and the piccolo might double that line one octave higher (see Figure E.4). The flute and piccolo have a similar timbre. They do differ slightly, though, and while the intensity of the doubled line will not change tremendously, its overall effect will sound different than if the flute were to play the line on its own.

You can apply this principle as well, even if you are not using orchestral instruments in your arrangement. This is done by doubling a musical line and transposing this line one octave higher or lower. Doing this will add emphasis to the line, drawing more attention to it. In other words, use this technique only when appropriate; otherwise, attention will be drawn away from more important parts.

Figure E.4   Example of a doubled melodic part—the first staff played by the piccolo doubles the flute one octave (12 half-steps or semi-tones) higher.

You may also want to try doubling a third (three half-steps above for a minor third or four half-steps for a major third) or a perfect fifth (seven half-steps above or five half-steps below) to get a different color altogether.

When you double a line like this, you will want to adjust the volume level of the secondary part in order to make it sound farther away, so that the primary line sounds different—as opposed to simply hearing two parts playing the same line.

Large Voicing

When you lay out a harmonic progression using a piano or guitar, you might be using one hand with closed voicing, in which every note in the chord is not far from the other one. This is a good way to get the idea of where the chords should go harmonically. It is easier to play a chord progression when all notes are close by rather than when each note in the chord is far apart from the other note in the same chord, not to mention moving your fingers to other notes as the chords change. However, when adding instruments, such as harmonic pads, to your song, you might get a bigger bang for your buck if you space out the voicing a bit.

While still using the same number of voices, large chords will fill the space better than small chords (see Figure E.5).

Figure E.5   The upper staff displays a close voicing harmonic progression, while the lower staff displays a wider version of the same chord progression.

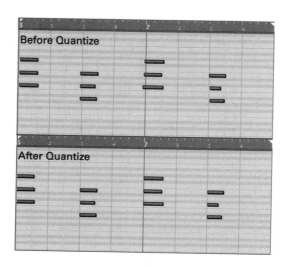

Figure E.6 An example of MIDI events before quantization (above) and after quantization (below).

Quantizing De-Humanizes

Quantizing is a technique often used with sequencers to tighten the rhythm of MIDI events in a musical part and to correct slightly sloppy playing. This technique places the notes you play on a grid of pre-established note values, such as quarter notes, eighth notes, or sixteenth notes, for example. As you record, any MIDI Note On event that's not entirely accurate—in light of the quantization value you have chosen—will be moved to the closest grid line defined by the quantization value in effect in Figure E.6.

Although it is useful to quantize MIDI events to improve the rhythmic integrity of your musical performance, quantizing can also remove some of the feeling from your performance. Sequencer software applications now offer different quantization options that allow you to control the degree of quantization and may also affect more then just the note's position in the time line. For example, it may affect the velocity level of notes that are played within this time line. When using these tools to adjust your timing, you should always listen to the result and try not to remove all the subtle variations in rhythm you played when recording. When the sequencer offers control over the amount of quantization, start with small changes, increasing slightly this amount until you are satisfied with the result without removing the human element from the performance.

MIDI Effects

With the prevalence of software instruments, MIDI instruments are more and more compatible with audio processing, since they use the computer's sound card to generate their sounds. Therefore, they are often treated as audio events and benefit from the effects processing available for any other digital audio event. However, since the musical parts are recorded

Figure E.7 The MIDI Arpeggio module in Cubase creates instant arpeggio lines from a MIDI input.

using MIDI, they are also considered MIDI events, and you can edit them as such in MIDI editors. In short, you get the flexibility of MIDI in terms of editing and the flexibility of digital audio in terms of processing. This allows for overall greater flexibility and also greater control over the types of effects you can achieve with MIDI sound modules.

Another addition to sequencers has been the implementation of integrated MIDI effects, which allow you to create variations on the MIDI events recorded, both in real-time and playback modes. Figure E.7 shows an example of such a MIDI effect. Here, you can create instant arpeggios using musical events recorded on a track or by playing real-time MIDI events through the MIDI effects module.

The techniques described below are, however, ways to accomplish certain MIDI effects without the use of software instruments or integrated MIDI effects. If you have a tool that offers a similar result, you will probably find it easier to simply use it. On the other hand, if your sequencer doesn't offer MIDI effects, here's how you can achieve a simulated echo using MIDI and a simulated auto-pan effect using control change messages.

MIDI Echoes

Adding an echo to a MIDI part might add a nice color to your overall music. This type of echo consists of repeating the note, notes, or pattern of a musical part at a specific interval a number of times, and each time it repeats, the velocity goes down a bit.

If you look at Figure E.8, you will find an example of a simple repeating pattern. In Figure E.9, you can see that this pattern is now more complex, since the same pattern has been copied over four times, and each time, the velocity level has been reduced by a quarter as well. The last repetition, in this case, plays at the quarter velocity of its first occurrence. This, in effect, creates the impression of an echo; however, no external processing is involved. It's only a repetition of the first set of MIDI notes that will give the illusion of echoes being played.

Here's how to create a MIDI echo effect without the aid of a special sequencing tool designed for the purpose:

1. Start by recording your original musical part. Long, sustained notes do not work as well as short notes in creating this effect, since you will be repeating the notes over, cutting sustained notes anyway.

2. Copy the MIDI part to another MIDI track below. If you want the echo to repeat three times, copy the same part on three separate tracks.

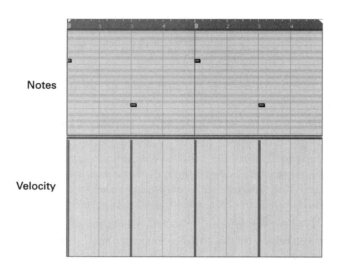

Figure E.8   Original musical pattern used to create an echo effect.

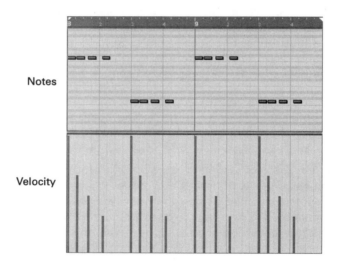

Figure E.9   The original pattern is repeated, each time with a lower velocity value, creating an echo effect.

3. Make sure each track is playing on the same MIDI port, MIDI channel, and instrument.

4A. If your sequencer offers control over the playback of your MIDI events, such as a velocity control, this will make things easier. If that's the case, all you need to do is set the velocity value for each track at a value lower than the preceding track. For example, the first track contains your original data, so you leave it alone. Set the velocity of the second track about 25% lower than that of the first track. Continue like this for each copied part, reducing each time by about 25% in this case, since you have three repetitions. In terms of values, it might look like this: The first track equals no change in velocity, the second track is −32 less than the first track, the third track is −64 less than the first track, and the fourth track is −96 less than the first track.

4B. If your sequencer does not support velocity control over tracks, you may edit the velocity controller in the appropriate editing window in order to make each repetition a bit softer than the preceding one.

5. Now that you have adjusted the velocity for each repetition, you will need to move each part in time. To do this, open the appropriate editing window (usually the piano roll type will do well for this) for the first copy (not the original recorded part).

6. Activate your quantization grid in this window to make sure your events will snap to the desired value. If you want your echo to follow at intervals of sixteenth notes, set your grid to snap to sixteenth notes.

7. Select all your events in the editing window for this first copy and move the events one-sixteenth note to the right (later in time). I'm using the sixteenth note as an example; you may want to use another value to determine the spacing of your echo. It's up to you.

8. Repeat steps 5 through 7 for the remaining copies of the original part, moving each copy one value more to the right—in this case, one sixteenth note every time.

9. Listen to the result once you are done and make adjustments as you see fit.

You may want to merge all the parts into a single part when you are done, having all copies appear on one track. To do this, you will need to consult your sequencer's documentation to find out how it handles multiple overlapping parts on a single track.

Rotating Pan

Another MIDI effect that can add movement to your song—without adding musical elements—involves panning a rhythmic pattern using controller number 10, which controls the panning. There are many ways to do this, depending on the sequencer you use; the easiest way would be to add pan automation through a MIDI mixer inside your sequencer. If your sequencer does not support MIDI automation mixes, you can add control change values in one of the edit windows, as shown in Figure E.10.

The idea in using this effect is to create motion, so rapidly changing the pan from a hard right to a hard left position (MIDI values 127 and 0) will be more effective than gradually panning from left to right. Panning a sound after its Note On message has been sent will likely not take effect until the next Note On message is received.

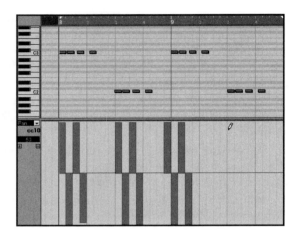

Figure E.10   Example of a MIDI panning effect.

Appendix F }

Review Questions: Answers

This appendix contains the answers to the review questions at the end of each chapter in this book.

Table F.1   Chapter 1 Answers

Question No.	Answer	Question No.	Answer
1	C	6	D
2	B	7	C
3	D	8	A
4	A	9	B
5	B	10	True

Table F.2   Chapter 2 Answers

Question No.	Answer	Question No.	Answer
1	B	6	D
2	C	7	D
3	C	8	A
4	B	9	D
5	A	10	True

Table F.3   Chapter 3 Answers

Question No.	Answer	Question No.	Answer
1	B	6	A
2	C	7	D
3	A	8	A
4	C	9	C
5	D	10	True

Table F.4   Chapter 4 Answers

Question No.	Answer	Question No.	Answer
1	B	6	A
2	C	7	C
3	C	8	B
4	B	9	C
5	D	10	False

Table F.5   Chapter 5 Answers

Question No.	Answer	Question No.	Answer
1	A	6	B
2	D	7	B
3	B	8	A
4	C	9	B
5	D	10	False

Table F.6   Chapter 6 Answers

Question No.	Answer	Question No.	Answer
1	B	6	D
2	C	7	B
3	B	8	C
4	C	9	A
5	D	10	False

Table F.7 Chapter 7 Answers

Question No.	Answer	Question No.	Answer
1	B	6	A
2	C	7	C
3	A	8	C
4	B	9	D
5	D	10	True

Table F.8 Chapter 8 Answers

Question No.	Answer	Question No.	Answer
1	C	6	A
2	A	7	C
3	C	8	B
4	B	9	C
5	D	10	True

Table F.9 Chapter 9 Answers

Question No.	Answer	Question No.	Answer
1	B	6	C
2	C	7	A
3	D	8	C
4	B	9	D
5	A	10	False

Table F.10 Chapter 10 Answers

Question No.	Answer	Question No.	Answer
1	D	6	B
2	A	7	A
3	C	8	D
4	D	9	B
5	C	10	False

Table F.11 Chapter 11 Answers

Question No.	Answer	Question No.	Answer
1	D	6	C
2	B	7	B
3	A	8	B
4	D	9	C
5	A	10	True

Table F.12 Chapter 12 Answers

Question No.	Answer	Question No.	Answer
1	B	6	B
2	A	7	A
3	A	8	C
4	C	9	D
5	C	10	False

INDEX